MARCEL PROUST

SELECTED LETTERS

[1880~1903]

Edited by Philip Kolb
Translated by Ralph Manheim
Introductions by J.M.Cocking

MARCEL PROUST

SELECTED LETTERS

[1880-1903]

ANCHOR BOOKS
ANCHOR PRESS/DOUBLEDAY
GARDEN CITY, NEW YORK 1984

PHOTO CREDITS

Marcel and his brother Robert Proust, and Proust as a soldier, courtesy Photo Harlingue-Viollet, Paris; illustration by Madeleine Lemaire, courtesy British Library, London; Nadar portraits of Mme Émile Straus, Madeleine Lemaire, Comtesse Greffulhe, Alphonse Daudet, Princesse Alexandre Bibesco, and Sarah Bernhardt, courtesy Visual Artists and Galleries Association, New York. All other photos are courtesy of the French Cultural Services, New York.

Design by Beverley Vawter Gallegos
Anchor Books Edition 1984

Library of Congress Cataloging in Publication Data
Proust, Marcel, 1871–1922.
Marcel Proust, selected letters, 1880–1903.
Translation of selections from Marcel Proust's Correspondence.
Includes index.
1. Proust, Marcel, 1871–1922—Correspondence.
2. Novelists, French—20th century—Correspondence.
I. Kolb, Philip. II. Title.
PQ2631.R63Z48 1983 843'.912 [B]
ISBN: 0-385-19288-6 (v. 1)
Library of Congress Catalog Card Number 81-43567

This work is a selection from Vols. I, II, and III of
Correspondance de Marcel Proust, edited by Philip Kolb
© Librairie Plon 1970, 1976.
English translation © 1983 by William Collins Sons and Co. Ltd
and Doubleday & Company, Inc.
Introduction and introductions to Parts 1, 2, and 3
© J. M. Cocking 1983

ACKNOWLEDGEMENTS

The preparation of this volume was made possible by a grant from the Translations Program, of the National Endowment for the Humanities, an independent agency of the United States Government. Special thanks are owing to the University of Illinois Research Board for its support of this project over the years, and to the staff of the University of Illinois Library for the use of its vast resources and the expert assistance of its personnel.

The following libraries have been of assistance in my work: Bibliothèque Cantonale et Universitaire, Lausanne; Bibliothèque Nationale, Paris; Bibliothèque Royale de Belgique; Brotherton Library of the University of Leeds; Carnegie Institute Library, Pittsburgh; Centre de Recherche pour un Trésor de la Langue Française; Dartmouth College, Butler Library; Harvard University libraries; Indiana University, Lilly Library; Jewish National and University Library, Jerusalem; New York Public Library; Pierpont Morgan Library; University of Texas Library; Yale University, the Beinecke Rare Book and Manuscript Library.

I'm very grateful to Catherine Carver for her meticulous assistance during the preparation of this volume.

P.K.

February 1982

CONTENTS

xi

LIST OF ILLUSTRATIONS

following page 188

Comte Robert de Montesquiou
Émile Zola with Maître Labori, 1898
Alphonse Daudet
Léon Daudet
With the Brancovans at Amphion, 1899

following page 308

Lucien Daudet
Bertrand de Fénelon
Prince Antoine Bibesco
Princesse Alexandre Bibesco
Marie Nordlinger
Mme de Noailles
Laure Hayman
Sarah Bernhardt
Louisa de Mornand
Proust after the death of his father

INTRODUCTION BY J. M. COCKING

There was a time when Proust's biographers and critics were on the defensive about his letters, aware as they were of the unprepossessing image those letters might conjure up. Philip Kolb's work in editing and presenting them, pursued with hardly a break over nearly half a century, has changed all that and revealed the wealth and variety of interests to be found there.

Proust's letters began to be known to the reading public in the late 1920s and the '30s; first, a few at a time, in the memoirs published by people he cultivated, or in periodicals; then, from 1930 onwards, in the old edition of the *Correspondance générale*. The first collected volume (1930), which revealed all the then known letters of Proust to Robert de Montesquiou-Fezensac, did very little for Proust's reputation as a correspondent. As a one-sided view of the relationship, it was like incense burning for a god; and, thought Proust's more serious readers, a dubious god. Montesquiou was known to the literary public as the model for des Esseintes, in Huysmans's novel *A rebours,* and for the Baron de Charlus, in *A la recherche du temps perdu:* the two images combined to reflect the essence of decadent aristocracy, arrogance, and vice. Montesquiou himself was little read in the '30s, and known only vaguely as a third-rate poet. So Proust the letter-writer made his first great impression as an uncritical and shameless snob, flattering his way to the social summits.

When the second volume of the *Correspondance générale* came out, in the following year, the situation was not much improved in the eyes of Proust's critics. Letters to another aristocrat, the Comtesse de Noailles; thus, unbounded flattery of another minor poet – second-rate rather than third, perhaps, but no great shakes. And little attention was paid to Proust's essay on Anna de Noailles's *Les Éblouissements* (1907), printed in the same volume as the letters, since it seemed to follow the same sort of pattern as the letters themselves. The letters in the four remaining volumes, which appeared from 1932 to 1936 – miscellaneous, often superficially socializing – did not reassure Proust's admirers; even his friendliest critics felt obliged to draw a distinction between the man and the writer, the personality and the genius.

This, of course, was a distinction more than suggested by Proust himself in his novel, in the passages dealing with the nature of literary vocation, and it was a theme he had worked out pretty thoroughly in an unpublished work, now in print as *Contre Sainte-Beuve*. He was bothered by what he judged to be his own moral shortcomings and anxious to keep the notion of art on a high spiritual level with the artist as a man of almost religious insight. Art, he reiterated, is life transformed, and the artist is separated from the man by the success of his metamorphosis. Style, he believed, is not a clever way of saying things but a quality of vision. He virtually gave his critics leave, therefore, to apologize for his letters and keep them well apart from his creative writing.

Philip Kolb was the first to see that Proust's letters were of more than trivial interest. As early as 1938 he spotted references to unknown writings that Proust was working at between 1895 and 1900, thought of then as the novelist's idle years; he was proved right in 1952, when the drafts of Proust's unpublished story of Jean Santeuil were revealed to the public. More important, Kolb set to work on the letters as they were then published – dated inaccurately or not at all, arranged in approximate and often improbable sequence – and played the ingenious detective. Through evidence converging from all angles – contemporary history, newspapers, weather reports, watermarks and internal cross-references – he put some order and coherence into them, and the book he published in 1949 became a bible for biographers.* He also collected quantities of previously unknown letters for the library of the University of Illinois at Urbana: originals, photocopies, snippets in sales catalogues. The final outcome of all this is the definitive edition of the letters now being published by Librairie Plon, from the first three volumes of which Kolb has made the selection here translated by Ralph Manheim.

The definitive edition is full of all kinds of interest. With everything properly dated and in order, and with the intercalation of a good many replies from Proust's correspondents, often for the first time in print, the letters now look very different and reveal a very different Proust and a different set of human relationships. The bridges between the man and the artist are discernibly there, in spite of Proust's attempt to demolish them; not only are some of the raw materials of the novel well in evidence, in the recorded substance of characters and events, but something of the sensibility and intellectual power that went into the making of the novel is to be seen growing and groping in the letters. In spite of the neurosis and egotism, there is a tremendous deal of common sense, wisdom, and even morality. The letters are still a far cry from the novel, of course; art is art. They show why the novel lacks what it does: an understanding of some kinds of human relationships. But they also help us to see its virtues more roundly and more clearly.

The inclusion in the full edition of many of Montesquiou's

---

* *La Correspondance de Marcel Proust. Chronologie et commentaire critique* (Urbana, Ill., 1949).

replies, for instance, makes him and his relationship with Proust look quite different. Philippe Jullian, in his interesting biography of Montesquiou, at last managed to separate the real personality from the caricatural images derived from des Esseintes and Charlus, and to show the side of him that Mallarmé's rather than Proust's biographers always knew: the very human being who was so touchingly kind to Mallarmé's young son in his final illness.† In these newly revealed letters, Montesquiou tells Proust a few home truths that can raise an appreciative smile in the reader – see the one translated here (letter 117). And when Proust praises Montesquiou for his virtues as an aesthete and a poet, there is beneath the unction a serious and acutely analytical set of observations that may be applied less truly to Montesquiou than to Proust himself. Proust is never quite blinded by his own pretences, even when desire to please can seem to get the better of his judgement or, hypocritically, to cover his genuine judgements with a veneer – see letter 35.

Sometimes we find Proust writing in a deliberately affected style, such as he will attribute to characters in his novels. 'Artemis the white goddess' and 'Pluto of the fiery eyes', invoked in letter 2, are typical of Bloch; and letter 74, to Maria Hahn, might have been written by Legrandin in a moment of delirium. A great many other passages which at first sight seem to be extravagant exercises in free fantasy or improbably strenuous hyperbole, often designed to please and flatter the recipient of the letter but proliferating into verbal self-indulgence, we can now, with our clearer idea of what Proust was trying to write, see as experiment and a flexing of linguistic muscle. The experiment is not only in the actual use of words and images but in thought, always subtle and often far-reaching, about the nature of language, the function of imagery, and the concept of literary style and meaning.

Such thought is to be found especially in the letters after 1904 to Anna de Noailles about her writing, where Proust's analysis of the poet's effects is leading him towards his own techniques for generating the kind of poetic aura, of magic and the light that never was, that every one of his readers has marvelled at in the first section of his novel, the evocation of Combray. But within the present selection there is plenty of evidence of Proust's attempts to analyse and understand his spontaneous responses to literature, music, and painting – for instance in his first letter to Anatole France, those in which he writes about Wagner and Ruskin, and in letters from his mother referring to his comments and judgements on writers and artists.

† Philippe Jullian, *Robert de Montesquiou, un prince 1900* (Paris, 1965).

The two sides of Proust's mind are perceptible throughout – sensitive responses and penetrating analyses. In letter 60 he tells Suzette Lemaire: 'I have never written a *line* for the pleasure of writing, but only to express something that struck my heart or my imagination'; exaggeration, perhaps, but essentially true. In letter 65 he is 'drunk with reading Emerson', but not thereby prevented from going off to hear one of the teachers at the Lycée Condorcet defend his thesis on 'The Modern City and the Metaphysics of Sociology'. In letter 69 he is sorting his impressions of Wagner, whose music, like Anna de Noailles's poetry, is to stimulate his thinking about aesthetic effects. But the most striking passage about music is in letter 71, which defines Proust's position within the Romantic world of nineteenth-century aesthetics. His mysticism of music marks him as a typical transcendentalist, and puts him close to the Symbolists. Yet he is a transcendentalist without belief in any definable metaphysical transcendence. His mystery is inherent in a particular kind of *human* meaning. And he utterly rejected the obscurity of style that some Symbolists cultivated. His own style is difficult until it becomes familiar, but it is never obscure. And he is a classical observer of manners as well as a Romantic prose-poet.

No less interesting are Proust's earliest attempts to size himself up, to pick out the reasons for some of his reactions to life, to look at himself objectively and sometimes through the eyes of his family and friends. Montesquiou sees through him as a valetudinarian; his relatives, and particularly his grandparents – as in the case of Jean Santeuil – see through him as one who takes too much pleasure in his own sensibility (see letter 7). But among those who know him, even the friends who mock what they came to label 'Proustification', criticism and disapproval are for the most part offset by affection and admiration.

Particularly interesting are the letters about his own homosexuality, which appeared for the first time in Kolb's definitive edition. The mixture of guilt and resolute enjoyment of his particular kind of sensuality is obvious from the start, as is the awareness. of how it would look if people knew, the adoption of poses to prevent them knowing, the intermittent defiance of outside opinion. This complexity of attitude was to give rise to some uncertainty in the theses about homosexuality in the novel, but also to a richness in the portrayal of a variety of homosexual psychologies. The most interesting in this connection are letters 5 and 12. Defending himself in the latter to Daniel Halévy, Proust writes: 'My ethical beliefs allow me to regard the pleasures of the senses as a splendid thing.' Later, writing when in Brittany with Reynaldo Hahn about his character Jean Santeuil, he evoked not only the strong sensory stimulus of seaweed and cider apples but 'sweet and impotent kisses, arms tight-knit in embraces and legs twined round legs, caresses which intensify the silence'. When guilt evaporates, sensuality becomes lyricism; and this is one of the driving forces of Proust's most poetically effective prose.

For years he hesitated between what might roughly be called a Romantic and a Classical image of himself as a potential author. What often worried him was the difficulty of ordering and systematizing his experience, whether of knowledge or of lyrical feeling. He feared his own dilettantism. Look at letter 46, where he says his intellectual development was arrested when he left school and that his writings 'have been the products solely of imagination and sensibility, the two ignorant Muses which require no cultivation'. He still has the illusion, he goes on, that he 'might have been something else, which is comforting and sad and undoubtedly an illusion'. By no means an illusion, however. Intellectual development, for Proust, was to be not systematic philosophizing or anything of the kind, but a continual sharpening of his powers of insight and of independent but value-dominated judgement.

His insights and judgements are already seen to be developing in some quite early letters. See, for instance, the account of human interaction between Mme Bessière and his uncle in letter 4, and the portraits of some of his schoolmasters in letter 6. For a seventeen- or eighteen-year-old these are remarkably observant and shrewd. In letter 8 he is already beginning to set up his notion of what he later called three-dimensional psychology, warning Robert Dreyfus against the assumption that human character is consistent and all of a piece. Typically, the theorizing is almost medieval in its meticulous demonstration. His relationship with Antoine Bibesco sets the earliest patterns of his theories about friendship; with Bertrand de Fénelon he suffers acutely enough to begin to become set into his prejudices – so wonderfully transformed into particular fictional situations in the novel – about romantic love and jealousy.

Altogether, then, the letters are neither trivial nor, in the witness they bear to so many features of *la belle époque*, merely picturesque. But there *is* plenty of local colour, and a pronounced period flavour. Letter 62 was written to Mme de Brantes with gold ink on violet paper; not without some practical inconvenience, as the letter itself reveals: 'But I shall tell you about it some day or write about it with more convenient ink.' Brittany must have seemed a delightfully primitive contrast to life in Paris; there Proust found it impossible to buy paper of any kind, and wrote whole sections of the *Jean Santeuil* drafts on the backs of old letters, bills, any odds and ends of paper he could lay hands on. And so he wrote to Robert de

Billy in September 1895 (letter 78) on the backs of two visiting cards, and promised more when he could find paper to write on.

In the early years of the new century we note his increasing involvement with friends in a social class above his own, with feelings that range from warm friendship to the equivalent, in the case of Bertrand de Fénelon, of passionate love; and reactions from the friends in question can awaken in Proust irritation, resentment, and even rebellion if their behaviour towards him carries any implication that they consider him socially inferior, or are mocking his hypersensitive and eccentric ways. Outside these emotional subtleties and complexities there is his admiration for their aristocratic manners, and his obvious enjoyment, though from the sidelines, of their high-spirited and often arrogant behaviour.

His observation of their ways and of his own reactions is meticulous; and, on a grander scale, so is his observation of groups and classes. For instance he writes to Reynaldo Hahn about a dinner party at the Daudets (letter 82) and records generalizations about the differences between aristocrats and middle-class intellectuals that will be at the root of a number of fictional situations in his novel. The aristocrats are sensitive, intelligent, and accomplished in the exercise of their one art, which is graciousness; in almost every other respect they are gross and stupid. The intellectuals are not only socially insensitive but strangely blinkered within their own sphere of literature. The former are fascinating and eventually disappointing; the latter are exasperating. The Daudets, moreover, are anti-Semitic – particularly disturbing to Proust's sense of loyalty to his mother's side of the family. This dinner party, in November 1895, took place of course before the Dreyfus Affair became critical and brought so much anti-Semitism into the open. Proust seems to have swallowed what he must in the way of private humiliation and resentment; later he joined the vocal Dreyfusards and found the moral courage to protest against Montesquiou's anti-Jewish witticisms and to declare his own ancestry. But it was in the novel that he took his full revenge, portraying the Dreyfus Affair through the absurd prejudices of the anti-Dreyfusard faction.

Apart from his comments on class reactions to the Affair, where the interest is sociological in very general terms but not specifically political, there is not much historical reference in the novel; nor is there much to be found in the letters in this selection. He sometimes comments on day-to-day events as any intelligent reader of *Le Figaro* might do. But there is no sign of awareness of the major political changes in the Third Republic: the definitive political victory of the bourgeoisie, the increased influence of the financiers and the industrialists, the establishment of Radicalism as the majority political attitude, with lip-service to the Revolution and the Nation, hostility to aristocracy, Church, and Army, and real interest in wealth and material prosperity. Unlike Balzac, Proust is not much interested in the eco- nomic mechanisms of social change, only in the repercussions of such change on social groupings, conventions, and rituals. Until, it must be said, political moves awaken his aesthetic sense because they threaten what he takes to be the bases of the French cultural edifice he respects and loves. When, under the minister Émile Combes, the law of 1901 against the reli- gious orders was strictly enforced, depriving them of the right to teach in France, Proust saw clearly that Radical anti-clericalism was changing the 'feel' of French life, and wrote a vigorous protest (letter 251) to his friend Georges de Lauris, who had defended the government's measures.

In all such matters – the Panama scandal, the Dreyfus Affair, the 'affaire des fiches' – Proust is placed rather like Jean Santeuil in the pas- sages about the scandal involving Charles Marie: portrayed as a criminal but a close friend of the family. Proust's family was socially involved with a good many political eminences – with the President of the Republic, Félix Faure, for instance, at the time when Faure felt obliged to refuse to acknowledge that a political error had been made over Dreyfus. Proust had therefore a dual perspective on many contemporary events, and it was only with the passage of time, with reflection on these events in the isola- tion of his cork-lined room, and with the maturing of his judgements, that detachment took precedence over the automatic assumptions arising out of personal familiarities and of the spontaneous identification in his early life with middle-class wealth, comfort, and cosiness.

The sequential and exactly dated order of the letters in Philip Kolb's full edition helps the reader to follow Proust through his successive efforts to write a novel about Jean Santeuil between 1895 and 1900; to plan a better kind of novel after abandoning this first attempt, but without making further headway; to please his mother by translating Ruskin even when enthusiasm waned and the devoted service of the disciple degener- ated into rather grudging hackwork. The most exciting references to Proust's developing sense of vocation come in letters later than those in- cluded here. But in many ways these earlier letters reveal what Proust was later to call the 'fundamental notes' of a personality, on which the subse- quent music of a human sensibility is based. Their interest is varied and subtle, and in Ralph Manheim's excellent translation they are suitably styl- ish and agreeable to read as well as faithful to the original French.

Cambridge
February 1982

EDITOR'S NOTE

Recipients of letters are identified in a note on the first letter to each; a cross-reference at the first mention of that person in the text directs the reader to the identifying note.

Proust rarely dated his letters in full; the dates given here in square brackets are supplied by the editor, the portion of the date that is dubious being followed by a question mark.

The following abbreviations are used in the notes:

CG   *Correspondance générale de Marcel Proust*, tomes I–VI (Paris: Librairie Plon, 1930–36)

CMP   *Correspondance de Marcel Proust*, texte établi, présenté et annoté par Philip Kolb, tomes I– (Paris: Librairie Plon, 1970–)

Pléiade v   Marcel Proust, *Contre Sainte-Beuve, Pastiches et mélanges, Essais et articles*, édition de Pierre Clarac et Yves Sandre, tome v de l'édition de la Pléiade (Paris: Éditions Gallimard, 1971)

References to the individual volumes of Proust's *Remembrance of Things Past* are to the 3-volume English translation (London: Chatto & Windus; New York: Random House; 1981):

vol. I   *Swann's Way* and *Within a Budding Grove;* vol. II   *Cities of the Plain*, translated by C. K. Scott Moncrieff and Terence Kilmartin; vol. III   *The Captive; The Fugitive; Time Regained,* translated by C. K. Scott Moncrieff and Terence Kilmartin, and by Andreas Mayor.

The translation is based on *À la recherche du temps perdu*, texte établi par Pierre Clarac et André Ferré, tomes I–III de l'édition de la Pléiade (Paris: Éditions Gallimard, 1954), © Éditions Gallimard 1954, and is © Chatto & Windus and Random House, Inc., 1981; quotations here are by permission of the copyright owners.

PART ONE

[1880~1895]

INTRODUCTION TO PART ONE

The first letters in this part show Proust in his relations with his grandmother, his mother, and some of his school friends. Those to Jacques Bizet, Robert Dreyfus, and Daniel Halévy are very revealing about his adolescent homosexuality. In one letter he writes of the beginning of his acquaintance with Laure Hayman, which was to continue for quite a while and to offer him a glimpse of the *demi-monde;* she was to be the principal model for Odette de Crécy. In letter 11 he consults his much-admired philosophy teacher Darlu – whose great influence over his thinking Proust was later to deplore – about his psychological problems, which he presents as a sort of Romantic *mal du siècle;* this amounts to reading his own experience in terms of literary patterns, which is typical of the way his mind is working at this stage in his development.

While still at school at the Lycée Condorcet, Proust wrote the first of the letters in which he attempted to draw close to the objects of his fascinated admiration by conveying an amalgam of concern and flattery; he offered his incense in this case to Anatole France (letter 13). The letter shows clearly that France was, for the young Proust, exactly what Bergotte was to be for the young Marcel of the novel.

Proust was just eighteen when he left school with the first prize in French composition and the third place in his class. In that same summer of 1889 there was a new law about military service. It reduced the term from five years to three but rescinded the option whereby, until then, young men who could equip themselves at their own expense and had a good secondary education could volunteer and get off with one year. Proust hastened to take up this option while it was still open. Later he was to look back at his military service with some nostalgia, as a time of comradeship and escape from the ordinary; but the letters written at the time – mainly those of his mother in reply to his – show a more realistic picture of a square peg in a round hole. He fared not too badly, however; his influential acquaintances made things a little easier for him.

In October 1893, after prolonged and at first very desultory attempts to study, Proust passed the exam for the *licence* in law, which precipitated the next great trial of his young life: the choice of a career.

3

With as much ingenuity as determination Proust managed not to choose one. The letters in which he consulted Charles Grandjean about qualifications for various posts, which he hoped would be undemanding, are amusing. The outcome, in 1895, was a job at one of the national libraries – a job which turned out to be neither prestigious nor interesting. Proust escaped by claiming indefinite sick leave, and saved himself for his literary pursuits.

Meanwhile his social life was taking him outward and upward from the family circle. By 1893 he was adopted by Madeleine Lemaire, who, when she was not painting roses, kept a salon in which Proust took note of behaviour that was to enter into his imagining of Mme Verdurin and her little clan. There he met Robert de Montesquiou-Fezensac. This was his first contact with the aristocratic world, of which, to be sure, Montesquiou was a very eccentric example, regarded by his own family as an oddity; Proust did his best to use him as a link with a more traditional aristocratic milieu.

In 1893 too, Proust began to prepare the collection of poems, essays, and short stories that was to be published in 1896 as *Les Plaisirs et les jours*, after a delay occasioned by Mme Lemaire's tardiness in providing the illustrations. Perhaps more important was the beginning of his acquaintance with Reynaldo Hahn, which was to do a good deal to inspire his first attempt at a novel, the story about Jean Santeuil. They met in 1894, probably in May at one of Mme Lemaire's receptions. That summer and the following they stayed with her at her country house, called Réveillon; but on the second occasion, in 1895, they deserted her and went off together to Brittany. There they met the American painter Alexander Harrison; Marcel's meeting with Elstir, when he is with Robert de Saint-Loup at Rivebelle, is based on this particular memory. The letters Proust wrote from Beg-Meil correspond in substance to the earlier drafts for his abortive novel, eventually published in 1952. The letters expose the roots of *Jean Santeuil* as the latter exposes some of the roots of *À la recherche du temps perdu*.

J.M.C.

1
TO PAULINE NEUBURGER[1]

47, rue Nicolo, Passy

Auteuil,[2] 5 Sep[tember 1880]
Dear Cousin,

Thank you very much for the books you sent me. The one I have returned to you interested me enormously.

I am going to Dieppe tomorrow, and am so glad that I shall be able to amuse myself reading.

We send kisses to your sisters and your mother.[3] I hope to see you soon.

Your little cousin
Marcel Proust

1. Proust's second cousin, the eldest daughter of Gustave Neuburger, director of the Rothschild bank, by his second wife, née Laure Lazarus.

2. 96, rue La Fontaine, Auteuil, the country estate of Proust's great-uncle, Louis Weil (see letter 4), where the family spent much time.

3. Mme Gustave Neuburger was a cousin of Proust's mother; one of her daughters, Louise, was to marry the philosopher Henri Bergson (1859–1941) in 1892.

2
TO MADAME NATHÉ WEIL[1]

Hôtel de la Paix
[Salies-de-Béarn, summer 1885 or 1886]
Dear Grandmother,

You won't thank me for this letter. In fact, since the dressing-down I got the other day, I'm very much afraid of another scolding. But Mme Catusse[2] promised me a little aria if I started doing a portrait of her for you, a big aria if I finished it, and all the arias I wanted for the whole thing. This doesn't mean a thing to you, does it? But if you, who know what feelings singing arouses in me, had yesterday heard a certain voice, so deliciously pure and marvellously dramatic, you would understand why despite my hurry to go out and play croquet with my friends, I am sitting down at the desk of Mme Biraben, our hostess,[3] to describe Mme Catusse to you.

I'm really embarrassed. Mme Catusse is to see this portrait, and even though I am doing it, I swear to you by Artemis the white goddess and by Pluto of the fiery eyes, as if she were never to see it, it gives me a certain feeling of shame to tell her that I find her charming. Yet that is the sad truth. Mme Catusse must be between twenty-two and twenty-five. A charming face, two bright, gentle eyes, a face worthy of figuring in the dreams of a painter enamoured of perfect beauty, framed in lovely black hair (Oh! what an unbearable task, to defy Musset and to tell you, Madame, especially when one thinks so, that you are beautiful, very beautiful.[4] But the divine melodies of Massenet and Gounod will make up to me for my woes). The waist is slender, delightfully shaped. But nothing equals the face, which one never wearies of contemplating. I own that the first time I saw her I only thought her pretty, but her delightful expression has charmed me more each day, and now I am stricken dumb with admiration.

But that will do. Mme Catusse would take me for an imbecile, and I leave the celebration of her physical charms for a letter that she will not see.

Mme Catusse's conversation consoles me for my many sorrows and for the tedium that emanates from Salies for anyone who has not enough 'double muscles', as Tartarin would say, to search the freshness of the nearby countryside for the grain of poetry indispensable to existence, which, alas, is utterly lacking on the terrace filled with chit-chat and tobacco smoke, where we spend our days. I bless the immortal gods for sending a woman so intelligent, so amazingly cultivated, who teaches me so many things and gives forth a charm so penetrating. But I curse the genii inimical to man's peace of mind, who have obliged me to talk such nonsense in the presence of a person I am so fond of, who is so charming and has been so good to me. It's torture. I would have told you how my stay here has enchanted me, how her departure would grieve me. I would have tried to paint her features eloquently, to give you an idea of her inner beauty; I would have liked to show you her grace, to tell you of my friendly feelings towards her. But never! My role is stupid enough as it is.

Enraged until those 'melodious accents' *Delight my ear and lull to sleep my sorrows,* I embrace you.
Hello, Grandma, how are you?

Marcel

1. Proust's maternal grandmother, née Adèle Berncastel (1824 – 90).

2. Mme Anatole Catusse, a friend of Mme Proust. See letter 139.

3. I.e. the proprietress of the hotel at Salies, in the Pyrenees, at which Proust was staying with his mother.

4. Proust is paraphrasing the passage in Musset's dialogue *Il faut qu'une porte soit ouverte ou fermée* in which the Comte declares his love for the Marquise.

3
TO ANTOINETTE FAURE[1]

[Paris, 15 July 1887]

My dear Antoinette,

Would you believe that Mama has torn up a letter I wrote to you. The handwriting was too bad. Actually, I am inclined to think that my great praise of our good general, that 'simple and sublime' soldier, as the *Petit Boulanger* calls him, aroused Mme Jeanne Proust's old Orleanist-republican sentiments.[2]

The streets of Auteuil (where I spent only the day of the 14th) had never been as lively as yesterday. Don't you find the refrain

Gais et contents nous allions triomphants

rousing? Or

C'est Boulange, lange, lange,

shouted by everyone, women, workmen, even children from five to eight years old, who sing it perfectly in tune – and with passion.[3]

Though the man is terribly vulgar, always beating the big drum, still, this enormous, unforeseen enthusiasm, so *romantic* in the midst of our humdrum monotonous existence, stirs everything that is primitive, untamed, warlike in one's heart.

You see that I'm no great philosopher, all that I find is adjectives when I look for the reasons that (forgive the string of 'that's) make me want to shout: He will return.[4]

7

I have nothing to tell you about life in the Champs-Élysées. Blanche is still as gentle as ever, still that angelic, mischievous and resigned look. Marie Benardaky is very pretty and more and more exuberant.[5] She had a fist fight with Blanche, who was defeated and who (there's no connection) sends many thanks for your letter.

The day before yesterday at the examination I wrote for five hours running without a moment's rest. I arrived at the Sorbonne at 9.30 and left at a quarter to four. The exam went on from 10.30 to 3.30. There were 120 or 130 of us, that is, the first two (or rarely three) in each division of all the lycées. The subject was history.[6] I'm going to hear Paulus one of these evenings. I'll give you an account of the performance.

Should I give your girl friends some message from you? I go to the Champs-Élysées almost every day now.

I wish you and those of your friends whom I know a pleasant vacation.

Give my affectionate regards to M. and Mme Faure, to Mlle Lucie,[7] Mlle Marcelle and her sister, etc.

Marcel Proust

1. Daughter of Félix Faure (1841–99), then deputy for Le Havre, later President of the Republic.

2. The political career of General Georges Boulanger (1837–91) was then at its height. As Minister of War in 1886 he had had the princes struck from the army list, and one of his last acts as Minister, on 20 May 1887, was to reject the demand of members of the Orléans family for reinstatement and to accept that of the princes Murat. The *Petit Boulanger* (Little Baker), published at Bordeaux, was the weekly organ of the Boulangist National Republican Party.

3. The lines ('Happily, triumphantly we marched') are from the General's campaign song 'En revenant de la revue' (On the Way Home from the Parade), referred to in *Swann's Way* (1. 438). The song was the creation of the music-hall singer Paulus (see below); Edmond de Goncourt wrote in his journal for 15 June 1887: 'Is it generally realized that if Boulanger succeeds in playing the role of Bonaparte in France, he will owe it largely to Paulus's song?'

4. Boulanger's appointment as commander of the XIII Army Corps at Clermont-Ferrand, undoubtedly with the intention of removing him from Paris, led at his departure on 8 July to a stormy demonstration at the Gare de Lyon. On 19 November a revue, *Il reviendra* (He Will Return), was staged at the Alcazar. Proust's enthusiasm for Boulanger was short-lived; his name does not even appear in *Remembrance of Things Past*.

5. This is the Marie de Benardaky whom Proust (in a letter of 1918 to the Princesse Hélène Soutzo) was to call 'the intoxication and despair of my

youth' and from whom he borrowed the salient features of Gilberte. Of Russian descent, she was then aged thirteen. Her arrival in the Champs-Élysées with her younger sister, Nelly, is described in *Jean Santeuil* (46 ff.), where Proust supplies accurate details about the girls' parents.

6. In 1887 Proust won second prize in history and in geography at the Lycée Condorcet and was thus entitled to sit the state examinations.

7. Antoinette Faure's elder sister.

4
TO HIS MOTHER[1]

[Auteuil], Saturday 24 September [1887]
My enchanting little Mama,

Let me first tell you that my stomach is *divine*, that I have again sacrificed to Grandmother, a very costly sacrifice for me, assure you that you will have *Pêcheur d'Islande*, but on Grandmother's advice probably from the Auteuil lending library because it's too late for the other,[2] then tell you about an experiment, and finally give you a bit of chit-chat, all this at a gallop, because I'm going out.

Here's the experiment. (I'm all mixed up.) I was *sure* I was going to digest well at night. But then came *transparent* nights with the feeling one has when asleep, about to wake up soon, etc., dreams, *foul* taste in my mouth on waking. One night (the night of the Louvre) I go to bed, I'm really worried about my digestion, but I've taken tea very late and eaten a heavy dinner (3 desserts). On waking I let out a spontaneous cry of surprise, exquisite taste in my mouth, calm, perfect sleep. Consequently I feel much better that day. The next afternoon I go to the Bois as usual on foot, then Uncle's carriage, etc. Troubled sleep, disgusting taste in my mouth.

So this is what I say to myself.

The *only* day followed by a good night was like this:

No Bois except in a *coupé*, because I called for Uncle outside the Louvre, not at the Acacia Gardens.

The next day I try not going to the Bois.

I take tea, I dine (by pure chance) very substantially, even provoking some comments on Grandmother's part.

No bad taste in my mouth.

Now for the chit-chat. Yesterday Nuna came to dinner. My uncle hauled her over the coals because she had the audacity to say: 'I

9

don't care for Ingres.' Heated discussion. My uncle said Nuna was IN-
COMPETENT to speak of *painting*.³ She said that wouldn't stop her
from saying the same thing in front of anybody. 'Then people will
say: there's a little woman who thinks well of herself.' And so it went
on crescendo. My uncle flew into such a rage that Nuna was all on
edge. She pretended to laugh and said: 'At least I'm glad I've helped
your digestion.' They were both as white as a sheet.

A week ago Nuna split her sides laughing because my uncle,
while holding forth about painting and sculpture, had got Raphael
mixed up with Dürer. That was in the garden, at night after dinner.
Suddenly a shadow flitted by. My uncle had just gone out to pee and
was hurrying back in for fear of catching cold. Nuna in a stricken
voice: 'Wasn't that your uncle who just passed?' 'Yes.' Horrified:
'Then he heard it all.' No. Not a thing.

A thousand kisses.

Marcel Proust

1. Mme Adrien Proust, née Jeanne-Clémence Weil (1849–1905), came of a
well-connected middle-class Jewish family from the region of Metz, in Lor-
raine.

2. When in Paris, the Proust family ordinarily used Delorme's lending library,
at 80, rue Saint-Lazare. In Auteuil they may have patronized Mlle Juvelet, at
15, rue de Passy. Pierre Loti's novel *Pêcheur d'Islande* had appeared in 1886.

3. Louis Weil (1816?–96), brother of Proust's maternal grandfather, was the
principal model for Uncle Adolphe. A businessman, owner of a button-and-sil-
verware factory, he was both irascible and kind-hearted. His quarrels with his
niece Mme Bessière, née Hélène Weil (called 'Nuna'), did not prevent him
from treating her generously. Since she was unhappy (and in financial straits, he
settled an income on her, provided her daughter with a dowry, and stipulated
in his will that his heirs were to continue her income.

5
*TO JACQUES BIZET*¹

[Spring? 1888]

My dear Jacques,

Under the stern eye of M. Choublier,² I have just raced
through your letter, propelled by my fear. I admire your wisdom,
while at the same time deploring it. Your reasons are excellent, and I
am glad to see how strong and alert, how keen and penetrating your

thinking has become. Still, the heart – or the body – has its reasons that are unknown to reason,[3] and so it is with admiration for you (that is, for your thinking, not for your refusal, for I am not fatuous enough to believe that my body is so precious a treasure that to renounce it required great strength of character) but with sadness that I accept the disdainful and cruel yoke you impose on me. Maybe you are right. Still, I always find it sad not to pluck the delicious flower that we shall soon be unable to pluck. For then it would be fruit . . . and forbidden. Now, to be sure, you think it poisoned . . . So let us never think or speak of it again, but prove to me by a friendship as long and tender as, I hope, mine for you will be, that you were right.[4]

Yours affectionately,
Marcel Proust

1. Jacques Bizet (1872 – 1922), son of Mme Émile Straus (see letter 17) by her first husband, Georges Bizet, composer of *Carmen*. He entered the Lycée Condorcet in 1887.

2. The letter was evidently written during the class of A. Choublier, professor of history and geography at Condorcet, under whom Proust studied from 1887 to 1889.

3. A paraphrase of one of Pascal's *Pensées:* 'Le cœur a ses raisons que la raison ne connaît point.'

4. Some time after this, Bizet gave Proust a photograph of himself as a child, on the back of which he wrote: 'To my dearest friend (with Cléry), 18 February 1889. J. Bizet.'

6

TO ROBERT DREYFUS[1]

96, rue La Fontaine,
Auteuil, Tuesday [28 ? August 1888]

My dear friend,

The gentleman in question is a thin, wizened, fussy little man.[2] Extremely intelligent and cultivated. Marvellously agile and penetrating mind. Almost subtle in his refinement. His teaching is rich, *lively* and most *distinguished*. A rigorous, virtuous thinker. Much more intelligent and, above all, intellectual than artistic. Still, he admires Leconte de Lisle. But finds him very 'odd'! I can see him now, all movement, all flame – his little eyes lively – taking on the expression of a psychological vivisectionist – 'that predilection for the strange, the exotic!' – But all in all his course is remarkable, a firm, flexible intellectual discipline; he is full of information and ideas, a most reliable, most intelligently cultivated guide for this year's circular journey from Homer to Chénier by way of Petronius. A bit too 'elevated', too 'serious', smacks a little too much of the classroom and the literary journal, but you stand only to profit, and beyond any possible doubt, now that our poor Gaucher is dead,[3] he is *by far the best* professor of rhetoric. I told him about you – without knowing you would have him – a year ago. I'll do it again in the same terms. I wouldn't dare repeat my words to you, because it strikes me as almost obscene and 'physically' disagreeable to say such things straight out, but I assure you that he'll be prepared to admire you. – Cucheval is not polite, cold, and stiff like him, but vehemently, broadly coarse. A ferocious *schoolmaster*, crude and uncouth – but all in all, I assure you, it's quite pleasant. This Brunetière, so callow and 'direct', is not lacking in savour.[4] It's rather amusing to let oneself be guided by two such different minds. Even if you were to be considerably Cuchevalized, it would do you no harm. Don't go taking him for an imbecile because he makes idiotic jokes and because he's a savage, insensitive to exquisite combinations of syllables or contours. In all other respects he is excellent, a welcome change from the imbeciles who speak in polished sentences. That is something he just can't do. It's delightful. An ideal professor and not in the least boring.

M. Dupré is an infinitely more amiable, nicer man. I have learned to appreciate the charm of his affectionate, sensitive mind in the body of an old soldier. But he's a bore. It's true that he knows Dierx and Leconte de Lisle (the works).[5] But what good will it do you to hear modern authors spoken of by a man who has too many reservations about liking them? It will bore you, in fact it will make you stamp your foot and gnash your teeth. You will have endless discussions, because he's a good sort and not at all strict. But what then? He will come out of them modernized. But you?

In short, Dauphiné is a lecture course, Cucheval a class, Dupré often a conversation. But the lecture course is remarkable, the class excellent, and the conversation boring.

Would you be a good boy – as you often are – and let me tell you a few little things that will relieve my mind. This is why. I beg you not to make fun of me, I wouldn't think of measuring myself with you. I think much too well of you for that, and M. Jalliffier[6] can tell you that these are no empty words. But what we have in common with a few others is that we know something of literature and love it, that we have other ways of looking at Art, and that we judge translations of writers or artists in accordance with very different rules. Well, I beg you – for your own sake – don't do what I did, don't proselytize your teachers. I could do it, thanks to an infinitely liberal and charming man, Gaucher. I wrote papers that weren't at all like school exercises. The result was that two months later a dozen imbeciles were writing in decadent style, that Cucheval thought me a troublemaker, that I set the whole class about the ears, and that some of my classmates came to regard me as a poseur. Luckily it only lasted for two months, but a month ago Cucheval said: 'He'll pass, because he was only clowning, but fifteen will fail because of him.' They will want to cure you. Your comrades will think you're crazy or feebleminded. For several months I read all my French papers aloud in class, I was hooted and applauded. If it hadn't been for Gaucher, I'd have been torn to pieces.[7]

Now, since you say you will write, this is what will interest me most. First what are you doing? And then tell me about the 'amiable person ill concealed behind the initials D.H.'. Intellectually I believe I know, and M. Jalliffier, who spoke about him to me for over an hour, has confirmed me in my idea, but really, what is he driving at? Why, after having been very pleasant to me, does he drop me *completely* and make it very clear to me, and then after a month of cutting me dead he comes and greets me. And his cousin Bizet? Why does he speak of his feelings of friendship for me and then drop me even worse?[8]

What do they want? To get rid of me, to annoy me, to mystify me, or what?

I used to think they were so nice.

Of course I'm telling you this very much in confidence, between friends. Don't mention it to anyone. But you are their friend, you must know.

And mine, too. You must tell me, because when one doesn't know what to think, one is in danger of being too cold or making a nuisance of oneself.

Oh! Making a nuisance of myself, that has always been my nightmare. I think I've done it this time. You'll tell me, won't you? I'll be very grateful.

Marcel Proust

P.S. Desjardins's articles[9] are very interesting.

What he is attempting is, I think, the finest thing a man can do. But the work itself (especially in the light of recent events) strikes me – so far at least – as scamped and incomplete.

Forgive my handwriting, my style, my spelling. I don't dare reread myself. When I write at breakneck speed. I know I shouldn't. But I have so much to say. It comes pouring out of me.

1. Robert Dreyfus (1873 – 1937), one of Proust's friends at the Lycée Condorcet. Later a journalist on the staff of *Le Figaro* and a historian, he kept every letter he received from Proust.

2. Oswald Dauphiné (1846 – 1924), who had just been appointed professor of rhetoric at Condorcet.

3. Maxime Gaucher (b. 1829), literary critic on *La Revue bleue*, had been Proust's teacher of French and Greek during the year 1887 – 88; he died on 24 or 25 July 1888.

4. Victor Cucheval-Clarigny, Proust's teacher of Latin in 1887 – 88, termed his pupil's progress in Latin mediocre and thought him 'erratic and harebrained'. Fifteen years later, Proust ridiculed his teacher in his 'Salon de la princesse Edmond de Polignac' (*Le Figaro*, 6 Sept. 1903), where a lady's footman asks: 'Your name, sir.' 'Monsieur Cucheval.' (The name in French sounds more or less like *cul de cheval* [horse's arse]. – Tr.) 'Sir! I asked you your name.' Etc. (Pléiade v. 466) Here Proust compares Cucheval with the eminent literary critic Ferdinand Brunetière (1849 – 1906), from 1893 editor of the conservative *Revue des Deux Mondes*.

5. M. Dupré substituted for Gaucher during his last illness. Léon Dierx (1838 – 1912) and Charles Leconte de Lisle (1818 – 94) were leaders of the Parnassian school of poets.

6. Régis Jalliffier had been Proust's teacher of history and geography in 1884 – 85. His name at least is suggested by M. Jacomier, professor of ancient history in *Jean Santeuil*.

7. Another schoolfellow, Pierre Lavallée (see letter 55), remembered Proust's essays, 'so rich in impressions and images, already quite "Proustian" with their sentences larded with asides and parentheses. . . . I can still see and hear Marcel reading his papers aloud, and the excellent, the charming M. Gaucher commenting, praising, criticizing, then suddenly overcome with laughter at the stylistic boldness, which actually delighted him.' (*CG* IV. 3)

8. 'D.H.' (Daniel Halévy; see letter 12), Jacques Bizet, and Dreyfus were the three 'intelligent boys' in the class, of whom Proust writes in *Jean Santeuil* (225 – 27). They thought Jean / Marcel 'insincere and affected' and felt an 'inexplicable antipathy' towards him (534).

9. In stories and articles appearing in *La Revue bleue*, Paul Desjardins (see letter 26) was attacking religious scepticism and literary dilettantism.

7

TO HIS MOTHER

[Auteuil, Wednesday 5 September 1888]

For you, my dearest Mama[1]
my last sheet of fancy paper.

What issues from my mouth will be the purest truth.
Fine walk yesterday evening. Took Georges[2] to the tram. For
ten minutes I kept him at a distance so he'd let it go without him. It
worked. Unfortunately, during the last few minutes, when I saw the
car was about to start, I was so delighted that I partly gave myself
away. He started running after it! It's such fun being with him.

Accidents during the evening. Long night, but *rather* unpleasant. And up until then my eyes had not been very dry. Still wretched
over your departure. I even brought a sermon from my uncle[3] down
on my head. He said my unhappiness was simply 'egoism'. That little
psychological discovery gave him such pure joy, such pride and satisfaction that he went on moralizing without mercy. Grandfather was
much gentler and only called me an idiot very calmly, Grandma just
laughed and shook her head, saying it didn't prove at all that I loved
my mother. I don't believe anyone but Auguste, Marguerite and Mme
Gaillard realizes how unhappy I am. As for Victoire and Angélique,
they naturally think I have a 'little female acquaintance', who will dry
my tears![4] But this morning I got up early and went to the Bois with
Loti.[5] Oh, my dearest Mama, how wrong I was not to do that before,
and how often I will in the future. The moment I arrived, it was delightful, sunshine, cool, all by myself I laughed for joy; it was a joy to
breathe, to smell, to move my limbs. Like that time at Le Tréport or
Illiers, during my Augustin Thierry year[6] – and a thousand times better than my walks with Robert. And *Le Mariage de Loti* added still
more to my well-being – I felt as if I had been drinking tea – I read
it on the grass beside the little lake, which was violet in the half-shade,
then the sun flashed down here and there, making the water and the
trees sparkle:

In the glitter and charm of the hour[7]

Then I understood, or rather felt, how many sensations this
charming line of Leconte de Lisle expresses! Him again!

Grandfather has given up tea entirely. Orange blossom. Ballet
is a great man now, because he said that Grandfather was quite right

not to blow his nose. One might even speak of a supernatural coincidence – how very supernatural, indeed! 'You would only irritate!'[8] I behaved very well at table, I didn't catch a single furious look from Grandfather. Just a bit of a remark because I was *rubbing* my eyes with a handkerchief. A vestige of grief.

Tell Robert that His Majesty's workmen have completed the instrument designed for such momentous affairs of state, but they (as is only fitting, see the novels of Dumas) don't suspect the importance or even the nature of what they have done. To me it looked many times too big, like a trumpet for the Last Judgement. Victoire said it was a scream, she can't imagine what it could be used for![9] Kiss Robert and yourself many times for me. The least annoyance I may have caused you fills me with remorse. Forgive me.

Many many kisses.

Marcel

P.S. The Crystal Palace trousers have just been delivered. Too tight. They will be brought back this evening without fail, altered. Robert's have been returned.

1. Proust's mother was at Salies-de-Béarn with her younger son, Robert (1873 – 1935), known in the family as Dick.

2. Georges Weil (1847 – 1906), Mme Proust's brother. A lawyer, he became a judge at the Tribunal of the Seine department, and later vice-president of the same Tribunal.

3. I.e. Louis Weil.

4. For this supposed liaison, see letter 10.

5. *Le Mariage de Loti* (*Rarahu*) was published anonymously in 1880; the author, Julien Viaud (see letter 111), later took the pseudonym Pierre Loti.

6. During a stay with his father's relatives at Illiers, near Chartres, in the autumn of 1886, Proust was reading *La Conquête de l'Angleterre par les Normands* and considered the historian Augustin Thierry (1795 – 1856) one of the world's great prose writers. Cf. *Swann's Way* (1. 169 ff. and *passim*), in which the Narrator, after hours of reading, walks 'the Méséglise way'. His desire to express the emotions he felt on these walks gives him the ambition to become a writer.

7. 'Dans l'étincellement et le charme de l'heure', a line from 'Épiphanie', in Leconte de Lisle's *Poèmes tragiques* (1886).

8. The recommendation of Dr Gilbert Ballet (1853 – 1916), a colleague of Proust's father; with perhaps an echo of Corneille's *Cinna* (IV. ii), where Augustus cries: 'Desiring to be feared, I only irritate.'

9. The servant Victoire was no doubt joking. The 'instrument' in question was a lavatory bowl, a novelty at that time.

8

TO ROBERT DREYFUS

[L'Isle-Adam, 7 September 1888]

(The monogram is that of Joyant,[1] with whom I am staying at l'Isle-Adam, but write to me at Auteuil, I shall be going back this evening.)

My dear friend,

Were you trying to tell me politely that Halévy thinks I'm cracked? I must tell you that I don't quite understand.

I do not believe that a type is a character. I *do* believe that what we think we can know of a character is purely a product of association of ideas. Let me explain, while at the same time admitting that my theory may be wrong, since it is entirely my own.[2]

Suppose then that in life or in a literary work you see a man weeping over someone else's misfortunes. Since whenever you have known someone to experience pity, that person was good, kind and sensitive, you will infer that this man is sensitive, kind and good. For in our minds we construct a character from a very few traits, with the help of our opinions which presuppose other traits. But this reasoning is most hypothetical. *Quare*, if Alceste shuns his fellow men, Coquelin attributes it to an absurdly foul disposition, Worms to a noble contempt for the base passions.[3] *Item* in life. Halévy drops me, making sure I know that he's doing it on purpose, then a month later he comes and greets me. Now, among the different persons of whom I am composed, the romantic, to whose voice I pay little attention, says to me: 'He does it to tease you, to amuse himself, to put you to the test, but then he has regrets and doesn't want to abandon you entirely.' And this person represents Halévy as a whimsical friend, who really wants to know me.

But the distrustful person, whom I prefer, tells me it's much simpler, that Halévy can't bear me, that my ardour struck him – him, so calm and reasonable – first as ridiculous and then as intolerable – that he wanted to make me feel just that, that I've been a nuisance, and to get rid of me. Then, when at last he saw that I wouldn't bother him any more with my presence, he spoke to me. This person doesn't know whether Halévy's little act was brought on by pity, indifference or moderation, but he does know that it means nothing and it worries him very little. To tell the truth, it interests him only as a psychological problem.

But there's the question of the exponent: is it x or is it y? That's the crux. If it's x (the sum of the phenomena of friendship), the break amounts to no more than a caprice, a test, or an access of ill humour, and the reconciliation is everything.

If it's y – antipathy – the reconciliation is nothing, the break is everything.

Forgive me. I've taken a whole letter to expound my theory, and now Joyant is calling me. My letter will be for another time. But on this question you can further my psychological investigations. Because you know perfectly well whether Halévy said to you (and I wouldn't hold it against him): What a pest that Proust is!

Or: That Proust fellow is rather nice.

True, there's a third solution, the most likely:

That he hasn't spoken of me to you at all.

I'm just an inert element.

Enlighten me about this little problem. I'll answer any questions you like.

Three apologies:

1) For not answering you sooner: but my mother went away and then my brother. Then my trip to the Joyants'.

2) So badly written and hurried in every respect: Joyant is waiting for me.

3) For bothering you with this . . . It interests me! . . .

Yours ever,

Marcel Proust

1. Édouard Joyant (1872 – 1953), Proust's classmate in rhetoric at Condorcet in 1887 – 88.

2. This is the earliest known mention of Proust's theory that each individual is made up of many selves – a theory he was later to put into practice in *Remembrance of Things Past*, where certain characters appear illogical or inconsistent, as did people he observed. His formulation of it here may owe something, despite his disclaimer, to an article he is almost certain to have read: 'Hamlet' (*Le Temps*, 5 Oct. 1886), by Anatole France (see letter 13), Proust's favourite author at the time.

3. The principal character in Molière's *Le Misanthrope*, as interpreted by two of the leading actors of the day at the Comédie-Française: Constant-Benoît Coquelin and Gustave-Hippolyte Worms.

9
TO ROBERT DREYFUS

[10 ? September 1888]

My dear friend,

It's such a beautiful day that I'm stirred by the whims of a *grand seigneur*. I would like to order up a play. By that I mean, to see a number of friends, to step out of myself, to be serene or passionate or extravagant or obscene according to the way I feel or my physical disposition, and indulge myself in the spectacle not only of the stupidities of most, but also of the originality or simply the character of a few. I would like to tell J.B. [Jacques Bizet] that I adore him, and X and Y that I'm decadent. Unable to indulge in this royal pleasure today, I shall compensate myself by driving to the Acacia Gardens in a carriage. That, to my taste, is the height of Parisian beauty in 1888. I would gladly analyse it if I were a journalist, which would amuse me a good deal, so much so that I wanted to start a newspaper at the Lycée. It blooms on soft white shoulders in sometimes exquisite textile fantasies. A certain grand courtesan, for example, whose bared nape has just the charming roundness of those amphoras in which the patient Etruscans expressed their whole ideal, their whole consoling dream of grace, the corners of whose mouths are the same as in the naïve virgins of Luini (Bernardino) or Botticelli, which I very much prefer to those of Raphael – bang, where am I? – wait while I reread, oh yes, this courtesan, I say, embodies more charm in the cunningly undulating folds of her violet dress than any number of 'salons'; above all, she's more modern and so very sincere. I mean that without imitation (such as occurs involuntarily in painting or poetry), without preference for idealism or brutality, such women express naturally what they regard as the height of beauty and elegance, with extremely rare and precious materials, tissue of a pink more adorable than that of the sky at six o'clock, blue crêpe as deep as still water. I'm afraid that in writing about these things I must sound a little like Georges Ohnet.[1] What consoles me is that what I like about them is not what appeals to Georges Ohnet, and that the changing reality is not very significant in itself.

Another pleasure, *ma chère*, would be to speak ill of our friends. Since I am play-acting and am not really myself, there's no crime in speaking ill of them. Of myself as well. I would even like to paint my portrait, a little corner of my portrait: 'Do you know X, *ma chère*, that is, M.P.? I must own that I rather dislike him with his everlasting grand impulses, his busy manner, his grand passions, and his adjectives. Most of all, he strikes me as utterly mad or utterly hypocritical. You be the judge. I'd call him a "great man for declarations". After knowing you for a week, he gives you to understand that he has quite a feeling for you and while pretending to love a comrade like a father he loves him like a woman. He visits him, proclaims his great affection wherever he goes, follows him everywhere. An occasional chat isn't enough for him. He needs the mystery and regularity of assignations. He writes you feverish letters. Pretending to joke, to turn phrases, to parody, he tells you that your eyes are divine and that your lips tempt him. The nasty part of it, *ma chère*, is that after making a fuss over B he drops him and cajoles D, whom he soon leaves to fling himself at the feet of E and a moment later into the lap of F. Is he a wh——, is he mad, is he a charlatan, is he an imbecile? Methinks we shall never know. Perhaps, come to think of it, he's all these at once. I don't know if all this is odious, absurd, or sincere. I'm more inclined to think that it doesn't mean a thing. In any case, *ma chère*, never respond to his ardours, if ever he kindles them for you. Because they tell me he keeps certain letters . . . Anyway, he holds the key to quite a few little romances. I'd like to have a serious talk with him. – No, he'd kiss me.'

I give you permission, dear friend, to show this letter to D.H. [Daniel Halévy], though I've written it at a mad gallop, racing with the clock, because I'm due for a riding lesson.

And so I leave you, having expiated my sins by this confession – if it is one. It probably is. And yet, as Lemaître[2] says, one might just as well assert the contrary, and in my opinion with greater justification. What do you think? If that's a portrait, it's not very flattering and would flatter me less than the portrait I make myself of you – according to you – draped in your contempt of the common man and offering him the spectacle of an imaginary, extremely ironical Dreyfus.

It goes without saying that if you show this letter to D.H., you must absolutely forbid him to mention it to anyone, even, or especially, to his brother.[3] In spite of what I just said, don't be afraid of my showing your letters to anyone. I presume that if D.H. sees this portrait, he will say the same of me as before: 'It's too sincere to be sincere.' He'd be perfectly right.

Because I am convinced (it's one of the few things I am convinced of) that there are certain things it would be odious to say of oneself, except by way of transcendental clowning. And that too is bad taste. So perhaps I'd rather you didn't show this letter to H. after all.

Yours,

Marcel P.

1. A popular playwright and novelist (1848 – 1918). In *Swann's Way* (1. 280), Mme Cottard, an admirer, after remarking that Odette de Crécy 'worships' his *Serge Panine*, adds complacently, 'like everything that comes from the pen of M. Georges Ohnet, it's always so well written.'

2. The critic Jules Lemaître (1853 – 1914); he had attacked Georges Ohnet in *La Revue bleue* (27 June 1885).

3. Daniel Halévy's elder brother, Élie Halévy (1870 – 1937), the future historian and professor at the École des Sciences Politiques.

10

TO ROBERT DREYFUS

Isle-Adam [25 September 1888]

My dear Dreyfus,

A visit to Chantilly,
A visit to l'Isle-Adam,
A platonic passion for a famous courtesan,[1] ending in an exchange of letters and photographs.

A very uncomplicated intrigue, which ended very banally as those things do and led up to an absorbing liaison,[2] which threatens to go on at least a year for the greater good of the *café-concerts* and other places of the same kind, where one takes this sort of person. All this prevented me from redoing my answer to your last letter. I lost this answer, but I won't rewrite it, I'll give it to you by word of mouth, because it's too sensitive. Specifically, it says that the 'odious' and the 'transcendental clowning' in my last letter applied to my portrait of myself, which was ignoble, and not to yours of you, which was charming and not the least bit odious. There has been a misunderstanding and I was very much pained by your angry tone. I want you to know that I have always spoken with *the most scrupulous frankness*, that if I had any fault to find with you, I would *not* disguise it, and that if my actions and words are sometimes in contradiction (I don't explain myself; proprieties which are almost obliga-

21

tions, as Labiche would say,[3] forbid me to), it's my words you must believe. My words are true, I give you my word of honour, and press your hand affectionately. Your letters are a great pleasure to me, and I miss them. Write to me immediately

> c/o Mme Duchauffour[4]
> l'Isle-Adam
> (Seine et Oise)

For the new school year, dear friend, I wish you brilliant success in your studies, sincere friends and beautiful mistresses.

Marcel Proust

1. Not Closmesnil, as Robert Dreyfus suggested – though she did briefly pose for Proust's portrait of Odette – but Laure Hayman (see letter 25). Proust took up with her in 1888 and not about 1891, as Robert de Billy supposed. The copy of Paul Bourget's *Gladys Harvey* (1889) which she gave Proust bears, along with the author's autograph dedication, this inscription: 'To Marcel Proust / Do not love a Gladys Harvey. / Laure Hayman / October 1888.'

2. According to Dreyfus, this was with a pretty Viennese girl, whom Proust had met at the Perrin dancing school in the rue de la Victoire. The liaison was perhaps not so absorbing as Proust let it be thought.

3. Eugène Labiche (1815 – 88), author of successful comedies and burlesques.

4. Édouard Joyant's grandmother.

11

TO ALPHONSE DARLU[1]

[Tuesday 2 October 1888]

Dear Sir,

This morning you spoke to us about young people who too soon acquire unfortunate habits of thought, who split into two parts, so to speak, and who can neither do nor think anything without their consciousness studying and analysing their acts or thoughts. I trust you will forgive me if I, your pupil of only two days, take the liberty of consulting you on a moral problem, as it were. In these two days I have conceived so great an admiration for you that I feel an irresistible need to ask you for some important advice before embarking on the study of philosophy.

You spoke so well of such a disorder that, if it had not been for the presence of my comrades, I could hardly have stopped myself from asking you what remedy there is for it.

When at the age of about fourteen or fifteen I began to retire into myself and to study my inner life, it was not a source of suffering, by no means.

Later, when I was about sixteen, it became intolerable, most of all physically. I experienced extreme fatigue, a kind of obsession. Now it is not at all like that. Since my health, which used to be delicate, has become almost good, I have been able to react against the exhaustion and despair caused by this constant cleavage.

But though my suffering has changed almost entirely in character, it is no less intense. It has become intellectualized. I can no longer take complete pleasure in what used to be my highest joy, the works of literature. When, for instance, I read a poem by Leconte de Lisle, even while I am savouring the infinite delights of former days, my other self examines me, amuses itself looking for the causes of my pleasure, finds them in a certain relationship between me and the work, specifically, it imagines conditions diametrically opposed to beauty, and ends by killing nearly all my pleasure. For more than a year I have been unable to judge anything in a literary light, I am devoured by the need for set rules by which to judge works of art with certainty. But in that case, to cure myself, I shall have to destroy my inner life or rather the constant contemplation of my inner life, and this strikes me as frightful.

Undoubtedly this situation occurs frequently in young persons of my age, whom ill health obliged in the past to live a good deal to themselves.

I am sure you know what manner of thinking can rid one and cure one of this disorder, if it is one.

I hope, sir, that you will put it down to my extreme admiration and my infinite desire to know what you think of all this, and forgive me for the oddness and perhaps indiscretion of confiding *intimate* thoughts to a stranger.

But thanks to the little I have heard you say, I already feel that I know you. I beg you, sir, not to make the least reference in class to this letter, which for me is above all a kind of confession.

Your student and profound admirer,

Marcel Proust

1. Marie-Alphonse Darlu (1849 – 1921), professor of philosophy at the Lycée Condorcet, later Inspector of Public Education; he published no books.

12

TO DANIEL HALÉVY[1]

[Autumn? 1888]

My dear friend,

You gave me quite a little thrashing, but your switches are so flowery that I can't be angry with you and the fragrance of those flowers has intoxicated me enough to soften the harshness of the thorns. You have beaten me with a lyre. Your lyre is delightful. So I would be delighted if . . . But I will tell you what I think, or rather chat with you as one chats with an exquisite boy about things quite worthy of interest, even if one is reluctant to speak of them. I hope you will be grateful to me for my delicacy. To me indelicacy is an abomination. Much worse than debauchery. My ethical beliefs allow me to regard the pleasures of the senses as a splendid thing. They also tell me to respect certain feelings, a certain refinement in friendship, and especially the French language, an amiable and infinitely gracious lady, whose sadness and delight are equally exquisite, but upon whom one must never impose obscene poses. That would be to dishonour her beauty.

You think me jaded and effete. You are mistaken. If you are delicious, if you have lovely eyes which reflect the grace and refinement of your mind with such purity that I feel I cannot fully love your mind without kissing your eyes, if your body and mind, like your thoughts, are so lithe and slender that I feel I could mingle more intimately with your thoughts by sitting on your lap, if, finally, I feel that the charm of your person, in which I cannot separate your keen mind from your agile body, would refine and enhance 'the sweet joy of love' for me, there is nothing in all that to deserve your contemptuous words, which would have been more fittingly addressed to someone surfeited with women and seeking new pleasures in pederasty. I am glad to say that I have some highly intelligent friends, distinguished by great moral delicacy, who have amused themselves at one time with a boy. . . . That was the beginning of their youth. Later on they went back to women. If that were the ultimate end, what, good God, would they be, and what do you think I am, or more especially shall be, if I have already purely and simply finished with love! I would like to speak to you of two masters of consummate wisdom, who in all their lives plucked only the bloom, Socrates and Montaigne.[2] They permit men in their earliest youth to 'amuse themselves', so as to know something of all pleasures, and so as to release their excess tenderness. They held that these at once sensual and intellectual friendships are better for a young man with a keen sense of beauty and awakened 'senses' as well, than affairs with stupid, corrupt women. I believe those old Masters were mistaken,[3] and will tell you why. I accept only the general tenor of their advice. Don't call me a pederast, it hurts my feelings. If only for the sake of elegance, I try to remain morally pure. You can ask M. Straus[4] about my influence on Jacques. And it is by a man's influence that his morality is judged.

M. Darlu has announced that he is going to question me, so I break off this beginning of a letter. But tell me what you mean by saying that your hands are not pure. . . . ——, ——.

Affectionately . . . if you permit this chaste declaration.

Marcel

1. Daniel Halévy (1872 – 1962), a schoolmate of Proust at Condorcet. Son of the author and Academician Ludovic Halévy, who was a cousin of Mme Émile Straus, he became a biographer and critic, co-editor with Charles Péguy of the *Cahiers de la quinzaine.*

2. Proust later realized that he was mistaken about Montaigne; he is nowhere mentioned in *Remembrance of Things Past* in connection with homosexuality.

3. In *Cities of the Plain* (II. 824 – 25; 985) and in *The Captive* (III. 210 – 11), homosexuality is termed a 'malady', a disorder of the nervous system.

4. Émile Straus (1844 – 1929), lawyer and financier; he was Jacques Bizet's stepfather.

13
TO ANATOLE FRANCE[1]

[About 15 May 1889]

Dear Sir,

It occurs to me that you have just read M. Chantavoine's article[2] and that an expression of passionate sympathy might console you if, as seems possible, those unintelligent pages have had the power to grieve you.

For the last four years Saturday has been my red-letter day, the day when *Le Temps* brings me the purest of joys. For four years I have read and reread your divine books, to the point of knowing them by heart.[3] For four years I have loved you so much that I believe I understand you a little. And indeed, if I ever have enough talent, I shall try to write what I think of you, and I assure you that my article will give you more pleasure than that of your 'colleague' M. Chantavoine.

In the meantime I content myself with loving you, with trying to understand you more fully and with reading your books to the more intelligent of my comrades at Condorcet, where I have won you some staunch friends! I have gone so far as to catechize those retarded professors who did not know you. What joy it has given me this year to find in my professor of philosophy, who is a great thinker,[4] a highly intelligent love for your books.

You have taught me to find a beauty I did not appreciate before in books, ideas, and people. You have beautified the universe for me, and I am so much your friend that not a day passes without my thinking of you several times, though I have some difficulty in imagining your physical presence.[5] With the memory of the hours of exquisite delight you have given me I have built, deep in my heart, a chapel filled with you.

I suffered so much at seeing you publicly denigrated in that article that I have taken the liberty of writing to tell you how cruelly it afflicted me.

A student of philosophy[6]

1. The well-known novelist; 'Anatole France' was the pseudonym of Jacques Anatole François Thibault (1844 – 1924).

2. On 15 May 1889 the *Journal des débats* published a highly disparaging review by Henri Chantavoine of Anatole France's recently published novel *Balthasar*.

3. An exaggeration: the weekly chronicles by Anatole France had been appearing in *Le Temps* for only a little over three years, since 21 March 1886.

4. In a note to his translation (1906) of Ruskin's *Sesame and Lilies*, Proust wrote of Darlu: '. . . the most admirable teacher I have known, the man who has had the greatest influence on my thinking . . .' But a few years later he had changed his mind, writing in a notebook: 'No one has ever had such influence on me (as Darlu, and I have recognized it to be bad)' (*Le Carnet de 1908* [1976], 104 and n. 430).

5. In *Swann's Way* (1. 104), the Narrator imagines Bergotte as 'a frail and disappointed old man'. Later (*Within a Budding Grove*, 1. 589), he is surprised to meet 'a youngish, uncouth, thickset and myopic little man, with a red nose curled like a snail-shell and a goatee beard' – the spit and image of Anatole France as he was when Proust first met him.

6. The handwriting of the original letter, the chronology, tone, and ideas show that this 'student of philosophy' can only have been Marcel Proust.

14
FROM HIS MOTHER

Saturday four o'clock [14 December 1889]

My dearest boy,

How dreadful that you've been deprived of leave. I was so glad Finaly went to see you yesterday.[1] If only I could do the same. I wouldn't send Robert if you have a friend. That's the kind of duplication that no one fully enjoys.

I am counting on a good long letter tomorrow, which will have to substitute a little for your company.

Your grandmother is on milk today – still in homeopathic doses – she only consents to take it if it has no taste of milk.[2]

I shall try to see Finaly and get some news of you. But from what I know of his character, I fear he will have stopped at the *Gebäude*[3] and not tried to penetrate your life and state of mind.

Oh well, my dearest, a month has passed, only eleven pieces of the cake remain to be eaten, and one or two slices will be spent on leave.[4]

I've thought of a way of making the time seem shorter to you. Take eleven bars of the chocolate you're so fond of, make up your mind to eat one and no more at the end of each month – you'll be amazed how quickly they go – and your exile with them. I believe I'm talking nonsense, giving you stupid advice that will only aggravate your dyspepsia.

Robert has just come up for a moment with Joyant, they seem to be very good friends. Joyant has grown enormously, I didn't dare tell him so.

Goodbye, my dear boy. Keep well and win the battle, the reward will be your happiness and ours.[5]

I love you tenderly.

J.P.

---

1. Proust was at Orléans doing his year of military service. His visitor, Horace Finaly (1871 – 1945), son of the banker Hugo Finaly, had been his contemporary in Darlu's philosophy class at Condorcet.

2. Mme Nathé Weil, now in her last illness, died on 3 January 1890, at the age of sixty-five. (Homeopathic doses = very small quantities.)

3. I.e. the 'building' – the external aspect or façade.

4. Proust had enlisted on 11 November 1889 as a 'one-year volunteer', and been inducted into the 76th Infantry Regiment as a private.

5. A paraphrase of Corneille, *Le Cid* (v. i): Chimène to Rodrigue, 'Sors vainqueur d'un combat dont Chimène est le prix.'

15
FROM HIS MOTHER

Auteuil, Wednesday one o'clock
[23 April 1890]

Dear boy,

Have you spoken to M. Kopff[1] about your hemi . . . doloritis?

Your father thinks it will be possible to take up the *Figaro*'s remarks orally – on Saturday.

He urges you, however, to cut down on your *fromages à la crème*. (Think a number, then take half, etc.)

My darling, I am permeated with Loti, and with him I say for the benefit of those so unfortunate as not to understand him: 'If they knew with what a shrug of my shoulders I . . . their disdain.'

I never tire of rereading these lines:

'And I should like, for the first appearance of this blessed figure in my book of memories, to welcome her if possible with distinctive words, with words made for her, such words as do not exist, and which, all by themselves, would bring healing tears to the eyes, words of infinitely consoling gentleness.'[2]

How happy you have made me, my boy, in finding me this to read. Sometimes in Madame de Sévigné I also find thoughts and words that give me pleasure. She says (in criticizing a friend for her conduct towards her son . . .):

'I know another mother who counts herself for nothing, who has wholly given herself over to her children.'

Doesn't that apply perfectly to your grandmother? Except that she wouldn't have *said* it.

And then this, speaking of anxieties she does not dare express:

'Another great friendship, my dear child, might be made from all the feelings that I hide from you.'[3]

There will be only three issues of *Le Temps* with Paul's article. I will send them to you. (The first is yesterday's.)[4] Robert is going to Boutroux's class today and will not miss another.

'*Philo sum et nihil philo mihi etc.*'[5]

My pet, this morning, since your father wasn't coming home, I had lunch at half past ten with Robert, then I saw to wiping the keyboard of my son's piano, the candle was stalactizing the dust on it, then – conscientiously practised exercises for an hour – while Robert read his physics book beside me.

Then – stiff and rheumatic – I stopped and dictated algebra problems to Robert, which he wrote on the blackboard. Then a little while ago your father came in, I saw him for a moment before he admitted a patient, and now I'm writing to my pet – and then I'm going out – to see Lebel, my hatter (who is at least the equal of Pepita and Clarinda).[6]

Adieu, my darling, I kiss you tenderly with a pedal point to be sustained until the next kiss.

Your white lilac is drooping, but the *Vergissmeinnicht* is quite fresh.

With infinite tenderness,

J.P.

Your father will be at home Sunday morning, then Monday consultation. All this is as sure as eggs is eggs.

No swimming or riding for the present, your father says.

1. Dr Pierre-Albert Kopff (1846–1907), an officer in the army medical service and an acquaintance of Proust's father.

2. From chapter 5 of Pierre Loti's semi-autobiographical *Roman d'un enfant* (1890). The sentence quoted above reads more accurately: 'Those people do not imagine all the contempt I have to offer them in return for their shoulder-shrugging.' Loti is evoking his earliest memories of his mother, and expressing his contempt for readers who cannot comprehend such sentiments.

3. The quotations are from letters of Mme de Sévigné to her daughter, Mme de Grignan, of 26 June and 21 July 1680.

4. Paul Desjardins, 'La Demoiselle du Collège de France: Histoire de la rive gauche', *Le Temps*, 23, 24, 25 Apr. 1890.

5. Étienne-Émile-Marie Boutroux (1845–1921) was professor of history and philosophy at the Sorbonne. Proust admired him almost as much as he did Darlu. The motto is apparently a playful allusion to Terence's 'Homo sum:

humani nihil a me alienum puto', referring to Robert Proust's passion for philosophy.

6. Lebel-Stritter, at 259, rue Saint-Honoré, specialized in 'round hats for ladies'.

16
TO HIS FATHER[1]

[Orléans] This Tuesday 23 September [1890]
My dearest papa,

If I haven't begun my correspondence with you before, it's because my leave was spent mostly in bed (Mama has probably written to you about it) and I had so much to do yesterday (my first day back) that I wasn't even able to write to Mama. I hope you liked Maupassant. I don't believe he knows me, I've only met him twice, because of his illness and his trip, but he must know more or less who I am.[2] I don't feel at all bad (except my stomach) and I'm not even suffering from the general melancholia, brought on by this year of absence which, if not its cause, can at least serve as a pretext and excuse for it.

But I am finding it very hard to concentrate, to read, learn by heart, remember.

Today, since I have very little time, I send you only this brief sign that I am thinking of you with constant affection. Until tomorrow, my dearest papa, remember me to the delightful poet, your neighbour, and tender my respects to Mme Cazalis . . .[3] Imagine, to the infinite horror of the Derbannes some Cabourg housemaids, catching sight of the traditional soldier boy, blew me a thousand kisses. The housemaids of Orléans – by me forsaken – are avenging themselves. And I am punished, if M. Cazalis will permit me to quote a line from one of his most beautiful poems,

For having scorned the flowers of their bare breasts.[4]

Ever so affectionately,

your son
Marcel Proust

I resumed my training yesterday.

1. Dr Achille-Adrien Proust (1834–1903), eminent physician, pioneer in the new science of hygiene, in which he held the chair at the Paris Faculty of

Medicine, and Inspector-General of the Sanitary Services. This is the only extant letter written by Proust during his military service.

2. Proust seems to have been introduced to Guy de Maupassant (1850 – 93) at the house of his friends the Strauses.

3. Dr Henry Cazalis (see letter 96) published verse under the pseudonym Jean Lahor. Dr Proust was apparently taking the waters at Aix-les-Bains, where the Cazalis family had a house.

4. Proust had returned on 22 September 1890 from a leave spent at Cabourg as a guest of the Derbannes. In Jean Lahor's poem 'Salomé' (1875), the line quoted – which refers to John the Baptist – reads: 'Qui jadis dédaignait les fleurs de ses seins nus.'

17
TO MADAME ÉMILE STRAUS[1]

[22 November 1890]

I am all the more pleased with your letter because I thought you were angry with me. I don't know why. Don't scold me for the chrysanthemums[2] or my friendly sentiments. The things are sad enough in themselves and anyway they are much too unimportant to worry you. Besides, Madame, you will surely be grateful to me for the infrequent flowers I send when I tell you that they invariably spare you a letter from me. And humble as they are, they will always be more beautiful and more subtly tinted than my prose. When I lack the strength of will to concentrate my affectionate thoughts, I have to write or do something. So I will come on Sunday though not on future Sundays, but at one o'clock as soon as I have my frock coat, because my jacket is too frightful.[3]

Marcel Proust

1. Mme Émile Straus, née Geneviève Halévy (1850 – 1926), widow of the composer Georges Bizet. A brilliant conversationalist, who kept a salon, she was one of Proust's models for the Duchesse de Guermantes.

2. French horticulturalists had just begun to grow giant Japanese-style chrysanthemums. Robert de Billy (*Marcel Proust: Lettres et conversations* [1930], 69, 70) tells how at about this time his parents were overcome 'with amazement' at the arrival of three of these splendid blooms, which Proust had sent him along with some verses he had written for his friend.

3. Having just returned from his year of military service, Proust was in need of re-outfitting himself.

18

TO MADAME ÉMILE STRAUS

[Some time in 1891 ?]
The truth about Mme Straus

At first, you see, I thought you loved only beautiful things and that you understood them very well – but then I saw that you care nothing for them – later I thought you loved people, but I see that you care nothing for them. I believe that you love only a certain mode of life which brings out not so much your intelligence as your wit, not so much your wit as your tact, not so much your tact as your dress. A person who more than anything else loves this mode of life – and who charms. And because you charm, do not rejoice and suppose that I love you less. To prove the contrary (for you are well aware that what one does proves more than what one says – you who sometimes say and never do) I shall send you more beautiful flowers and you will be angry, Madame, since you do not deign to favour the sentiments with which I have the painful ecstasy to be

The most respectful servant
of your Sovereign Indifference
Marcel Proust

19

TO FERNAND GREGH[1]

9, boulevard Malesherbes,
this Thursday [2 ? June 1892]
My dear Fernand,

I have just reread your 'Soir', and despite the objections of Jacques Bizet, who claims to have the 'authorities' on his side, I much prefer it to your 'Banlieue' and your 'Amours défuntes'[2] just as I prefer Baudelaire's 'Le Voyage' to Musset's 'Silvia'. Yet I adore 'Silvia' and 'Banlieue' and 'Amours défuntes'. I have only glanced through the rest, the charming 'Conte métaphysique' and 'Pessimisme', which is not quite so pleasant, it seems to me. But it ('Pessimisme') will make an excellent impression in twenty years when a painter, drawing inspiration from the illustrious Fernand Gregh, enters a grandiose painting in the competition for the medal of honour, representing the last man killing the last woman. At the bottom he will have copied the whole 'passage' that inspired him. And the art critics, some of whom will prefer the man's *geste*, some the woman's imploring gaze, and still others the 'cosmic' background, will consider the painting inferior to the writer's description.

After this praise, may I give vent to a reproach, the violence of which you may perhaps put down to my poor health? How stupid you must all be to have accepted 'Meditation on the Suicide of One of My Friends' by Monsieur what's-his-name.[3] The marquis and the vicomte in *Les Précieuses ridicules* are two lackeys who ineptly ape their masters' way of speaking. This article might have been written by Barrès's lackey.[4] Moreover, it smacks of an indulgence towards usurers, promissory notes, loans, which can only dishonour the editors of *Le Banquet*. Did this young man (Maxime) really exist? If he did, I pity him for serving as a model for the most repugnant of *fin-de-siècle* chromos. But of course he never existed! Why would a person disgusted with everything, disillusioned with everything (an attitude for which the author professes an exasperating admiration which he obviously regards as most 'distinguished' and 'intelligent'), borrow money, sign promissory notes and resort to usurers?

Now perhaps you will tell me that my articles are worse. Maybe so, but I am *on Le Banquet*. Its purpose is to publish our productions. But when we take an article from outside, it oughtn't to be so stupid that we would reject it if it were written by one of us. Really, such conduct shows a journal up and dishonours it. Publishing bad articles on fashion does not dishonour. But to write such stuff about death! When I have turned down military articles by an officer. They would have been a thousand times better and *less compromising*. I am sick at heart that *Le Banquet* should publish such an article. Louis de la Salle's verses[5] are beautiful both as to form and as to colour.

Tender thoughts from your affectionate

Marcel

1. Fernand Gregh (1873 – 1960), poet and author of a book about his friendship with Proust. He was one of Proust's models for Bloch.

2. These three poems, as well as the two *contes philosophiques* mentioned below, all by Gregh, appeared in issue no. 4 of *Le Banquet*, a periodical founded by Gregh, Jacques Bizet, Daniel Halévy, Robert Dreyfus, and Proust. 'Banlieue' (Suburbs) and 'Amours défuntes' (Dead Loves) are presented as

'posthumous poems' and attributed to Henry Chalgrain. Proust was taking no great risk in expressing his preference for 'Soir' (Eventide), since it alone of all these pieces bears Gregh's signature. The first number of *Le Banquet* had appeared in March 1892, when its founders were all about nineteen or twenty. It was supposed to be published monthly, but the eighth and last number did not appear until March 1893 – although, as Robert Dreyfus observed, that year had as many months as usual.

3. The author whose name Proust affects to forget was Léon Blum (1872 – 1950), the future Premier of France. Despite his position on the editorial board, Proust was unable to prevent the publication in *Le Banquet* of two further articles by this same author. His antipathy to Blum seems to have lasted until January 1919, when Proust learned that the man he so detested was trying to obtain the cross of the Legion of Honour for the author of *Within a Budding Grove*.

4. Cf. the play by Molière. The essay-novels of the nationalist politician Maurice Barrès (1862 – 1923) were popular at the time.

5. Comte Louis-Georges Séguin de la Salle (1872 – 1915), poet and essayist. His sonnet entitled 'Pholoé' (*sic*), dedicated to Proust, appeared in *Le Banquet* no. 4.

20

TO MADAME ÉMILE STRAUS

[Friday 24 June 1892]

When you receive this bouquet, Madame, I shall be taking examinations at my School of Political Science. I am writing to you because I hope it will bring me good luck and because I shall no doubt be detained too long to call on you. I have been taking examinations all week and hope to have done with them tomorrow morning. But my professor has gravely threatened my divine Saturday, my day of true happiness, by scheduling my examination for the afternoon rather than the morning. I have passed up to now and hope to do so again tomorrow,[1] so proving to you that you are quite mistaken in thinking me lazy or interested only in society. I work very hard. I know I have no business praising myself to you. But whom can I trust to do it for me? M. Straus? And as for the virtues of industry and application, to which I lay claim because you esteem them, perhaps it is no great sin to boast of them, since they imply great difficulty in understanding

things and dealing with them. I find Jacques [Bizet] quite charming at
the moment and hope you will not be more severe in your judgement
of

Your respectful, affectionate and sincere

Marcel Proust

1. On Wednesday, 22 June 1892, Proust – now studying law at the Sorbonne – took an oral examination in Albert Sorel's course on Diplomatic History from 1818 to 1878 and obtained the mark of 4¾ out of a possible 6 with
the comment: 'Highly intelligent'. On Thursday the 23rd he was questioned on
Albert Vandal's course in Oriental Affairs and was marked 5 out of 6, with the
comment: 'Generally good responses'. The examination which threatened to
spoil his 'divine Saturday' was in Anatole Leroy-Beaulieu's Survey of Contemporary Europe. His thoughts may have been elsewhere, for his mark was only
4¼ out of 6, without comment.

21

TO JACQUES-ÉMILE BLANCHE[1]

This Friday [29 ? July 1892]

My painter!

Now that the Saturdays which brought us together are over,[2]
since my law examinations (4 and 5 August) will be going on until
after your likely departure, you will forget me completely. It seemed
to me that the only way of guaranteeing myself against your forgetfulness was to associate your permanent and beloved thirst with your
memory of me. Therefore accept this little gift, which will remind
you of it and satisfy it,

from your sincere friend,

Marcel Proust

whom you will kindly tell when you are leaving, so he can go and bid
you goodbye.

1. Jacques-Émile Blanche (1861 – 1942), prominent painter and art critic. He
did portraits of Leconte de Lisle, Gide, and many others.

2. Blanche had just completed his portrait of Proust as a young dandy, for
which he had done a first pencil sketch at Trouville on 1 October 1891.

22
TO ROBERT DE BILLY[1]

This Friday at Les Frémonts,
where I am with Louis de la Salle[2]
[19? August 1892]

Thank you for your regards, my dear Robert. We are thinking of you at Les Frémonts, where Mlle Mary[3] speaks to me every
day of you and your nobility of soul. But I am amazed at this young
lady's moral, almost religious preoccupations. True enough, Mme
Cahen is not at Saint-Moritz, but believe me, she has no more connection with the W[eisweiller]s than Picherel can have with Mme de
Pourtalès, though they are both Protestants.[4] So you see she wouldn't
have lowered you in anyone's esteem. I won't give you the news of
Trouville, because I know it would amuse you less than [Aubert]
Mme Baignères.[5] (Aubert must be pleased at my putting his name instead of Mme Baignères.) But I think of you constantly with faithful
affection. Write to me at Les Frémonts. Tell Aubert I love him dearly
and don't forget your friend Marcel, who embraces you with all his
heart.

M.P.

My dear de Billy,

Marcel is kind enough to let me add my regards to his, a traditional formula but in this case sincere. Horace [Finaly] asks me to
say the same for him.

De la Salle

1. Robert Jules Daniel de Billy (1869–1953), later a diplomat. Proust made
friends with him at the time of his military service.

2. Les Frémonts, the estate on a hill overlooking Trouville which Proust used
as a model for La Raspelière, has the fabulous 'three views' described in *Cities
of the Plain* (II. 1031–32). Proust and Louis de la Salle were visiting the
Finalys, who had rented the villa from the Arthur Baignères's.

3. Cf. Fernand Gregh, *L'Âge d'or* (1947), 166: '. . . the centre of the family
was Mary Finaly [1873–1918], a delightful girl, by turns laughing and serious,
with whom we were all a little in love.' She married Roger Thomas de Bar-
barin in 1897.

4. Comtesse Louis Cahen d'Anvers, née Louise de Morpurgo, was famous for her elegance; Paul Bourget was said to be in love with her. The Comtesse Edmond ～ ～ ～ alès, née Mélanie de Bussierre, had been a great beauty of the ～ ～ ～ Proust is commenting on the social differences among Jewish, ～ ～ ～ ant, members of Parisian society.

～ ～ ～ ssed out and 'Madame Baignères' added between the lines. ～ ～ ～ the acquaintance of Edgar Aubert (1869–1892), son of a ～ ～ ～ e, the previous winter, through Robert de Billy. Aubert and ～ ～ ～ -Moritz.

～ BERT DE BILLY

> Les Frémonts, Trouville.
> This Monday [29 August? 1892]

～ bert,

～ ord from my bed before I fall asleep . . . thinking of ～ rd on this paper to which you are so unjust. For ～ h concerned with categories as you are, it is even ～ to confuse Mme Straus's this year's travelling paper ～ ne Sulzbach than to have associated Mme Louise ～ Weisweillers in your other letter. To finish up with this paper and defend it against you, you horrid little rascal, Captain Walewski wrote yesterday to ask me where I had found this 'ravishing paper'.[1] I will conceal from you no longer that it costs 95 centimes at the Trois Quartiers. But is that a reason why it should be ugly, you who buy such disturbing neckties for a song (I wish you could see my Liberty ties in every possible tint).

I'll write you more another time. But don't boast about the length of your letters. Segonzac[2] keeps writing me ten-page ones. At last I've found the friend of my dreams, affectionate and given to letter-writing. It's true that he only puts on one stamp and I always have 30 centimes to pay at the post office. But what won't one do when one loves? I slip back under the covers but first press your hand most affectionately. I even, if it gives you pleasure, embrace you, as well as our dear Edgar Aubert.

> Marcel Proust

Do you know that my neighbour Mme Straus[3] has made me a devotee of the races and alas I've lost!

37

1. Charles-Zanobi-Rodolphe, Comte Colonna-Walewski, grandson of Napoleon I, a captain in Proust's regiment during his military service at Orléans. He is said to have served as model for the Prince de Borodino in *Remembrance of Things Past*. The paper in question is a pink laid paper, 259 × 141 mm, water-marked 'SOUTHERN CROSS / FINE QUALITY'.

2. Comte Pierre de Segonzac (b. 1871).

3. Mme Émile Straus had taken a villa, the Manoir de la Cour Brûlée, near by at Trouville.

24
TO ROBERT DE BILLY

Friday morning [23 September 1892]

I'm very sad, my dear Robert, and I wish you were here with me so we could talk about Aubert[1] together. Did you know that when I was left alone in Paris – after my parents went off to Auteuil – I began to like him very much and his return to Paris was one of the joys I was most looking forward to. He was so sure of returning, always saying '*In any case* I shall be back next year.' Now those words break my heart. I believe he still expected a good deal out of life, found it still full of promise, and that makes it even more heartrending. And then his charming sadness, his distrustful, almost anxious uncertainty about everything he was planning to do, strike me now as presentiments. Thinking of these things, we can only find reasons to love him more and to heighten and appease our grief. I have a photograph of him, on the back are some verses translated from the English, I don't remember them but they are rather sad, I think. And some letters, the last two of which I was reproaching myself the *day before yesterday* with not having answered. I beg you to write and tell me what his illness was, whether he knew how serious it was, what relatives he has left behind, whether they resemble him, tell me all the details of your trip with him; a thousand things that would not have interested me before, but are so precious to me now because they are the last things I shall know of him.

My dear friend, with love,

Marcel

1. Edgar Aubert died in Switzerland, of appendicitis, on 18 September 1892.

25
TO MADAME LAURE HAYMAN[1]

This Wednesday morning
[2 November 1892]

Dear friend, dear delight,

Here are fifteen chrysanthemums, twelve for your twelve when they have faded, three to complete your twelve; I hope the stems will be excessively long, as I requested. And that these flowers, as proud and sad as you – proud of being beautiful, sad that everything is so stupid – will give you pleasure. I thank you again (and if my examination were not on Saturday, I should go and thank you in person) for your kind thought for me. I should so much have liked to attend that eighteenth-century party, to see those young people who, you say, are so witty and charming, gathered around you. How well I understand them! That a woman who is merely desirable, a mere object of lust, should divide her worshippers and incite them against one another is only natural. But when a woman, like a work of art, reveals to us the most refined charm, the subtlest grace, the most divine beauty, the most voluptuous intelligence, a common admiration for her forges a bond and makes for brotherhood. The worship of Laure Hayman makes men co-religionists. And since this goddess is very special, since her charm is not accessible to everyone, since to fathom it one needs rather refined tastes, a sort of initiation of mind and feeling, it is only fitting that the faithful should love one another, that the initiate should understand one another. And indeed your shelf of Saxe (almost an altar)[2] strikes me as one of the most charming things to be seen anywhere – such a thing, I believe, as has rarely existed since Cleopatra and Aspasia. And so I propose to call the present century the century of Laure Hayman, the reigning dynasty being that of the Saxes. – Will you forgive me all this foolishness and permit me after my examination to bring you

My affectionate respects
Marcel Proust

On second thought, it would rather embarrass me to walk into your rat's nest of Saxes. If you don't mind, I would rather on visiting you see the man whom I desire above all to see.[3] Then if they find me a bore they will at least not find me indiscreet. And I shall not have to fear the vengeance of dukes or counts for having disturbed any Saxes.

1. Laure Hayman (1851 – 1932), Proust's principal model for Odette, was born at the Hacienda de la Mariposa, in the Andes. Daughter of an engineer, she seems to have been descended from the painter Francis Hayman (1708 – 76), Gainsborough's teacher, and had English, Belgian, and French blood in her veins.

2. Saxe = Dresden china, but is also an allusion to the royal princes of the Saxe family, who frequented Laure Hayman's salon.

3. Probably the novelist Paul Bourget (1852 – 1935). See letter 10, n. 1.

26
TO PAUL DESJARDINS[1]

This Monday morning [December 1892]

Dear Sir,

Forgive me for not having subscribed yet to *L'Action morale*.[2] I was unable to, but shall do so now.

In the hope of being enlightened, I take the liberty of submitting to you an impression made on me by the first issue, that you were kind enough to give me. I read with stupefaction that one should favour[3] a useless and as it were sensuous (like perfume) charity rather than a utilitarian charity (utilitarian not in the virtuous intention of the giver, but in producing a result appropriate to the receiver) which, says the article, leaves the soul dry. These words would not have surprised me (even if they displeased me) in M. Renan's *Marcus Aurelius*, M. France's *Thaïs*, or M. Barrès's *Jardin de Bérénice*.[4] Since these great artists consider charity exclusively (and in my humble opinion it is a weakness on their part) in an aesthetic light, they are careful not to divest it of this charm of 'uselessness', the most artistic sort of elegance.

But that you should allow such things to be written in your journal – that is the cause of my stupefaction.

Haven't you banished pure aestheticism from art itself (and this, it seems to me, is the excessive element in your doctrine and amounts to a confusion of two ideas) only to inject it into ethics, where it has no business.[5] Suppose someone were to pour perfume over the feet of a poor man instead of clothing him: wouldn't he be cultivating the artistic pleasure of performing so splendidly useless an act rather than the virtue of wanting to do the poor man good? Consequently a utilitarian intent is implicit in this sort of charity rather than in the charity which strives to do the most good to the object of its love.

What language! I am sure you think I am abusing your permission to dispense with literary pretensions[6] in writing of these matters.

Pardon my indiscretion, but you know the extreme importance I attach to everything that issues from your admirable mind as well as to those men whose good will has rallied round your thoughts and feelings.

Rest assured, sir, of my affectionate esteem,

Yours sincerely
Marcel Proust

1. Paul-Louis Desjardins (1859–1940), critic and philosopher, member of a distinguished family of upper-bourgeois intellectuals.

2. The first issue of the *Bulletin* of the Union for Moral Action appeared on 7 November 1892.

3. Proust first wrote 'que vous recommandez' (that you favour), then changed it to 'qu'on devait recommander'.

4. Ernest Renan, *Marc-Aurèle et la fin du monde antique* (1881), vol. vii of his *Histoire des origines du Christianisme*; Anatole France, *Thaïs* (1890); Maurice Barrès, *Le Jardin de Bérénice* (1891).

5. In *Swann's Way* (I. 130), Legrandin, quoting a poem by Desjardins, adds: 'Perhaps you have never read Paul Desjardins. Read him, my boy, read him; in these days he is converted, they tell me, into a preaching friar, but he used to have the most charming watercolour touch. . . .'

6. The first number of the *Bulletin* carried the notice: 'In these pages there should be no pretension to literary form . . .', repeated in each issue for the first year of publication.

27
TO MADAME ÉMILE STRAUS

Thursday, upon leaving you.
[December 1892 or the first months of 1893]

Madame,

I love mysterious women, since you are one, and I have often said so in *Le Banquet,* in which I would often have liked you to recognize yourself.[1] But I can no longer love you wholly, and I will tell you why, though it's useless, but you know how one spends one's time doing things that are useless or even quite harmful, especially when one loves, even if less. You believe that in making oneself too accessible one lets one's charm evaporate, and I think that's true. But let me tell you what happens in your case. One usually sees you with twenty people, or rather through twenty people, for the young man is farthest away from you. But let us suppose that after a good many days one succeeds in seeing you alone. You only have five minutes, and even during those five minutes you are thinking of something else. But that's nothing so far. If one speaks to you of books, you find it pedantic, if one speaks to you of people, you find it indiscreet (if one informs) and curious (if one enquires), and if one speaks to you of yourself, you find it ridiculous. And so one is a hundred times on the point of finding you a lot less delicious, when suddenly you grant some little favour that seems to indicate a slight preference, and one is caught again. But you are not sufficiently imbued with this truth (I don't believe you are imbued with any truth): *that many concessions should be granted* to platonic love. A person who is not in the least sentimental becomes amazingly so if he is reduced to platonic love. As I wish to obey your pretty precepts condemning bad taste, I won't go into detail. But give it a thought, I beseech you. Have some indulgence towards the ardent platonic love borne you, if you still deign to believe and to countenance it, by

> your respectfully devoted
> Marcel Proust

1. One of several possible allusions to Mme Straus in *Le Banquet* is this: 'At last he made the acquaintance of a woman whose intelligence was revealed only by a subtler grace, who contented herself with living and did not dissipate the enchanting mystery of her nature in over-precise conversation. She was as gentle as graceful, agile, deep-eyed animals, and as disturbing as the memory, almost effaced in the morning, of our dreams. But she did not trouble to do what two others had done for him: to love him.' (*Études* I, 'Les Maîtresses de Fabrice', *Le Banquet* no. 2 [April 1892], 41)

28

TO ROBERT DE BILLY

This Tuesday [10 January 1893]
My dear little Robert,

I hardly dare write to you. I am not worthy to, I'm not doing a thing and luckily Paul Baignères,[1] by having me pose for a portrait, has been providing a pretext for my recent inactivity. Otherwise I'd have been devoured by remorse for my inertia, and it would have grieved me to abandon my innocent little body to such a nasty beast. I think of you every night as I go to bed, every morning as I get up, and all the time, all the time. I wouldn't have thought it possible – to such a point. There has been no great change in my sentimental life, except that I have found a friend, someone who is to me what I would have been to Cachard, for example, if he had not been so cold. That is the young and charming and intelligent and good and affectionate Robert de Flers. Ah! you other Robert, hurry back to Paris to learn how one must love one's friends.[2]

Poirson would not be pleased at the way you speak of him. Did you know that his mother's letters are filled with heraldic devices showing an upraised arm. One day M. Étienne Ganderax saw them and exclaimed: 'It's the left hand,' a joke which the Baignères seemed to relish more than the Poirsons.[3]

Did you know that M. Secrétan has honoured Paris with his visit. Since he stayed with Desjardins, we saw a good deal of him, as you can imagine. I wouldn't allow myself to express an unfavourable opinion of so admirable a master, if it were only my own. But Desjardins himself thought he was beneath contempt, that he had lost all understanding of himself, that he was bourgeoisified, Swissified, Calvinized. His debate with Ravaisson, Brochard, Séailles, etc. was grotesque.[4] 'These young people have lost all respect for the masters,' as Laure Baignères[5] says.

I embrace you with all my heart and beg you to write to your little Marcel, who is parched with longing for you.

Yours,
Marcel Proust

1. Paul-Louis Baignères (1869 – 1930), son of Arthur Baignères (see letter 29).

2. Robert de Billy was in Berlin, on his first diplomatic posting. Proust's friend Edward B. Cachard was the son of an American lawyer, Henry Cachard, counsel to the American Legation; his mother, née de Chazournes, seems to have been French. For Robert de Flers, see letter 93.

3. The family of Paul Poirson (1836 – 95), minor playwright, lived in place Malesherbes. Étienne Ganderax and his brother Louis (1855 – 1940), director and co-founder of the *Revue de Paris*, were often at the Baignères's.

4. Charles Secrétan (1815 – 95) was professor of philosophy at the University of Lausanne; his meeting with the other philosophers, old and young, mentioned here took place on 6 January 1893.

5. Mme Henri Baignères (see letter 29).

29

TO ROBERT DE BILLY

This Thursday [26 January? 1893]

My dear little Robert,

You can't imagine how much I miss you. My frivolity, which often makes me dwell in the present, has not impaired my feeling of friendship for you here. And I think of you all the more desperately because I cannot see you, because your charm no longer perfumes my daily life, your gaiety or wisdom no longer consoles me for my cares, and your advice no longer steers me towards the true and the good. I have been deeply moved by a package that has come to me through Boissonnas.[1] It is a memento that Edgar Aubert chose for me. Alas, he himself will come no more, he has gone away for longer than you. The days, which are turning mild and bright again, give me an illusion, precise to the point of hallucination, of those times, going home with him, when he was so charming, so witty, when he would glance at one or shake one's hand so very gently to make up for something rather sharp or ironic that he had just said. I remember that lunch with him, the *allée à la paume* in the Tuileries, and his English at the Finalys'.

You complain that no one tells you anything. But you see, I don't dare tell you anything, because I go out so much that you'd lose all respect for me if I told you about it. Do be kind enough to give me another list of the four examinations I should take[2] and the books I should read, I've lost the one I had. Don't forget. Tell me if I'm mistaken in thinking Edgar was friendly with Mme de Lareinty and Mme de Chaponay, two ladies I meet rather often, I could speak to them of him. Was it Mme de Lareinty or Mme de la Tremoïlle whom Caro asked what she thought about love – and who replied brusquely: 'I often make it but never speak of it!'[3] – The Baignères (I can speak of this because it has nothing to do with society) played charades the other day with the de Trazes at the house of a Mme Bourdet. It was wonderfully hilarious. J. de Traz as an old bourgeois in a bathtub, hidden under a sheet, but his foot sticking out so the chiropodist could cut his corns. It was sublime. M. Arthur,[4] once as an old Jew and another time as a member of the Institute, presiding over a meeting of the Geographic Society and inviting the members to attend the Wednesdays of Mme Henri Baignères, 'whose profound knowledge of cards cannot fail to be useful to you.' M. Arthur Baignères is an old

Proust's father, the distinguished physician Dr Adrien Proust,
and his mother, the former Jeanne Weil.

Marcel Proust, aged six (right), with his younger brother,
Robert, known in the family as Dick.

As a schoolboy, Proust (about 1885) played in the Champs-Elysées with the thirteen-year-old Marie de Benardaky, whom he was to call 'the intoxication and despair of my youth'.

Proust's admired teacher, Alphonse Darlu (front row, second from right), with his 1888–89 class in philosophy at the Lycée Condorcet; Proust is at the extreme left in the second row. Above, the main courtyard of the Lycée, which Proust attended from 1882 to 1889.

Anatole France, Proust's favourite author at the age of eighteen; the portrait is by Raymond Woog. France was later to contribute a preface to Proust's first published book, *Les Plaisirs et les jours.*

Proust as soldier, aged eighteen. He enlisted in November 1889 as a 'one-year volunteer', and served his term at Orléans as a private in the 76th Infantry Regiment.

Proust in 1890, still sporting a crew cut after his return from military service; he complained that his wardrobe needed extensive refurbishing.

In 1891, with his mother and brother, Dick (right). Mme Proust was in mourning for her mother, Proust's beloved grandmother Mme Nathé Weil, who died the year before.

Above, Mme Emile Straus, photographed by Nadar in 1887. A brilliant conversationalist, she kept a salon which Proust began to frequent about 1890.

Proust as a young dandy, in the portrait Jacques-Emile Blanche painted of him in 1892.

lecher, he told me how he took advantage of his position on the stage
to look down the bodices of his sister-in-law Laure and the other
ladies, and added: 'One could see their bosoms, they were like the inside of a trunk. Some had packed only six pairs of socks, others a
dozen, and still others nothing at all. My sister-in-law must have been
leaving on a long trip. . . .'[5] Seydoux has no doubt told you about
L'Invitée and how at the interval when I went over to bid Mme Aubernon good evening, she exclaimed so loudly that the whole audience up-
stairs and down craned their necks to look at us as they do when
there's a fight in the house.[6] I haven't seen a single one of your friends.
As Seydoux and M. de Neufville never came to see me, I never called
on them either. I haven't been able to return the call Boissonnas paid
me with you. I haven't been to see Rivière for fear of another dinner
with his parents, nor Trarieux for fear he would read to me, or rather
because I haven't had time. I often see Gregh, La Salle, Waru, Bizet,
Paul Baign[ères], who is doing my portrait, Jacques Baign[ères], Car-
bonnel, Henri de Rothschild, Segonzac, J. de Traz, but no one as
often as Robert de Flers, who comes to see me almost every day. Do
you know a new acquaintance of mine – observe that I don't say a new
friend, because you would think I was as quick to love as I am to forget – who lives in your avenue Kléber, his name is Chasseloup-Laubat?
I dined the day before yesterday with one of your colleagues, M. de
Florian.[7] Ah, my dear Robert, what art there is in his greeting, his
handshake, his walk, his repose, his silence, his conversation, his courtesy, and that superior politeness, his wit. He is the most accomplished
diplomat I have ever seen and his wife seems to be a superior person.
Write to me, love me, and give me the list requested by
Your little friend for ever
Marcel Proust

Constant (from the École) sends his regards.

P.S.   I went to see your parents recently, they are in excellent health
(including your grandmother).

1. Jean Boissonnas (1870 – 1953), one of Proust's schoolmates at the Lycée
Condorcet and then at the École des Sciences Politiques; he later entered the
foreign service.

2. To prepare for examinations for his law diploma; see letter 31.

3. The Baronne de Lareinty, née Puységur, then owned the actual château of
Guermantes at Lagny (Seine-et-Marne). The social decline of the Marquise de
Chaponay, née de Courval, whom Proust later admitted having taken as one of

the models for his Marquise de Villeparisis, was a consequence of her being divorced at a time when such a thing was unusual. Elme-Marie Caro (1826 – 87) was professor of philosophy at the Sorbonne.

4. Arthur Baignères (1843 – 1913), remembered as one of the wittiest men of his day, published two collections of stories (*Histoires modernes* and *Histoires anciennes*) in a somewhat old-fashioned style which Proust likened to that of Sainte-Beuve.

5. Cf. *Cities of the Plain*, where Swann casts 'an attentive, serious, absorbed, almost anxious gaze into the depths' of the Marquise de Surgis's corsage (II. 733).

6. Jacques Seydoux (1870 – 1929) was another of Proust's schoolmates at Condorcet. *L'Invitée*, a comedy by François de Curel, was staged at the Théâtre du Vaudeville on 19 January 1893. Robert de Montesquiou left a satirical portrait of Mme Raoul Aubernon, née Lydie Lemercier de Nerville (1825 – 99), in his *Professionnelles Beautés* (1905).

7. Xavier-Louis-Joseph de Froidefond, Comte de Florian (b. 1850), a career diplomat.

30
TO ROBERT DE MONTESQUIOU[1]

9, boulevard Malesherbes.
This Saturday evening [15 April 1893]

Sir,

You gave me leave to call on you – the evening Mlle Bartet recited your poetry at the home of Mme Lemaire.[2] But I don't dare call without asking at what time of day I would not be disturbing you. You were already so kind to me last Thursday that perhaps you will be even more so and grant an appointment, preferably in the afternoon, to

Your most respectful, fervent and charmed

Marcel Proust

1. Comte Robert de Montesquiou-Fezensac (1855 – 1921), aristocratic descendant of several marshals and statesmen who figure in French history, including d'Artagnan, hero of Dumas's *The Three Musketeers*. Highly cultivated and a great wit, he was a prolific poet as well as a respected art critic. The speech and mannerisms of the Baron de Charlus were modelled on his.

2. 'Mme Lemaire has just resumed her Thursday receptions,' reported *Le Gaulois* for 14 Apr. 1893. '. . . Yesterday evening, in the presence of a distin-

guished audience, Mlle Bartet recited exquisitely several poems by M. José de Heredia and by Comte de Montesquiou-Fezensac. . . .' For Mme Lemaire, see letter 44.

31
TO ROBERT DE BILLY

This Friday [9 June 1893]

My dear little Robert,

What a joy! So you're really coming! I am glad with all my heart. What will be your impression of me? I couldn't really say, not too bad a one, I hope. My relations with society ladies have changed a little. Couldn't you alter yours with me so we can see more of each other? Anyway, I'm anxious and delighted at the thought of seeing you. If I had known you were coming, I'd have waited for you before giving my *dîner de camarades*. In case it amuses you, here is the table:[1]

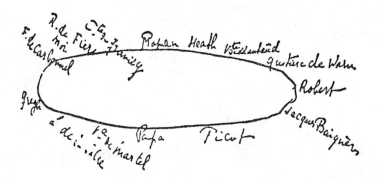

In the evening MM. Abel Desjardins, Paul Baignères, de Seligny, Pierre Lavallée, Pelletier, de Chamberet, Yeatman.[2] It's not quite complete, but that's it more or less. I think I shall spend the month of August at Saint-Moritz (if I pass my law exam). I've been strongly urged to do so by Robert de Montesquiou and Mme Howland,[3] both of whom you may have seen at Saint-Moritz, they are charming. Besides, I would know quite a few ladies there, and if I went, L. de la Salle would be kind enough to come along and stay with me. I shall ask you a good many questions about it and count on you to win my family over. I am being tutored in law along with Trarieux and Boissonnas. They claim that you've written horrid things about me, but you can see by this letter that I don't believe it for a minute.

Adieu, dear friend. Write me the date of your arrival and let yourself be embraced by your unalterably devoted

Marcel Proust

P.S.   My respects to Mme and M. Aliscé [*sic*].[4]

---

1. An incomplete version of the same seating plan is to be found on the back of a MS page of 'Mondanité de Bouvard et Pécuchet', published in *La Revue blanche* for July-August 1893. Willie Heath (see letter 44), to the left of Dr Proust in the original sketch, is here to the left of Mme Proust. In the original plan the young Comte Gaston de Chasseloup-Laubat, the 'new acquaintance' of letter 29, had the place of honour on the right of Mme Proust; here he is replaced by Comte Charles de Grancey. Segonzac has also disappeared from the final plan.

2. Proust had met Léon Yeatman (see letter 48) only recently.

3. Mme Meredith Howland, née Torrance, to whom Proust would dedicate his 'Mélancolique villégiature de Madame de Breyves' (see letter 36).

4. Henri Allizé (1860–1930), an acquaintance of Dr Proust, was a secretary at the French Embassy in Berlin, where the ambassador was his father-in-law, Jules Herbette.

32

TO ROBERT DE MONTESQUIOU

This Sunday evening [25 June 1893]

Sir,

I have been lying since this morning in this starry meadow, worshipping this heaven of flowers. I am dazzled by all these perfumes, intoxicated by so much light, and like the lotus-eaters, I have given up all thought of returning and wish I did not have to. I am too moved to compare this book to *Les Chauves-souris*.[1] But with regard to what is not an object of reasoning, for the divine reason that apprehends it is exempt from time, space, and relationships, with regard to what like music or faith is purely mysterious, I believe that there are here more lines that give an intimation of it, incarnate it, and so manifest it. After the fourteen most marvellous lines you have written (which begin with *At sunset they dance their pavanes*) there comes this divine movement:

> *Blinded eyes, peacocks bereft of all their luminaries,*
> *Yet even more*
> *Beloved of poets!*

It makes one's heart stop, and one doesn't know why. At this level, art no longer carries its explanation with it. Certain phrases of Wagner have this sweetness and certain of Leonardo's glances – and these lines as well:

> *. . . weep with*
> *With the star of gold, silvered by its gentleness.*[2]

Your Venetian glasses, those goblets so proud and sad in form, have nuances which, as Michelet says of pearls, 'madden the heart'.[3] Your verses are the mysterious honey that is as sweet as the sunlight. I could thank you endlessly if my thanks kept pace with my happiness. But in concluding I must also thank you for the lofty words that I heard from you yesterday and that still resound for me in the rich music of your voice. You have in me a frank, affectionate, respectful and true admirer.

Marcel Proust

I am awaiting your photograph with impatience. If one of these days I send you a magazine with something of mine in it, do not dwell on the absurdity of it following so closely on your gift of *Le Chef des odeurs suaves* – an absurdity for which I should have to take responsibility if I had harboured the ridiculous thought that this earthworm could be regarded as an exchange for your starry firmament.[4]

---

1. Montesquiou had just sent Proust *Le Chef des odeurs suaves* (The Master of Sweet Scents), his second collection of poems (1893), which deals almost entirely with flowers. The mention of the lotus-eaters is an allusion to the poem 'Invite', inspired by the well-known passage in the *Odyssey*. *Les Chauves-souris* (The Bats; 1892) was Montesquiou's first book of poems.

2. 'Au coucher du soleil ils dansent leur pavane / . . . Yeux crevés paons privés de tous leurs luminaires / Pourtant plus adorés / Des poètes encor!' is a quotation from 'Pavones', a poem about peacocks in *Le Chef des odeurs suaves*. 'Pleurez avec / Avec l'étoile d'or que sa douceur argente' is from the poem 'Laus noctis', in *Les Chauves-souris*.

3. A reference to poems XLVII – XLIX in *Le Chef des odeurs suaves*.

4. An allusion to Victor Hugo's *Ruy Blas*, II. ii.

33
TO ROBERT DE MONTESQUIOU

9, boulevard Malesherbes,
this Wednesday [28 June 1893]
Dear Sir,

Since 'one does not send a photograph through the post', since I am not expected to call on you until Easter or at the earliest New Year's Day, and since two of your friends, Mme Lemaire and the Princesse de Wagram, have done me the honour of inviting me this week, would you be so kind as to bring me the said photograph, promised but impossible to lay hands on, on Thursday or Saturday to the rue de Monceau or the avenue de l'Alma. I shall also ask you, if they attend one or another of these affairs, to point out to me some of those lady friends in whose circles you are most often spoken of (the Comtesse Greffulhe, the Princesse de Léon).[1]

Accept, sir, the expression of my devoted admiration,

Your sincerely respectful
Marcel Proust

1. For the Comtesse Greffulhe, see letter 34. The Princesse de Léon, a great friend of Montesquiou, ceased to bear that name on 6 August 1893, when her husband's father died and he became the eleventh Duc de Rohan.

34
TO ROBERT DE MONTESQUIOU

[Sunday 2 July ? 1893]
Dear Sir,

I have at last (yesterday at the home of Mme de Wagram) seen the Comtesse Greffulhe.[1] And the same feeling that decided me to impart to you my emotion on reading *Les Chauves-souris*, compels me to choose you as the confidant of my emotion of last evening. Her hair was dressed with Polynesian grace, and mauve orchids hung down to the nape of her neck, like those 'hats of flowers' M. Renan speaks of. It is hard to judge her, because to judge is to compare, and because in her there is no feature that can be found in any other woman or anywhere else. But the whole mystery of her beauty lies in the brilliance and especially the enigma of her eyes. I have never seen a woman so beautiful. I didn't ask to be introduced to her and I shall not even ask that of you, for apart from the indiscretion that might imply, it seems to me that speaking to her would agitate me rather painfully. I would like her to know what an enormous impression she made on me, and if, as I believe, you see her often, would you tell her? I hope to displease you less by admiring the woman whom you admire above all things and whom I shall henceforth admire after you, with you, and as Malebranche said, 'in you'.[2]

Your respectful admirer,
Marcel Proust

1. Comtesse Henri Greffulhe, née Princesse Élisabeth de Caraman-Chimay (1860–1952). A beautiful, energetic woman who played a leading role in Paris society, she was a patroness of musical and artistic events and one of Proust's models for the Duchesse de Guermantes.

2. Nicolas de Malebranche (1638–1715), metaphysician, author of *Recherche de la vérité*. He was, of course, speaking of the deity.

35
TO ROBERT DE MONTESQUIOU

This Monday evening [3 July 1893]
Sir,

Many thanks for the photograph. But the dedication is too modest if, thus isolated from the poem it summed up, it purports to define you. I believe that you are equally the sovereign of things eternal.[1] Let me explain my meaning:

I have long been aware that you far transcend the type of the exquisite decadent, whose features (never as perfect as yours, but often met with nowadays) have been imputed to you. But in these times without thought or will, in a word without genius, you alone excel by the twofold force of your meditation and your energy. And this, I believe, is something that has never been seen, this supreme refinement accompanied by the energy and creative power of earlier epochs, and what one might almost call a seventeenth-century intellectuality, so little of it has there been since. (Incidentally, I believe one might demonstrate – and not just for the pleasure of the paradox – that both you and Baudelaire have a seventeenth-century quality. The taste for maxims, the – lost – habit of thinking in verse. Did Corneille ever write a finer line than this:

She sees her soul more clearly in the declining light;

or a more Cornelian one than this:

Those whom proud delicacy condemns to live dry-eyed.)[2]

And this, I believe, is what has preserved so pure in you a generosity so rare in our time, what has enabled the subtlest of artists to write verses which embody the most powerful thought and would be assured of a place in an extremely choice anthology of philosophical poetry in France, what transforms the Sovereign of things transitory into the Sovereign of things eternal, and finally what makes it impossible to foresee the character of your future work, as is always the case where there is spontaneous outpouring, a wellspring, true spiritual life, in a word, freedom. All this for the greater happiness of your respectful and grateful

Marcel Proust

1. The photograph in question bears the inscription: 'Je suis le Souverain des choses transitoires' (I am the Sovereign of things transitory), the first line of Montesquiou's poem 'Maestro', in *Les Chauves-souris*.

2. 'Elle y voit mieux en elle au déclin des clartés' and 'Ceux que la pudeur fière a voués au cil sec' are both lines from 'Laus noctis', in *Les Chauves-souris*. Proust slightly misquotes the second, writing 'ceux' for 'Vous': 'You whom, etc.'

36
TO DANIEL HALÉVY[1]

[Paris, Friday 4? August 1893]

My dear Daniel,

Here's my answer. I'm delighted with the verve of your abbé. You've hit on the right tone straightaway. It bothers me that L. de la Salle (1) talks about my love affair. This makes matters easier for me. But it would be better if it came to light in the letter I am going to write him; (2) makes him a lieutenant, that's bad, he's an NCO. Otherwise he wouldn't be able to send him to me with a letter; (3) says that I shouted his praises. I won't say any good of him in the whole novel and, even though I possess information that might help me in my adventure, I'll pretend to attach no importance to it. It will come out in spite of me. Naturally the rest of you will know the truth, but you'll be tactful enough not to speak of it. I am answering you by return. Let's keep on this way. But of course we shall arrange the letters afterwards so that the answer will never come immediately after the letter. Later on I'll ask leave to change the name of the Princesse d'Alériouvres. In a short story I've just finished Mme de Breyves is née Alériouvres,[2] and Mme de Breyves's reputation might suffer from the resulting confusion.

Your devoted friend
Marcel Proust

Write to me at 9, bd Malesherbes until Monday morning and even after that with *Please forward*, until you hear from me. But I must tell you that with one or two exceptions the letters must be a lot longer than yours, which is very funny but too short. They should be several pages long.

What should I do with La Salle's letter and yours? Send them to Gregh? But think of all the Baignères commenting on them at Clarens.[3] It's worrisome. Well anyway, let me know.

1. This letter accompanies Proust's contribution to an epistolary novel he was writing in collaboration with his friends Halévy, Gregh, and Louis de la Salle, for which they seem to have taken as their model *La Croix de Berny* (1846), by Mme de Girardin, Théophile Gautier, Joseph Méry, and Jules Sandeau. Some fragments of the unfinished work survive in MS, three of them in Proust's hand and one in that of Louis de la Salle; the young authors seem to have lost interest before they had done much more.

2. 'Mélancolique villégiature [Melancholy Summer] de Madame de Breyves'.

3. Fernand Gregh was visiting the Baignères family at Clarens.

37
TO DANIEL HALÉVY

Saturday [19 August 1893]

Dear friend,

La Salle has done his letter over and is returning it to you. No, nothing should be changed in your letter and 'though it kill me', I won't say another word about it – and I'm only saying this by way of answering you. I shall be for a few days more at the Pension Veraguth, Saint-Moritz, Upper Engadine, Switzerland, where your letter has reached me along with Louis de la Salle of all people. Has Chalgrain[1] written? Of course we won't have a letter followed directly by the answer to it. We shall intersperse them as in Hervieu's novel.[2] A thousand affectionate thoughts.

Yours,
Marcel Proust

La Salle is reading *L'Intrus*[3] and is delighted with it.

I'm taking precious care of your letters, and I beg you to do the same with all those you have. Even if we do nothing with this *Cross*,[4] it will be amusing to read it from end to end.

La Salle has been generous enough to sacrifice his first letter to my love affair. I'm very glad. The first was mediocre despite the fine sentence at the end. This one is an exquisite 'masterpiece'.

He will write to you, because this letter is an answer to a request I had sent him for information about Givré, the man I love. He has answered me and he will inform you in a letter that will take the place of the one we are omitting, which you know and have sent me.

If you have any criticism of my part, you would oblige me by telling me.

1. Gregh's pseudonym (see letter 19, n. 2).

2. *Peints par eux-mêmes* (1893), by Paul Hervieu (see letter 172).

3. *L'Intrus* (The Intruder) was the title under which d'Annunzio's novel *L'Innocente* was published (1893) in French.

4. See letter 36, n. 1.

38
TO MADAME ANTOINE-ÉMILE BLANCHE[1]

Saint-Moritz,
Sunday 20 August [1893]

Madame,

If I did not wire M. Jacques yesterday, it is because I read of your great misfortune in the papers only yesterday. I wish I could see you and speak to you of my grief and give you at least the comfort of knowing how much those who like myself did not have the good fortune of seeing Dr Blanche very often admired him and what affection they felt for him. I am heartbroken not to have been able to bid him goodbye. He was so well when I saw him two weeks ago that I felt sure of seeing him again on my return. As soon as he fell ill and I half-suspected that you might lose him in the more or less distant future, I reproached myself for not having taken greater advantage of his friendliness to me. And I promised myself then that I would see him often. How much intelligence, charm and sublime goodness one forfeited by not going to see him now and again. It saddens me to think that I was too timid a fortnight ago to ask his leave to embrace him as I longed to do but did not dare. On my return I shall ask you for a photograph of him, so as to have always before me that gaze, which gave me a feeling of profound happiness, the memory of which now fills me with infinite sorrow. Madame, I have always been greatly moved by your kindness to me. My deep and respectful sympathy for you makes me share your grief and adds to my sorrow over the death of M. Blanche. As for Jacques's unhappiness, I cannot tell you how deeply it affects me. If there is any being so exquisite that his suffering sickens one more than that of others, and seems more unjust, it is he. Please be so kind as to embrace him for your respectful and very sad friend

Marcel Proust

1. Mme Blanche, née Louise-Émilie-Félicité Baron-Châtillon (1819? – 95), mother of Jacques-Émile Blanche. The death of her husband (b. 1820), the distinguished alienist, son of the founder of the famous psychiatric clinic, was reported along with that of Charcot in Le Figaro, 17 Aug. 1893.

39
TO ROBERT DE BILLY

Hôtel des Roches-Noires, Trouville.
But write to me before the end
of the month! or I'll be gone.
[Between 6 and 16 September 1893]

My dear little Robert,

You complain of my silence but don't tell me where to write to you. Well, I think you must be back in Berlin. I have had a lovely trip and after spending three weeks at Saint-Moritz and one on Lake Geneva, here I am with Mama at the Hôtel des Roches-Noires at Trouville. As for my impressions, you will read them in *La Revue blanche* – not in the enclosed issue, which is the one that was long promised and appeared late, nor even in the next, which will carry a very melancholy short story of mine – but in a later one.[1] People? I prefer not to speak of them because I don't want my stern Robert to tease me about my social ways. I only want to ask you a musical question about a lady – who is neither a duchess nor a princess, so don't condemn me – but only a Protestant, so you may have met her – with whom I became rather friendly there, since we have friends in common: Mme Jameson. I very much admired her talent at the piano, I saw a greatness in it – and I must say that sensitive and competent judges of music, the Princesse Brancovan, who is a friend of Paderewski and herself a great musician, Mlle d'Harcourt – as well as Mme Henri Baignères, whose sound judgement is known to you and who is not famous for her indulgence, agreed with me. But now Mme Straus says: 'Yes, of course she has a vigorous organism, takes excellent care of the apartment and polishes everything in sight' (which is very witty but should be saved for someone other than this woman who strikes me as such a great musician) 'and plays in an odious, anti-artistic way.'[2] Even if you have never heard her, you must – since she no doubt graces with her talent all those soirées where Trarieux acts the pretty boy and Boissonnas smirks, where MM. Vernhes and Picherel frown and glare under the ferule of Mme Mirabaud – and where Seydoux, forgetting he's a Barbantane,[3] goes looking for the young girl who will purify his morals – know what to think of her talent. I am not asking your opinion to form my own. The impression she made on me was too powerful to be effaced by a word from someone else, but I shall say: I definitely have no taste – or the contrary.

I am really at a loss because, my father insists, I have to make up my mind about my career. The Cour des Comptes[4] tempts me more and more. This is how I look at it. Unless I want to spend my life abroad, a career at the Ministry of Foreign Affairs in Paris would be just as boring as the Cour des Comptes.

Maybe the Cour des Comptes would be – for me – harder to prepare for, but wouldn't that be very largely compensated for by the absence of the period of apprenticeship which would absorb all the attention I am capable of? The rest of the time I would just amuse myself.

Ah, my friend, more than ever your advice in this would be

precious, and I suffer sorely from your absence; may a good letter ex-
punge it through the all-powerful miracle of the communicability of
spirit. – Is the bench not too badly discredited? What is left, considering that I am determined to become neither a lawyer nor a doctor nor
a priest nor – .

Ah, my dear Robert, you can imagine the thought that pursued me throughout my beautiful trip, the thought of him who loved
us so dearly and who is no longer with us, in whose clear eyes an
unparalleled charm was mingled with irony and tenderness, faith and
disillusionment. Poor Edgar, I reproached myself for the pleasure I
took in looking at Lake Geneva, which he would never see again.
Write me the date of his birthday, which I never knew, not even
when I received your letter with the crushing news. Give me his parents' address at the same time. Never having written to them, I would
like on that day to send them the sympathy of a friend of their son.

As ever, Robert,
Marcel Proust

1. The story, 'Mélancolique villégiature de Madame de Breyves', appeared in
the issue of 15 Sept. 1893; the prose poem 'Présence réelle' (Bodily Presence),
inspired by his stay in the Upper Engadine, did not appear in the review until
December 1893.

2. The pianist was probably Mme Conrad Jameson, née de Portal, who lived in
the boulevard Malesherbes and had a château near Coppet, in Switzerland. For
the Princesse Rachel Bassaraba de Brancovan, see letter 158, n. 3. Mme Straus's
observation is echoed by Mme de Cambremer-Legrandin, of her mother-in-
law, in *Cities of the Plain* (II. 843).

3. The sister of Jacques Seydoux was married to the Marquis de Barbantane.
M. Legrandin was to be in a similar situation, having a sister who marries into
an aristocratic family, the Cambremers.

4. A court whose function it is to control government expenditure.

40
TO HIS FATHER

9, boulevard Malesherbes
Thursday 10 a.m. [28 September? 1893]

My dearest papa,

I have kept hoping that I would finally be able to go on with
the literary and philosophical studies for which I believe myself fit. But

seeing that every year only subjects me to more and more practical discipline, I prefer to choose at once one of the practical careers you have suggested. I shall start studying in earnest with a view to the examination either for the Ministry of Foreign Affairs or for the École des Chartes, whichever one you prefer.[1] – As for a law office, I should vastly prefer going to work for a stockbroker. And I assure you, I wouldn't stick it out for three days! I still believe that anything I do outside of literature and philosophy will be just so much time wasted. But among several evils some are better and some worse. In my most desperate moments I have never conceived of anything more horrible than a law office. By helping me to avoid that, the foreign service would strike me not as my vocation, but as a remedy.

I hope you will see M. Roux and M. Fitch here. I believe Delpit is staying with M. Fitch. Let me remind you (for fear of a gaffe) that he is Mme Guyon's brother.[2]

I am delighted to be back again at the house whose charm consoles me for Normandy and for no longer seeing (as Baudelaire says in a line of which, I hope, you will feel the full force)

> . . . *the sun shining on the sea*[3]

I embrace you a thousand times with all my heart,

Your son
Marcel

P.S.   Would you be so kind as to write to Mama and tell her whether during your stay at the Brouardels', you have seen Kopff in connection with my officer's examination.[4]

---

1. Having completed his law course (his diploma bears the date of 10 October 1893), Proust was being urged by his father to take some advantage of his studies. The École des Chartes, founded in 1821, offered a three-year course of training for palaeontologists and archivists.

2. Mme Félix Guyon, née Delpit, had two brothers: Édouard Delpit (1844 – 1900), a man of letters, and Albert Delpit (1849 – 93), novelist, poet, and playwright. Dr Proust's gaffe would have been to confuse the latter, who died on 4 January 1893 from abuse of chloral hydrate, with the former. Dr Félix Guyon (1831 – 1920), a prominent urologist and surgeon, known for his love of puns, has been regarded as one of the models for Dr Cottard.

3. 'Le soleil rayonnant sur la mer', from 'Chant d'automne', in *Les Fleurs du mal*.

4. Dr Proust had been staying with his close friend Dr Paul-Camille-Hippolyte Brouardel (1837 – 1906), professor of forensic medicine. Dr Kopff was now

chief medical officer at army headquarters in Paris. As a reservist in the French Army, Proust was supposed to undergo the annual obligatory twenty-eight days of 'refresher' training. (In fact he was never well enough to serve.)

41
TO ROBERT DE MONTESQUIOU

[October 1893]

Dear Sir,

Your kindness to my friend Robert de Flers has provided me with your address. I am making use of it to ask your advice in connection with a project in which, I hope, you will find a certain respectful graciousness.

It is my intention, by way of simplifying a form that is often needlessly complicated, to write a few newspaper or magazine articles. And as you will not be surprised to learn since I have often told you how I felt, I would like the first to be an essay about you. In it, if 'Your Grace' agrees to help me, I would show how very much you differ from the run-of-the-mill decadents of our day. I would show your strength of will, the richness of your intellect, and how much of the seventeenth century there is in you, in short, everything that I have already taken the liberty of saying to you. For I believe that, in so far as it is desirable, through success and by acting on public opinion, to achieve the temporal embodiment of a great spiritual force, that is what your concern, or rather the concern of those who admire you, should be. This I would say *first* because I believe it to be true and *secondly* (or perhaps first in point of feeling) because, in the present state of public opinion, I believe it to be the *only thing* that can benefit you. The incomplete Montesquiou that most people conceive of suffices to enchant persons of feeling. I am convinced on the other hand that a good many intellectuals remain to be won over. This I would not undertake to do, for I lack the authority and have only love in my favour, but what does it matter who says 'Read', if those who read love, since love is a charming and excellent path to understanding. If the project appeals to you, do you approve of the title (which would seem paradoxical with regard to the legendary Montesquiou, but which my essay would soon show to be appropriate to the real one): 'Concerning the Simplicity of M. de Montesquiou'? Would it please or displease you were I to pass on (without of course saying that I heard them from you) your ideas about *success*, to wit, that a man of talent should earn money by his books? (I would connect this with my praise of your *will.*) If, incidentally, you tell me one of these days that I can come to Versailles and consult you in person, it would give me no trouble and infinite pleasure![1]

Accept, Sir, my most respectful and faithful regards.

Marcel Proust

1. Montesquiou replied on 20 October 1893: 'Thank you for your kind attentions and intentions with which, I hope, hell will not be paved. You will find me delighted to discuss them with you if you care to come here for lunch at about twelve o'clock on Monday 30 October.'

The essay on Montesquiou, which seems to have been drafted at Évian in August 1893, remained unpublished in Proust's lifetime. Cf. *Contre Sainte-Beuve* (Pléiade v. 405 – 9).

42
TO PIERRE LOUŸS[1]

This Monday [23 October 1893]

Dear Sir,

As you can imagine, my ardent, intimidated sympathy for you was enhanced by grateful pleasure on receiving *Méléagre.* Was it to favour me with the semblance of an exchange,[2] which, for all its ingenuity, loses none of its kindness? I liked the *Vie de Méléagre* enormously, the subtle and graceful beginning, the charming, gentle and tolerant middle part, and the beautiful ending. I have no Greek[3] and barely know French, two circumstances that make it hard for me to judge the qualities of your translation as a translation, but I am certain of the others and ready to vouch for them. Forgive the uncouth appearance of my letter, but I am in bed, I wanted to thank you before going to sleep – and my pen has nothing to press on. Will you, too, be taking lunch on Monday with our common (but so refined) friend Robert de Montesquiou? If not, do come to see me one day or give me leave to call on you. In the meantime, rest assured, etc.

Marcel Proust

1. Pseudonym of Pierre Louis (1870 – 1925), novelist and poet, best known for his novel *Aphrodite* (1896).

2. Louÿs's *Les Poésies de Méléagre, précédées d'une vie de Méléagre*, a life of the Greek poet and a translation of his Epigrams, had just been published;

evidently he had sent it in exchange for a copy of *La Revue blanche* containing one of Proust's pieces.

3. Proust had had five years' study of Greek at the Lycée Condorcet.

43
TO CHARLES GRANDJEAN[1]

9, boulevard Malesherbes
This Saturday [4 November 1893]

Sir,

If you could see me for a few moments one morning without too much inconvenience to yourself – I won't even mention the great pleasure it would give me and which I would not have dared request for selfish reasons – I would like to ask your advice, which would be infinitely precious to me at a time when I am deciding on a career. My parents attach so much importance to it that I must regard it as a duty to ask an opinion which is so precious to me – and beg your pardon for disturbing you.

Respectfully yours
Marcel Proust

1. Charles Grandjean (1857 – 1933) had a distinguished career as archivist of the Senate and Inspector-General of Historic Monuments. As a student in Rome he had frequented the salon of the Princesse Julie Bonaparte. He was a long-time friend of Anatole France.

44
TO ROBERT DE BILLY

Sunday [5 November 1893]

My dear Robert,

I have been hoping you would arrive – But I cannot wait to inform you of a certain project and even to entrust you with a mission which has been made rather *urgent* by the delay I have incurred in waiting for you to return. Here it is. This year I am publishing a collection of short pieces, most of which are known to you. I had thought from the start of dedicating this little book to two men whom

I knew only a short time but whom I loved and still love with all my heart: Edgar Aubert – and Willie Heath, whom I believe you did not know, he died of dysentery hardly a month ago.[1] After a most distinguished life he died with a heroic resignation which, if he had not died in the Catholic faith to which he was converted at the age of twelve (he had been born a Protestant), would be identical to what you wrote to me about Edgar's death. However, the mediocrity of my book, the great licence of certain parts, the futility of a public homage, which is always inferior to the unexpressed memory, dissuaded me from putting the impulse of my heart into practice. But a new development has now changed my mind. Mme Madeleine Lemaire is going to illustrate my little book.[2] Consequently it will find its way into the libraries of writers, artists, and persons of standing in all walks of life, who would otherwise have remained unaware of it and who will keep it only for the illustrations. I would so much like this élite, who would have appreciated Edgar and Heath if they had known them, to learn at least, through my humble testimony rendered in a short preface, what men they have lost. Heath's family seemed pleased with my project. Since I have never had any correspondence with Edgar's family, I should like you to write to them for me. I shall be glad if my idea appeals to them, but of course I shall withdraw it if they prefer – understanding in advance the feelings that will dictate their response. Let them decide my conduct, which will seem good to me if in carrying out – or not carrying out – my project I can contribute however little to the consolation that the inconsolable admiration he has bequeathed to us all can bring to his family.

When you tell me what decision has been taken,[3] my dear Robert, I shall ask you in what terms you will let me speak of Edgar's affection for you.

Until then, my dear friend, I remain your affectionate and devoted

Marcel Proust

If you are coming back to Paris, come soon, before my career is decided.

Please give Mme and M. de Billy my grateful and respectful regards.

1. Proust's English friend Willie Heath died in Paris on 3 October 1893.

2. Mme Lemaire, née Jeanne-Magdeleine Coll (1845 – 1928), a society hostess famous for her musical evenings, was a successful painter of flowers. She

illustrated the original de luxe edition of Proust's *Les Plaisirs et les jours* (1896; translated as *Pleasures and Regrets*, New York, 1948).

3. 'Owing, I believe, to certain misgivings on the part of the Aubert family, the book appeared with only the dedication to Willie Heath' (Robert de Billy, 'Une Amitié de trente-deux ans', in *Hommage à Marcel Proust* [1927], 28).

45
TO CHARLES GRANDJEAN

This Sunday [12 ? November 1893]

Dear Sir,

If I did not thank you at once, it was because I thought I would be going to Louveciennes today for lunch with your neighbours the Beers and intended, without notifying you because I did not want you to stay at home on my account, to drop in on you, tell you how grateful I am – and bother you some more. But something has prevented me from going to Louveciennes.¹ In Paris I go to the rue de Monceau now and then. But they tell me every time that you are not coming back – which saddens me, since I know it is in part because you are not well.

You give me terrifying, that is, excellent arguments against the École des Chartes. But bear in mind that it will take me at least two years to prepare for the Cour des Comptes and that I am bound to fail once. And even if I succeed, I would by then have almost finished at the École des Chartes. At least I would have nothing left to do but my thesis, which I would do on my own. As for the École de Rome, you had told me that in any case I could go there without a fellowship. But what you say about Rome without the École de Rome is indeed more attractive.²

And now, before settling for that sinister Cour des Comptes, what would you say to this? That I go and see one of the directors of the Louvre (I believe I know only M. Heuzey) or that I arrange for a meeting with M. Reinach (Saint-Germain) or M. Saglio (Cluny) or M. . . . (Versailles).³ And ask to be attached to their museum as a volunteer. During that time, if I find it appeals to me, I could, as you think best, prepare for the École des Chartes, study for a *licence* in letters,⁴ prepare for the École du Louvre, or simply devote myself to work of my own – so as to make a future *career* of whichever one, and in the meantime the distinguished and discreet setting of an existence which I would try to inspire and improve by the study of the beautiful things surrounding it. From the standpoint of reflection and literature, Versailles and Saint-Germain strike me as more suitable, but possibly the Louvre or Cluny would be more interesting and offer more future (for curators), meaning, I suppose, that they contain more of the past.

But alas, your so marvellously critical mind will prick this new balloon – actually, I hope so, for you dissipate my mirages, which are the greatest danger, so sparing me cruel awakenings. Since sooner or later one must stop dreaming one's life and live it, I would incur great disappointments – the greatest of all, to have wasted one's life – if your experience and your intuition did not correct my too imaginative and too ill-informed good intentions.

Please pay my respects to Mme Grandjean.

Your grateful and devoted

[*No signature*]

1. The Grandjeans, who lived at 80, rue de Monceau, were staying with Mme Grandjean's mother, Mme Camille du Locle, on her estate at Louveciennes. Edmond and Guillaume Beer, great-nephews of the composer Meyerbeer, owned the nearby château of Voisins; Proust had apparently been invited to lunch there by Mme Guillaume Beer, née Elena Goldschmidt-Franchetti (1874 – 1949), who later published under the pseudonym Jean Dornis.

2. See letter 43. Grandjean had been advising Proust about the possibility of his becoming a museum curator.

3. Léon-Alexandre Heuzey (1831 – 1922), archaeologist, professor at the École du Louvre and curator of oriental antiquities and ancient ceramics; Salomon Reinach (1858 – 1932), philologist and archaeologist, then curator of the museum of Saint-Germain-en-Laye; Edmond Saglio (1828 – 1911), archaeologist, curator at the Louvre, and from 1893 director of the Cluny museum; Pierre de Nolhac (1859 – 1936), poet and historian, appointed curator of the Versailles museum in 1892.

4. The degree of *licence ès lettres*, corresponding to a B.A.

46
TO CHARLES GRANDJEAN

[Monday 13 ? November 1893]

Dear Sir,

I knew you to be capable of the utmost delicacy and generosity, of the most ingenious, diverse and indefatigable charity, and yet I was amazed at the miraculous kindness of your writing again as you have done.

Very well, I renounce the École des Chartes, not without a regret, I must say, inspired not by it but by the École de Rome. Could I go there otherwise? And undoubtedly the picture you paint (so clear, so vivid that only you could have done it) is bleak. But is the Cour des Comptes – or diplomacy in Paris – any more enjoyable? But I think that if you thus demolish all this, it is to build on its ruins the independent, aesthetic city of which we have been dreaming together. And when you have hit on the material means by which I might do that, will you be . . . how shall I put it . . . so kind – and the kindness you have already shown me can be qualified only by a superlative, as rare as what it denotes – as to write and tell me about it.

Please tender my respects to Mme Grandjean and give my regards to your little boy.

Your sincerely grateful
Marcel Proust

You are very much mistaken in supposing my intellectual development to be far advanced. Since my last year at the *lycée*, it has not only been suspended but has gone astray and regressed. That, I believe, is why my writings have been the products solely of imagination and sensibility, the two ignorant Muses which require no cultivation. I still have the illusion that I might have been something else, which is comforting and sad and undoubtedly an illusion.

47
TO CHARLES GRANDJEAN

This Sunday [19 ? November 1893]

Dear Sir,

My parents leave me *free* but feel that my plan doesn't amount to much of a career,[1] they ask me precise questions, whether one can really be attached to a museum, whether the doctorate really *entitles* one to attend the École de Rome and the École de Rome to a paid position in a museum, because the post as Inspector of Fine Arts is only a possibility, and in the meantime they would like me to have something definite to count on. Does the École du Louvre confer the same rights as the doctorate, and which way (*licence* and doctorate, or École du Louvre) would be best? Finally, would there be as much time for writing in a museum as at the Cour des Comptes? It would embarrass me to ask you all these questions, were it not for my confidence in your kindness and patience. And if I had not been afraid of disturbing you, I would have gone to consult you in person.

Now, as to all this precise information, should I ask M. Poincaré to get it for me, which would be easy for me to do. If on the other hand you have occasion to see M. Roujon or M. Benoit, could you yourself enquire?[2] We shall do whatever you think best. But as for the question of more or less free time, I believe that no one could know better than a museum person.

As for Mme Lemaire, since

your goodness extends to the entire realm

of my occupations,[3] she writes that she will not have time to start her drawings before her return to Paris, that she will do them in a way that is easy to reproduce by an inexpensive process (something I had not asked of her and which bears witness to her exquisite simplicity, she is a woman who thinks only of others and hasn't one jot of artist's vanity), that she has no publisher, that only M. Boussod has reproduced her illustrations,[4] but that he is not a publisher and that I should therefore do as I see fit. What should I see fit?

I hope Mme Grandjean has recovered from her migraine. Please continue to believe in my respectful gratitude,

Your devoted
Marcel Proust

1. Cf. *Jean Santeuil*, 25: '. . . Nevertheless, we have several very definite ideas about his future, not that we should ever wish to go against our son: we want him to be perfectly free to choose, so long, that is, as he sets his mind on a regular career, the Law for instance, or the Foreign Service.'

2. Raymond Poincaré (1860–1934), the future President of the Republic, had been Minister of Education and Fine Arts since April 1893. Henri Roujon (1853–1914) was director of Fine Arts from 1891 to 1903. Camille Benoit (1852–1923) was curator of the Louvre museum.

3. Cf. Racine, *Athalie*, II. vii: 'Votre bonté s'étend sur toute la nature'. ('Realm' is here substituted for 'nature' in the quotation, to make it fit Proust's purpose. – Tr.)

4. The firm of Boussod and Valadon had issued two books illustrated by Mme Lemaire: Halévy's *L'Abbé Constantin* (1887) and *Flirt* by Paul Hervieu (1890).

48
TO LÉON YEATMAN[1]

This Monday morning 18 December [1893]
Dear friend,

I was sorry to have missed you, but it was after half-past three when you came – I waited for you until then, and you were supposed to come at *half-past one*. Robert was expecting to see you and he would have thanked you for your thought, which touched him, but he is working too hard to accept such diversions, though greatly tempted. I shall not be at Faguet, I have a lesson with M. Mossot[2] until seven o'clock. If not *Napoléon*, would you care to drop in on *Phèdre* – or *La Dame aux camélias?* Saturday night I went with some ladies to see *Gigolette*, which just made me sick. . . .[3] The eldest of the seven male Weisweillers

Seven sons, the noble hope of an illustrious house!

was there.
Day follows day and the Weisweillers are all different.[4]
Thank you again for Thursday. When can we see each other? I shall not be free tomorrow Tuesday evening.
Please give your mother my respectful thanks, and accept, dear friend, the affectionate thoughts of your

Marcel Proust

Oh, those C's![5]

All will be winter once more in my heart (Baudelaire).[6]

1. Léon Yeatman (1873 – 1930), whom Proust met at the Sorbonne. They studied law together, and Yeatman became a lawyer.

2. M. Mossot, professor of rhetoric at the Lycée Condorcet, tutored Proust – possibly in Latin – when he was studying for his *licence* in letters.

3. *Napoléon*, an epic drama by Léopold Martin-Laya, was playing at the Théâtre de la Porte Saint-Martin. Sarah Bernhardt was giving twenty performances of *Phèdre* that season, at her Théâtre de la Renaissance, where she and Lucien Guitry were also performing in *La Dame aux camélias*, by Dumas fils. *Gigolette*, by Pierre Decourcelle and Edmond Tarbé, opened at the Théâtre de l'Ambigu on 25 November 1893.

4. The banker Charles Weisweiller had six or seven sons and two daughters. Cf. *Phèdre*, II, i: 'Six frères, quel espoir d'une illustre maison'. (The following sentence, so pointless in English, is a play on the French saying, 'Les jours se suivent et ne se ressemblent pas', 'Day follows day and no two are alike', or, more idiomatically: 'Tomorrow is another day'. – Tr.)

5. What Proust actually wrote was 'Quelles C . . . ries!', a pun which on the one hand means roughly, 'Oh, those C's!' – an allusion to his peculiar way of elongating the bottom of the letter *c* – and on the other stands for 'Quelles conneries', meaning 'What a lot of nonsense!'

6. 'Tout l'hiver va rentrer dans mon être', from 'Chant d'automne', in *Les Fleurs du mal.*

49
TO LÉON YEATMAN

This Thursday [21 December 1893]
in bed,
midnight

Dear Léon,

What well-chosen – and better entertained – guests! What a delightful evening! How intelligently you gather young people, and all of them charming. But most of all, how well you entertain them. Dear friend, may you never lose (but of that I have small fear, seeing that you have so great and good a mentor as Mme Yeatman) that art so rare – and hard to preserve. Some otherwise charming women are like the Princess Badrul Budur,[1] whose words and everything she touched, even chrysoprase and gems, were instantly transformed into toads. In their presence men of wit become dull, the best matched friends are bored with one another. Preserve that exquisite art and your home will be one of the few that people are happy to visit.

A single black mark in this delightful picture, my agitation, which I feared to betray if I opened my mouth. Still, I calmed down at dinner. I have never eaten so much – and, I would add, so well – if I had not been so deterred from enjoying it. And for such stupid reasons. I was feeling very well this afternoon and were it not for my stupidity I would have felt very well this evening.

I thank you again, dear friend.

Marcel Proust

1. A character in the *Thousand and One Nights*. Cf. *The Guermantes Way*, where those 'sham men of letters, the pseudo-intellectuals whom Mme d'Ar-

gencourt entertained . . .' picture Oriane de Guermantes, 'whom they would never have an opportunity of knowing personally, as something more wonderful and more extraordinary than Princess Badroul Boudour . . .' (II. 464).

50
TO ROBERT DE MONTESQUIOU

Tuesday morning [1 May 1894]

Dear Sir,

Forgive me (I have been rather ill) for not answering you sooner. I believe I can reconcile your serious preconceived occupations and the kind thought that follows by interpreting this last as permission to come to Versailles on Friday between two and three o'clock. You will have been able to work with Léon Delafosse[1] before then. And yet I shall have a great pleasure that was denied me in the original plan. We shall be able to go for a walk or to stay at your place, accordingly as one or the other choice seems to prolong the pathways of our dreams more naturally.

Until Friday then. I am beginning to fear that one of these days I shall involuntarily fall into the so complex and many-faceted character, so different from myself, which you persist in evoking. Your brandishing its shadow will make it become flesh. . . . And what will be left of me then? Simple of mind and complicated of character is too much. Couldn't we invert the terms and at last obtain an identity?

Affectionate respects,

Marcel Proust

1. Léon Delafosse (1874 – 1951 ?), talented composer and concert pianist; one of the models for Charles Morel. Proust introduced him to Montesquiou, who became his assiduous patron and remained so until they quarrelled three years later.

51
TO HORACE DE LANDAU[1]

This Thursday [24 May? 1894]
Dear Sir,

I was ill on New Year's Day[2] when I meant to write to you. I don't know why it is just today, almost five months later, that, ill again, I write to wish you all happiness, for I have thought of you so often since I last saw you that I might have written to you *every* day. Don't tremble in retrospect!

Perhaps you will find my wish for your happiness a little vague. But that is the nature of prudent wishes. I am required to write essays[3] proving that some sort of happiness exists. Since I am a good pupil and a good son, I write them; since I am a poor philosopher, I make a botch of them. But above all I don't believe it. I believe that everyone has his own private happiness – when he has it. And to wish someone a happiness he might not want would be most imprudent. I don't know exactly what you desire, and that is why I make my wishes extremely vague. But I have little fear of their not coming true. You have happiness within you: that is the safest, if not the only, way of having it. In any case, whatever may be the happiness you dream of (to dream of it is already to have it in the most ideal sense of the word, which as a good idealist I believe to be the only true one), I am sure it is a happiness of the very best quality. (The only compensation for habitual and prolonged absence is that it enables one to write certain endearments which are so unjustly forbidden in conversation.) I hope that you are very well, that I shall be at Trouville[4] or you in Paris, that I shall be able to plunge for a moment into the reddish-grey waves of your beard, the bright blue of your eyes, and the pale blue of your cravat, shake your hand and tell you how much you are loved and admired by your respectful

Marcel Proust

---

1. Horace de Landau (1824–1903), great-uncle of Horace and Mary Finaly. Born in Odessa, he made his fortune in Italy as representative of the Rothschild interests at the time of the Risorgimento; his library in Florence was rich in old books and incunabula.

2. On 13 January 1894 Proust had written to Montesquiou apologizing for having been unable to present his greetings for the New Year because he was suffering from 'pleurodynia'.

3. Perhaps by M. Darlu, in preparing Proust for his examination for the *licence* in letters.

4. M. de Landau had purchased Les Frémonts, the estate at Trouville (see letter 22), for his niece Mme Hugo Finaly.

52

TO GABRIEL DE YTURRI[1]

This Thursday morning [2 August 1894]

Dear M. de Yturri,

I shall do my best to change the hour of my Monday 4.30 lesson, but if I am unable to, I shall count on your kind help in obtaining another audience, for I want very much to see the Comte, and to see you before your departure.

As for the 'bad impression' created by the question of the magazines,[2] make no attempt to dissipate it, for the good reason that such a thing *can* not be because it *should* not be. To tell the truth, I behaved very well in this whole affair. M. de Montesquiou does not know all about it, and I don't know yet whether I shall ever tell him the whole story, but what little he knows is, I can't say to my credit, for one deserves no credit for being devoted to a man so eminent and charming – but at all events can only please him. Thus, since I behaved well, I esteem M. de Montesquiou's perspicacity and nobility of character so highly that I can only feel certain of his gratitude. I therefore give you back your 'Let's have more jokes about articles',[3] which thereby loses a good part of its meaning, since you do not joke about matters concerning your glorious friend – and how right you are!

I cannot tell you how much your sympathy touches me and how highly I value it. I hope you will never cease to play your role of intermediary – and with what grace, power and charm – between M. de Montesquiou and me.

Until Sunday, as I fervently hope,

Yours very sincerely,

Marcel Proust

1. Gabriel de Yturri (1864–1905), Argentinian friend and devoted secretary of Robert de Montesquiou.

2. Proust had written to Montesquiou in mid-June 1894 that, as none of the magazines seemed willing to publish his article on the Comte's 'simplicity' (see letter 41), he was thinking of founding a magazine himself for that express purpose.

3. Proust's acrimony is explained not only by Yturri's irony at the expense of his article but by the fact that Montesquiou had got an 'intermediary' to answer Proust's letter instead of writing himself.

53
TO ROBERT DE MONTESQUIOU

This Sunday [12 August 1894]
Dear Sir,

Is an attack of rheumatic fever sufficient excuse for my being so late in thanking you for troubling to write me a few words on the day of your departure?

I experienced a most pleasant emotion at seeing our great poet Verlaine turn critic to speak of you in terms not the least soured by the rivalry of an equal, terms full of aptness and charm, which, falling from such a height, have great weight.[1] I have returned to Versailles with M. France, the only companion with whom I could have been happy in that place, where I had seen you and where you were no longer. I have no need to tell you that you were spoken of constantly with affectionate veneration and that your memory is much to be thanked for so graciously and nobly accompanying or rather guiding us on this excursion, which it diverted and embellished. I have not yet seen your charming friend M. de Yturri. I mean to ask him for an appointment soon, so as not to go to Réveillon[2] before speaking with him. You have no doubt heard that Mme L. de Montesquiou has thrown 30,000 francs into the English Channel.

At which the fishes now dilate their eyes
Dazzled by the glow rising from the depths.

The pious whim of a devoted and well-read relative wished to make a reality of the 'carp embroidered with gold'.[3]

I send you, *cher maître*, my kindest and most respectful regards and hope the Engadine will do you good.

Marcel Proust

1. Paul Verlaine, 'À propos de Desbordes-Valmore', *Le Figaro*, 8 Aug. 1894.

2. The château of Mme Lemaire, in the Marne; see letter 57.

3. On 9 August 1894, the cutter in which Comte Louis de Montesquiou, with the Comtesse and the Marquis and Marquise d'Aramon, was crossing the Channel sank off Saint-Malo. All on board were saved except for a sailor and his young nephew – but, reported *Le Figaro* for 10 Aug., 'Nearly all the luggage was lost, including a travelling case containing some 30,000 francs.' The quotations are from Montesquiou's poem 'Annulate', in *Les Chauves-souris*, commemorating the loss of some rings in a deep lake.

54

FROM HIS MOTHER

Rueil, Tuesday 2.30 [11 September 1894]

Dear boy,

I have just arrived at Rueil to visit your little brother,[1] but his room, it seems, is full of people, interns from Ivry and all sorts of brothers in arms, so I have discreetly withdrawn to a room at the back of the house, and that is where I am writing. Your father – at Vichy, much upset by the news of his son's fall – took the train and walked in on us yesterday evening, just like that! as your grandfather would say. He was pleased with Dick's looks, humour, and appetite and will go back as soon as he has moved him to Auteuil, the time to be arranged with Dr Guinard,[2] who will be coming soon (but too late for me to tell you what he says because of the post).

Poor Dick says that – except for the first day – he has spent 'the most delightful' hours at Rueil. The entire household (Giguel) at his beck and call: 'Halloo, mine host, bring wine and of the best. . . .' And his visitors kept for lunch or dinner, etc. – His room has a view of the Seine, with a lovely backdrop of trees and greenery.

Well, I cannot thank Providence enough that he escaped serious injury. It's as miraculous as falling from the fifth floor and getting up unhurt. The elder Chauveau left yesterday morning for his 28 days.[3] The younger Chauveau is replacing him and staying here. So much for his steady care. Now the surgical intern from Ivry has come to bandage him, etc. – and then a succession of others at irregular intervals. I knew he was having friends for lunch today, and that's why

I came late, but still too early, as you see. I shall write tomorrow to tell you how many days your father is staying in Auteuil.

J.P.

Dick's accident happened Saturday afternoon – at Rueil – there was no one on the road. – Sunday he saw no one but me, Chauveau and Dr Guinard. And yesterday M. de Gourlet came to see how he was doing![4]

1. On Saturday, 8 September 1894, Robert Proust, while riding a tandem bicycle with a girl friend at Rueil, on the outskirts of Paris, collided with a coal cart, which passed over his thigh.

2. Dr Marie-Aimé-Désiré Guinard (1856 – 1911), a surgeon.

3. See letter 40, n. 4.

4. M. de Gourlet (or Degourlet) was Inspector of National Palaces. Mme Proust fails to mention another circumstance, of which Proust later wrote: 'Years ago, when a 3-ton truck ran over Robert's thigh, Mama fraternized at his bedside with the little cocotte who was taking care of him . . .' (letter to Mme Catusse, June 1915).

55
TO PIERRE LAVALLÉE[1]

Hôtel des Roches Noires
Trouville, Calvados
Sunday [16 September 1894]

My dear Pierre,

I shall be in Paris in a week and then I will tell you about the extraordinary incidents which might have been tragic and which have delayed my correspondence to the point of leaving you without an answer. As for my friendship, rest assured that it's exactly the same, affectionately devoted. I am at the Hôtel des Roches Noires, Trouville. It would be charming of you to write to me here, or better still come and see me, as Hahn[2] is doing. You will find a musically tainted Marcel, possibly Romeo and Julietizing to excess, but in any case remaining

Your sincerely devoted
M.P.

I shall doubtless be in Paris Sunday, Sunday week, that is. Mightn't you be in Trouville before then?

1. Pierre Martin-Lavallée (1872 – 1946) was in Proust's class at the Lycée Condorcet in 1887. They became friends a few years later, when they were both studying law. Lavallée became a librarian, in charge of the collections at the École des Beaux-Arts.

2. Reynaldo Hahn; see letter 56.

56
TO REYNALDO HAHN[1]

This Sunday morning [16 September 1894]
Trouville – [Hôtel des] Roches Noires – Calvados

My little Master,[2]

Your note dated Friday evening arrived only this morning, whereas a letter posted in the evening arrives the next morning. – ? – The weather has been delightful, moonlight nights, of which you will read what you call an interpretation.[3] Mme Straus, to whom I have spoken of your 'adorable qualities' and then some, will be delighted to have you. And so, without wishing to inflict such a journey on you, I believe that if you are to spend two days at the seashore, this would be the best time – and at Trouville. If you can't, Mama is leaving soon, so you could come after she goes, to comfort me. But let me know, because then I shall stay on at the hotel after Mama leaves, on the assumption that you will probably stop here, since it's the best hotel. If you are not coming, or if you are coming later, I shall stay at the Strauses' after Mama leaves, or more likely at Étretat with a friend.[4] Why 'Marcel the pony'? I don't care for this novelty. It makes me think of Jack the Ripper or Louis the Headstrong.[5] Don't forget that it's not a nickname and that I am really and truly, Reynaldo,

Your pony
Marcel

Have you seen M. Carvalho?[6] – You are hard on *Lohengrin*, I think. The herald and the king throughout, Elsa's dream, the arrival of the swan, the chorus of judgement, the scene between the two women, the refalado,[7] the Grail, the leavetaking, the gift of the horn, the sword and the lamb, the prelude – isn't all that beautiful?

75

1. Reynaldo Hahn (1874–1947), French composer and conductor. Born in Caracas, Venezuela, he was a child prodigy and entered the Paris Conservatory when only eleven. He was nineteen when Proust met him and they struck up a friendship which lasted until Proust's death.

2. In English in the original.

3. Evidently Proust had just written the two little pieces which appear in *Les Plaisirs et les jours* as 'Sonate au clair de lune' and 'Comme à la lumière de la lune' (cf. *Pleasures and Regrets*, 130–34, 161–62).

4. Léon Yeatman.

5. Louis le Hutin, King Louis X of France. 'Pony' in French is a fairly common term of endearment.

6. Léon Carvaille, known as Carvalho (1825–97), was director of the Opéra Comique, where Hahn hoped for a production of his opera *L'Île du rêve*. Carvalho turned it down, but it was later produced by his successor.

7. The theme beginning with the notes ray fah lah doh (DFAC).

57
TO SUZETTE LEMAIRE[1]

Trouville [Hôtel des] Roches Noires (Calvados)
[17 or 18 September 1894]

Mademoiselle,

If the intensity of a constant thought is felt at a distance, you must be overwhelmed by the persistence of my company. I may be at Trouville, with Le Havre before me and M. Straus behind me – not that he bothers me at Saint-Fiacre, on the contrary, he is charming during these holidays – but I am still at Réveillon, walking on the sand and in the park, trying to write to you in French but speaking Loute[2] language. I have come to find it quite natural that a certain door should not always open and to insist. . . .

Alas, the conversation of the people I meet and the monotony of the dishes I eat make it cruelly clear to me that I have changed. The sympathetic confidence I inspired in you at Réveillon worries me a little now, and I shall tell you why. At Réveillon it filled me with joy, it didn't trouble me in the least: I had returned it a hundredfold in anticipation, and I found it perfectly natural. Now, far from you and alone, examining your gift of sympathy, I find it so precious that I sometimes wonder if I am not unworthy of it. And I would so much like to think that I am not. Because of all this, the moment when I see you again will be infinitely welcome to me. What at a distance seems complicated, painful and difficult becomes mild and simple in your presence. You will say that to deserve your friendship one need not be very remarkable, but only (1) love you very much, (2) love you more, and (3) love you still more. In that case, I believe I shall meet the conditions for being your friend without blushing too much at my unworthiness.

I hope you have worked a lot since I left. I think that for the present work is what can give you the greatest pleasure and that you owe it to others, to yourself, and even to your gracious and innocent models. I also hope very much that your mother is working – and on something besides illustrating my little things which, in having even a bit of her time, are being given much more than they deserve. But her great kindness gives me pleasure, and the dove, the chrysanthemums, the pansies, Violante's castle,[3] merge in my memory with the living occupants of Réveillon to add to my gratitude and my regrets.

In the letter I received from Hahn this morning, he tells me that he has seen M. Carvalho but not what was decided, and I'd have very much liked to know.

Yesterday Mama and I went out with the Strauses. In the evening we saw the Porto-Riches and we talked about your friend Mme de Mailly, whose so romantic and so touching story seems tragic when I hear of de Reské's indifference and duplicity.[4] M. Schlumberger is at Mme Straus's. The princess of Monaco may come and stay for a day or two.[5] Apart from the Strauses, the only people I know here are Mme Trousseau and Mme de Galliffet. But I am told the Duezes are at Villerville.[6] They asked me to come and see them again this year, and I shall, only too glad of the chance to speak of you to friends of yours.

Dear Mlle Suzette, do you know *La Nuit d'octobre* (by Musset)? If not, I shall send you a few extracts. Will you countenance a letter now and then from your little friend, who loves you ever so respectfully with all his heart.

Marcel Proust

Tender my respects to Mme Lemaire, Mme Herbelin[7] – and to Loute, whose extreme importance and high station I have understood since Réveillon.

1. Suzanne (called Suzette) Lemaire (1866? – 1946), only daughter of Mme Madeleine Lemaire. Like her mother, she painted flowers. She never married.

2. Mme Lemaire's dog. Cf. *The Prisoner*, when the pensive attitude of Mme Verdurin, burying her face in her hands as she listens to music, gives rise to the suspicion that she is asleep: 'A regular noise which was not musical gave me momentarily to think that this last hypothesis was the correct one, but I realized later that it was produced by the snores, not of Mme Verdurin, but of her dog' (III. 253).

3. Illustrations for *Les Plaisirs et les jours*.

4. In the end, however, the celebrated Polish tenor Jean de Reszke (1850–1925) married the Comtesse de Mailly-Nesle, née Marie de Goulaine.

5. Gustave Schlumberger (1844–1929) was to write: 'On a stool at the feet of Mme Geneviève Straus one constantly saw the bizarre Marcel Proust, still a young man, who since then has written books admired by some and quite incomprehensible to others, including myself' (*Mes Souvenirs, 1844–1928*, vol. I [1934], 305 ff.). The Princesse de Monaco, née Marie-Alice Furtado-Heine (1853–1925), widow of the Duc de Richelieu, was – or so the distinguished Sorbonne professor Antoine Adam has asserted – the model for the Princesse de Luxembourg.

6. Mme Armand Trousseau, née Tamburini, and her husband had a villa at Trouville. The Marquise de Galliffet, née Laffitte, daughter of one of the founders of the Jockey Club, was a cousin of Mme Arthur Baignères; she is mentioned in *The Guermantes Way* (II. 416) and in *Cities of the Plain* (II. 1032). Ernest-Ange Duez (1834–96), a painter, had a house at Villerville.

7. Mme Lemaire's aunt, née Jeanne-Mathilde Habert (1818–1904), a well-known miniaturist, who had done portraits of Delacroix, Rossini, Guizot, Rosa Bonheur, Dumas père and fils, Mérimée, and Thiers.

58
TO ROBERT DE MONTESQUIOU

Trouville, this Tuesday morning
[18 September 1894]

Dear Sir,

An accident – in which my brother was injured – has complicated my life of late and prevented me from sending you two requests concerning my affairs. One of them also has to do with Mme Lemaire, who would be glad of a reply in the affirmative. It is this. Would you authorize me, in the preface to my book, to quote one or two of the brilliant and beautiful lines you wrote on the flyleaf of the copy of *Le Chef des odeurs suaves* which you gave Mme Lemaire. And here is the second. I think I shall dedicate the principal stories or poems in my book to masters whom I admire or friends whom I love. Would you, at least in the first of these capacities, allow me to dedicate one of them to you? You were kind enough to trouble to write me such a nice letter from the Engadine. But 'it leaves me with a sweet and sour memory, like those autumn days when the sun is shining and a cold wind is blowing' (*Le Lys rouge*).[1] Perhaps I should do better here to use the felicitous adjective 'bitter-sweet' with its indubitable undercurrent of melancholy – which you made into French by applying it to Mme Desbordes.[2] The fact is that for some time your letters, whose intellectual and aesthetic quality I continue to value, have neither begun nor ended with a friendly word, and I suffer from their coldness of feeling. Before going to Réveillon for a month, not a day of which passed without our speaking of you, I had occasion to see your friend M. de Yturri one afternoon, and I succumbed once more to the charm of his graceful wit. What civilized refinement and what a wildcat, what gentleness and what readiness to leap! – I hope Saint-Moritz has done you a great deal of good and that I shall be able to see you soon.

Believe, dear sir, in my faithful admiration and respectful attachment.

Marcel Proust

1. Proust is quoting freely from *Le Lys rouge* (The Red Lily), the novel by Anatole France which had appeared in July 1894.

2. Montesquiou, in an essay of 1894 on the poetry of Mme Desbordes-Valmore (1786 – 1859), had spoken of 'ce doux-amer génie' (that bitter-sweet genius).

59
TO REYNALDO HAHN

Saturday evening [Hôtel des] Roches Noires
[22 September 1894]

My dear friend,

I'm a little sad this evening because of Mama's going away tomorrow and take it as a pretext for spending five minutes in your company to console myself. I hope you agree to my latest suggestions. Of course you won't be as comfortable here as if I had a villa, but the room I shall give you is on the first floor, overlooking the sea and next to mine. And Mme Straus is just about the best I have to offer. I am working on a long piece and think it's rather good. I shall use it as an excuse for omitting from my volume the story about Lepré, the opera, etc.[1] which you are having copied.

I love you, my very dear friend.

Marcel Proust

Do not scorn the reception I would give you at the hotel as insufficiently sumptuous, and if you don't come, let it not be any fear of meagre hospitality that deters you. – And don't leave me on tenterhooks by letting the letter you will be kind enough to write me moulder for a week in your pocket. Some of the letters I have received from you have taken four days rather than twelve hours.

1. The novella 'La Mort de Baldassare Silvande, vicomte de Sylvanie' was to lead off the contents of *Les Plaisirs et les jours*. The omitted story is not in the MS of the collection, but appeared later in a magazine. Rediscovered only recently, it was published in book form by Gallimard in 1978, under the title *L'Indifférent*.

60
TO SUZETTE LEMAIRE

[25 or 26 September 1894]

My dear Mademoiselle Suzette,

I am going to see Reynaldo, and then you will know what's what. You could not have been kinder to me and you have done me a world of good. I slept last night, something I had not done for a long time – and if I woke I felt dear little hands, cool, industrious hands – on which tears fall and from which are born flowers that might easily be mistaken for those of the garden or field – and alas, the tears too resemble other tears – before this parenthesis I was saying that if I woke I felt your dear little hands, so adroit and so cool, resting on my forehead, and I assure you that it was not unpleasant. . . . I repay them in licit kisses for all the good they have done me[1] (I have just corrected *licit*, which was not legible, and thinking it to be one of the important words in the sentence . . .).

Reynaldo is still an angel, or rather he has been even more of an angel in the last few weeks. I know a lady who wouldn't say that, who detests him.[2] The fact is, she loves him . . . and nothing so distorts one's judgement. Yet this lady is good and he is good. And nothing comes of it except that they hurt each other terribly. I will say with Schumann's lovely song 'A Man Loves a Woman',[3] which Reynaldo sings:

The story is a common one
But no less sad for that.

Yes, Paris will be Réveillon, at least for your friends, who will devote themselves entirely to you. I can speak at least for myself. I presume that Reynaldo feels the same way and I leave you the pleasure of hearing him say so himself. I have the impression that you are leading a very literary life in spite of your lovely walks in the woods, the glorious trophy from which is turning red in the letter that brought me its last golden lights. But though it would interest me a good deal to know what you are reading, don't, I implore you, speak to me of what I write. Not that I don't feel a deep and heartfelt joy when I think you have liked it. Since I have never written a *line* for the pleasure of writing, but only to express something that struck my heart or my imagination, to tell me you like what I write is to tell me you like me, and that cannot leave me indifferent. . . . But I haven't an ounce of vanity (unfortunately), not even of author's vanity, and when it seems to me that you feel obliged, as with a man of letters, to say a word either of criticism or praise, it makes me sad and gives me the impression that I am becoming a man of letters, instead of remaining purely and simply a man who bears you feelings of the most respectful friendship.

Marcel Proust

1. It seems possible to find in 'La Mort de Baldassare Silvande' a confession of platonic love for Suzette Lemaire: 'Supernatural as a Madonna, gentle as a nurse, I have adored you and you have cradled me. I loved you with a tenderness whose delicate sagacity no carnal pleasure ever spoiled. And in exchange have you not brought me an incomparable friendship, such lovely tea, conversation by nature richly graced and how many fragrant roses! You alone, with your maternal and expressive hands, knew how to soothe my fevered brow. . . .' (*Pleasures and Regrets*, 18)

2. A veiled reference to Mme Lemaire's authoritarian character, a trait which appears in Proust's portrait of Mme Verdurin.

3. *Dichterliebe*, no. 11, a setting of Heine's poem 'Ein Jüngling liebt ein Mädchen'.

61

TO ROBERT DE MONTESQUIOU

This Tuesday evening [2 October 1894]

Dear Sir,

I have just had the pleasure of receiving your double reply. Please be so good as to thank M. de Yturri, who was kind enough to be its – always eloquent and well-informed – herald. I communicated your first authorization to *that Flora*

Who immortalizes them, while the other makes them die[1]

and who like me will be glad of it and grateful.

As to the second, I shall respond to your hesitation by taking (from my publisher, as soon as he can dispense with it, in less than a month, I think) the manuscript or proof of the obscure tale to which you will be asked to add the prestige (it will have no other) of your name,[2] the syllables of which, to every well-born ear and well-behaved imagination, are so rich in past, present and future. You will judge whether this lane is not too poorly paved or ill-frequented to allow of writing a name so glorious and so dear to literature on its wall. Often, indeed, in obscure streets where the houses have no style and the crossings no prospect, the passer-by is set to dreaming by the name he reads on entering. From you I expect the same support as the rue Théophile Gautier, or whatever, expects from the author after whom it is named. As for the company, which I believe to be good, because it includes only those whom I admire or love, it will not always be illustrious. But rest assured of the company of M. France or M. de Heredia, which you will undoubtedly find desirable, since you yourself often seek theirs. On the other hand, my portraitist M. [Jacques-Émile] Blanche and M. Ferdinand de Montesquiou[3] will not figure in this volume. I should be glad if you were to permit me, one of these days, to come to Versailles and thank you for all this, and on the same occasion I should ask you for still more, namely, the affectionate treatment merited by my most respectful devotion.

Marcel Proust

1. '. . . la Flore / Qui les immortalise où l'autre fait mourir', from a set of five poems by Montesquiou dedicated to Mme Lemaire, from which Proust had asked permission (see letter 58) to quote in the preface to his book.

2. 'La Confession d'une jeune fille' (cf. 'A Young Girl's Confession', *Pleasures and Regrets*, 31 – 47) was to have been dedicated to Montesquiou.

3. Ferdinand de Montesquiou had perhaps incurred his relative's displeasure, as so many of the Comte's family did at one time or another.

62

TO MADAME DE BRANTES¹

Friday 23 Oct[ober 18]94²

Madame,

It is said that the light of the stars has been on its way for a long time when it reaches us. Something of the sort happens with delayed letters. . . .

I assure you that I have not only been thinking of you but also meaning to write to you for a long time. Perhaps you will forgive me for having seemed indifferent to the magnificent success of Monsieur your son,³ which gave me the keenest pleasure, when you know that my brother had just been in a dreadful bicycle accident – a cart filled with sacks of coal and weighing five tons ran over his thigh. Now after a month's rest, by some miracle, he is walking as well as ever.

What we don't know is whether he will take up bicycle riding again.

At the time I had to answer letters for him from worried friends – and then I was absorbed by three short stories and lots of poetry.⁴ The whole, I hope, will give you an impression of enormous progress after the feeble little things I used to turn out.

I've written so much that it didn't even occur to me to present myself at the October examination for the *licence* in philosophy. That will have to wait until April at the earliest. However, I don't know yet when I shall be able to send you the most sumptuous copy, which will be reserved for you, of my little volume, or rather, what with all the pieces I've added, my fat volume. . . . Mme Lemaire, you see, has become interested while working on it and after doing a great many drawings is beginning to do . . . water-colours. All this may take a long time to produce. I add that a musician of genius – aged twenty – is composing music for the poetic part of the volume, and M. France is writing a preface. This musician is not Delafosse (though

83

this summer he wrote a setting for one of my poems).[5] But neither the poem nor the piece is in this volume – in connection with which I seem now to have committed (having as unwitting accomplice the kindness of your friend Mme de Fitz-James) a frightful gaffe!

But I shall tell you about it some day or write about it with more convenient ink.[6]

From your charming and inspired cousin I received a letter from Saint-Moritz in August and one from Versailles three weeks ago. Before going to Trouville I spent a month at Mme Lemaire's. . . .

But this is too much about myself. You are so kind that I take advantage of you. But I hope at least that this will entitle me to ask for long reports about yourself, Madame your daughter and Monsieur your son.

Believe me, Madame, with all my heart very respectfully yours.

Marcel Proust

I was grieved to hear of M. Chauvelon's disgrace.[7] I hope you will give me an opportunity to do you other services and shall try to make them more durable.

1. Mme Sauvage de Brantes, née Louise de Cessac (1842 – 1914), was a cousin of Robert de Montesquiou.

2. Proust's uncharacteristically precise dating seems in this case unreliable; 23 October 1894 was a Tuesday.

3. Paul de Brantes (1864 – 1950) was promoted to the rank of captain in the 1st Regiment of Chasseurs on 11 October 1894.

4. I.e. 'La Mort de Baldassare Silvande', 'La Confession d'une jeune fille', 'La Fin de la jalousie' (The End of Jealousy), and the poems 'Portraits de peintres et de musiciens' (Portraits of Painters and Musicians).

5. Reynaldo Hahn composed the music for the 'Portraits de peintres'. Another poem, 'Mensonges' (Lies), with music by Léon Delafosse, had been published in April 1894.

6. The letter is written with gold ink on violet paper.

7. Émile Chauvelon, a brilliant young man from the town of Authon (Loir-et-Cher), who was a protégé of Mme de Brantes. Through Robert de Flers, Proust had obtained an appointment for Chauvelon as a teacher at a Paris *lycée*. The consequences of his 'disgrace' seem not to have been very serious, for he was to have an honourable academic career.

63
TO SUZETTE LEMAIRE

CONFIDENTIAL

Thursday, All Saints Day
[1 November 1894]
Mademoiselle,

Your sarcasm about my 'Orleanist occupations' has not offended me. At the most it makes me sad. It was perfectly natural of you to find my *démarche* awkward (I thought so myself and only did it to avoid being disobedient). To pretend, as a mere M. Straus would not do,[1] that all this was brought on if not by snobbery, then at least by inveterate social climbing, is very strange. It is likely that if my advisers (to whom, I own, I should not have listened) had thought that for any reason Paulus or Amaury had more influence on the Lévy brothers, they would have asked me to get them to speak. And if I had known Paulus and Amaury, whom I would have been neither more nor less proud to know than Mme X or M. Z but whom I might have found more amusing, I would have complied with the same idiotic deference for Mme Ernesta's opinion.[2]

I have been really ill these last few days (and I am still very tired, but less so than Mme Ernesta thinks, she has been wanting to send me far away for a rest ever since Mme de Thèbes[3] told her that my health was in a bad state), which has greatly distressed me, because it prevented me from writing to you, especially at a time when I had the impression (I am not speaking of your Orleanist pleasantries, which don't matter) that my credit with you is terribly on the decline.

My dear little Mlle Suzette, sweetest of women, the only intelligent young girl in the whole world, my good little Mlle Suzette, my little mother, my darling little sister, don't scold me, don't tell me I'm touchy and quick to take offence. Don't tell me, not because it's not true – it is – but because I already know it. It is true, but only with people I like. You'll say that's an odd way of showing my appreciation, I should save my touchiness for people I don't like. But where did you ever hear that one loves people to give them pleasure? One loves people because one can't help it. But where you are concerned there are more people who can't help it than with anyone else. That's all. You have reason to be proud. But not to be happy. I am still too young to know what makes for happiness in life. But I know for sure that it's neither love nor friendship.

My dear Mlle Suzette, I know this is illegible. Perhaps that's a bit of coquetry, an attempt to hide from you all the nonsense I'm writing. Another time I shall be calmer. But if you knew the threefold sorrow with which my life is barred, like those well-fortified cities one sees in Élisée Reclus's Northern Europe volume,[4] you would forgive me. I kiss your little hands that know how to do such pretty things and that will know how to guide me, a culprit wishing to beg forgiveness, to the feet of Madame your mother.

Your little
Marcel

1. This ironic reference to Émile Straus seems to prefigure the quarrel, a year hence, which would keep Proust away from the Strauses for a time.

2. The singer Paulus (see letter 3) and the actor Ernest Amaury: in other words, prominent men who were not members of 'society'. It is not known what member of the Orléans family Proust induced to intercede with Messrs Calmann-Lévy, who had agreed to publish his book. But since he begs Mme Lemaire's pardon, the *démarche* must have had something to do with the illustrations she was doing for the volume. His move had evidently been suggested by Mme Louis Stern, née Ernesta de Hierschel (d. *c.* 1926), who published under the pseudonym of Maria Star.

3. Proust relates his consultation with Mme de Thèbes (1865 – 1916), the celebrated palmist, in *Jean Santeuil*, 45 – 46.

4. None of the nineteen volumes of the *Nouvelle géographie universelle: la terre et les hommes* (1875 – 93), by Élisée Reclus, bears the title 'L'Europe septentrionale'. Proust may have been thinking of *L'Europe méridionale* or *L'Europe du Nord-Ouest*.

64
TO ROBERT DE MONTESQUIOU

3 January [1895]

Mon cher maître,

I am sending you a copy of the manuscript of the short story that is dedicated to you in a book.[1] I shall give you this manuscript, but may I ask you, if you don't mind, to send back this copy on your return to Paris, because Mme Lemaire will need it for another month. I hope you don't dislike the story too much and that you will accept the gift of it. 'A small thing, to be sure,' as Theocritus says, 'but every gift is dear to us that comes from a friend' ('The Distaff', quoted from memory).[2] To this little gift I add my best wishes for the new year, filling this empty traditional formula with all my oldest and newest feelings for you. Two years ago and one year ago I didn't dare hope anything of a new year, either for myself or for others. I had the feeling that years may change but characters do not, and that the future, one's dreams and desires, was fulfilled only by that selfsame past from which one would have liked it to be so different, that it gave off the exact same sound as all the good and bad bells we had previously set in motion. I am beginning this year with a keener sense of divine grace and human freedom, with confidence in at least an inner Providence. Accordingly I am expressing an individual wish, not just repeating a general formula, when I wish you a happy new year with all my heart, and, to borrow another saying, good health as well. And if your kindness, in accord with tradition, wishes to return my good wishes, you can offer me nothing better, nothing more honourable or more welcome, than the persistence – transcending the ephemeral fragility which so often goes with these things – of your clearsighted and friendly benevolence.

Please convey my respects and good wishes to Mme de Brantes,[3] and my good wishes to M. de Yturri.

Your respectful, admiring and devoted

Marcel Proust

1. 'La Confession d'une jeune fille' (see letter 61). In the event, none of the stories in the published volume, *Les Plaisirs et les jours*, bore dedications.

2. Idyl xxvIII.

3. *Le Gaulois* for 4 Jan. 1895: 'Comte Robert de Montesquiou will be spending another month with Mme de Brantes at the château de Fresne, where he is putting the finishing touches to a volume of poetry. . . .'

65
TO REYNALDO HAHN

[Friday 18 January 1895]

My dearly beloved child,

This morning I shall go to the Bois if I get up soon enough, for I am still in bed, drunk with reading Emerson.[1] Come and see me before a quarter to two – at that time I shall be going out with Yeatman to hear M. Izoulet defend his thesis on the Metaphysics of Sociology, the Holy City.[2] It's open to the public, you ought to come with us. – Or rather, come before a quarter past twelve for lunch. Otherwise, after the thesis at the Sorbonne I shall try to meet you at Mlle Lemaire's at about six. She has written to say that my poems (to you) were good. I replied that one is always inspired when speaking of what one loves. The truth is that one should never speak of anything else. These poems are the only ones of mine that you would give me pleasure by showing around and reciting as much as possible. In the Catholic liturgy, you see, real presence signifies ideal presence. – No, I haven't got that quite right.

> I am your pony
> Marcel

1. Possibly his *Essais de philosophie américaine*, translated by Émile Montégut (1851), or *Sept Essais*, translated by I. Will [Me Mali] with a preface by Maurice Maeterlinck (Brussels, 1894).

2. J. B. L. Izoulet-Loubatières (1854 – 1929), professor of philosophy at the Lycée Condorcet, was defending two theses, the first in Latin on Rousseau, the second entitled *La Cité moderne et la métaphysique de la sociologie*. The session, which was tumultuous, seems to have taken place on 18 January 1895.

66
TO ALPHONSE DAUDET[1]

This Friday [22 February 1895]

Sir,

If I haven't thanked you sooner, it is because I was not quite well and I hope you will forgive me. I am looking forward to hearing your sons' stories next Thursday.[2] I shall try and find an old photograph of Goethe skating in Frankfurt, as well as two pages of Lamartine's *Confidences* to illustrate M. Lucien's skating reminiscences.[3] But he probably has both.

I cannot tell you, sir, how touched I am by your kindness. My fondest dreams when I was a child could not have held out a prospect as unlikely or as delightful as that of being so graciously received one day by the Master who even then inspired me with passionate admiration and respect.

Your respectful admirer and servant,

Marcel Proust

1. The famous novelist Alphonse Daudet (1840–97), author of *Tartarin de Tarascon* (1872) and many other books. For his two sons, Léon and Lucien, see letters 151 and 97.

2. Under Sunday 24 February 1895, Edmond de Goncourt wrote in his journal: 'I dine this evening with Léon and Lucien [Daudet], who have just returned in 72 hours from Stockholm . . . , both marvelling at those hyperborean landscapes and Léon quite stricken with *snow madness*, having been tempted for a moment to press on as far as the North Cape.'

3. Cf. Lamartine, *Les Confidences* (1848), Book v; and see Annie Barnes, 'Proust et les patins de Goethe', in *The Artist and the Writer in France. Essays in Honour of Jean Seznec* (Oxford, 1974).

67
TO PIERRE LAVALLÉE

[7 or 8 April 1895]

My dear little Pierre,

You can't possibly imagine how sad I am. At least you will see from a few pages I shall show you when you get back that I did not go about like a blind man at Segrez, that I *saw* enough to leave me with regrets and memories.[1] Think of me now and then on the river bank or at night under the stars, I shall show you that I thought of both sights with an emotion that Reynaldo has deigned to find contagious. I am still dragging my sadness around Paris, unable to make up my mind whether to go to Dieppe or stay in Paris. How shall I express my gratitude to your whole family for a kindness whose charm I have long known and prized, and the limits of which, I am now certain, I shall never know. I hope your charming brother is with you and that Mme R. Lavallée no longer has cause for concern over her mother's health.[2] I should hate to see each year bringing her new suffering on her mother's account. If anyone deserves, because of her exquisite kindness, to be spared such trials, it is Mme Lavallée.

Your tender and devoted friend,

Marcel Proust

1. Proust had been obliged by an attack of asthma to leave Segrez, where he was staying with the Lavallées. The 'few pages' were apparently those entitled 'Promenade', in *Les Plaisirs et les jours* (cf. 'A Walk', *Pleasures and Regrets*, 117–19).

2. Pierre Lavallée's brother, Robert Martin-Lavallée (1867–1903), had married Juliette Giraudeau; her mother was to die before the end of the year.

68

TO REYNALDO HAHN

[Friday morning 26 April 1895]

My poor child,

My boy, it's all the fault of Mme Lemaire. She wouldn't let me go to Mme E. Stern's alone but insisted on accompanying me (with Mlle Suzette). At eleven o'clock, when I wanted to go, she asked me to wait a few moments. I complied, mostly because I was still vaguely hoping that you would turn up at the Daudets'. Had they deceived me in telling me it was eleven o'clock, or had more time passed since then than I thought? When I got to the avenue Montaigne and saw people leaving the ball[1] and no one arriving, I had a feeling that it must be very late. I had to go in, because I didn't want to confess to Mme Lemaire that I had only one thought, which was to join you, my friend. Alas, I went in to Mme Stern's, I didn't speak to a soul, I came out again, I can assure you, in less than four minutes, and when I reached the rue Cambon it was after half-past twelve! Flavie[2] told me all! Wait for my boy, lose him, find him, love him twice as much on hearing that he had come back to Flavie's to get me, wait two minutes for him or make him wait for five, that for me is the true, throbbing, profound tragedy, which I shall perhaps write some day and which in the meantime I am living.[3] All this to show that the incident is important enough to go on about. Can I see you today, I must be at Mme Legrand's in the rue de Bourgogne[4] at two o'clock. Would you like me to call for you after class at a quarter past three? I'd very much like to. I don't dare make any more plans with this weather, which like Montesquiou can change its intentions towards us from one minute to the next.

Your boy,
Marcel

Can you give me this morning's *Gaulois*, I want to see if the Brancovan ball has been announced.[5] I'll return it to you shortly.

1. Under Thursday 25 April 1895, Edmond de Goncourt's journal notes: 'Big dinner party at the Daudets'. The Ganderaxes, Charpentiers, the Lemaires mother and daughter, Montesquiou, Brochard.' At the so-called 'pink cotillion' that same evening at the home of Mme Edgar Stern, née Fould, at 20, avenue Montaigne, the name of Marcel Proust figures in the list of guests reported by *Le Gaulois* for 26 Apr. 1895.

2. The Marquise de Casa Fuerte, née Flavie Lefebvre de Balsorano (d. 1905), lived at 42, rue Cambon.

3. Proust may have recalled this incident when, in *Swann's Way*, he describes the emotions of Swann on the evening when he arrives at the Verdurins' after Odette has gone (I. 247 – 50).

4. Mme Gaston Legrand, née 'Cloton' de Fournès – the model, it would seem, for Mme Blanche Leroi in *Remembrance of Things Past;* she lived at 12, rue de Bourgogne.

5. *Le Gaulois* and *Le Figaro* in the following week announced 'soirées dansantes' at the home of the Princesse Bassaraba de Brancovan for Tuesday the 7th and Monday the 20th of May 1895.

69
TO REYNALDO HAHN

[May ? 1895]

Forgive me: this letter was mixed up with mine when they were brought to me in bed, I didn't look at the envelope and I opened it. . . . Here it is. Enclosed.

It is possible, even probable, that I shall come and wish you good evening after dinner (at about half-past nine). Don't send word if you won't be there. I am not dining at home and shall be delighted in any case to walk that little way, which is my 'road of hope' and always has been, come to think of it. In the days when I went to the avenue Marigny every morning to see Mme de Chevigné pass, I always took the rue la Ville l'Évêque, the place des Voitures, the same itinerary.[1]

I was extremely bored at *Tannhäuser* up to the solo. And in spite of the general cries of admiration, Elisabeth's languishing prayer left me cold. But how beautiful the whole last part is. I definitely disagree with you about the phrase 'legendary rather than human', though it sounds so well *in the voice* of our friend[2] and goes so well with her type of beauty. – The more legendary Wagner is, the more human I find him, and in him the most magnificent artifice of the imagination strikes me only as the compelling symbolic expression of moral truths.

[*No signature*]

1. Reynaldo Hahn lived in the rue du Cirque, the next street after the avenue Marigny. The Comtesse Adhéaume de Chevigné, née Laure de Sade (1860–1936), lived in the rue de Miromesnil; for a time in 1892 Proust waited every day to see her pass, as the Narrator waits in *The Guermantes Way* (II. 55–67) for the Duchesse de Guermantes to pass.

2. Mme Straus had alleged – a statement with which Hahn seems to have been in agreement – that the public's infatuation with 'legendary and mystical works' was undermining the popularity of 'human works' (such as the operettas of her own father, Fromental Halévy). When *Tannhäuser* was first produced in Paris, in 1861, it was received with boos and catcalls. On 13 May 1895, after thirty-four years of neglect, it was again performed at the Opéra, and greeted this time with wild enthusiasm.

70
FROM MADAME HENRI GAUTHIER-VILLARS (COLETTE)[1]

[Spring 1895]

Sir,

I have read your letter, my husband has gone out and left it for me to answer, which I don't mind in the least, far from it. You can't imagine the pleasure your letter gave Willy, because you are the only person (actually, I believe Fénéon[2] made the same observation) to have seen so clearly that for him a word is not a representation but a living thing, and much less a mnemonic sign than a pictorial translation. I'm bumbling a bit, but I know very well what I mean, and I feel that you understand me perfectly, because, as your letter shows, you know that my Willy is an original mind (though he hides it with pious care) whom the reading of shopworn expressions or incoherent metaphors sickens to the point of nausea, a man in sum far more inclined to translate his thought into hieroglyphics than into tropes such as (Nonoche the cat put her paw on that)[3] such as 'embrace a career' or 'ventilate' those 'burning questions which unauthorized individuals put on the agenda at committee meetings'.

I've said enough about him. Now I want to tell you how beautiful and perceptive we thought your glosses on painters[4] the other evening. You mustn't spoil them as you do by reciting them badly, that's a terrible thing to do. We had some hope of seeing you at the avenue Hoche⁵ last night. It would give me pleasure to see you there and to chat on Wednesday evening. It seems to me that we have quite a few tastes in common, a taste for Willy among others.

Colette Willy

1. Sidonie-Gabrielle Colette (1873 – 1954), later a novelist of distinction, was married at this time to the journalist Henri Gauthier-Villars (1859 – 1931), who used the pen name 'Willy'.

2. The art critic Félix Fénéon (1861 – 1944) was then editorial secretary of *La Revue blanche*, to which Colette's husband contributed.

3. An ink blot in the MS, made by the cat whose portrait Colette published in 1908, in the volume *Les Vrilles de la vigne* (Tendrils of the Vine).

4. The set of Baudelairean poems, 'Portraits de peintres', of which Proust had given a reading.

5. Mme Arman de Caillavet (see letter 120) received on Sunday in her apartment at 12, avenue Hoche.

71

TO SUZETTE LEMAIRE

[Monday 20 May? 1895]

Dear Mlle Suzette,

You've got me quite wrong. I don't conceal my Wagnerism from Reynaldo, why should I since he shares it? The point we disagree on is this: I believe that the essence of music is to arouse the mysterious depths (which literature and generally speaking all finite modes of expression that make use either of words and consequently of ideas, which are determinate things, or of objects – painting, sculpture – cannot express) of our souls, which begin where all the arts aimed at the finite stop and where science as well stops, and which for that reason can be termed religious. This doesn't make much sense when said so quickly, it deserves a longer conversation.

Since Reynaldo, on the contrary, believes that music is always subordinate to the word, he regards it as a way of expressing sentiments of a particular kind, nuances of *conversation*, if you will. You are aware that a Beethoven symphony (which to me is not only the most beautiful of music but also fulfils the highest *function* of music, because it operates outside the particular and concrete – is in essence, that is, quite apart from the particular external objects to which it may attach, as vague and profound as our emotion) bores him dreadfully. He is far too much of an artist not to admire it profoundly, but that's not what music is for him and basically it doesn't interest him. I have never concealed from him our disagreement on this all-important point. And if I said 'while Reynaldo isn't listening', I merely meant to remind you of the fact that he was not of that opinion. If I were to praise Amaury in your presence, I would be quite capable of saying, 'I hope Mlle Suzette isn't listening.' To tell the truth, I don't like to discuss Reynaldo's musical opinions in company. In the first place it would be most presumptuous of me. I am only too well aware how much condescension there is in your kindness or his, when he consents to talk music with me or you painting. And I would not invite ridicule by opposing the opinion of an ignoramus to that of a specialized artist. Besides, general discussions of that sort are sterile. It is quite clear to me that Reynaldo's way of looking at music follows quite naturally from his temperament as a literary musician. His attitudes, believe me, are not the fruit of his theories, his theories, as always, are his marvellously agile mind's justification of his temperament. One does not fight a temperament and I have too profound an admiration for his to have any desire to fight it. Lastly and especially, the discussion of music soon gets on Reynaldo's nerves, it pains him. If I think I have something theoretical to say to him, I satisfy my conscience by saying it when alone with him.

What bliss that you are coming back. You will find me shaky in health, but very glad to see you.

Kindly tell Madame your mother that I haven't had time to get the little story I wrote about her and about you published in a paper. (I tried *La Patrie*, but failed, and *La Presse* too.) I know it means nothing to you, but it would give me so much pleasure! If she doesn't want to send it to *Le Gaulois*, on the pretext that she would seem to be asking them to praise her (which is absurd, as I venture to say respectfully, considering on the one hand who she is and on the other hand who I am. When you think of all the famous people who have glorified her, the praise of an unknown like me can only irritate her. And M. Arthur Meyer would be well aware that she was doing it to give me pleasure and not for her own sake). If she won't send it to *Le Gaulois*, I should be pleased if she would, as she offered to do, put me in touch with *Le Gaulois* so I can get them to publish a page of mine. Once they have taken two or three things of mine, I can easily slip them my little story about Mme Lemaire, who would then no longer be responsible for it. In *Le Château de Réveillon* there are a number of short unpublished pieces which would do nicely for *Le Gaulois*. For instance, 'Dîner en Ville', which I presume to regard as more literary than many of the stories in *Le Gaulois* and yet of the right kind.[1]

You are coming back, so I won't have any more letters from you! But we shall be able to talk together and that will give me so much pleasure. Dear Mlle Suzette, I am very fond of you. How pleasant it will be to see you both, sometimes dressed very simply and sometimes in 'rare and marvellous' gowns. I think it is because of my illegible writing that you read 'fortified cities in Élisée Reclus'; I don't think I ever said anything of the kind.[2]

Robert de Flers is back.

Till tomorrow evening perhaps[3] . . . what a joy!

Marcel Proust

1. The story about Mme Lemaire and her daughter seems to have been lost; Arthur Meyer (1844 – 1924), managing editor of *Le Gaulois*, published neither this nor 'Un Dîner en ville', though other pieces by Proust appeared in the paper. *Le Château de Réveillon* was the original title of Proust's *Les Plaisirs et les jours*, in which 'Un Dîner en ville' was included (cf. 'A Dinner in Society', *Pleasures and Regrets*, 48 – 58).

2. Proust had evidently forgotten what he had written six months before. See letter 63.

3. At Mme Lemaire's soirée on Tuesday 21 May 1895, *Le Gaulois* notes (22 May) the presence of the 'young poet M. Proust'.

72
TO ROBERT DE MONTESQUIOU

9, boulevard Malesherbes
9 a.m. [27 May 1895]

Dear Sir,

To give words to the theme which has prompted some of Hahn's lovely variations, some of my worst poems will be heard tomorrow in that same studio[1] where such beautiful ones have been heard, and where even more beautiful ones, as Mme Lemaire hopes and leads others to hope, will yet stir your admirers! If amongst all the fine pieces of music that will be played tomorrow, you might derive some pleasure from discerning, in a young man's verse, not only admiration for yours but imitation as well, if it might please you to hear certain skies 'sadder for being blue' as a faithful though feeble echo of august hands 'more beautiful for being bare', I would ask you to come early, for Risler,[2] who is coming expressly from Chartres to play the 'Portraits de peintres', must go back to his regiment that same night and will be obliged to leave us at eleven o'clock.

Your respectful and affectionate

Marcel Proust

1. *Le Gaulois* for 29 May 1895 reports on a 'brilliant musical evening' at Mme Lemaire's on the 28th, devoted to the works of 'the distinguished composer Reynaldo Hahn' and featuring his settings of 'finely wrought poems by M. Marcel Proust. Each of the "Portraits de peintres" is a little gem.' Among those in attendance was Comte Robert de Montesquiou.

2. The pianist Édouard Risler (1873 – 1929), later professor at the Paris Conservatory. Proust may have taken him as one of the models for the 'young pianist' favoured by the Verdurins.

73
TO REYNALDO HAHN

Half-past 8
[Spring – summer 1895]

Alas, my poor little Reynaldo,

I must tell you straight away – no luck. After going to Mme Fould's, then doing the avenue Montaigne and the avenue Marigny step by step (because I had made a mistake and first taken the avenue d'Antin on leaving you),[1] then to Mme Ernesta's, where they told me you had sent to enquire but they had found nothing, I decided to give the faubourg Saint-Honoré another careful going-over, and then, my poor boy, I found one sheet and then another in the gutter, right next to the sewer opening. And nothing more. I went back to Mme Ernesta's and asked them to speak to the street sweeper, and to me poor Isis, searching for the scattered limbs of Osiris, the porter replied: 'Ah, but there must have been seven or eight of those papers when Madame went out. I pushed them out into the street in obedience to the wishes of Madame, who dislikes to see papers in front of the door!' And I, when like Isis I should have been roused to fury by the cruel Anubis, answered gently, but went over the faubourg again in vain, picking up crumpled newspapers at every street corner and from every flowing gutter, and 'finding not that which we sought'. I stopped in again at your place and at a quarter past eight decided to go home. And here I'm sending you these poor little scraps, though I hardly know why, whether they will help you to establish the truth or to invent some little falsehood, traffic accident, or something. Don't laugh at me for using such a beautiful envelope for these filthy papers, *disjecta membra poetae*.[2] A thin envelope, you see, would have made the papers *look fat*, and you might have thought at first that I had found the proofs and sent them, and had a recurrence of the same despair as before. And that is why I'm writing on such thin paper, so you won't think the envelope is thick before you open it. . . . I'm telling the bearer to go to Otto's before going to M. Dettelbach's. He'd have given you the proofs if they had been there.[3] See you this evening.

Your pony,
Marcel

1. Mme Léon Fould, née Ephrussi, lived at 38, cours la Reine, Mme Louis Stern ('Mme Ernesta') at 68, faubourg Saint-Honoré. (The avenue d'Antin is now the avenue Franklin D. Roosevelt.)

2. A few mud-stained sheets – apparently proofs of a chapter from Albert Lavignac's *La Musique et les musiciens* (1895) which Hahn had been correcting – were enclosed with this letter, in a large envelope bearing on the back the initials 'MP' and addressed to Hahn c/o Mme Dettelbach, 13, rue Christophe Colomb. *Disjecta membra poetae*: Horace, *Satires* i. v. 62.

3. Not the proofs of n. 2, above, but prints of some photographs which Proust had ordered from the photographer Otto, 15, rue Royale.

74
TO MARIA HAHN[1]

[Dieppe, August 1895]

Mademoiselle,

Now I don't know what to do about 'Baldassare', because I shall have to send it to a magazine and then I won't see your annotations. Yet your opinion is just about the *only* one that matters to me, and if when it appears in the volume people talk or write about it, that

will interest me much less than the opinion of the most intelligent of
women. So I don't know what to do. If the comments only come to a
few lines, you might copy them for me. . . . In any case, I should like
you to send 'Baldassare' to

Mme Proust
9, boulevard Malesherbes

who will send it to the managing editor of the magazine in question.[2]
My nerves are frayed from insomnia, but I am enjoying my visit here
thanks to Reynaldo, and you are associated with all my impressions,
oh, my sister Maria, confidante of my thoughts, beacon to errant
sadness, protectress of the weak, helpmate of the sick, source of
goodness, spice of wit, sparkling rose, courageous kindness, breeze
upon the sea, song of happy oars, shuddering sea foam, glory of morning, perfume of friendship, soul of the nights which you dazzle with
your brilliance (friendly lights), which you enliven with your games
(Puck and Titania), which you cause to vibrate with your laughter,
by turns echo and voice of the spirit, which you startle discreetly
with your dresses; O charm without limit but not without measure,
you who lend your frocks a moral charm, modesty or nobility, literary qualities, conciseness, a veil spread over too much brilliance, but
who endow your counsels, your speech with supreme elegance which
makes them resemble your frocks, who brighten them benevolently
with the smile even of your eyes, O you, who are all men's sister, in
the sense that Mary, whose gentleness you share, is their mother, but
whom, come to think of it, I prefer to keep just for myself and
Reynaldo, sail of hope in the darkness of my life, guiding beam on the
pathways of the sea, retrieved country of noble souls banished into
this vile world, intelligent adviser of Levadé,[3] obedient daughter of
God, heady flower of the right road, delicious flute of the wind that
brings the lost skiffs home.

Respectfully your
Marcel

1. Maria Hahn (1865 – 1948), sister of Reynaldo; in 1899 she married Raymond
de Madrazo.

2. Mlle Hahn had been reading Proust's novella 'La Mort de Baldassare Silvande' (see letter 59) and had written her comments in the margins of the
manuscript, which he now wanted sent on to *La Revue hebdomadaire*.

3. The composer Charles Levadé; see letter 85.

75
FROM HIS MOTHER

Sunday [25 August 1895?]

My darling,

It's your letters that are sweet, your idea of hugging me un-starched made me burst out laughing.

At the Louvre? I gave Watteau regards from you and Hahn,[1] then I cast myself at the feet of Leonardo and Titian (and so many others!!!). At this season and in the morning the rooms are almost deserted. The occupants are mostly poor wrecks, old women in spectacles, who, though perched on top of ladders to be as close as possible to their models, don't succeed in stealing their celestial fire.

And among the public a few English ladies, whose main concern it is to keep abreast of their catalogues.

Suddenly the calm was shattered by a thundering voice and an uninterrupted flow of words.

Alarmed, I see a group of English ladies and gentlemen emerging, all with binoculars slung over their shoulders (the straps of which strangely divide the airy shirtwaists of the ladies into eastern and western hemispheres), following in the footsteps of a guide, who leads them at a furious pace, stunning them with the names of persons and gods of whom, as poor Louise used to say, 'Old as I am, I can safely say I have never heard of such a thing in all my life'.[2] Listening ecstatically, they kept on running for fear of losing him. As they were leaving the *salon carré* and entering the *grande galerie*, the man negligently thrust out his middle finger behind him and said without turning round: '*This, Charles the First, by Van Dyck.*'[3] Since the tone said: a minor work, they hardly looked. 'Kings of England,' they said. 'Oh, we've got them at home.' And they hurried on to catch the guide, who had already entered the next gallery.

[*End of letter missing*]

1. Hahn had just composed the music for Proust's poem about Watteau, in the 'Portraits de peintres' series, while he and Proust were staying with Mme Lemaire at Dieppe.

2. Aunt Léonie, in *Swann's Way* (I. iii), uses this same turn of phrase in expressing her surprise that an artist should have come to Combray to copy a stained-glass window in the church.

3. In English in the original.

76
FROM HIS MOTHER

[Wednesday or Thursday 28 or 29? August 1895]

[First four pages missing]

. . . the book is very nicely written. It's like one of Voltaire's *contes*, but seen through the little lens of Montesquiou's penholder.[1] Dick with his unpardonable negligence about writing has been tormenting me since Sunday, but this morning the atoning letter came at last. It was high time! Just a little longer and I'd have written to General Zurlinden.[2] Your father is (still, I believe) at Carlsbad. Since our letters can never match up with one another, they make me feel as one does at the Salon when, looking for the title of a portrait, one mistakes the catalogue number and finds: 'Still life'. – Your father, having learnt of the stifling sensation you had on arriving, has been discussing the likelihood of its not lasting, etc. . . .[3] He will spend 2 and 3 September here. (He arrives on the 1st – morning or evening – and leaves on the 4th for Vichy.)

A thousand affectionate kisses, my darling.

[No signature]

Do you keep giving Mme Lemaire my heartfelt thanks?

1. Cf. the poem 'Peintresse', in Robert de Montesquiou's latest volume, *Le Parcours du rêve au souvenir* (The Journey from Dream to Memory; 1895), which ends: '. . . closing an eye, one squints . . . / Through the hole in a penholder.'

2. Robert Proust was at Reims, doing his year of military service. General Zurlinden, here whimsically evoked, was Minister of War at the time.

3. On 10 August 1895 Reynaldo Hahn had written from Dieppe to his sister Maria: 'The poor boy [Marcel] has had a touch of asthma and feels somewhat stifled – we don't know the cause of it.'

77
TO GABRIEL DE YTURRI

Hôtel Fermont, Beg-Meil (Finistère)
[September 1895]

Dear Sir and friend,

Since I was changing address from day to day, no post has been forwarded to me on this pilgrimage to abodes made illustrious by Sarah Bernhardt, for I started with Belle-Île and am now at Beg-Meil. A delightful spot, where Norman apples ripen at the edge of the rocks, mingling the smell of cider with the perfume of the seaweed, on the shore of a fantastic Lake Geneva, where, however, there are not even any water closets. And indeed, this would be just the place to air Vigny's line:

Never leave me alone with nature.[1]

For it is to nature that we consign everything, and I assure you that nothing is so *irritating* as the excessive zeal of the nettles, which try to make themselves *indispensable*, if you will forgive the pun,[2] and their way of doing it is piquant but harsh.

It is in this primitive and delightful spot that your regards have reached me, and I thank you for them without delay, at the same time begging you to convey my tribute of admiration and devotion to the great Poet. As for you, from whom I await an explanation of your mysterious card, too hard perhaps on one of our friends, who, believe me, has charming qualities, please accept my thanks and best wishes.

Marcel Proust

1. From *La Maison du berger.*
2. 'Indispensables' seems to have been a current euphemism for lavatory paper.

78
TO ROBERT DE BILLY

[Beg-Meil, September 1895]

My dear Robert,

Luckily I have this card on me, because I am in a village where there is no paper. It's called Beg-Meil, the apple trees come down to the sea, and the smell of cider mingles with that of the seaweed. This mixture of poetry and sensuality is just about right for me, but I am prevented from fully enjoying it by my fear that they neglected to inform you at the Ministry of my dropping in on my way through Paris. I wanted to tell you how kind you had been to Robert [Proust] and how touched I was that you are always doing so much for us. When I have some paper, I shall write to you about Brittany, and anyway I shall soon be passing through Paris again. Pay my respects to Mme de Billy and take a look now and then at the contents of *La Revue hebdomadaire*. I have just sent them that 'Baldassare Silvande' which you corrected for me one evening in the lamplight and of which you disliked only certain parts, and you will soon find it published there.[1] I am reading a stupid book by Balzac, the title of which begins with *Splendour and Misery*, the rest of it cannot be mentioned to a married man, and *Heroes*, who should all march abreast to cripple M. Izoulet, who has got a head start on them.[2]

Yours,

M.P.

1. The novella appeared in *La Revue hebdomadaire* for 29 Oct. 1895.

2. Balzac's *Splendeurs et misères des courtisanes* (1838 – 47), and *Les Héros: le culte des héros dans l'histoire*, a French translation (1888) by J. B. L. Izoulet-Loubatières of Thomas Carlyle's *Heroes and Hero-Worship* (1841). The implication is that M. Izoulet has crippled Carlyle's prose.

79
TO PIERRE LAVALLÉE

[Beg-Meil, September – October? 1895]

My dear Pierre,

Reynaldo joined me in writing you a beautiful letter almost a month ago. If you have a moment, be a good boy and answer it, because we shall be leaving Brittany soon if we are to go to Segrez, and to settle our plans we must have some idea of yours. I don't need to tell you that if, because of other people you may have invited or for any of a thousand reasons it would be less convenient for you to have us at Segrez this year than some other, it would be absurd of you to stand on ceremony with us and not tell us so quite frankly. You would have all the less ground for regrets as the resorts we should substitute for Segrez would be very near Paris, so we would be able to come and see you. – I'd have liked to see your charming cousin Atthalin to congratulate him on his success, which gave me real pleasure. I don't know whether I told you in our letter how happy I was for our government's sake to see your uncle in that post, and how afraid I was for your uncle's sake that the post would be terribly fatiguing.[1]

Forgive this ridiculous paper, the only kind to be found in this wild country. Alas, there's no pleasure in writing to you from here, it takes letters more than three days to reach Paris, and the burning friendship I send you will have cooled and frozen in the mists of three nights before it reaches you. May your heart warm it up again. My address for telegrams is *télégraphe restant Beg-Meil Finistère*. But you won't need it. As for letters, it's best to send them to Paris to be forwarded, because I have no idea how much longer we shall stay here.

[*No signature*]

1. André Laurent-Atthalin (1875 – 1956) had just been admitted to the École Polytechnique. His father, Gaston-Marie Laurent-Atthalin (1848 – 1912), was appointed Procureur de la République on 3 September 1895.

80
FROM HIS MOTHER

[Wednesday evening 23 October 1895]

[*First two pages missing*]

He was intending – said his mother-in-law – to send you his speech and eeven to Georges![1] This 'eeven' reduced poor Georges to the level of the pariahs, whose feet are washed by the queen once a year.

As I write, Dick has arrived – for the night. – He is reading the order of the day to the troops at reveille tomorrow morning.

You used to laugh over the dialogue between a gentleman and a locomotive: 'Do you smoke, Madame?' But what do you think of the locomotive who, bored at having to spend all her life on the tracks, went out to take the tram in the square? It would be as funny as it is terrifying, if a poor woman hadn't been killed![2]

A thousand affectionate kisses, my darling. I'll add one more tomorrow when the post comes.

Dick has gone to bed, sends love and falls asleep.

J.P.

Thursday morning at half-past 8

Good morning, my darling, I've received your letter; and am racking my brains to figure out what I could have written you that was 'witty'. It doesn't matter.

'Since I am crept in favour with myself
I will maintain it with some little cost'[3]

Your little brother sends much love and so do I, my darling.

1. Probably the speech delivered by Henri Bergson at the prize-giving ceremony for the state examinations, 30 July 1895: 'Le bon sens et les études classiques'. Bergson's mother-in-law, Mme Gustave Neuburger (see letter 1), was a cousin of Mme Proust and her brother, Georges Weil.

2. At the Gare Montparnasse on 22 October 1895, the brakes of an incoming express failed and the locomotive demolished the buffers, destroyed a newspaper kiosk, and broke through the front wall of the station, almost falling down on the busy place de Rennes, where the horse-drawn trams stopped. A newspaper vendor in the square was killed by a falling segment of wall. (*Journal des débats*, 23 Oct. 1895)

3. *Richard III*, I. ii, quoted in English.

81

TO JACQUES-ÉMILE BLANCHE

Réveillon par Courgivaux (Marne)
[5 or 6? November 1895]

My dear friend,

Mama has made me very sad, writing that I shall never see Mme Blanche again, that the admirable woman who loved you so dearly has left you forever on this earth. Her aspect, her conversation delighted my imagination no less than her kindness moved my heart, for with all her intelligence and goodness, she was someone very special, full of set and singular opinions which lend her memory extraordinary precision, originality and relief. Her originality is the indestructible tie that will bind the sympathy and tenderness of so many to her memory, without fear of its fading or blurring. Her memory will remain as living as the portrait you did of her. You had already seen her dying many times. But then you were alone with your sorrow, and now you have Mme Jacques Blanche beside you,[1] to remember with you. Please give her my respectful regards. At a time when so much of yourself and your childhood is taken from you, she, I am sure, will restore some of it.

Yours,
Marcel Proust

1. Blanche's mother, Mme Antoine-Émile Blanche, had died on 3 November 1895, four days after his marriage to Rose John-Lemoinne.

82
TO REYNALDO HAHN[1]

[Friday 15 November 1895]

Dinner yesterday at the Daudets with my little dear one, M. de Goncourt, Coppée, M. Philipe, M. Vacquès [*sic*].[2] Noted with sadness (1) the frightful materialism, so surprising in 'intellectuals'. They account for character and genius by physical habits or race. Differences between Musset, Baudelaire and Verlaine explained by the properties of the spirits they drank, the characters of certain persons by their race (anti-Semitism). Even more astounding in Daudet, a pure and brilliant intellect shining through the mists and storms of his nerves, a small star on the sea. All that is most unintelligent. The narrowest view of the mind (for everything is a view of the mind) is one in which it has not yet gained sufficient self-awareness and believes itself to be derived from the body. (2) None of them (I always exclude Reynaldo, in whose mind I never cease to admire all the nuances of truth, as sublimely distinct as the nuances of the sky in the sea) understands anything about poetry. Daudet's comparison of Musset and Baudelaire is about as true as if one were to say to someone who knew neither Mme Straus nor my concierge: 'Mme Straus has black hair and black eyes, a rather large nose, red lips, a rather good figure' – and the same about my concierge, and the other would reply: 'Why, they're identical.' True enough, a certain overworked rhetoric might lead one to liken Musset to Baudelaire from the standpoint of composition, although they have about as much in common as Bossuet and Murger.[3] If you were to describe your impressions of the ocean to someone who had never seen it, he might imagine it to be the same as a switchback. A person who has no feeling for poetry and who is not moved by Truth, has never really read Baudelaire. Hence these statements made by Coppée and Goncourt. (3) Sentences spoken by Daudet (in the director's garden), Daudet all over, acute observation, but musty-smelling, a trifle vulgar and pretentious for all his sharpness. He's the Céline Chaumont of the novel.[4] (4) Mme Daudet charming, but how bourgeois! A poor young fellow arrives, he doesn't know anyone but her son, who isn't there. In spite of herself she does everything possible to freeze him out, in five minutes he has become the 'intruder', and from time to time she says: 'I don't know Monsieur, I've never laid eyes on him before.' The same with me. When I called on her for the first time and thanked her for letting me come, she replied: 'M. Hahn asked me to.' Monstrous! The aristocracy certainly have their faults, but show a true superiority when thanks to their mastery of good manners and easy charm they are able to affect the most exquisite affability for five minutes, or feign sympathy and brotherhood for an hour. And the Jews (detested in that household in the name of I don't know what principle, since He whom they crucified is also banished, from their son's wedding, for instance)[5] have the same quality though in another way, a kind of charitable self-esteem, a cordiality without pride, which is infinitely precious. How pitiable Mme Daudet looks in her treatment of poor M. Philipe, by contrast with Mme de Brantes or Mme Lyon,[6] whom in this respect I find it natural to lump together. From the viewpoint of art, to be so lacking in self-mastery, so incapable of playing a part, is abominable, made all the worse by her dumpy figure. One almost yearns for the obnoxious grace of Don Juan in his scene with M. Dimanche, the inane grace of M. de Florian, or the repulsive grace of the Duc de Gramont.[7] But great intelligence and sensibility (though slightly exasperating and sometimes false) are here, and extremely interesting. In sum, a charming person.

Daudet is delightful, the son of a Moorish king who might have married a princess of Avignon, but simplistic in his intelligence. He thinks Mallarmé is fooling the public. One must always assume that a pact has been made between the poet's intelligence and his sensibility of which he himself is unaware, that he is its plaything. It's more interesting and more profound. Laziness or narrow-mindedness to be explained by a physical pact (with charlatanesque intention) with his disciples. If it were that, it would cease to interest us. And it cannot be that.

[*No signature*]

1. Pages torn from a notebook, with jottings by Hahn on the back of one page.

2. Edmond de Goncourt (1822 – 96), who also left an account of this dinner party in his journal for 14 November [1895]; François Coppée (1842 – 1908), Parnassian poet, member of the French Academy, harshly treated in Goncourt's journal; Charles-Louis Philippe (1874 – 1909), author of realistic, rather sordid novels, among them *Bubu de Montparnasse* (1901); Dr Henri Vaquez (1860 – 1936), cardiologist and professor of medicine.

3. Jacques-Bénigne Bossuet (1627 – 1704), theologian and moralist, bishop at the time of Louis XIV, was noted for his sermons; Henry Murger (1822 – 61) wrote the well-known *Scènes de la vie de Bohème* and other books about Parisian low life.

4. Proust is comparing Daudet as a novelist to the brilliant but frivolous comedienne and variety entertainer Marie-Céline Chaumont (1848 – 1926).

5. Léon Daudet's first marriage, in 1891 to Jeanne Victor-Hugo, was a civil ceremony, at the Mairie in Passy.

6. For Mme Daudet, see letter 87. Mme Charles-Léon Lyon-Caen, née Louise-Marguerite May, wife of a member of the Institut de France, was a highly cultivated Jewish society woman.

7. In Molière's play, the aristocrat Don Juan flatters the merchant, M. Dimanche, in order to take advantage of him. Like the Comte de Florian, Agénor, Duc de Gramont, father of Proust's friend the Duc de Guiche (see letter 208, n. 1), was a diplomat.

83
TO ROBERT DE MONTESQUIOU

[Friday 13 December ? 1895]

Mon cher maître,

> *This mark of honour that he accords the family*
> (*Le Cid*, Act I)[1]

touches us infinitely and I thank you with all my heart for consenting to come on *Saturday* (and not on Friday as your letter has it). – As for the role of travelling salesman for your wit, which had no need of one, I abandoned it long ago, and to take it up again is the one thing I would not do to give you pleasure. In those days, to be sure, thanks to the phenomenon which makes the body follow the soul, my voice and my accent may well have taken on the rhythm of this borrowed thought. If anyone has said more than this, and if they have spoken of caricature, I invoke your axiom: 'A remark repeated at second hand is rarely true.'[2] I, so scrupulous and anxious about everything else in my life, am very much at ease when it comes to you, since the only sentiment I have allowed to overflow in public is my admiration for you, which, God be praised, is in no danger of drying up. I was therefore somewhat humiliated to see that my 'latest creations', as you call them, were held to be not very creative, and that you address me with the contemptuous tolerance that a Fuster[3] might inspire. No, I shall send you my most recent creation, a very sad story,[4] which alas! and happily is also an imitation of you. In the hope that you will relish it, I shall send you this artistic honeycomb, filched from the mournful hive at the feet of which I lay my affectionate and most admiring respects.

Marcel Proust

1. Scene iii: 'Cette marque d'honneur, qu'il met dans ma [*not* la] famille.'

2. Albert Flament (see letter 134) describes a dinner held on 12 December 1895 at the house of Alphonse Daudet, at which, at about one o'clock in the morning, Proust 'imitated with virtuosity . . . the piercing cries of M. de Montesquiou', and repeated his imitation in the cab while taking M. Flament home (*Le Bal du Pré-Catelan*, 1946). As for the Comte's 'axiom', Proust was to put it into the mouth of Charlus in *The Guermantes Way* (II. 582).

3. Charles Fuster (1866–1929), poet, publicist, and man of letters, managing editor of *L'Année des poètes*, in which three of Proust's 'Portraits de peintres' appeared in 1895.

4. I.e. 'La Mort de Baldassare Silvande'.

84
TO J. HUBERT[1]

[Friday 27 December 1895]
Dear Sir,

I really have no luck with you: yesterday evening I missed you. This morning I get up at an hour that is for me very early! and you're out again. At this disastrous juncture it would seem that business must always be mixed up with friendship and that I shall never be able to pay you a visit or leave my card on you without asking a favour of you. Since you had the unfortunate idea (forgive me, I am joking) of advising Mme Lemaire to do new headpieces, she seems to have concluded with truly feminine logic that there was no longer any hurry, and after doing a third of one headpiece, she ordered models for God knows when with a view to doing designs with figures, which could take a year or two, and now she has dropped the book and is doing watercolours for Benguet or Boussod. Would you kindly write her a letter, saying: 'Madame, the final deadline has now passed, if you do not send me everything, we shall not be able to publish this year, or at least I can make no promises, for if we are not ready at the end of the season, it will be best to wait until next year. If you still have some of the separate illustrations to do, then by all means hurry up and do them, but anyway send the rest of the book, or we shall not have time enough. We shall have no difficulty in interspersing the headpieces among your fifty little drawings. Since they have no definite subjects, they can fit just as well in one place as in another.'

If you write this in a firm tone (which, however, will not be domineering, for you will not say 'I need the book', but merely observe: 'If I don't get the book, we shall have to publish next year') and at this point, I am pinning my hopes on the friendship of Mme Lemaire, who, since she has been holding me over the baptismal fonts of letters for the last four years[2] (I am greatly honoured to have such a lovely godmother, which is all very well, but it's getting to be high time), will not wish to hold me up for another year.

I have been hearing great things about you lately and I learned how your unique competence gave wings for a time to a certain publication, and how its quality has fallen off again since you left it. Ignorant as I am, I would never dare express an opinion to an expert like yourself, and say that the book might have more unity if the drawings, reproduced by zincography or otherwise, were all in black and white, reserving the colour for the de luxe editions.

But I am too certain that in all such matters you will always be right to express a preference, which coming from one who knows nothing can be no more than a fancy or a prejudice.

I hope you are not as penetrated and racked by this fog[3] as I am. I feel most discouraged. If one of these days you think you might still be in the rue Auber at about four o'clock or half-past six (for I usually work from two to six) and will drop me a note to let me know, it will give me great pleasure to come and chat with you a while, which will always be a source of pleasure and profit to

Your

Marcel Proust

1. M. Hubert was in charge of production at the Calmann-Lévy publishing house.

2. At the time of this writing, Proust had been busy with *Les Plaisirs et les jours* for scarcely more than two years (see letter 44, of 5 November 1893, for the first mention of the projected book).

3. 'Another gloomy winter day,' reported *Le Figaro* (28 Dec. 1895); on the 27th 'a dense fog covered the city'. Proust's letter is dated from this report, of the only day of fog in Paris between 1 November 1895 and 1 March 1896.

PART TWO

[1896~1901]

INTRODUCTION TO PART TWO

Proust was to work intermittently at the drafts of *Jean Santeuil* for another five years or so, and echoes are heard in his letters; he was especially anxious to reassure his mother that he was forging ahead. Meanwhile, in 1896, Mme Lemaire having at last produced her illustrations, *Les Plaisirs et les jours* was published, with a preface which Mme Arman de Caillavet extracted from Anatole France. Although M. Hubert, the production manager at the publishers, revealed to Anatole France his doubt about the merits of Proust's prose style, France himself wrote in his preface that the book reminded him at once of Petronius and of Bernardin de Saint-Pierre. The expensive, limited edition meant comparatively few readers, and though many of the press notices were quite complimentary, what reputation the book won for Proust was that of a rich dilettante.

In December 1896 Proust met Reynaldo Hahn's English cousin, Marie Nordlinger, who was to give him a great deal of help over his Ruskin translations. The relationship with Montesquiou became more stormy as it became closer. But it always survived the strains – as when, in December 1895, Montesquiou had got wind of the fact that Proust was giving popular imitations of his mannerisms, and of his extraordinary voice, behind his back. Proust tried to forestall Montesquiou's reproaches; Montesquiou saw through his ploy and told him so.

Relations with Reynaldo Hahn became rather cooler in 1896, and he seems to have been replaced in Proust's affection by the pretty and rather effeminate Lucien Daudet. Early in 1897 the journalist Jean Lorrain, who himself had a rather lurid reputation, published a sarcastic review of *Les Plaisirs et les jours* with the implication of homosexual relations between Proust and Lucien. Proust fought a duel with Lorrain; they exchanged shots with no bloodletting.

In December 1897 the Dreyfus Affair took a new turn when *Le Figaro* published facsimiles of the document that had given rise to Dreyfus's conviction, together with the handwriting of Comte Esterhazy, who, in the eyes of the Dreyfusards, was the chief suspect. In January 1898 Zola published *J'accuse*, his famous letter to the President of the

Republic asserting that there was an Establishment conspiracy to prevent justice; he was promptly arrested and brought to trial. An officer in the case, Colonel Picquart, who had discovered some forged documents in the official dossier, was himself imprisoned and, in September, placed in solitary confinement. At this point Proust came into the open as a Dreyfusard and collected signatures for a petition on Picquart's behalf.

This entry into the Dreyfus controversy brought Proust into a closer relationship with the Brancovan family; this can be seen in his letters to Prince Constantin de Brancovan and to his sister, the poetess Anna de Noailles.

By the end of 1899 the *Jean Santeuil* project was petering out. Encouraged if not directly persuaded by his mother, Proust began to study Ruskin with a view, first, to writing about him, then to translating some of his work. In October of that year he was reading *The Seven Lamps of Architecture* at the Bibliothèque Nationale. In December 1899 he wrote to Marie Nordlinger (letter 163) that his attempt at a novel reminded him of Casaubon's futile work in *Middlemarch* – as a 'collector of ruins'; for the last fortnight, he said, he had switched to writing about 'Ruskin and certain cathedrals'. The year 1900 saw the appearance in various periodicals of the first fruits of these studies: an obituary on Ruskin in January; 'Notes and Reminiscences: Ruskinian Pilgrimages in France' in February; three essays on Ruskin and Amiens in April and August. His 'Ruskin period' was to go on for another four years or so.

In May 1900 Proust went to Venice with his mother and met Marie Nordlinger there. In October Proust's family moved away from the centre of Paris, in the interests of his mother's health, and Proust went to Venice again while the move was going on. His own health took a turn for the worse at about that time; asthma and hay fever kept him indoors a good deal.

The first letter from Proust to Prince Antoine Bibesco to have survived (not translated here) was sent from Évian, where Proust was staying in September 1899. The correspondence went on for a long time; two hundred or so letters have survived. In 1901 the letters to Bibesco came thick and fast and testify to an increasingly close friendship. From then onwards Proust met more and more young aristocrats and spent a good deal of time in their company in the early years of the new century.

J.M.C.

85
TO MARIA HAHN

[1895 or 1896]

Mademoiselle and dear friend,

This is what I wanted to tell you. Levadé's[1] attitude towards me has changed completely, he is now, like everyone else (if you forgive this bit of conceit) being very nice to me. His indifference or hostility troubled me less than I can say, to my mind they demonstrated (still the same conceit) a lack of taste which made me find him uninteresting. Nevertheless, his sympathy, or, rather, for that may be going too far, his affability gives me great pleasure by opening my eyes once again to the undeniable charm of his talent, character and mind. But in a life where we are all obliged to give our attention to so many more considerable changes, this change might not have made me inflict a letter on you and pay so much attention to it, had I not seen in it the work of three collaborators who to my mind are worthy of the highest interest: I am referring to your goodness, your intelligence in its aspects of tact, intuition, subtlety, etc., and your kindness to me. Of course you will deny all this, for people who like to do good and know how to, do so in the dark. If I may venture on a very small scale to compare myself with you, it is likewise in the dark, in silence, that I smooth the path for those I love, here dispelling a prejudice, there little by little fostering a sympathy, at my happiest when, in the presence of my finished handiwork, they do not see the strings I have pulled, which I always take pains to conceal. If for an instant I have had the temerity to compare myself with you, it is to show you that I understand all the delicacy of your nature and that, without sharing your wonderful qualities, I am able to understand them. Your life is very different, dear Mlle Maria, and I would wish it to be as decked with joys as mine at present is thorny with sorrows. But flowers, as a Romantic might have said, like to bend over the abyss. May the flower you are continue to dispense fragrance and grace over the abyss that I am. May we never allow any enemy, any ruse of others, any misunderstanding between us, or any spirit of irony to break our holy alliance. In our alliance there is no calculation on my part, though I know how much more you can do for me than I for you, I who cannot even imagine ever being in a position to do anything for you. But you know that in such matters the ways of God are most obscure, and that it is often the ant that helps the lion out. And at all events, two friends who sustain each other in life triumph over all obstacles, or rather, they would triumph, because it never happens: in any case, my great desire to please you makes me accept all your kindnesses without embarrassment, since with you I am never wanting in tenderness.

Yours,
Marcel Proust

1. Charles-Gaston Levadé (1868 – 1948), the composer mentioned in Proust's pastiche of Flaubert, 'Mélomanie de Bouvard et Pécuchet' (cf. *Pleasures and Regrets*, 110). See letter 74, in which Mlle Hahn is described as his 'intelligent adviser'.

86
TO J. HUBERT

Dear M. Hubert, [January 1896]

But I never *sent* Reynaldo to you! He says he went to see you to talk about his music and has *told* me what you told him (elegant repetition). Your letter is full of affectionate remarks and I thank you sincerely for them. As for Mme Lemaire, rest assured that she has done nothing and will do nothing as long as you ask nothing of her. If you will permit me not to give you a piece of advice but to express a wish, write to her immediately, saying you need the two insets (or more, I don't remember how many are lacking) and asking when you can go and pick them up. Otherwise we shall be no further advanced a month from now. And specify which stories you need insets for, so she won't take uncertainty as a pretext for further delay. I believe you should ask her for:
 – two insets for 'Baldassare' with headpiece and tailpiece;
 – two insets for 'La Fin de la jalousie' with headpiece and tailpiece;
just say you need them (without detriment to the little drawings you will ask for later on, after the book is made up). And say 'This is all I ask of you (while reserving the right to ask you for floral designs at the last moment and for the cover) but this I need as soon as pos-

sible. When can I pick them up?' Remember that on 25 December she said she would give you everything in a week! She hasn't done a thing since she saw you last!

Don't you think I'm an awful bore? But it's your fault, because you wanted me to get busy again with the book. I shall come soon and thank you for your letter. It moved me deeply. Think of me as a friend who is very grateful to you for it and for employing all your precious artistic experience in his favour.

Yours,
Marcel Proust

87
TO MADAME ALPHONSE DAUDET[1]

Saturday morning [4 January 1896]
Madame,

I have just read your 'Notes sur Londres'.[2] I was charmed by so much art and still more captivated by so much life. For an hour you gave to my eye the visual acuteness of yours, to my sensibility the subtle and quivering chords which belong only to you, to my intellect all the manifold penetration of your intelligence. For an hour, through the suggestion of your sentences, which like the other sort of suggestion redoubles the power of the patient's senses, nature and life appeared to me as rich and varied and alive as to you. I take the liberty of thanking you with this brief note. I am not surprised that a sentence of yours should have such power, for it is not just a beautiful creation, it is a unique, living, agile creature; or rather, a spirit of life, which penetrates all creatures by turns, takes on their form and brings them to us chained but still alive, almost free, like the animals in the zoological gardens, of which you speak so well. The old conventional architecture of the sentence is at every moment dissolved by this spirit of life, and it (the sentence) recomposes itself spontaneously on the basis of a new and living structure. It is a capricious sort of charm, continually jolting one's sensibility, which skips and jumps with you, twists and turns, like a scholar's afterthought or a painter's retouchings. And something else that I relish infinitely is your consummate conciseness, as in 'the big birds have *room to fly in* [la place de leur vol]'; 'rocks receiving and *retaining the sun* [gardant le soleil]'; 'SURVIVAL IN A CAPTIVATED HEART [LA SURVIE DANS UN CŒUR TOUCHÉ]'.[3]

It is thanks to this classical perfection that so much life is beautifully summed up. Each word becomes an image, each object a poem, and to speak of your article as you speak of those butterfly cages, which contain no more flitting, whirling grace perpetually escaping from matter, from the cocoon of facts in which we remain imprisoned, than it does, I shall say of your language that all your necromantic characters are illuminated with magic eyes, which at every moment look at us, arrest us, and charm us.

Accept, Madame, the offering of my charmed respects.

Marcel Proust

Would you be kind enough, Madame, while tendering my respects to M. Daudet and giving my regards to M. Léon Daudet, who has been so kind to me, to press the hand of Lucien, my liking for whom is growing little by little into a feeling of very real friendship.

1. Mme Daudet, née Julia-Rosalie-Céleste Allard (1844–1940), the wife of the writer. She was herself the author of poems and essays.

2. Mme Daudet's 'Notes on London (May 1895)' was first published in *La Revue de Paris* (1 Jan. 1896) and later appeared in book form (1897).

3. The last phrase was inspired by homage paid to the effigies of Chaucer, Dickens, Thackeray, Sir Walter Scott, Shakespeare, and others in Westminster Abbey.

88

TO REYNALDO HAHN

Twenty minutes to midnight
[March 1896]

My dear little Reynaldo,

Seeing that Delafosse had played, Mlle Suzette had sung and I had forgotten my notebook at Mme Lemaire's, which obliged me to go back because of *'Méchant'*,[1] I didn't get to your place until eleven o'clock. I knocked and even–just once–rang. I heard no sound, saw no light, no one opened, and I've come home feeling very sad. Don't you do anything but sleep?

They will bring you this note tomorrow morning and will not give me your answer until ten o'clock (that way I shall be at M. Neveu's at eleven) unless you write *on the envelope* that it should be given to me before ten o'clock, but don't unless there is some point

why I have so long delayed writing to tell you how amazed, how moved and overwhelmed I was at your so touching, so beautiful, so 'chic' thought of the other day. When the cyclist with your wreath caught up with the flowerless burial procession (such was my uncle's wish), when I found out that it was from you, I burst into tears, less out of grief than admiration. I was so hoping you would be at the cemetery so I could take you in my arms. Of course they couldn't put your wreath on the hearse. But when we got to the cemetery and Mama was told about it, she wanted my uncle to be buried with that one wreath, since you were the only one who didn't know, and that's what was done. One could say of you, as of that woman of the seventeenth century, that 'kindness and generosity were not the least of her *élégances*'. All that seems worth talking about at length. Shall we do so one of these days?

With my respectful admiration.

Yours,
Marcel Proust

92

TO ROBERT DE MONTESQUIOU

This Tuesday morning [19 May 1896?][1]

Dear Sir,

Yesterday I did not answer the question you put to me about the Jews. For this very simple reason: though I am a Catholic like my father and brother, my mother is Jewish. I am sure you understand that this is reason enough for me to refrain from such discussions. I thought it more respectful to write this to you than to answer you in the presence of a third person. But I very much welcome this occasion to say something to you that I might never have thought of saying. For since our ideas differ, or rather, since I am not free to have the ideas I might otherwise have on the subject, you might, without meaning to, have wounded me in a discussion. I am not, it goes without saying, referring to any discussion that might take place between the two of us, for then I shall always take an interest in any ideas on social policy which you may choose to expound, even if I have a most fitting reason for not sharing them.

Yours,
Marcel Proust

1. It seems possible that this letter followed a discussion of Émile Zola's article 'Pour les juifs' (On the Jews), in *Le Figaro*, 16 May 1896.

93
TO ROBERT DE FLERS[1]

TELEGRAM

M. Robert de Flers
8, rue Lincoln

[Tuesday evening 26 May 1896]

My dear Robert,

I hear you've been crowned by the Academy.[2] What a joy, what good news! I am *delighted*, and Mama, whom I have just told, is radiant. It's an advance for the Academy – indeed, very much in advance – anyway, my boy, it's a step.

Mme Lemaire had told me if I saw you to tell you to be sure to go and applaud Reynaldo this evening,[3] but I have been too ill to go. I hope your grandfather well.[4]

Till this evening perhaps

Marcel

1. Robert Pellevé de la Motte-Ango, Comte, later Marquis, de Flers (1872–1927), a long-standing friend of Proust. He became a successful author and playwright, collaborating with Gaston de Caillavet (see letter 152) and Francis de Croisset, and was on the staff of *Le Figaro*. He may have been one of Proust's models for Saint-Loup.

2. The news – now more than ten days old – that Flers had won the Prix Montyon, awarded by the Académie Française, for his book *Vers l'Orient*, had been published in *Le Temps* and *Le Gaulois* for 14 May 1896.

3. Reynaldo Hahn's Breton choral work *Là-bas* was performed at a soirée at Mme Lemaire's on 26 May 1896; according to *Le Gaulois* (27 May 1896), Proust was among the guests.

4. This sentence is Proust's only concession to telegraphese. Flers's maternal grandfather, Eugène de Rozière (1820–96), senator from the Lozère, palaeographer and member of the Academy, had only a few weeks to live. His correspondence with Proust has not been preserved.

94
TO PIERRE LAVALLÉE[1]

[About 12 ? June 1896]

My dear Pierre,

Like someone whose name figures by itself on a deed of gift to which several of his friends have contributed, I feel somewhat ashamed to hear people speak of my book and to inscribe to you a book which might just as well be yours, if you, having like me, better than me, dreamt of it all your life had, instead of me, troubled to write it. Though I have managed to put into it even the things to which I attach the greatest importance – such as a certain feeling about transmigration, which I have no need to define more closely when speaking to you – what is there to love in it which might not be found, and with greater distinction and purity, in you, and which is not the common heritage of our souls, the native soil in which our sympathies are joined, the very foundation of our friendship, older and more durable than ourselves and than that friendship itself.

But in any case, this particular copy deserved a special inscription. A book read by you, especially if it is a copy of my book, cannot resemble any other. How many meanings hidden from others, what – relative – depths known to you alone, will come to light, if you are the reader.

I say my book as though I were never to write another. You know well enough that that is not true. If I can finish the one I have undertaken[2] and begin others, I beg you not to begrudge me the inspiration of your tenderness, the reward of your understanding. Fecundate and love my faults, which to you are the best part of me. Our good qualities are not so much ours, and to relish them there is no need of so warm a tenderness, so close a resemblance.

Your grateful friend
Marcel Proust

1. The letter was written on the flyleaf of copy no. 29 of the special rice-paper edition (thirty copies printed) of *Les Plaisirs et les jours,* published on 12 June 1896.

2. I.e. *Jean Santeuil.*

95
TO ÉDOUARD ROD[1]

[28 June 1896]

Dear Sir,

I can't tell you how proud I am, how overwhelmed, grateful and delighted at the graceful and gracious words you have been kind enough to devote to me in yesterday's *Gaulois* and which I have just this minute read.[2] I would have gone at once to thank you, if I were not detained at the bedside of my grandfather, whose strength is failing from hour to hour and whom we have lost hope of keeping with us much longer.[3] Still, I believe Mama is not quite so sad when I am here, so I should not like to go as far as Auteuil. I showed her *Le Gaulois,* and she was very proud and as happy as it is possible for her to be at the moment.

Your grateful admirer
Marcel Proust

If ever you have a moment's time, I should very much like you to read the first story in my book ('La Mort de Baldassare Silvande') which you may not find too displeasing.

1. Édouard Rod (1857–1910), novelist and critic of Swiss origin, long resident in Paris. He wrote more than forty novels, some of them widely read at the turn of the century.

2. In *Le Gaulois* for 27 June 1896, Rod wrote at length of Anatole France's 'marvellous preface' to *Les Plaisirs et les jours,* adding: 'And this singular mixture of freshness and maturity has produced a book highly characteristic of our time. How can there be such qualities of observation in so youthful a mind?' That Proust sensed the reservations behind this complacent mention of his book is indicated by his postscript.

3. Nathé Weil died two days later, at the age of eighty-two.

96
TO HENRY CAZALIS[1]

[Late June 1896]

Mon cher maître,

Many thanks for the precious elixir of wisdom and beauty, which I am proud to receive from your noble, adroit and beneficent hands.[2] It is contained in little phials which one opens one by one, like that anaesthetic, amyl, I believe, which is employed in your art and which spreads a magic calm over our ills. But this calm is short-lived. The virtue of your wisdom is not thus limited in time. And the mind that has once reflected them will continue to turn over your magnificent calm images, scarcely broken by vague movements of agitation. For each of these quatrains is like an inland sea and renders the sound, brief but indefinitely prolonged, of the rising or rather falling tide. Falling towards suffering, towards death. At the risk of outdoing Al-Ghazali, Cazalis would add: Towards Life.

I know you are indulgent to the young. When my book comes out at 3 francs 50 (the present edition is a de luxe one and they don't give me any copies) I shall permit myself an unequal exchange.[3]

Your respectful friend
Marcel Proust

While sorting some two-months-old papers, I find this note.[4] Will you forgive me? I know that in the meantime Mme Lemaire has sent you our book.

1. Dr Henry Cazalis (1840 – 1909), physician and poet (as 'Jean Lahor'), one of the founders of the Parnassian school, and the friend of Maupassant and Mallarmé; he was also the author of several books on hygiene.

2. Cazalis had sent Proust a copy of his *Quatrains d'Al Ghazali*, published in June 1896.

3. More than a year later, on 20 September 1897, Robert de Flers reported to Proust that Calmann-Lévy refused to consider publishing an edition at 3 francs 50 until the 15-franc de luxe edition was completely sold out. They had printed 1,500 copies of the latter, and in 1918 1,171 copies remained unsold.

4. Unposted, presumably, until the end of August 1896.

97
TO LUCIEN DAUDET[1]

[Late June – early July 1896]

[Beginning of letter missing]

. . . of *L'Enterrement d'une étoile*. I have so much to say about it that I'd have liked to write to your father.[2] But I don't dare, it's too absurd. To your mother or your brother I can just manage to write. It's not that they have less talent. But, well, your father . . . You understand. And besides, I'm always afraid he might say

'Surely it is too late to be speaking of it now.'[3]

But these things of your father's affect me so that I would never want to stop talking of them entirely, because they continue to live in me, or to die (in the case of *L'Enterrement d'une étoile*). I am still caught up in the excitement of that stormy day, just as I still hear the sound of the engrossing pen, and still see, in the *Lettres de mon moulin*, the flock of pigeons we were talking about the other day.[4] This survival in the imagination is the hallmark of immortal works, and your father's are just that. My dear friend, it will be so much nicer if you embrace him and say: Marcel Proust admires you very much. I entrust all this, as I do many other things, to your heart and mind, which are two very amiable little intendants.

À bientôt,

Your friend
Marcel Proust

Do you know who M. Perret is? He has done a long long article about me in *La Liberté*,[5] too flattering, but it struck me as very well done. Naturally!

1. Lucien Daudet (1878 – 1946), younger son of Alphonse Daudet. At this time he was studying painting, though he later became a writer.

2. In exchange for a copy of *Les Plaisirs et les jours,* Alphonse Daudet had sent Proust his *L'Enterrement d'une étoile* (The Funeral of a Star), published about the same time; 'a doleful little book,' said its author, 'which will break your heart if you read it.'

3. A paraphrase of Musset's line, 'Sans doute il est trop tard pour parler encore d'elle', from 'À la Malibran' (*Poésies*, II).

4. Cf. Daudet's story 'Les Vieux' (The Old People), in *Lettres de mon moulin* (Letters from My Mill; 1868).

5. Paul Perret (1830 – 1904), novelist and critic, had just reviewed *Les Plaisirs et les jours* in *La Liberté*, 26 June 1896.

98
TO REYNALDO HAHN

[Friday 3 ? July 1896]
My good little Reynaldo,

I've wired you my answer. I would be glad if rather than incur the fatigue of another trip, you would benefit for a while from your 'good Germany', as the Queen says in *Ruy Blas*. I am not, like the Lemaires, hostile to all places where we cannot be together.[1] I am delighted to know you are in peaceful surroundings and want you to stay as long as possible. I assure you that if the rare moments when I am tempted to jump on the train so as to see you straight away became intolerably frequent, I would ask you to let me join you, or beg you to come back. But this is quite unlikely. Stay as long as you enjoy it. Just tell me from time to time in your letters no mosch,[2] have seen no mosch, because, even though you imply as much, I'd be happier if you'd say it now and then. And I am happy – *without self-abnegation* – that you're staying on. But I shall also be very happy, ah, my dear little Reynaldo, very very happy when I'm able to embrace you, you whom along with Mama I love best in all the world. To finish up about plans and as quickly as possible (for I am determined not to write you anything that will irritate or annoy you, since at this distance I can't soothe you with the thousand little pony endearments that I reserve for your return), if you come back, I shall probably be in Paris or rather Versailles with Mama, in other words not at all far from your beloved Saint-Cloud. Then at the end of August I'd go to the seashore with Mama for a month or a little more, near your Villers, to Cabourg for instance. If you prefer Bex, I'll go to Bex with Mama or possibly without her, but then I think I shall have to take her to the seashore, which will be good for her, I think. But plenty of mountain air might do as well. Actually, she only wants to spend a month with me, she wants me to 'have a good time' for the rest of the season. But do you prefer Bex to some other place in Switzerland? If so, that settles it, unless I hear that it's too hot, too scorching. And anyway, if we can't see each other at all, we'll think of each other. As for the Lemaires, I believe they will soon be going to Dieppe. Then Mme Lemaire is expecting to rent something near Versailles (but all this is terribly vague, and 'if you want my honest opinion', I think she'll be going to Réveillon) (where Mlle Suzette, who can't leave her 'poor old aunt'[3] alone, is determined to go in any case) (here bear in mind that Mme Lemaire, who doesn't feel well at Réveillon and can't work there, keeps hesitating for fear of upsetting her daughter, whereas her daughter hasn't for one minute thought of giving up Réveillon. This is only a statement of fact, you mustn't conclude that I think the mother better than the daughter, for they are both good and the daughter in spite of everything is more affectionate). But they are quite resigned to not seeing us this summer. Still, I think it would give them pleasure if in October we went either to Réveillon or to Mme Lemaire's country place, and I must admit, my dear little Reynaldo, that I think it would be rather lovey (here Reynaldo: 'What's that you said? Rather lovey? Do my ears deceive me?'). You'd have died laughing if you had been here yesterday for the return of Clairin[4] (very much changed, poor man) (like a miserable liar I told him you had asked for news of him in your last letter). After our Édouard [Risler] had made fun of Clairin to Mme Lemaire, she took pity on him and the poor man had the disappointment of seeing all his blazing memories of Egypt extinguished one by one on the shore of a Mme Lemaire as impassive as a treacherously smiling lake. After a while, though, she began listening to his talk about art with that air of profound earnestness which comes of a profoundly absent mind. Or rather I think she did listen, and the upshot was something like this:

> CLAIRIN: Because, you know, the Greeks took everything from them; the Ionian Greeks, I mean.
>
> MME LEMAIRE: Oh yes.
>
> CLAIRIN: And then they brought out heads, every one of them resembling those excessively thin heads of the Fourth Dynasty in the Siena museum.
>
> MME LEMAIRE: Oh yes, indeed. How very strange!
>
> CLAIRIN: And their Sphinx whom they call the Father of Terror.
>
> MME LEMAIRE: Oh yes.
>
> CLAIRIN: He's well named. They are so keenly aware of the feeling that comes over us under the Egyptian sky.
>
> MME LEMAIRE, *hearing the word 'Egyptian', interrupts:* Oh yes.
>
> CLAIRIN, *continuing:* Under the Egyptian sky, in the Egyptian night, when it looks [so much] as if the stars were about to fall that in their paintings they represent the stars hanging on strings.
>
> MME LEMAIRE: Oh yes, how curious that must be; it must indeed be (*emphatically*) very curious . . . (*Silence, smiling . . .*) Our Jotte[5] . . . (*Laughing*), etc. . . .

Mme Lemaire was delighted with the Castellanes' fête.[6] I can't quite make out what it was like.

Mme Lemaire said to me: 'It was just like the *grand siècle,* pure Louis XIV, you know.'

Mme de Framboisie said to me: 'You'd have thought you were in Athens.' And our Tur[7] said in *Le Gaulois:* 'One felt one was living in the days of Lohengrin.' You see that I can't tell you anything very precise about the period the 'young Comte' reconstituted. *Le Gaulois* was full of pearls on the subject. For instance, you know that to say that the army must bow to civil law, the Romans used the phrase *'cedant arma togae'*, the toga being the garment worn by men performing legislative functions. Meyer writes that in the ballet they put on at the Castellane fête, terrifying warriors appear, but they are soon joined by beautiful young women, who disarm them, and at this point our Tur cries out: *'cedant arma togae!'* I haven't space to tell you everything, I only add this: You know, there were 3,000 people at that fête. *Le Figaro* adds solemnly: 'All of Parisian society was there. We shall give no names. For though the whole of society was there, it was there incognito, because of the death of Monseigneur the Duc de Nemours.'[8] Seeing that no masks were worn, I can't help wondering what their incognito consisted of. It's a good dodge for going out when in mourning. I'd have a lot more to tell you, but it's getting late and I embrace you with all my heart. Embrace your sister Maria for me.

Marcel

Mama isn't doing too badly. She seems to be bearing up better under her great grief[9] than I expected.

---

1. This was the attitude attributed to the Verdurins in *Swann's Way* (I. 205 – 8). Hahn was in Hamburg visiting one of his sisters.

2. Apparently a word, meaning homosexual, in the private language used by Proust and Reynaldo Hahn.

3. Mme Herbelin.

4. Georges-Jules-Victor Clairin (1843 – 1919), a painter, who did portraits of Sarah Bernhardt and other celebrities. He completed the decoration, begun by Pils, of the staircase at the Paris Opéra.

5. Jotte, or Jojotte, was the Lemaires' nickname for Clairin; it no doubt inspired the name Chochotte for a member of Mme Verdurin's 'little band'.

6. A sumptuous fête given by Comte Boni de Castellane and his wife, née Anna Gould, in the Bois de Boulogne on 2 July 1896. Cf. *Le Gaulois* for 3 July 1896.

7. I.e. Arthur Meyer, of *Le Gaulois*.

8. Louis-Charles-Philippe-Raphaël, Duc de Nemours, born in 1814, died 26 June 1896.

9. At the death of her father, on 30 June 1896.

99
TO HIS MOTHER

[Monday evening 6 July 1896]

My dear little Mama,

Here are *Blondel's cards*.[1] I'm *heartbroken* about not going to Passy, but it was half-past seven when I finished with the Montesquiou gang (he didn't ask anything disagreeable of me, it was to make arrangements for France's Mme Desbordes journey Monday). If by any chance (I'm sure you won't, but one must think of everything) you meet Yturri or Montesquiou tomorrow (they were determined to go and see you, I had to beg them not to), if I am not going to Douai on Monday with France for Mme Desbordes,[2] it's because you absolutely don't want me to attend these festivities at such a time. – I'm very sad at not seeing you: Very sad for too many reasons. And yet, to what purpose? When one sees, as we saw the other day, how everything ends, why grieve over sorrows or dedicate oneself to causes of which nothing will remain. Only the fatalism of the Moslems seems to make sense. My hay fever has been acting up in the last two days, I don't know why. I had to smoke before dinner.[3] Don't come in to say good-bye tomorrow if I'm not awake, because I'm not on very good form, and the time I spend sleeping, provided I don't dream, will at least be that much spared from my black gloom.

Curious to hear about your conjugal country dinner, I kiss you tenderly.

Your little
Marcel

Must we write to Blondel? These came in an envelope addressed to me without a letter. I think it would be better if you did it. But give me exact instructions. Let me kiss you again. If I knew where to find you – ?

Think of Jean[4] for *La Revue. Panem et circenses.*

1. Blondel, a stationer, was at 2, place de Rennes.

2. On Monday, 13 July 1896, a monument commemorating the poet Marceline Desbordes-Valmore was to be unveiled at Douai, her native city. Robert de Montesquiou had arranged the ceremony, at which Anatole France was to speak.

3. Proust smoked medicated cigarettes and burned powders to relieve his asthma.

4. Presumably their manservant, Jean Blanc.

100
TO LUCIEN DAUDET

[16 or 17 July 1896]

My dear boy,

It is a very great misfortune and I sympathize with you most especially because you are so kindhearted and M. de Goncourt was very fond of you. He owed your parents the only comforts of his old age and perhaps of his life. And for all the grief it must have given you, I find it beautiful that he should have died in your home, surrounded by all of you.[1] And so gently! For when it comes to death, sudden is gentle.

I, on the other hand, want to know it when I die, if I am not too ill. But in his case, I think it was even finer as it was. My dear boy, you were always so good to him. I remember your worry over *Manette*, your joy at the little present he gave you, your unhappiness when you were afraid of his falling out with your parents,[2] your determination to remain friends with him yourself. My dear boy, it's not unusual to admire the people one loves. But it is unusual to love the people one admires. In any case I feel for you and hope above all that your father is not too shaken by his grief.

Yours,
Marcel Proust

131

1. Edmond de Goncourt died of pneumonia on 16 July 1896, at 1.30 A.M., in the Daudets' house at Champrosay.

2. Goncourt's play *Manette Salomon* opened on 29 February 1896. Later that spring the Daudets objected bitterly when Goncourt published portions of his journal in *L'Écho de Paris*, which on 31 March 1896 had printed a drawing by Steinlen showing Léon Daudet licking the boots of the Duc d'Orléans. But in April Léon Daudet was stricken with typhoid fever, and the family forgot about everything else.

101

TO REYNALDO HAHN

[Between mid-July and 8 August 1896]

Reynaldo, I had a spell of bad humour this evening, you mustn't be surprised or take it amiss. You said, I'll never tell you anything again. If that were true, it would be a breach of your oath; even untrue, it's still the cruellest of blows. That you should tell me everything has been my hope, my consolation, my mainstay, my life since the 20th of June.[1] For fear of making you unhappy, I hardly ever speak of it, yet I think of it almost all the time. Besides, you said the one thing that to me is really 'cutting'. I would prefer a thousand insults. I often deserve them, more often than you think. If ever I don't deserve them, it's at moments of painful effort when, glimpsing a face, finding resemblances between names, or reconstructing a scene, I try to fill in the gaps in a life which is dearer to me than anything else, but which will be a source of sorrow and torment to me as long as it remains unknown to me even in its most innocent aspects. Alas, it's an impossible task, and when in your kindness you try to satisfy my curiosity with a little of your past, you are undertaking a labour of the Danaïds. But if my fantasies are absurd, they are the fantasies of a sick man, and for that reason should not be crossed. Threatening to finish off a sick man because his mania is exasperating is the height of cruelty.[2] You will forgive these reproaches because I don't often make any and always deserve some myself, which will appease your pride. Be indulgent to a pony. Would you find many masters with the qualities you demand of a pony, etc.[3]

M.P.

1. The date, it seems, on which Hahn had promised to tell Proust 'everything'.

2. Proust was to transform this diagnosis of his own jealous mania into art, in Swann's jealousy of Odette in 'Swann in Love' and in the Narrator's jealousy of Albertine in *The Prisoner*.

3. A paraphrase of Beaumarchais, *Le Barbier de Séville*, II. ii.

102
TO REYNALDO HAHN

Établissement Thermal & Casino
Mont-Dore (Puy-de-Dôme)[1]
[18 or 20? August 1896]

My dear little Reynaldo,

If I don't wire, it's because in case you've left I wouldn't want them to open my telegram. And yet I'd terribly like you to know straight away. Forgive me if you're angry with me, but I'm not angry with you. Forgive me if I've hurt you, and in future don't tell me anything since it upsets you. You will never find a more affectionate, more understanding (alas!) and less humiliating confessor, since, if you had asked silence of him as he has asked a confession of you, your heart would have been the confessional and he the sinner, for that is how weak he is, weaker than you. Never mind, and forgive me for having added, out of egoism as you say, to the sorrows of your life. But how could it have been otherwise? It might be great, but it would not be natural, to live in our time as Tolstoy asks us to do. But of the substitution it would be necessary to make, the little detour, if one is at last to get back into life, I cannot speak to you, for I know you don't like it and that my words would be taken amiss. Don't worry about having grieved me. For one thing it would be only too natural. At every moment of our life we are the descendants of ourselves, and the atavism which weighs on us is our past, preserved by habit. And if bad seed has been mixed with the good, the harvest will not be entirely a happy one. 'The fathers have eaten sour grapes,' says the Bible, 'and the children's teeth are set on edge.'[2] Actually, I'm not at all upset. No, that's wrong. I am rather upset over what's happening to Chicot; if he must die, I'd at least like the king to know all he has done for him. If I had sorrows, they would be relieved by the pleasure that Bussy is having at the moment. And my own joys or sorrows would not seem much more real to me than those of the book,[3] to which I resign myself. So you see, I have no sorrows, only an enormous tenderness for my boy, whom I think of, as I said of my nurse when I was little, not only with all my heart, but with all me. The other day I had a letter from our dear Mlle Suzette, it was charming and of the utmost interest, as they say. But how she loves to be pitied. She told you that she hadn't let me notice her grief, but she writes to me that she conceals her distress from you. There's too much artifice in all that. One would like her to reread Vigny's 'Mort du loup'.

To pray, to scream, to sigh, one's as cowardly as the other
. . . Suffer and die in silence

(That's not quoted very accurately.)[4] I realize that smacks of a Stoic wisdom which doesn't do anybody much good and certainly can't be expected of a young girl except in Corneille. But frankly, what do you think of this business of telling you how she hides her sorrow from me and vice versa. She strikes me as the kind of person who would turn her back to prevent you from seeing her tears but only after making sure that you'd seen them in the mirror. An artful way of arranging to be pitied for her sorrow and admired for her heroism. Her soul isn't as base as all that, there's no great calculation in it, and I hope it's natural. But you have to admit that it comes naturally to her to be very affected. It's all so theatrical. 'Why, Mother, what's wrong?' 'Oh, nothing. A moment's weakness . . . the heat . . . these roses . . . oh, my dear boy, you can see that I've never been so well in all my life, that there's nothing nothing nothing wrong. . . .' Whereupon she falls down dead, or if you prefer, 'that I've never been so happy, so gay' and she bursts out sobbing. Let us take care, my dearest, not to sympathize with grief only when it takes the forms that are congenial to us and disturb us the least, but let us never imitate theatrical display and the artificial demonstration of often imaginary sorrows. I didn't wire you that I was coming home tomorrow for fear of preventing you from going to Villers. Just as well, for I may stick it out in spite of Mama's discouragement and determination to take me home. We were wrong in condemning this treatment. The trouble is that they are haymaking all round here. You know Mme de Sévigné too well not to know all about haying.[5] It's lovely but bad for me. Mme Conneau was here, we were both invited to dinner by a Dr Schlemmer, to whom Hillemacher dedicated a melody and who has studied harmony. I have no great faith in him but he's very intelligent.[6] He is not my doctor here. I'm in the middle of the second volume of *La Dame de*

Monsoreau and I'm also getting on, but more slowly, with Rousseau's *Confessions.* Today I'm all music, I'd like to hear you sing

The invisible hand of the saints

and many other things.

You must have received three copies of *Les Plaisirs et les jours,* one for you (which is not a present, I told Calmann to send it to you at his expense), one for your sister Elisa, and one for your cousin. I have been working a little[7] in the last two days. I haven't come to any decision about my 28 days.[8] Tell me in your next letter if, after what I've said, you consent to be released from your little oaths, and if in September you would like to go to Switzerland or somewhere else. Otherwise, even apart from the 28 days, I may spend September in Versailles, but not because of you, bad boy, it won't bind you in any way. What a lot of pages! and I haven't said anything yet about the little Baudelaire book. That will have to wait till next time. And have you received the appendix to Mme de Sévigné with the facsimiles?[9]

I embrace you tenderly, your sisters too, except the one with the jealous husband. I, who am no longer jealous but have been, respect jealous people and have no wish to cause them the slightest unhappiness or to lead them to suspect any secret.

Marcel

1. A spa in the mountains of central France where Proust and his mother were spending the last three weeks of August.

2. Ezekiel 18:2.

3. Dumas *père's La Dame de Monsoreau* (1846), in which Chicot the jester and Bussy d'Amboise figure.

4. 'Gémir, pleurer, prier, est également lâche, / . . . Puis, après, comme moi, souffre et meurs sans parler', from Alfred de Vigny's poem 'La Mort du loup', in *Les Destinées.*

5. Cf. *Lettres de Madame de Sévigné,* letter of 22 July 1671 to Coulanges.

6. Dr Georges Schlemmer had a villa at Mont-Dore; Mme Conneau, née Pasqualini, was a singer. The Hillemacher brothers, Paul (1852 – 1933) and Lucien (1860 – 1909), were both composers.

7. I.e. on *Jean Santeuil.*

8. See letter 40, n. 4.

9. A fine album published by Hachette in 1868 and presented as a supplement to the 1862 Monmerqué edition of the *Lettres de Madame de Sévigné*. Suzette Lemaire had given a copy to Reynaldo Hahn.

103

TO CHARLES MAURRAS[1]

[28 August 1896]

Sir,

Obliged by illness to interrupt a cure at Mont-Dore, I am back in Paris for the moment. And I have just read *La Revue encyclopédique*. You find the books you touch precious, without stopping to think that it is you who have turned them into gold by touching them. Quite amazed at the metamorphosis, I thank the amiable magician you are with all my heart; sudden as your enchantments are, they endure in the memories they have embellished. And some day the spellbound reader who reads you will believe it was because of some injustice that my book failed to endure and that perhaps I had some talent. In the meantime I am very grateful and very proud that you should have said such charming things about me.[2] Beautiful things as well, but that is no more than I expected of so great a friend of the Muses!

'For you beautify the praise, O goddesses'

of the blessed Comatas himself, who in his prison as a man and as a critic is fed with divine honeycomb.[3] And what delightful words you have written about the man of genius who is our master, M. France.[4]

Your devoted
Marcel Proust

It would give me great pleasure if *La Revue encyclopédique* could return my photographs.

1. Charles Maurras (1868–1952), poet, critic, and essayist, later active as a right-wing political journalist and co-editor with Léon Daudet of the monarchist paper *L'Action française*.

2. In his essay 'Un Poète, deux Pamphlétaires, un Sociologue et un Moraliste', in *La Revue encyclopédique*, 22 Aug. 1896, Maurras classified Proust as a moralist, but observed that *Les Plaisirs et les jours* 'shows such a wide variety of talents that one is bewildered at having to register them all in so young a writer'.

·3. In the ancient fable the goatherd Comatas is shut up in a cedar chest because he has sacrificed too many of his goats to the Muses. But the Muses send him bees to feed him with their honey, and when the chest is opened three months later he is quite alive. (Cf. Theocritus VII. 78 f.)

4. Maurras had also praised Anatole France's preface to Proust's book.

104
TO REYNALDO HAHN

[Paris, 28 or 29 August 1896]

My dear boy,

I've come home because I was ill, but I didn't write to tell you for fear of upsetting you. I just had a bad cold with fever, etc., and yesterday too I stayed in bed until four o'clock. Today I'm fine and I want to thank you straight away for your letter. I don't know why you say it's not good. I took pleasure in reading it. You misunderstood mine. I don't know what could have made you think I doubted the sincerity of your 'tone'. Oh, my dear boy, I shudder to think that you could ever have believed that. I assure you that as I see it, this sadness of yours is not just the sombre beauty of your character, not only your moral but also your intellectual depth, the genius (which I take in the ancient sense, so that for once your modesty need not show itself, for it would show itself to be ill-informed) of your music, the ballast of pleasure one must jettison in order to rise to a great height. It is the height to which you have risen and from which you will fall without fail if you abjure it, like those men who might have been great if . . . (*Tu Marcellus eris*) but whom you will on the contrary surpass if < from the noble repentance of imperfect life you rise to a life of serenity >[1] no, it's not for me to say such things. I have no right to as yet. – As for the 'little detour',[2] it doesn't mean a thing. It made you angry, but really, my dear silly, there's no harm in it.

· ·

You say, with the quick elegance which I admire in your letters, comparable to the most *telling darts* of the seventeenth century: 'Tell me what I think of it.' That is far superior to Mallarmé's lines[3] (and what I say isn't as stupid as it looks because it's of the same period). It would not be enough to tell you, like the Chevalier de Méré: 'From time to time you write letters one takes pleasure in reading, especially if one has good taste; but they always cost dearly and I do not believe one could write more than two of them in one day. [Jean-

Louis Guez de] Balzac once told me that before being satisfied with a certain note to the Mayor of Angoulême he had spent more than four mornings on it. And yet I find nothing either beautiful or unusual in that note, etc.'[4] As for Mallarmé, while it's always pedantic to *explicate* a literary and especially a poetic charm, any such efforts become ridiculous when applied to a purely occasional quatrain, one of those poems we term fugitive, meaning no doubt that they flee from a mind rash enough to attempt to pin them down and analyse them. And yet, since it amuses my little *Kunst*[5] to see me floundering, and since he takes an interest in everything to do with Mallarmé, I will say, speaking of this poet in general, that in all likelihood his *obscure* and *brilliant* images are still images of things, since we cannot conceive of anything else, but reflected as it were in a dark polished mirror of black marble. Thus at a great funeral on a bright day the flowers and the sun are upside down and black, as mirrored in blackness. And yet it is still the 'same' spring that 'is kindled', but it is a spring in a catafalque. –

As for the particular little piece which I am asking Jean to take from its hiding place and to put in this letter after having registered it,[6] its charm, like that of many of Mallarmé's poems, seems to me to consist in this: its way of passing, under a cloak of archaism (as though from Malherbe to Voiture, or rather backwards from Malherbe to Desportes), from an inflexible, pure, almost bare classical form to the wildest preciosity. The two first lines are magnificent in their simplicity. I would add that even if we value it for its own sake this unadorned simplicity admirably evokes a broad vision of summer. But the 'Méry', so sixteenth and seventeenth century in quality, the sixteenth and early seventeenth century colour of these lines

The year unchanged in its course,

etc. – thanks as much to the mythology of time, the pomp, etc. as to the language – are a charming artifice of taste, moving them as it were [the lines] in the direction of preciosity. Since this preciosity is in essence quite modern and typical of Mallarmé (true, we often find modernity if not Mallarmé in the sixteenth century), this artifice, while making the transition acceptable, does not prevent it from being exceedingly piquant. Add that with all this preciosity the images remain exquisitely sincere and natural (I mean borrowed from nature). This *thirsty* foot drinking like a plant gives us a marvellous idea of the parts of our body, those obscure beings which seem indeed to live an obscure life of their own (I'm so tired my words repeat themselves and I no longer know what I am saying), this foot drinks like a root and after that, true enough, it feels happy, as if it had slaked its thirst.[7] And the foot fêted by the water, that too is delicious, the water gives so much an impression of being *en fête*, with its thousands of stirred-up ripples, murmuring sparkling caresses at the 'feet' of the beauty which treads on them. Anyway it's a great joy to find so much archaism, grandeur, mythology, good taste, and nature in a few simple lines. That 'in the last analysis' is their charm. Mallarmé's charm is that he solemnizes life, and that is indeed the role of the poet. – Whew!

Dear boy, I never gave the impression of thinking we wouldn't triumph over our little difficulties. And it is not, as you say, the general, time-honoured opinion that it can't be done. For it is only too evident that superior persons, thinkers, saints, etc. believe that one can do what one wills, or rather that one is as good as what one wills, or rather, as what one is able to do. (In other words, that our will, our power over ourselves, is the measure of our worth.) That excludes the common herd. But precisely on this point he [the thinker] seems to believe in freedom. That would account for his extreme severity towards these failings, which he would doubtless treat more leniently if he thought them inevitable. Incidentally, I don't believe it's a special problem. The problem of freedom does not have to be taken up afresh with each new category of action. I embrace you and ask your forgiveness for this boring letter. I'm so far behind in my correspondence and I wanted to begin with you. I have some little things to tell you which would amuse you. But I'm too tired. They will keep till another time. For today you'll have to content yourself with the tedium. Stay at Villers a long time so as to build up your strength for Saint-Cloud. I strongly approve of the summer plan, even though you make fun of it. I don't think I shall emulate it, though Mama seems rather to favour it. (Not at Villers, at Saint-Cloud.) Very best regards, especially to Mlle Maria and to your sisters in general, since you have the good fortune to be in the midst of them, like Apollo among the Graces.

Marcel

I had a little trouble at Mont-Dore which almost developed into a duel but it's over now (so let's not say any more about it). In that connection M. Bérardi's behaviour to me (he was the only person I knew there) was beyond all praise, perfect. I mention the incident only in order to praise him.[8]

1. Passage deleted by Proust. The phrase 'Tu Marcellus eris' is from *Aeneid* VI. 883, implying a promise from heaven that will not be fulfilled.

2. See letter 102.

3. Hahn had enclosed with his letter Mallarmé's 'Quatrain pour Méry', written for the name day of his mistress Méry Laurent, née Marie Louviot, on 15 August 1896: 'Méry, l'an pareil en sa course / Allume ici le même été / Mais toi, tu rajeunis la source / Où va boire ton pied fêté.' (Méry, the year unchanged in its course / Kindles the same summer here, / But you rejuvenate the source / In which your fêted foot has stopped to drink.)

4. From *Les Oeuvres de Monsieur le Chevalier de Méré* (Amsterdam, 1692).

5. Proust perhaps confuses the German word *Kunst* (art) with *Künstler* (artist).

6. The MS of the quatrain, first published in 1948, was found among Hahn's papers after his death.

7. In *The Prisoner* Proust was to develop a similar idea in connection with Albertine, who, 'stretched out at full length on my bed, . . . reminded me of a long blossoming stem that had been laid there; . . . as though by falling asleep she had become a plant' (III. 63 – 64).

8. The incident in question perhaps inspired certain aspects of the episodes in *Jean Santeuil* (548 f., 558 ff.) when Jean fights a duel. Gaston Bérardi (1857 – 1925), writer and composer, was director of *L'Indépendance belge* and other publications.

105
TO REYNALDO HAHN

[3 or 4 September 1896]

My dear little Reynaldo,

Forgive me for not writing. But I have been reading a great deal and roaming about a good deal, and I'm so tired after that treatment and the cold I caught there,[1] that I don't feel very energetic about writing. Yesterday I numbered the first ninety pages of my novel. I had *La Belle Gabrielle* sent from a bookshop, but apart from the unpleasantness of exchanging Dumas for Maquet, I had the impression without cutting the pages that the characters left up in the air in *Les Quarante-cinq*, Ernanton de Carminger, Rémy le Hardouin, Diane de Meridor, and Henry III, aren't in it. If it's a sequel only in the sense that it follows 'in the order of time' I prefer to read *La Reine Margot* (are Bussy, St-Luc, Chicot, etc. in it?) or some Dumas of a different period (tell me again what you think about this) (I prefer the ones without love or dark passions, I particularly want sword fights, policemen à la Chicot, royalty, good humour and victorious Innocents). I've finished *La Cousine Bette*. There are really amazing things in it. But at the end of the first volume of Sainte-Beuve's *Port Royal* (appendix) there's an attack on Balzac (the one who wrote *Cousine Bette*) by Sainte-Beuve that's more amusing than Lemaître's article on Ohnet.[2] I went to the Louvre the day before yesterday (do you like Quentin Matsys's man with some gold-pieces, a little convex mirror showing what's going on in the street, some pearls, etc. in front of him and his wife beside him) and to the Jardin des Plantes with Mme Arman [de Caillavet]. But the menagerie was closed. Still, we saw the bears. Those wild animals, the lions, etc. are really *Les Rois en exil*.[3] And their jungles etc. etc. are really a *Paradise Lost*. That whole park, so exotic and so Parisian, breathes a sadness further increased by the ravages of the latest hurricane.[4] On the way back we saw M. France strolling on the embankment. We stopped the carriage and Mme Arman said in a tone of ironic congratulation: 'So there we are, going about our little affairs all alone. . . . A fine kettle of fish . . .' It seems they had quarrelled about a bookseller or something. And M. France said: 'Oh, Madame, you want everything, don't you, not to pay your debts, the pleasure of a clear conscience, and the esteem of your friends. Well' (laughing uproariously), 'Madame, you're asking too much, indeed you are, you'll manage not to pay, your conscience won't trouble you, because it's not very demanding, I should say not, but the esteem of your friends, no, that's asking too much, it can't be done.' And Mme Arman, somewhat aggrieved, said: 'Monsieur, you are too disagreeable, go away.' When she had driven off, M. France sang her praises and said to me: 'She really has a strange cast of mind for so good a woman, because, you know, Mme Arman is good.' It's true that she is charming. Dear boy, write to me at once whether, now that you like the sea again, you'd be willing to stay on with me, not at Villers, but near by, after the 15th, etc. Write in detail, love me (your 'on the sand recumbent' was a marvellous stylistic touch).

Affectionately,
Marcel

Something to make you laugh: this old telegram from Cazalis which we received at Mont-Dore and had to pay 3 francs for and which outraged Mama's instinct for concision and economy in equal degree. Did I write to you that I recently ran into Coco Madrazo at dinner time and he came up and dined with me?[5] I think so but I'm not sure.

1. I.e. at Mont-Dore.

2. Sainte-Beuve, in the article cited, accused Balzac of trying to write *Volupté* – Sainte-Beuve's own novel – all over again in *Le Lys dans la vallée*. Jules Lemaître had demolished the novels of Georges Ohnet in *La Revue politique et littéraire* (*Revue bleue*), 27 June 1885.

3. Proust is alluding to Alphonse Daudet's novel *Les Rois en exil* (Kings in Exile; 1879).

4. On 26 July 1896 a hurricane uprooted trees in the Jardin des Plantes and other Parisian parks.

5. Dr Cazalis's telegram was evidently to thank Proust for the copy of *Les Plaisirs et les jours* sent him by Mme Lemaire (see letter 96). Frédéric de Madrazo (1878? – 1938), called Coco, was the son of the painter Raymond de Madrazo (later the husband of Maria Hahn) by his first wife, née Ochoa.

106
FROM HIS MOTHER

Tuesday evening seven o'clock [20 October 1896]
My darling,

I have just received your letter – (which is charming).[1] The little card I sent you a while ago must have seemed rather dismal. I was standing up in the post office next to a gentleman who was watching me because he wanted my pen – I'll send the magazine to the rue Lincoln at once – your letter stopped me in time. I thought I was supposed to send it to you. In the meantime I've read the letters to Mme Hanska. Your father is putting off reading Pozzo di Borgo, so as not to delay the mailing and will content himself with Vandal's Russian Alliance.[2]

My darling, I think you must wait a few days to see if you acclimatize yourself and your oppression lets up before you come to any decision. I hope you will feel better – but if you are suffering, why not, rather than Paris, consider Illiers (where you were as wonderfully well in cold weather as unwell in warm weather) which would present a good many advantages. (Mme Brouardel says Fontainebleau is very damp.) You really need good air, my pet, to repair all the harm done by the summer and since there are good places for you, we shall just have to find them. I've taken my poor exile's books and begun *Wilhelm Meister*. Please tell me if Wilhelm Meister's ideas should be taken as those of Goethe. De Flers is as sweet as can be and speaks most affectionately of you. It seems he tried to persuade his grandmother to settle at Fontainebleau because of you! saying it would do her good.[3] A thousand thousand kisses, my dear boy, I am waiting impatiently to hear what sort of night you have had and whether you have managed to break all ties with that insidious Trional.

Sandford and Merton[4] had sent your overcoat yesterday afternoon. So Eugénie has mailed your hat all by itself. Where am I to look for your umbrella to send it to you? It is not here.

[No signature]

1. Proust was staying in Fontainebleau, at the Hôtel de France et Angleterre.

2. Robert de Flers lived at 8, rue Lincoln. The magazine on its way to him was the *Revue de Paris* for 1 Oct. 1896, containing Balzac's 'Lettres à l'Étrangère' and an article by Comte Pozzo di Borgo entitled 'France et Russie en 1817'. Fortunately for Dr Proust, Albert Vandal's article, 'L'Aurore d'une alliance', was in a different magazine, *La Revue hebdomadaire*, for October 1896.

3. Mme de Rozière's husband had died in June of 1896.

4. The tailoring establishment Sandt et Laborde was at 11, boulevard Malesherbes (next door to the Prousts); Mme Proust refers to it jokingly by the title of the English novel by Thomas Day (1748 – 89).

107
TO HIS MOTHER

[Fontainebleau]
Wednesday morning half-past nine
[21 October 1896]

My dear little Mama,

It's pouring. I had no asthma last night. And it's only just now, after a bad sneezing fit, that I had to smoke a little. I haven't been very easy since then, because I'm uncomfortable in bed. You see, my good side is next to the wall. In addition to which, all the canopies, curtains, etc. (impossible to take them down because they're fastened to the wall) make me very uncomfortable because I am forced always to be next to the wall.[1] All the things I need, my coffee, my tisane, my candle, my pen, my matches, etc. etc. are to the right of me, so that I keep having to lie on my bad side, etc. To which add a new bed etc. etc. My chest was very clear all day yesterday, morning and afternoon (except at bedtime as usual) and last night as well. (It's now that I'm most uncomfortable.) But I don't have wonderful nights like in Paris, or at least recently in Paris. And once I wake up, instead of feeling good in my bed, my only desire is to get out of it, which is not a good sign, whatever you may think. Yesterday the rain didn't start until four o'clock, so I was able to go for a walk. I didn't care for what I saw. The little fringe of forest that I saw is all green. The town has no character. I can't describe to you the terrible hours I spent yesterday between four and six (hours which I move back to before the telephone call in the little story I sent you, which I beg you to *keep* and remember where you are keeping it, because it will be in my novel.)[2] I don't believe any of my various states of distress ever rose to such a pitch. I can't even try to tell you about it. Needing someone to talk to, I went to the station at eleven o'clock to meet Léon Daudet, who was coming back from Paris. He absolutely wants to take his meals with me. Which will mean taking *pension* with Jean. The hotel is certainly remarkable. But no one speaks to me, probably because the servants have only worked for some sort of Doudeauville. 'I am well.' I can't say 'I am unwell' and tell them all about it, or have pleasant little chats with them as with Mme Renvoyzé or at the Fermont,[3] etc. etc. You've seen the price. I think it will be further swollen by the fires I'm obliged to keep up and the lamp because at this time of year there's no lighted parlour, one only has one's room. I have nothing to read and I wonder if Reynaldo has forgotten my books. If moving weren't such a business, I'd change rooms so as to have a bed turned the other way. I kiss you tenderly. I've received another letter from Reynaldo this morning, it will amuse you and I'm saving it for you.

Your little Marcel

P.S. I've just spoken to the chambermaid, she is going to put my bed a different way, head to the wall (because they can't take down the canopies), but the bed will be in the middle of the room. I think I'll be more comfortable that way. It's raining twice as hard. What weather!

I'm surprised that you don't mention the price of the hotel. If it's exorbitant, wouldn't I do better to come home? And from Paris I could go to Versailles every day and work.

2ND P.S. Léon Daudet wants us to go to Marlotte and stay at a cheaper hotel, he knows an asthmatic who is happy there. But I think it's a lot further from Paris, not as many trains, etc. What do you think? Then I wouldn't have Jean Lazard[4] any more, I think. . . . Do ask Papa for something to stop my nervous laugh. I'm afraid of irritating Léon Daudet.

3RD P.S.   No Trional.

4TH P.S.   Brissaud[5] who knows this part of the country so well could have told us the relative merits of Nemours, Marlotte, etc. etc.

1. Cf. *Jean Santeuil*, 367: '. . . his eyes fell on the bed which until then he had not noticed, an enormous bed suffocating under a tester with hanging draperies on every side (they could not be opened, being firmly fixed to the walls and ceiling) and a pink quilt which gave off a stuffy smell. He imagined himself lying there, unable to sleep, thinking of his mother. . . .'

2. The story became a part of *Jean Santeuil* as the chapter 'He Telephones to His Mother', in Part VI (368 – 70).

3. The Duc de Doudeauville was a society character, perhaps satirized in the play *L'Habit vert*, by Robert de Flers and Gaston de Caillavet, in which a character cuts short unwelcome interlocutors by saying in a loud voice, 'I am well.' At Orléans, during his military service, Proust had rented a room from a Mme Renvoyzé; in September and October 1895 he and Reynaldo Hahn had stopped at the Hôtel Fermont in Beg-Meil.

4. Jean Lazard, a friend of Proust's living at Fontainebleau; not to be confused with the Prousts' manservant Jean, mentioned above.

5. Édouard Brissaud (1852 – 1909), an eminent physician, had just published a treatise on *L'Hygiène des asthmatiques* with a preface by Dr Adrien Proust. Proust was to use certain of Brissaud's traits for Dr du Boulbon, who attends the Narrator's grandmother in *Remembrance of Things Past*.

108

FROM HIS MOTHER

Wednesday two o'clock [21 October 1896]

My darling,

This morning I received your note and then your manuscript. Since I wanted to speak with you on the telephone and was sure of reaching you only in the morning, I left the pages in the envelope and have read them only now. They are very sweet but so sad, my poor pet. They make me unhappy thinking of the sadness you felt. The story of a deported convict's arrival at the Île du Salut couldn't be more heartbreaking.[1]

I can't help wishing you were more unfeeling, though I don't like that kind of person, rather than see you invaded by an oversensitive melancholy.

'Monsieur, couldn't you reduce it to silence?' – not your melancholy, because it 'expresses itself very well' – but yourself, who ought to equip yourself with a heart 'less tender and less easily swayed'.[2]

You announced (over our dear little telephone) – an important letter, which I am to answer point for point – it hasn't come yet. Your father is still very eager to know how Versailles would agree with you. If it did, I would go and find a house there and set it up in advance.

I sent out calls for your umbrella – I can't resign myself to its not having lived for so much as one morning.[3] Dick has quite won his father's heart by the way he has settled down to work. But Dick has reserved half his own heart for Abel [Desjardins],[4] who is his main preoccupation at the moment and wishes your father would bestow his affection on him. Dick was here yesterday evening when your telegram came. He loves you dearly.

I would have been glad to write and ask Yeatman to go and see you, but I was afraid it wasn't the right thing to do. I prefer to let you draft your decrees from Fontainebleau.[5]

As for the telephone, it's better that I should call you, it's much quicker now but one can't set a definite time, there are often too many people.

How many apologies you owe it for your past blasphemies! What remorse for having despised, disdained, rebuffed such a benefactor! To hear my poor pet's voice – for my poor pet to hear mine! Just your hello! 'That hello is admirable, I would rather have uttered that hello than an epic poem.'[6] You see, my pet, that the classics have not been neglected in your absence.

A thousand kisses, my dear boy.

[*No signature*]

---

1. Cf. *Jean Santeuil*, 365: 'This was his room. Hearing the words, he gave a start, suddenly seized by a desire to recoil a step or two, like a condemned prisoner at the very moment that he is being pushed into his cell.'

2. 'Monsieur, je vous prie de la faire redevenir muette' (Molière, *Le Médecin malgré lui*, III. vi); 'Mais un cœur à leurs vœux moins facile et moins tendre' (idem, *Le Misanthrope*, II. i).

3. Cf. Malherbe, 'Stances à Monsieur Dupérier': 'Mais elle était du monde, où les plus belles choses / Ont le pire destin, / Et, rose, elle a vécu ce que vivent les roses, / L'espace d'un matin.'

4. Abel Desjardins (1870 – 1951), younger brother of Paul; it seems Robert Proust had persuaded him to take up medicine.

5. An allusion to the decrees sent from Fontainebleau by Napoleon when he retired there.

6. 'Cet hallo est admirable et j'aime mieux avoir fait cet hallo qu'un poème épique' (Molière, *Les Précieuses ridicules*, sc. ix).

109
TO HIS MOTHER

[Fontainebleau]
[Thursday morning 22 October 1896]
My dear little Mama,

My asthma is back down to the Paris level (I mean it's no worse than in Paris, at least I don't think it is). I sleep a good deal less (at least than in Paris lately). There's a little noise here after all, and that bothers me a good deal. I'm terribly sorry I can't comfort you with news of some sort of pleasure. But so far I haven't had one minute of gaiety or reverie, or even of well-being. But perhaps it's only that it always takes me so long to get started. Yesterday I walked in the forest for two hours, in the rain. But it didn't hurt me. When I got back, I was so sleepy I was unable to work, though I couldn't sleep. After dinner Léon Daudet took me out driving in the forest until a quarter past twelve, so I haven't been too sad (except from five to seven) but he insists on taking his meals with me. That makes for a lot of talk at the table, which I detest. I still haven't received the books Reynaldo was supposed to send, so I have nothing to read. I make do by picking up the Du Barry from time to time. But I had it with me (by mistake) on the train, and the smell of the railway carriage reminds me of the unhappiness of my departure. You weren't the same on the telephone yesterday. 'That's not your voice.' No, I won't settle at Versailles or anywhere else. If I don't stay at Fontainebleau, I'll come back to Paris and not stir out of it until I have to, when we all go away. But I shall take a room at the Réservoirs or in a less luxurious hotel in a less beautiful spot, and go there to work every day. But

I've lost my faith in country places; from here at least I can get home easily and I'd be taken care of if I fell ill. If I don't happen to telephone you today, here are the books you might send, but *immediately*. Balzac, *Le Curé de village, Le Ménage de garçon, La Vieille Fille, Les Chouans.* – Shakespeare, the volumes with *Julius Caesar* and *Antony and Cleopatra* in them. The first volume of *Wilhelm Meister* and *Middlemarch* by G. Eliot. I embrace you with all my heart. I have a little of what Papa calls intercostal pain in the chest (but no difficulty at all in breathing, it's not at all the same as at Mont-Dore or in Paris when I was in pain, and I breathe perfectly all day).

The weather is still the same, which didn't stop them from having a big hunt yesterday that one could hear in the distance. If Courteline[1] comes for dinner one evening with Léon Daudet, should I let Robert know? Léon Daudet thought Jean Lazard charming. As for me, I agree with Papa at least.

A thousand kisses,

Marcel

I haven't taken any more Trional, because with no consolation at hand I don't want to run the risk of being sad the following night, but I haven't been sleeping any better. I forgot to tell you that this hotel (formerly the mansion of the Duc d'Aiguillon, I believe) is very beautiful. – Maybe that is what drives pleasure out of it. – I have my fire kept up all day and I'm afraid of the bill. But I'm especially horrified at the thought of what may have slipped away through the hole in my trouser pocket yesterday.[2]

1. Georges Courteline, pseudonym of Georges Moineaux (1861 – 1929), satirist, author of often hilarious plays and short stories.

2. In a second letter to his mother of 22 October 1896, written at 11 P.M., Proust reported that the lost money – 'I suspect theft,' he said, 'because, come to think of it, the money was not in the pocket with the hole in it' – was 'taking on fantastic proportions. . . . More than 30 francs! . . . I have been ravaged by remorse, harried by guilt, crushed by melancholy.' Mme Proust, forbearing as always, replied the next day, 'Your letter makes me fear that what [money] I sent yesterday may not have been enough. Let me know at once if I should send more, so you won't get all edgy and upset with waiting. If you could flourish there the expense would be only too welcome.'

110
TO FERNAND GREGH

[Shortly after 4 November 1896]
Dear Fernand,

I've just received your book.[1] Thank you very much for sending it. Reading it I shall delight in looking, as I would for old friends, for your intelligence, your pride, your sensibility, your distrustfulness and your trustfulness, the childlike soul in which a mature mind is undoubtedly awakening, your mature mind which is still – parts of it – bathed in the soul of a child.

I also thank you very much for the inscription and for remembering that I was exceedingly fond of these poems. It's true that such things are easy to remember.

Your admirer and friend
Marcel Proust

I marvel, when I think how hard it is for me to write ten lines of verse, to see hundreds (perhaps thousands) which all seem beautiful. Regardless of whether you should continue to write poetry, you will never regret having written this. It will always be present in what you do, something akin to the excellence of your prose. And better.

1. Gregh's book of poems *La Maison de l'enfance* had just been published. For a sequel to this letter, which was not posted, see letter 112.

111
TO PIERRE LOTI[1]

[14 or 15 November 1896]
Sir,

I was on the point of writing to you to express my admiration and gratitude, when I learned of the misfortune that has struck you.[2] Though all those whom your genius has made acquainted with your heart have a right to grieve with you at this time, I am only too sensible of how far those, who like myself never met your mother and can call no memory of her to your mind, must be from you. I ask you only to accept my respectful sympathy.

Marcel Proust

1. Pseudonym of Julien Viaud (1850–1923), naval officer and novelist; his best-known books include *Pêcheur d'Islande* and *Madame Chrysanthème*.

2. Proust's gratitude was for a note Loti had written, thanking him for a copy of *Les Plaisirs et les jours*. *Le Figaro* for 14 Nov. 1896 announced the death of Mme Viaud, the novelist's mother, at the age of eighty-eight.

112

TO FERNAND GREGH

[24 November 1896]

My dear Fernand,

I am covered with shame for not having thanked you yet. A fortnight ago I had a letter ready for you, but there were two little things which, as you are inclined to be touchy, you might have taken amiss, and so for fear of wounding you I didn't send it.[1] I've been meaning to write to you every day since then. But then I waited for Reynaldo to return the book, so as to be better able to speak of it. At the moment he still has it, but I wouldn't like you to suppose that I'm not thinking about it. I'm sure you have run into some of the many people I've discussed it with, and no doubt they told you, if they have repeated even a small part of what I said, that my delay in giving you my opinion does not mean it was bad. What I have read struck me as really *beautiful*, and I am amazed to think that at your age and despite the various trains of thought which impel you in other directions (for you are not exclusively a poet) you have been able to produce a work at once so weighty, so consistent and so transparent. There is no point in my writing you my impression of what characterizes your poems and yourself. You know that I know; we can talk about it whenever you like and if an opportunity presents itself I shall be glad to *write* about it. I only wanted to tell you how very pleased I am at your success, which seems considerable, to judge by what I hear and read. And I am delighted because your book really represents many things. That is why I didn't want to send you a letter in which you might have found a barb, for it would not be very clever to respond with superficial bits and pieces to the piece of inner life which your book is. I don't know whether you will continue to write poetry, whether that is what you are made for. In any event your prose will always be tinged with poetry. You know that earth over which the waves have passed, if only once, keeps the softness of shellfish and algae. Or rather the image would be more apt if I said that earth once lifted by a volcanic eruption stays lifted. And from its fields the newest ears of corn grow highest. At the very least your poetry will remain on the high level of your prose. It gives me pleasure to tell you all this. I know you were hard on my book.[2] But that no doubt was because you thought it bad. For the same reason, finding yours good, I am glad to tell you so and to tell others. I am especially glad that others should be speaking well of it, which is more important for you.

 À bientôt, my friend,

Marcel Proust

1. See letter 110. Proust may have feared his friend would take offence at his references to Gregh's 'pride', his 'distrustfulness', and his 'childlike soul', and also at his praising the quantity, rather than the quality, of the poems.

2. In a short review in *La Revue de Paris* for 15 July 1896, Gregh had expressed no opinion of *Les Plaisirs et les jours* itself but had spoken only of Mme Lemaire's illustrations, Anatole France's preface, and the piano pieces by Reynaldo Hahn.

113
TO FERNAND GREGH

Friday 18 December 1896

Dear friend,

 Not having seen you for a long time and wishing to talk with you about your poems,[1] I dropped in to see you at the *Revue* the day before yesterday and left my name. Now, in leafing through *La Revue de Paris*, I see in the announcements of gift books a notice on *Les Plaisirs et les jours.*[2] I tremble at the thought that you may have seen a connection between my visit and the 'article', which may already have appeared, but of which I was unaware. For you are too perceptive not to realize that such a thing would be utterly ridiculous on my part. Anyway I shall try to get hold of you one of these days.

 In the meantime, best wishes,

Marcel Proust

1. *La Maison de l'enfance.*

2. This second notice by Gregh, in *La Revue de Paris* for 15 Dec. 1896, praised not only the preface and the illustrations but the book itself.

114
TO MADAME LAURE HAYMAN

[Late December 1896]

Fair sweet and cruel Friend,

You told me some harsh truths yesterday. They are dear to me because they are friendly and come from you. But you will agree that even if they are the fruit of pure friendship, they are nevertheless bitter fruit.

I would like at least to clear myself of one reproach, which strikes me in a sensitive spot, because it is literary. I am speaking of 'as one might say' [*comme qui dirait*]. Anatole France, who is with me at the moment, assures me, and authorizes me to tell you, that this locution is irreproachable and not at all vulgar. I have no need to tell you that I will gladly sacrifice it to you and that I would rather be mistaken with you than right with the whole Academy. And so would [Anatole] France.[1] Yes, it would be delightful to be mistaken with you. *Felix culpa*, as the Church Fathers say.

I throw myself at your feet, beg your absolution and embrace you tenderly and *absentmindedly*.

Marcel Proust

P.S.   If you haven't received my Saxe[2] yet, it's because I haven't yet found a piece that's worthy of you. I shall try and get it to you tomorrow.

1. Anatole France, elected the previous January, was received on 24 December 1896 into the Académie Française.

2. I.e. Dresden china; but cf. letter 25, n. 2.

115
FROM HIS MOTHER

Thursday evening
[late 1896 or early 1897 ?]
My dear boy,

Your letter has done me good – your father and I were feeling very badly. I assure you that I didn't mean for one moment to say anything whatsoever in front of Jean and if I did it was quite unintentional. Let's never speak or even think of it again. From now on let the broken glass be what it is at temple – a symbol of indissoluble union.[1]

Your father wishes you good night and I kiss you tenderly.

J.P.

I have to come back to the subject after all: be sure not to go into the dining room with bare feet, because of the glass.

---

1. Cf. 'Jean's Quarrel with his Parents', in *Jean Santeuil*, 206 – 18. When Jean's mother scolds him in the presence of a servant, he leaves the room, 'slamming the door so violently behind him that the glass ornaments fixed to its panels . . . were shattered.' In his own room he accidentally breaks a Venetian glass which his mother has just given him. His mother forgives him in almost exactly the words of Mme Proust's letter, which refers to the Orthodox Jewish marriage ceremony, when the couple drink wine out of the same glass and break it.

According to Céleste Albaret, in *Monsieur Proust* (1973), Proust broke the Venetian glass not by accident but on purpose, in what he called 'the only real rage of my life'. The rage, says Mme Albaret, was because he had asked his mother to buy him a pair of pale yellow gloves to wear when he went out with a certain demi-mondaine, and she had bought him grey ones instead.

116
TO MADAME LAURE HAYMAN

[Early January 1897]
Dear friend,

(Since you don't want '*Madame*' any more – and you are quite right: as I put on years, you stay the same, so that today I need have for you no other respect than that commanded by your mind, your noble character and your beauty.)

And so, dear friend, if I have been slow in sending you this vase, destined to bring you flowers with my New Year's greetings – it is because I wanted to find among the odd things from my uncle's household one that might remind you a little of him. This pin, which may do for a hat after having no doubt clasped a tie, does not strike me as ugly and will appeal, I hope, to your sentiment of friendship without too much offending your taste. Therefore accept it with the affectionate good wishes of one who awaits only a word from you to call on you as agreed.

> Yours,
> Marcel Proust

My respectful New Year's greetings to Prince Alexis[1] if he is with you at the moment.

You see how right I was the day we met to speak of presentiments and coincidences. Do you recall that we spoke of M. de Modène? I made his acquaintance that same evening. Perhaps he has told you everything I said to him about you. And yesterday again, in the presence of M. de Stuers, who, it seems, did a watercolour portrait of you without your knowing it, I had occasion to 'profess my religion'.

---

1. Prince Alexis Karageorgevich, of the Serbian royal family.

117
FROM ROBERT DE MONTESQUIOU

[First days of January 1897]

My dear Marcel,

It is the transparent subterfuge of those who feel themselves at fault to pretend to think they have been injured and try to hide their real guilt behind a false susceptibility.[1]

Coming from you to me, such innocent knavery can only amuse, on the one hand, our friends, who have long been aware of my indulgence towards your congenial and somewhat evasive person, on the other hand, myself, who, though often severe towards you when I judge you (as one of our masters would put it), have had, by way of comparison, only too many occasions to acknowledge your many virtues, among others honesty and delicacy. And I am pleased to do so when you are not present. Indulgence, however, has never meant sycophancy. And since you have not had the wisdom to banish those crippled peddlers the *tale-bearers* from the halls of your mind and drive them from the temple of your life – you can, when they inform you that I speak harshly of you, reply to them that I have nowhere spoken as harshly as I would to your face. And you will be speaking the truth. That *is the whole crux of the matter. Et nunc intellegite.*[2] And to come back to the matter of comparison which I have just mentioned, I have long thought and said that to draw comparisons between particular persons was to expose oneself to the worst injustice.

That is my New Year's gift. It is still my voice, crying out in the social wilderness where your good qualities are rather going to seed, but not so much as to blind you to your faults, from which you make the virtues of your books. Witness this:

'The practice of close friendship, so purifying when it is sincere, saved N. and N. from that curiosity which is the shameful amusement of most people in society.'[3]

For the rest, I see you seldom enough now that there is no need of my going into further detail and I can serve you up as new some old arguments (or call them bits of advice), whose *ugly faces* you will recognize and love if you recall and understand aright the words of my sage, who always began his Sermon by enumerating my merits, 'if it were not for which,' he never failed to add, 'I would never speak to you again.'[4] – Take the length at which I am speaking to you as a pledge of my interest – of which you will have better proof.[5]

Regards and best wishes,

RMF

1. Montesquiou was furious with Proust for amusing their friends with his 'imitations' of him (see letter 83), and had not forgiven him for failing to attend the ceremony at Douai in July 1896 in honour of Mme Desbordes-Valmore.

2. Cf. Psalms 2:10.

3. A quotation from 'Mélancolique villégiature de Mme de Breyves', in *Les Plaisirs et les jours* (cf. *Pleasures and Regrets*, 177).

4. Possibly an allusion to Ernest Hello (1828 – 85), a mystic and satirist whom Montesquiou admired.

5. Montesquiou was to include a chapter from *Les Plaisirs et les jours* in his anthology *Roseaux pensants* (Thinking Reeds), published later in 1897.

118

TO ROBERT DE MONTESQUIOU[1]

[Early in January 1897]

Dear Sir,

With all my faults, at least I have one good quality, to wit, that I am never tempted to belittle the favours which eminent persons are sometimes pleased to bestow on me, or to regard them as commonplace or no more than my due. I know the worth of four long pages from you and of the gift of your time, whose price I can estimate by the value of the works which it lends you, which you give back to it, and which it will keep.

And indeed, flattered by your kind words, I am sometimes impelled to cry out:

' 'Tis to me, if you please, that those words are addressed.'[2]

As for the witty reply you suggest, I shall not pass it on to the 'tale-bearers', for you have never told me what they quote you as having said. If you had, you would have ceased to exist for me, just as I should have ceased to exist for you, but as you advise, I regard their product as falsified.

I await your return to Paris with impatience, for then I hope to go and hear from your lips, amid fire and smoke, one or another of your pronouncements rich with meaning, as in ancient times I might have consulted the oracle. How often the desire for an answer with regard to *Le Curé de village*, *Mémoires d'Outre-tombe*, or *l'Éducation sentimentale* almost made me forget my hard feelings and set out once again for Delphi, where, at the feet of Pythia Montesquiou, I should be more in place than 'a certain little scribbler'.[3] Dear Sir, my admiration for you has re-

The highest mark being 20, this little epistolary exercise deserves no more than minus fifteen. The teacher

impertinent
impertinent

bitterness at not receiving a written appreciation of his book

insolent and stupid peepee

inadmissible direct criticism

insolent and untrue friendship can descend, not rise

frivolous

156

mained unchanged and always shall. I had merely ceased to harbour the slightest feeling of friendship. You, I have the impression, still give evidence of some for me, and like a certain character in comedy, I am only too ready to 're-enlist'.

Your admirer and friend,
Marcel Proust

1. Proust's reply to letter 117; it was returned to him by Montesquiou with marginal notes (here printed in small type).

2. A paraphrase of Molière, *Le Misanthrope*, i. ii. 261.

3. Possibly Albert Flament.

119
TO ALFRED FRANKLIN[1]

[10 January 1897]
Dear Sir,

Your past kindness is still so fresh in my memory that I am only too sensible of your reproof, transmitted to me by M. Marais, over my apparent delay in returning to the Mazarine [Library].[2] I therefore wish not so much to apologize as to acquaint you with what I believe to be my justification.

The present nature of my studies, even more than the state of my health, made it necessary for me to prolong my leave of absence. I therefore applied to the Ministry for an extension. Receiving word that this extension had been granted, I not only thought I was justified in not going to the Mazarine, but feared it would be incorrect to appear at the library during my leave of absence. The truth is that I often felt a strong desire to go there and work like any other reader. I was afraid you might regard it as tactless and indiscreet for a member of the staff to frequent the library during a leave of absence. If you would be kind enough to tell M. Marais how you feel about this, I shall be sure to act on your opinion. If it is favourable, I shall take frequent advantage of a privilege that would not only facilitate my studies but also enable me to see from time to time the colleagues and superiors whose benevolence and kindness I have so keenly appreciated.

If apart from this you have any orders to give me relating to my duties or my leave, I shall respond to your first call.

Yours faithfully
Marcel Proust

1. Alfred Franklin (1830–1917), French medievalist and historian, author of *La Vie privée d'autrefois*, in twenty-seven volumes. Since 1885 he had been director of the Mazarine Library.

2. See letter 88, n. 2. Paul Marais was on the staff of the Library.

120

FROM MADAME ARMAN DE CAILLAVET[1]

Sunday morning [7 February 1897]
My dear Marcel,

I thank you for your sweet thought and take you to my heart for being so brave and coming back to us safe and sound from your adventure. I wish the monster had come to some harm but even so it's fine of you to have attacked him,[2] considering the universal cowardice which had thus far given that ruffian impunity.

Come and see me as soon as you can, and rest assured of my friendship.

L. Arman de Caillavet

1. Mme Albert Arman, self-styled Arman de Caillavet, née Léontine Lippmann (1844–1910), Anatole France's Egeria and mistress for many years; mother of Gaston Arman de Caillavet, the playwright.

2. In *Le Journal* for 3 Feb. 1897, Jean Lorrain (pseudonym of Paul Duval, 1850–1906, journalist, poet, and playwright) had published an article containing ironic remarks about *Les Plaisirs et les jours* and about Mme Arman as well. Proust challenged Lorrain to a duel, which took place in the Bois de Meudon on 6 February. Two pistol shots were exchanged, but no one was hurt. After the duel Proust's seconds prevented him from shaking hands with Lorrain.

121
TO ROBERT DREYFUS

[10 February 1897]
My dear Dreyfus,

You may think it unkind of me to answer with a reproach a mark of sympathy which, let me tell you before all else, touched me deeply and for which I thank you with all my heart.[1] Still, I think it is more affectionate to profit by the occasion and bring up a matter which, I promise you, will be forgotten for good as soon as this letter is sealed, but which would otherwise have stayed with me in the form of unfriendly feelings towards you. Well then, I must tell you that I was horrified to hear recently that you had taken a most unfriendly attitude towards me. I have always spoken so well of you to everyone, and though I've never been able to prove it to you, I have always taken every opportunity to show my friendly feelings towards you, so much so that I thought your conduct disloyal and was very much offended. I believe, since you troubled to come on Sunday, that your feelings have changed for the better.[2] It remains for me only to ask your pardon for speaking to you of a matter which from now on will mean no more to us than if it had never been, to thank you with all my heart for your kind gesture, and beg you to count on my friendship.

Marcel Proust

1. Robert Dreyfus had called on Proust on Sunday 7 February 1897, the day after Proust's duel with Jean Lorrain.

2. Replying on 11 February 1897, Dreyfus mentioned 'a sentence [in your letter] which it is impossible to understand but several words of which, if they apply to me, portray me falsely . . .'. Nevertheless, he found the tone of Proust's letter so affectionate that he saw it as 'a precious vestige of our old friendship'.

122
TO ÉDOUARD ROD

[March 1897]
Sir,

Not knowing when I shall have the honour of seeing you, I am taking the liberty of writing you a letter to express my profound admiration for your novel *Là-Haut*, in my opinion the finest you have ever written.[1] As in nature, where increasingly general laws conspire with more particular phenomena, in your novel history, history captured at the moment of being enacted, provides a solemn background for individual passion, of which it is composed but which carries it onwards and transcends it, and you show individuals within the generations as the ebb and flow in the tide which is slower than they, but equally sure, more vast, and essentially identical. It is this panoramic painting, not only of places but also of events that I so loved in a novel like *Middlemarch*. But by situating yourself 'on the heights', you have seen objects and hours from a greater distance, spread over a wider area, in a silence which helps one to hear more clearly the mysterious sound of their coming. And in your book the changing times, the civilizations that come and go, form a contrast as admirable as the seasons you see taking possession of your entire upland meadow. What a beautiful page, your Alpine flora in the spring. I liked it ever so much more than the flora in *Le Lys dans la vallée*, itself so beautiful. But here every flower is restored to life not only in its form but with its soul. The rhododendrons have preserved their mischief (there is a certain boldness in *mischief*) and the paradisias their fragility. It is not a herbarium, it is not a picture, as in the legend it is an enchantment which has burst into bloom, the words smell good, the sentences undulate, corollas grow between the lines, one would like to stoop over your pages and pick the flowers. And you are no less a painter of the soul. Who, for instance, has ever spoken more eloquently than this: 'He experienced one of those moments, the delight of which once savoured leaves deep within you the seed of an eternal desire.' And if you have written no finer novel, to my taste at least you have written none more captivating. And just as a faint sound is more striking in the country, where we hear the slightest echo and vibration, than an uproar in the streets of Paris, so even the trifling events of life at the hotel interest me more than would extraordinary happenings.

Forgive me, Monsieur, for my inability to exercise more restraint, and accept, if you will, along with my intense gratitude for your kindness in sending me the book, the expression of my esteem and admiration.

Marcel Proust

1. Rod's novel *Là-Haut* (On the Heights) was published in March 1897.

123
TO CONSTANTIN DE BRANCOVAN[1]

[Sunday 14 March 1897]

My dear Prince,

Would it interest you to go to the Chamber of Deputies with me tomorrow? It is the session in which the government is supposed finally to justify its policy on Crete, and I think it will be interesting.[2] If so, be so kind as to call for me at half-past one. If you think you will not be able to come, please let me know, for I believe the seats are much in demand, I had considerable trouble in obtaining two seats, and I could oblige a friend. But most welcome to me would be this opportunity to spend the day with you.

Please convey my respectful greetings to the Princesse and believe me

Sincerely yours
Marcel Proust

The section where we shall be sitting is that of the President of the Republic.[3] But I do not think this will embarrass you in any way, for he does not attend the sessions, and there would be nothing official about your presence there.

1. Prince Constantin Bassaraba de Brancovan (1875 – 1967), son of the Princesse Rachel Bassaraba de Brancovan and brother of Comtesse Anna de Noailles (see letter 171). He later edited the magazine *La Renaissance latine*.

2. Greece had taken the disorders in Crete, then under Turkish rule, as a pretext for seizing the island, and the European powers – France, England, Austria-Hungary, and Russia – had landed troops on Crete in February 1897, to

prevent its annexation by Greece. Jean Jaurès called the French Government to account for its policy before the Chamber on 22 February and 15 March 1897.

3. I.e. Félix Faure, with whom the Proust family was on friendly terms.

124
TO ROBERT DE MONTESQUIOU

[15–20 April 1897]

Dear Sir,

I am writing, more to tell you how highly I should value your presence than with any thought of making you go to La Bodinière to listen to poems which you have heard only too often, and to tell you that at half-past four there will be a concert of Hahn's works, in the course of which your marvellous [Mme] Moreno will sing my 'Portraits de peintres'.[1] If, as I feel sure, you do not wish to attend, please be so kind as to leave with *your* concierge these tickets, which I send you after hesitating for some time to give you this mark of indiscretion and presumption along with this token of deference, and to disturb a poet for such paltry poetry, upon which, at great inconvenience to himself, he has already bestowed his indulgence one evening.[2]

I doubt if they will be of any greater interest to M. de Yturri, though in my thoughts the second ticket is addressed to him.

Permit me, dear Sir, to assure you of my affectionate admiration.

Marcel Proust

To spare you the trouble of taking a note down to your concierge, I have asked the bearer to wait for your answer.

1. *Le Figaro* for 24 Apr. 1897 gives an account of a 'modern music hour' at La Bodinière on the 21st, at which works of Reynaldo Hahn were performed following a lecture by Mallarmé. Among the performers was Marguerite Moreno, pseudonym of Lucie-Marie-Marguerite Monceau (1871–1948), of the Comédie-Française, who had often read Montesquiou's poems on such occasions.

2. Montesquiou had heard the 'Portraits de peintres' at Mme Lemaire's on 28 May 1895; see letter 72.

125
TO MADAME ÉMILE STRAUS

[June 1897 ?]
My dear little Mme Straus,

You mustn't think I love you less because I've stopped sending you flowers. Mlle Lemaire can tell you that I have been taking Laure Hayman out every morning and often bringing her back for lunch – which costs me so much that I haven't a sou left for flowers – and except for ten sous' [50 centimes'] worth of poppies to Mme Lemaire, I don't believe I've sent anyone flowers since the last time I saw you. You were lying in bed, as lovely as an angel who wasn't looking well, lovely enough, that is, to drive mortals mad. And since, for fear of giving you a headache, I didn't dare do it really, I now kiss you tenderly in my fancy.

Your little
Marcel

126
TO ROBERT DE MONTESQUIOU

[Wednesday evening 23 June 1897]
Dear Sir,

Pending the time when I can thank you in another way, permit me to tell you how happy I was, towards the end of a work the reading of which has enchanted my day, to find a page *about myself*,[1] as durable as the rest, whatever you may do and whether you like it or not, so that, thanks to your voluntary benevolence and to that involuntary power which causes whatever you write to be, as you say, 'tainted with immortality', I am now immortal like the work as a whole, a matter for investigation by future scholars, who will wonder who this unknown whom you called your 'friend' can have been. I thank you with all my heart, I shall begin to think I have talent and become insufferable. I hope to see you tomorrow at the home of Comtesse Odon de Montesquiou, for I may have a small favour to ask of you. Your admirer, for whose admiration your book provides a new object, I don't mean one more, but really and truly a *new* one.

Marcel Proust

1. Montesquiou had written a highly complimentary introduction to 'Un dîner en ville', the selection by his 'young friend' Marcel Proust included in his just-published anthology *Roseaux pensants* (see letter 117).

127
TO EUGÉNIE BARTHOLONI¹

9, bd Malesherbes
Wednesday [7 July 1897]

Mademoiselle,

I have just received your astonishing letter, astonishing be-cause along with the 'Monsieur' and the expression of your 'respectful good wishes', bearing witness to a 'young lady' of, as they say, 'the very best society', it includes sentences which can only have been written by a writer and which show a kinship with great writers. But not only with great ones. For somewhere in my book I spoke of hollyhocks as tall as young girls,² and when you have read that far, you will greet them I hope with affection as the elder sisters of your lovely foxgloves–. But great ones too. For in his *Roseaux pensants*, M. de Montesquiou speaks of the 'silken' pages of my book and elsewhere of my 'harmonious' verses. So you see, if you fight his influence, as he himself said, you are submitting to it. 'How utterly untrue, how little the young man knows me,' you are saying to yourself if you have read this far and if you have not been stopped at the very start by the frankly repugnant tone of this young man, who obviously doesn't know of any middle ground between writing 'polite compliments' and writing 'nonsense'. I have been awaiting with impatience–I am passionately on the lookout for–the irrefragable and mysterious information that every person who writes supplies about himself. With impatience and anxiety as well. For to see what had so little definition defining itself is at the same time to see it incurring limitation. A form is constituted precisely by its limits. As I opened your letter, all my fears and all my hopes were waiting. And some of both are already beginning to be realized. I can't tell you how much pleasure it would give me, were you to send me one of those foxgloves. Perhaps they will not have all the colour and all the elegance they preserved in a marvellous page of your letter, but I shall keep them in memory of you.

Deign, Mademoiselle, along with my thanks for the trouble

Proust's long-time friend, the Venezuelan-born composer and musician Reynaldo Hahn, whom he met in 1894, when Hahn was nineteen.

Proust and his friend the writer and playwright Robert de Flers, who sometimes acted as intermediary between Proust and his publishers.

Above, the society hostess Madeleine Lemaire, photographed by Nadar in 1891. Famous for her musical evenings, Mme Lemaire was also a successful artist and did the illustrations (as the one reproduced at left) for Proust's first book, *Les Plaisirs et les jours.*

Comtesse Greffulhe, photographed by Nadar in 1896. Patroness of musical and artistic events, she was one of the leaders of Parisian society. 'I have never seen such a beautiful woman,' Proust told Robert de Montesquiou on his first sight of her, when he was twenty-two.

you have taken in writing to me, to accept, for Madame your mother and yourself, my sincerest respects.

Marcel Proust

How many aggressive phrases come to my mind at this exact moment, the one about the 'polite compliments' recalled above, the quotation from Stendhal looked for in the carriage, *'Dominique, it's so well written'* 'Why must one always compare', etc. etc., but most of all the challenge, the lure, and the charm of a blond head, rosy lips and blue eyes.

1. Eugénie Bartholoni (1873 – 1951), called Kiki, was the daughter of Mme Anatole Bartholoni, née Marie Frasier-Frisel, *dame d'honneur* at the court of the Empress Eugénie.

2. Cf. 'The Tuileries' (*Pleasures and Regrets*, 114). Proust seems to have sent the Bartholonis a copy of *Les Plaisirs et les jours* after a musical evening at their house on 17 June 1897, at which some settings by Léon Delafosse of words by Robert de Montesquiou were performed.

128
TO REYNALDO HAHN

Friday evening [16 July 1897]

My dear little Reynaldo,

Would you please wire how your night was and whether I can make myself useful in any way.[1] Unless you tell me to, I won't come. I am thinking of you though, my poor boy. I love you with all my heart.

Marcel

The distance is nothing, my dear Reynaldo. I am always with you. And I pray God in His mercy to be with you too.

Tell your sister Maria how ill train travel and the country make me at the present time, so she will understand why I didn't come back after dinner this evening.

1. Carlos Hahn, Reynaldo's father, had died at his country home at Saint-Cloud on 15 July 1897.

129
TO MADAME DE BRANTES

[Paris, 19 July 1897]
Madame,

Many thanks for bothering to write to me. I am deeply moved by your kindness. If I think most particularly of you, I who have no need of a letter to think of you in these sorrowful days, as we approach the anniversary of a loss which you have no need of a date to remember because you do not forget,[1] but which the recurrence of comparable days makes you relive more cruelly. I remember it with the sadness aroused by a sympathy too soon interrupted, but also with the consolation of having then seen you give evidence of a delicacy I had long suspected and reveal the full measure of your sensibility and warm, faithful heart.

I am writing you all this from a horrid café, but no matter

'For thought can illumine a hovel'

as Baudelaire has said,[2] and the beautiful things we say to each other and the eminence of my reader are so far superior to the best water-marked stationery that this paper ceases to be unworthy of her. To it, then, I entrust my respectful greetings to Mme L. de Montesquiou. I used to think her delightfully pretty. I find her beautiful now that I know her lovely eyes have looked upon death without fear, reflecting only tenderness for the sailor who considered himself happy to die near her. 'Body of woman, so soft and tender, how sublime you can be!' There's some Villon for you![3]

It goes without saying that I shall not for the present write to Mrs Higginson about a matter so remote from her thoughts at this time. I don't think as highly as you do of the other lady you mention, I find her artificial, composed when not discomposed. What I like best about her is her weakness.

If you would care to come and dine one evening with the Comtesse Potocka,[4] I shall not for once take my dinner at the Parc des Princes. In the meantime, rest assured of my respectful good wishes.

Marcel Proust

I saw M. de Montesquiou the other day. He has left town.
I had a nice letter from Mme d'Eyragues[5] this morning.

1. Miss Mary Dutton, Mme de Brantes's companion, had died in Paris on 21 July 1896. Mme de Brantes had come to know Miss Dutton and her sister Mrs Higginson on the Isle of Wight, where Mme de Brantes had taken refuge in 1870 from the Franco-Prussian War.

2. Cf. Baudelaire, 'Le Voyage', in *Les Fleurs du mal:* 'Son œil ensorcelé découvre une Capoue / Partout où la chandelle illumine un taudis.'

3. For the near-drowning of the Comtesse Louis de Montesquiou, née Claude d'Aramon, see letter 53. Cf. François Villon, *Le Grand Testament*, lines 325 – 27: 'Corps femenin qui tant es tendre, / Poly, souef, si précieux / Te fauldra il ces maux attendre?'

4. The Comtesse Nicolas Potocka, née Emmanuelle Pignatelli (1852 – 1930).

5. The Marquise Charles d'Eyragues, née Henriette de Montesquiou-Fezensac; Proust was later to consider her when seeking models for the noble family in the novel he was preparing to write.

130
TO LUCIEN DAUDET

[Kreuznach, 23 or 24 August 1897][1]

What a rare and exquisite letter. If I thank you for it in a 'naked' letter, it is to tell you as quickly as possible to write and tell me, if you receive this in time, whether you are expecting to be in Basel. If so, I might manage to get there from Kreuznach and meet you. I think it's only five hours by train.

If you could recommend some good Balzacs (on the style of the *Vieille Fille* and the *Curé de Tours* and the *Cabinet des antiques* – or of *Goriot* and *Bette* – I'm now reading *La Muse du Département*), you'd be doing me a big favour. And who wrote *The Brothers Karamazov*?[2] – Has Boswelle's [sic] *Life of Johnston* [sic] been translated?

And is there something really beautiful by Michelet that I haven't read? – And what's the best of Dickens (I haven't read anything)?

Affectionately,
Marcel

1. Proust was staying with his mother, for the second time, at the German spa of Kreuznach.

2. At the age of twenty-six Proust had apparently read nothing of Dostoevsky, who later became his favourite Russian author.

131
TO MADAME DE BRANTES

1 September 1897
Oranienhof, Kreuznach
Germany

August clothes it in golden down,
Bite, o teeth, into the luscious
Fragrant peach, ready
And waiting on the espalier.
(*Mallarmé's latest*)[1]

And another bit of literary news that may interest you, France's next volume, the sequel to *L'Orme du mail*, will be titled *Le Mannequin d'osier*.[2]

Madame,

This fine photograph, which my imagination retouches to the point of perfect resemblance, which my memory varies with one or another hair-do or gown, has given me the greatest pleasure and I thank you for it with all my heart.

I shall first answer your questions. *Amitié amoureuse*, if I remember rightly, is by Mme Lecomte du Nouy, the wife not of the painter but of the architect.[3] It's made up of letters she wrote to Guy de Maupassant, whose mistress she was. As for the witticism 'At my age one rereads', it's not by C[hamp] Fleury, but by another of those hyphenated names, which is what misled you (as France says so wittily: 'the hyphen, that nobiliary particle of the democratic countries'), namely, Royer-Collard. Today it's a charming witticism, time has beautified it by casting a veil of oblivion over the circumstances that engendered it. Actually it was uttered in a fit of bad temper and narrow sectarian obstinacy that's not in the least attractive. Vigny, who had just been admitted to the Académie Française, was paying Royer-Collard the usual duty call. After the frostiest of receptions, Vigny grew angry and asked Royer-Collard if he had read any of his books. 'At my age one does not read, one rereads', was the only answer he could get out of the embittered old man.[4]

As for the questionnaire you send me about the 'twenty books', etc. etc., it's as merciless as the questionnaires of *Le Figaro* and *Le Gaulois*. The *Gaulois* questionnaire, sent to the most obscure readers, is a prodigious monument raised by journalistic imbecility to the reader's curiosity. Does it interest you to know where Isnardon spends his holidays,[5] Mlle Héglon's conception of life at the seashore, Paulus's opinion of how long Wagner's work will survive?

I have no desire to imitate their absurdity by falling into the trap set for me by your indulgence. (True, your questionnaire is as intelligent as theirs is stupid. But I can't help fearing that my answers would be of no greater interest. In any case they would be very different!)

I have been at Kreuznach for more than a fortnight for the sake of Mama's health and I don't know *one* person here. For the first few days there was still your friend 'Martine', as you call her, and thanks to that sauce Béarnaise,[6] which I found most savourous, the first part of my stay went down easily enough. But now she has been gone for over a week. She is really intelligent and her seriousness is sincere, something, I admit, that I hadn't believed up to now. But here, where there was no one to watch her, she was constantly with *Wilhelm Meister*, with Beethoven, with XXXX [*sic*]: so she must be really fond of them.

Before leaving, I saw Mme Potocka at Versailles and liked her even better than in Paris. And I must own that if I hadn't suddenly left for Kreuznach, I'd have gone to Versailles very often. I repeated to her the things I told you the evening of your departure, and which you were too modest to listen to. I believe that her friendship rejoiced in them.

'I send you', Dumas wrote to a lady, 'the homage of my *least* respectful sentiments.' Nothing is funnier than hearing you say in your letter: 'Mme Stern whom they call Ernest'! It's much funnier than you can even suspect. 'And I for my part see a million words in it,' as Molière says.[7] No, it's not a nickname, it's the poor lady's Christian name, well, not Christian because she's Jewish, but anyway the name *her parents* gave her: 'Ernesta'.

Alas, Marienbad is 18 hours from Kreuznach, and the only hope left me is to be able to write some day like Balzac: 'Ah, if you knew what Touraine is. Here one forgets everything. . . . My house near Saint Cyr-sur-Loire, on a hillside, near a charming river, covered with flowers, with honeysuckle, whence I look out over landscapes a hundred times more beautiful than the ones those scoundrelly travellers bore their readers with' (Letter to Victor Ratier, dated from La Grenadière).[8]

I read *La Duchesse de Langeais* because you said you liked it, but I didn't think much of it. And I have just finished *Une Ténébreuse Affaire*. In *Gobseck* I found portraits of old nobles, of the kind I need for my novel, and for which I go about gleaning sayings 'in the manner of Aimery de la Rochefoucauld',[9] and character traits, not of course to copy but as a source of inspiration.

In that you haven't helped me at all, you've never been willing to tell me anything. Mme de Béarn advised me to try and see a Mme de Laubespin, who it seems is just like that. But I prefer to be told of these things. In five minutes a clever woman or a man of taste can sum up the experiences of several years.

Anyway, I shall show you my Duc de Réveillon (I won't keep the name)[10] and you will tell me whether the tics, the prejudices, the habits I attribute to him are too exaggerated. I would like to know whether such oddities as your friend's left hand (and his wife on his left in the carriage) are based on something, at least for others if not for him. Have you known people who did that? And when one became intimate with them did they go on doing it? Would they have given their left hand (or shown some other mark of contempt which I'd be glad to know of) to M. Haas or M. Schlumberger?[11] In a word, was it because of not being *well born* or of not being in society?

This is a long letter, proportionate to your isolation at Marienbad. If you knew someone not too far from Kreuznach . . . But it's so unlikely!

Deign, Madame, to accept my respectful homage.

Marcel Proust

1. 'Août la dore et la duvette / Faut-il, ô dents que vous n'alliez / Savoureuse, odorante, prête / Mordre la pêche aux espaliers', from Stéphane Mallarmé, *Divagations* (1897).

2. *Le Mannequin d'osier* (The Wickerwork Woman), the second part of Anatole France's satirical novel *L'Histoire contemporaine* (A Chronicle of Our Times), was to appear that same month. *L'Orme du mail* (The Elm Tree on the Mall) had been published in 1896.

3. *Amitié amoureuse* [Loving Friendship], *Préface fragmentée de Stendhal*, by Mme H. Lecomte du Nouy, née Hermine Oudinot (1854–1915), appeared in 1896. Her husband was the architect André Lecomte du Nouy; his brother, the painter, did a portrait of Dr Proust.

4. The philosopher and politician Pierre-Paul Royer-Collard (1763–1845) was a lifelong republican, whereas Alfred de Vigny was an aristocrat and a royalist. The incident, which occurred shortly before Royer-Collard's death, is related by Sainte-Beuve in his *Nouveaux Lundis*.

5. Jules Huret, in *Le Figaro*, 14 Aug. 1897, asks the reader: 'Are you in favour of problem plays?' 'Should dramatic literature be analytic or synthetic?' etc. etc. In *Le Gaulois* for 18 Aug. 1897, M. Isnardon of the Opéra-Comique is

questioned: 'How do you spend your holidays?' 'What are your hopes for the next season?' (Answer: 'I have given up hope.')

6. The Comtesse René de Béarn, née Martine de Béhague.

7. Cf. *Les Femmes savantes*, III. ii.

8. A letter of 21 July 1830 (cf. Honoré de Balzac, *Correspondance*, ed. 1960, I. 561), here quoted freely and inaccurately.

9. Comte Aimery de la Rochefoucauld (1843 – 1928), noted for his aristocratic pride.

10. The first page of MS of the chapter of *Jean Santeuil* devoted to the Duc de Réveillon bears the letterhead of the Kurhaus-Hôtel Restaurant, Bad Kreuznach.

11. Charles Haas (1832 – 1902) was the first of several models for Charles Swann. Gustave Schlumberger (1844 – 1929), a surgeon who went into archaeology, frequented the salon of Mme Straus.

132
TO SUZETTE LEMAIRE

[Sunday evening 24 October ? 1897]
My dear little Mlle Suzette,

Thank you for the flowers and the thorns. The flowers are faded, but the things you say about Réveillon have a grace that will never pass. How fortunate you are to possess a grace that will never pass. I have no luck. The sweet things I want to say to a friend turn to monstrosities under my pen. What I want to say is that I never cease to think of you, that of this I choose to give you more lasting proof than a letter, and that I am very ill. And now it looks as if, worse than a Goncourt, I had been afraid to squander on friendship the wit (which alas I do not deem precious enough to be chary of) that I'm bent on reserving for 'literature' (good Lord!).[1] At last a handclasp will rejoin our disunited souls and our eyes will illumine what our minds have darkened.

Your letter was as lovely as any of George Sand's descriptions. What a splendid nature you have!

The 'Nuit d'amour bergamasque' struck me as charming and was given two rounds of applause.[2] I leave you now, to write to your mother, not without having tenderly embraced you despite your pointed 'dear Marcels'. And having asked you whether you might in very gentle, very respectful terms, communicate to Mme Herbelin some part of the sympathy, affection and veneration which my diffidence prevents me from expressing directly.

Marcel Proust

1. Presumably a reference to a previous letter, which has not come to light.

2. The first performance of Reynaldo Hahn's 'Nuit d'amour bergamasque' was given at the Colonne concerts on 24 October 1897. Henri Gauthier-Villars wrote in *L'Écho de Paris* (26 Oct. 1897) that although 'M. Marcel Proust, emulated by a few society ladies, applauded . . . vigorously', the piece 'seems to have left most of the audience cold'.

133
TO DOUGLAS AINSLIE[1]

[19 December 1897]
Dear friend,

I am so sorry not to have seen you. This death[2] has so upset me that I forgot everything. Except to notify you: yesterday I sent word to Durand's (from Weber's) that I couldn't come. And the fact is that I haven't left the poor Daudets since.[3] Lucien so unhappy (and very much touched by your regards which I gave him). – Then this evening I sent a message to the Continental, asking you to meet me at eleven o'clock. Alas, you had gone. I won't try to see you tomorrow morning, I am so utterly exhausted I shall sleep till one or two. If you haven't left, it would be awfully kind of you to come about two. In any case, don't fail to let me know when you come again in January. I shall be more available then, we shall go and look at the [Gustave] Moreaus and I shall try to obtain forgiveness for the apparent indifference with which, wholly taken up by the grief of my friends the Daudets, I have seemed, without at all meaning to, to respond to your charming attentions.

Yours,
Marcel Proust

Remember me to the Billys if you see them.
I shall send you *La Presse* as soon as I get them to publish a word about you.[4] I haven't been able to do so yet, because I've had to badger them to let me bid Daudet goodbye in their columns. I'll do it next week, I hope, soon in any case.

1. Douglas Ainslie (1865–1948), English poet, literary critic, and philosopher.

2. Alphonse Daudet had died at dinner on 16 December 1897.

3. Lucien Daudet was to write: 'I don't know how Marcel Proust and M. Reynaldo Hahn found out; they arrived during the evening, brotherly and in despair, and throughout the three days that followed they sustained me with their presence' (*Les Cahiers de Marcel Proust* [1927–35], v. 34).

4. No mention of Ainslie seems to have appeared in *La Presse.*

134
TO ALBERT FLAMENT¹

[Soon after 18 December 1897]
Dear Albert,

Only an event so tragic and so unforeseen could have so disoriented my thoughts and disorganized my days as to delay me in thanking you for an attention the *kindness* of which I am FULLY aware of, which is saying a good deal.² Since I have been so slow in thanking you, I take pleasure in adding my most sincere compliments for your article on Daudet,³ which I thought quite remarkable, I can truthfully say, superb. It gave me great pleasure to find in every line brilliant confirmation of the opinion I have held of you for some time. Every detail is brought out in a way that no one else could have done, you take possession of it as its rightful owner. For a man of letters there is a world of difference between Daudet's Christlike head, which everyone has spoken of, and your 'Spanish Christ displayed', etc. Your 'tilted head', with indication as to which side, shows a power of physical observation which I envy you, because I have always been lacking in it and without it objects are not pinned down, they float as in a dream. Your 'red screens' charmed me. On the other hand, a few bits of pretentiousness which you will have to get rid of (among the fine things, however, I forgot the 'patina of Rembrandt'). I assure you that I do not say as much to all my illustrious or, as you put it, not very noteworthy friends who write articles. But aren't we both at an age where we need to be encouraged? I have no one for that. You at least have me. . . .⁴

1. Albert Flament (1877–1956), a journalist, wrote columns of society gossip for several newspapers. He quotes this letter in his *Le Bal du Pré-Catelan;* the original has not come to light.

2. The unforeseen event was the death of Alphonse Daudet. Flament seems to have been instrumental in getting Proust's article on Daudet published in *La Presse* for 19 Dec. 1897.

3. Flament's article on Daudet, entitled 'L'Homme', appeared in *La Presse* on 18 Dec. 1897.

4. The end of the letter is missing in the printed text.

135
TO LUCIEN DAUDET

1 January [1898]

My dear little Lucien,

On this first of January when people think of the future, I am thinking with you of the past and of him whom we shall see no more, to whom I would have wished a happy New Year and good health. Dear boy, you will never know how near I feel to you. I don't seem to have been very good at showing it, since my letters and visits have gone unacknowledged. Or rather, you have so many letters to write, and not much inclination, I'm sure. All the same, don't forget me. The past years have brought you so much grief that I don't dare wish you anything for the new one. At least it will not efface the memories and sorrows that make me cherish you more than ever.

Yours,
Marcel

136
TO MADAME ALPHONSE DAUDET

[Soon after 22 March 1898]

Madame,

I was greatly moved yesterday to receive *Soutien de famille*.[1] Greatly moved, but hardly surprised; I wish I could be like your daughter, who thought that her father was only very ill. He was so alive in me that he seems to be still living, and it's sad having to send you the thanks one automatically addresses to him. I shall read it, and it will be a consolation for a grief that is rekindled in me every day (by the need for a piece of advice which I could ask only of

M. Daudet or the desire for a charm which he alone could dispense) to be able to speak of it with Lucien and with you. I am almost ashamed to speak of my health to you, who have seen that desperately ill man, who never spoke of his health, endure infinitely greater sufferings. But I should not like you to put it down to indifference if I do not go to see you, I won't even say often, but *every day*, for not a day passes but that my desire to go is so intense that I am deeply disappointed each evening not to have fulfilled it. But my health has put me into a strange situation: especially in the past few weeks, I don't begin to exist until four in the afternoon, and if I want to work a little and take the air for half an hour, it is already evening. Still, if one wants something for too long a time, one ends by doing it, because to live with a desire that is never fulfilled is no life. Especially now that I am utterly bereft because Lucien has stopped coming to see me. And I understand him, I even prefer it this way, I've had several choking fits, and it's better for me not to speak until the end of the day. But within two days I shall have been to see you in the late afternoon. You must be very happy, Madame, to have two such sons, the most remarkable I've ever known, the one stronger, the other more exquisite (and strong as well when necessary). Knowing what Lucien is for me, I can imagine what he must be for you. And it's not only by being so sweet and kind that he will give you pleasure, but by his talent as well. I can feel how his mind teems with ideas, it is so diversified, so universal that I sometimes think painting will not suffice to express it, that he will need another art, the art in which all those who have borne the name of Alphonse Daudet excel and of which so many of Lucien's letters that I am keeping for you and for many others are already delightful masterpieces bearing the mysterious smile of an epistolary Leonardo. I want him to be well in order that he may be happy, for he needs happiness, I think, to produce. He is one of those people who make us understand why the first question it is customary to ask is 'How are you?' Unfortunately, I am not the right kind of friend for him, I too am too nervous. He needs someone who, along with similar intellectual and moral aspirations, has the opposite sort of temperament, calm rather than agitated, resolute and happy. I should like to find him a friend of that sort, or become so myself. Accept, Madame, the assurance of my respectful sympathy. If it is sympathy, admiration, affection to think unceasingly of you and yours, with all my heart, with all my memories and all my hopes, no one more than I, Madame, can call himself your devoted servant.

Marcel Proust

1. *Soutien de famille* (Mainstay of the Family), a posthumous novel by Alphonse Daudet, was published on 22 March 1898.

137
TO PAUL REBOUX¹

Dear Sir,

[About mid-May 1898]

What makes me all the more sensible of the sympathy you have shown me in sending me your book is that it is no more than a return for the sympathy you have long inspired in me. I can tell you in complete sincerity that of all the young men now making their début in poetry (of course I can speak only of those I know) you are the most congenial to me, because, it seems to me, it is you who bring to it the most grace combined with the most simplicity. There is a simplicity in your poems, and that is the highest praise I could give someone like you, who knows all the refinements and has even invented some. But when one knows how to humanize them, the most marvellous complications become simple and touching, like those 'Black Irises',² which before reading you I had no liking for, but in the hidden depths of which you have discovered a heart of fire. The function of the poet is to go to the heart of all things. Like the Racinian heroine, nature can say of the poet that he 'has found the way to her heart'.³ There is no poppy so lowly but that he can kindle our feeling for it by initiating us into its charm. But he can guide us even to the complicated flowers which seem reserved for the unimaginative rich, showing their heart of fire, as in these black irises you have made us love. I have the impression that there is enormous talent in your book, that you are wonderfully gifted and skilful. I amused myself with a little game I never played before. I took each line in your book by itself and imagined I saw it quoted as a famous line in the middle of an article by, say, [Jules] Lemaître. Try it, you'll see that each one already has an aura of fame, as though entitled to it by right. From this point of view, look at 'Avenging Eros'. I'm sure it will amuse you. See how, in the perspective of a page of prose, inverted commas spring up of their own free will round
       'And ferocity glittered in his green eyes'⁴
and for all the rest.

    Forgive a letter that must be long for the reader, but is short for me, who would have many more things to write to you, which I shall be glad to say to you one day.

Yours very sincerely,

Marcel Proust

1. The twenty-one-year-old poet Paul Amilet (1877 – 1963), who wrote under the pseudonym Paul Reboux, had just sent Proust his second book of poems, *Les Iris noirs* (Black Irises; 1898).

2. An allusion to the first poem in the book, from which it took its title.

3. Cf. *Phèdre*, IV. vi: 'Aricie a trouvé le chemin de son cœur.'

4. '. . . Et la férocité luisait en ses yeux verts', from the last stanza of Reboux's long poem 'Éros vengeur'.

138
TO MADAME ALPHONSE DAUDET

[June 1898]

Madame,

Thank you ever so much for your kindness in sending me your book.[1] Lucien will tell you why I could not go and thank you in person. I read it with enchantment and reread it, I stop at every word, I would like to know how you manage to find the words 'streets ending in the waves',[2] rather than roads leading to the sea (I may not be repeating the exact expression, because I haven't got the book here at hand) and to give all those portraits their delightful substance, which has the freshness of your voice and the clarity of your gaze. I read and reread all these marvellous products of sensibility born of intelligent curiosity (the house of Mme de Beaumont, Mme Ackermann, the house of Chateaubriand), I examine these sentences, trying to understand how they were made, so as to try, when I write, to write streets ending in waves rather than streets leading to the sea. And I discover nothing, I remain enchanted, as though looking at a collection of miraculous butterflies, which give us the magic but not the secret of their colours.

Oh, when it comes to flowers, how helpless and unhappy I felt before those bluish spring flowers, I who had many times felt such joy in their presence but had never succeeded in writing anything to show

177

it. Those pages, which will be read by all lovers of literature, will always be inimitable. Or rather, no, I do hope you will have a disciple, your exquisite and gifted Lucien, to whom you will give the equivalent of your secrets, the transposition of your art. And we who see the swallow flying without ourselves being able to leave the ground, we shall see the young swallow, after barely trying his wings, follow his mother.

Accept, Madame, my humble respects and profound sympathy for the glimmer of happiness rising over your sorrow.

Marcel Proust

1. *Journées de femme* [A Woman's Days]. *Alinéas* (1898).

2. The phrase 'les rues aboutissant aux vagues' occurs in the chapter entitled 'Côtes bretonnes'.

139
TO MADAME ANATOLE CATUSSE[1]

[Soon after 6 July 1898]

Madame,

We didn't want to worry you by telling you Mama was going to be operated on[2] and actually no one was told. But now that she seems quite out of danger, now that she is really better, I wanted, knowing your great affection for her, to tell you that the operation she underwent was terrible. Mama doesn't know (how serious an operation it was, because of course she knows she was operated on) and perhaps we shall never tell her. It took almost three hours and we wondered how she could ever come through. I have just left her. She is feeling well and her doctors are quite satisfied. Even my poor papa, who was out of his mind for days and refused to be reassured by her improvement, is satisfied.

Deign, Madame, to accept the assurance of my sincere and respectful devotion.

Marcel Proust

1. Mme Catusse, née Marie-Marguerite Bertrin, was the wife of Anatole Catusse (1847–1900), former prefect of Nice, a councillor of state and tax official.

2. Mme Proust had just undergone a major pelvic operation, during which she almost died. She was in hospital for three months afterwards.

140

TO EUGÉNIE BARTHOLONI

[Summer 1898]

Mademoiselle,

What a pretty letter for a collection (all of which would be exquisite). How would we title it? 'Divers occupations of a melancholy summer.' A great many copies would be printed; but I am flattered and touched to have the original. So there you are in the mountains, and it's on mountaineers that your lovely eyes are casting their darts, an amused and devastating Diana. More than one will say with the wretched song

'That in the corner of your artful smile
His heart was caught.'

There haven't been any important events, or rather there have, but not the same ones for everyone. For some the great news is that M. and Mme Aimery de la Rochefoucauld (I'm referring to the husband and wife, no crisscrossing compliments) were twice in a row placed after the Wagrams. 'They've put a hundred years before a thousand,' the Comte cried out. And added: 'I don't say they shouldn't invite those people. I say they shouldn't invite me.'

For others, including myself, the events are rather those which are every day venomously distorted, when they are not passed over in silence, by your reactionary newspapers. As though the defenders of the Altar should not, more than anyone else, have been the apostles of truth, compassion and justice. In this you recognize the ideological sophisms of the incorrigible and verbose Dreyfusard, who, at least, will speak no more this evening, except to declare himself, Mademoiselle, your most respectful servant

Marcel Proust

If the pretty demoiselle de Pierrebourg,[1] with cheeks of milk beneath a rain of roses, is with you, tell her I am sorry I cannot pour out to her my sadness over what they have done to Picquart,[2] that Picquart whom I thank you for speaking of with so much intelligent sympathy.

1. Madeleine de Pierrebourg, daughter of the Baronne Aimery Harty de Pierrebourg (see letter 245), was later to marry Proust's friend Louis de la Salle.

2. In March 1896 Colonel Picquart of the Intelligence Service, after studying the dossier, had expressed doubts as to the guilt of Captain Alfred Dreyfus, tried and convicted of treason in 1894 and imprisoned for life on Devil's Island. On 13 January 1898 Picquart was arrested and confined in the fortress of Mont Valérien; in July of that year he was denounced by the Minister of War, Godefroy Cavaignac (1853 – 1905), and charges were brought against him before the High Court. Thereafter he was held for some weeks in the Santé prison.

141
TO MADAME ÉMILE STRAUS

[September 1898]

My dear little Mme Straus,

At the request of M. Labori, M. France is asking a few prominent persons to sign a petition in support of Picquart, which, M. Labori believes, might impress the judges.[1] New names would be welcome, and I have promised M. France to ask you to approach M. d'Haussonville, saying, if you like, that it's on behalf of M. France. The petition would be couched expressly in such moderate terms as in no way to commit the signatories on the Dreyfus case itself. And M. d'Haussonville is such a generous, high-minded man, perhaps he will not refuse.[2] M. France, like everyone else, believes that his name, which is outstanding from every point of view, would carry enormous weight for the future, not so much of the Affair, as of Picquart, which looks a good deal darker.[3] I say for his future, because the serenity of the man himself is such as to wring accents of tearful affection from France, who is ordinarily more detached. But since M. d'Haussonville seems too great a catch to be likely, if you do not succeed or prefer not to try, you could fall back on Dufeuille, Ganderax, or any other prominent person you know, Pozzi, for instance,[4] or anyone else you can approach without going to too much trouble. But for you such trouble will be a pleasure

Since you are beautiful, and he unhappy.[5]

But the matter is rather pressing. I'd have written to M. d'Haussonville myself, but since I hardly know him I was afraid of being ridiculous, and much worse, ineffectual. I have not seen you since the Affair, from being so utterly Balzacian (Bertulus, the examining magistrate in *Splendeurs et misères des courtisanes*, Christian Esterhazy, the provincial nephew in *Illusions perdues*, Du Paty de Clam, Rastignac arranging a meeting with Vautrin in some remote faubourg), became pure Shakespeare with its piling up of precipitate dénouements.[6] But why skim the surface of a subject which we shall have occasion to discuss at Trouville, where, I hope, Mama will be sent to complete her recovery, which is already under way.

Respectfully yours,

Marcel

Don't mention the Picquart petition except to possible signatories; it should be kept as quiet as possible.

1. Maître Fernand Labori, Picquart's defence counsel (see letter 157), was to represent him at the trial scheduled for 21 September.

2. A former deputy, Comte Othenin d'Haussonville (1843 – 1924) was a member of the Jockey Club and the Académie Française. He was careful at the start of the Dreyfus Affair not to divulge his sentiments, but showed his true colours when his name appeared on the first membership list of the Ligue de la Patrie Française, published in *Le Temps* for 1 Jan. 1899.

3. On 22 September 1898, by order of the Public Prosecutor, Picquart was to be handed over to the military authorities and confined in the Cherche-Midi prison; after 27 September he was held in solitary confinement, unable to communicate even with his lawyer, and was not finally released until 9 June 1899.

4. François-Eugène Dufeuille (1841 – 1911) had been head of the political cabinet of the Duc d'Orléans, pretender to the French throne; convinced of Dreyfus's innocence, he resigned his post in December 1897. For Louis Ganderax, of the *Revue de Paris*, see letter 28. Jean-Samuel Pozzi (1846 – 1918), a surgeon and member of the Academy of Medicine, was then senator for the Dordogne department.

5. Cf. Victor Hugo, 'Sept Odes', v. xxxiv, in *Toute la lyre, à Mme Judith Gautier:* 'Puisque vous êtes belle, et puisque je suis vieux.'

6. A reference to proliferating events in the Dreyfus Affair in the weeks since 25 August 1898, when Me Labori had submitted to the examining magistrate Bertulus, on behalf of Colonel Picquart, a complaint of fraud against Colonel Du Paty de Clam, deputy chief of the Third Bureau at the Ministry of War. Du Paty was a cousin of Cavaignac, who resigned as Minister of War on 4 September; on 12 September Du Paty himself, implicated in the guilt of Major Esterhazy, the real culprit, was retired from active service. The confession and subsequent suicide, on 31 August, of Colonel Henry, Picquart's deputy, who had forged crucial evidence in the case, led to several other resignations before the month of September was out.

142
TO HIS FATHER

[Trouville, September ? 1898][1]
My dear little Papa,

Mama just took the lift down to the garden, where she stayed from four to half-past six. Now she has gone back up again (in the lift) and isn't tired. I want to ask you for a consultation, by letter. Here's what it is. A young officer of Marines has just spent three years on Madagascar. He contracted an ailment there, some kind of blood poisoning. As long as he was there, he had no illness. But since his return, he has been having violent attacks of fever regularly every fortnight, they last from one to six days, with pains in his right shoulder and above his left buttock. Quinine (taken during his attacks) and Fowler's solution (taken continuously) have had no effect. Do you know of a remedy? – And if not, is there a doctor who really knows these colonial diseases? –

And now a bit of gossip. The painter Rolle, who is a friend of the Élysée, claims that Mme Faure is a strong Dreyfusard and shuts herself up with him [Rolle] to read the good newspapers, but that M. Faure and Lucie are very much against.[2]

With loving kisses,

Marcel

1. Proust and his mother were installed in a hotel at Trouville while she convalesced from her operation.

2. In *Cities of the Plain* the Prince de Guermantes, after the exposure and suicide of Colonel Henry, begins unbeknownst to his wife to read the Dreyfusard press, and instructs the Abbé Poiré to say masses for Dreyfus; the Abbé informs him that the Princesse has been doing likewise (II. 735, 736 – 37).

143
TO CONSTANTIN DE BRANCOVAN

[Towards the end of September 1898]
Dear Prince,

My brother has asked me to recommend to you (for no specific purpose, just in general) M. Heresco, a young doctor and former intern of the Paris hospitals, who is going to practise in Bucharest. He seems to be an absolutely remarkable man with a great future. Your good will could be extremely helpful to him.

Several times this summer I wanted to chat with you, at least in a letter, and I should have liked to write. But Mama was very ill and I was always with her, incapable of doing anything. Mariéton tells me that you've turned Dreyfusard. That gives me pleasure in many ways. First – let's not be egotistical – for the sake of the cause. If even ten persons who were well known and consequently above suspicion were to come out for revisionist ideas, the truth would not only be on the march,[1] it would have gone a long way. Next, I think this will be a further bond between us, and that gives me great pleasure. And lastly because, as Ibsen put it so eloquently, there is hardly anything which is not at once the object of our faith and of our doubt. Since Christ himself doubted on the Mount of Olives, a Dreyfusard is surely entitled to moments of misgiving, in which he asks himself: Have I espoused the truth? And every time I see some of those whom I regard as the most intelligent, the most amiable, and the best, among whom I number you (*littera non erubescit*),[2] sharing my opinion, I have the impression that this gives it greater force, and I feel comforted. If you have nothing to do one evening, let me know, and arrange to meet me about nine o'clock at Weber's or some such place; it would give me great pleasure to talk with you.

Your devoted
Marcel Proust

1. Zola had concluded an article in *Le Figaro* (25 Nov. 1897) with the sentence which soon became famous: 'Truth is on the march, nothing can stop it now.'

2. Cf. Cicero, *Epistulae ad familiares*, letter to Lucius Lucceius.

144
FROM HIS MOTHER

Trouville-sur-Mer, Calvados
Tuesday 6 p.m. [11 October 1898]

My darling,

I didn't write to you this morning, I was waiting to hear that you had left for Holland. I've received your 'Am in Paris' telegram

(Gabrielle brought it to me on the beach). I shall know by tomorrow's letter what made you give up your plan – you must have been tempted.[1] What was the obstacle? Your letter this morning was very nice – your father didn't miss a syllable of it – as for your mama, she is rereading it. I'm getting along ADMIRABLY.[2] Can you read? Your father says variations of a tenth of a degree are of no consequence. As for Dick – not only is he raving mad, but it takes two whole degrees.

A thousand kisses.

I will make the concession of writing to you only once a day.

[*No signature*]

1. Proust's visit to Amsterdam, to attend a Rembrandt exhibition being held there from 7 September to 31 October 1898, was merely postponed. An article he wrote about Rembrandt on his return to Paris was never published in his lifetime.

2. Written in large capital letters.

145
TO ROBERT DREYFUS

[9 November 1898]

Dear friend,

I am tearing this page out of a work notebook to beg your forgiveness. I wrote you the enclosed on the evening of the day I received your book.[1] I thought it had reached you. It hadn't been sent. Your note caused me to look for it, and find it. I look back in horror: since the day Mama went to the clinic to be operated on I've been letting the books people send me accumulate. I haven't even begun to answer. If a fortnight's silence has surprised you, what must others think? I'm truly unhappy about it. I haven't been able to read any more of your book except for the marvellous Cicero. And I've reread the end, which is superb.[2] Perhaps some echo of my praises has reached you. Again I ask your forgiveness and assure you that on the contrary I was deeply touched by an inscription which seems to put an end to a period that was not to my liking. It was the epitaph of those feelings of distrust, which come sooner or later to seem as strange as our schoolboy animosities and sympathies. You see that I was bound to be pleased and that on the contrary I overdid it, for we never change completely and a time comes when we return to the prejudices and instinctive antipathies of the very first day. Well, I thank you kindly for the intention and the attention, as they say in the *Journal des débats.*

Your devoted
Marcel Proust

[*Enclosure*]

[Between 24 and 29 October 1898]
Dear friend,

Many thanks for sending me your book. I shall write to you again if you don't mind, when I have read it. But even now I've been struck by the grandeur and simplicity of the beginning. In the sentence about gold and the land (I haven't got the book before me) there's a mysterious poetry that delights me.[3] It seems to me that you, greatly gifted like several members of our generation, have hit on a piece of work in which to show it. For what do the rest of us do? But you, perhaps, *exegisti monumentum. – Monumentum adolescentiae.*[4] I don't know if one can say that. I have the impression that the whole thing is written with great force. 'Political catastrophes' (or some other violent word) and social transformations! . . . And 'ideas, etc., that is to say, the circumstances'. I thank you, too, for the inscription that sums up a period in history which, though less important for humanity than the Agrarian Laws, nevertheless has its importance and had its bitterness for me.

Affectionately yours,
Marcel Proust

In tendering my respects to Mme Dreyfus, do tell her that I share the joy this work must give her and that its success will give her tomorrow.

1. *Essai sur les lois agraires sous la république romaine* (An Essay on the Agrarian Laws under the Roman Republic), published by Calmann-Lévy in 1898.

2. Chapter II of Dreyfus's book is entitled 'Marcus Tullius Cicero'; the last chapter, 'Caius Julius Caesar', deals with the attempt at agrarian reform under Caesar.

3. The sentence occurs in the first paragraph of the book: 'There is a wealth older than gold, namely, the land.'

4. 'You have erected a monument, a monument to youth', a play on Horace's ode (III. 30): 'Exegi monumentum aere perennius' (I have erected a monument more enduring than bronze).

146
TO LUCIEN MUHLFELD[1]

[November 1898]

Dear Sir,

Forgive me for not thanking you sooner: I hadn't read *Le Mauvais Désir*[2] yet.

Permit me to bring up two memories, which you will recall without difficulty because they relate to you. The first is my memory of an article you wrote about *Le Lys rouge*.[3] In it you sketched the grand and beautiful idea at the base of *Mauvais Désir*, but there was no way of knowing whether you would come back to it. For among our ideas for books many are called but few are chosen, and innumerable seeds perish for every one that germinates.

My second memory, a melancholy one, but brightened today by a happy disclaimer and an already glorious ray of light, is of the day when I learned from you with startled faith and saddened sympathy that you were giving up writing, feeling that you had neither the vocation nor the talent for it, that your life's happiness and the fulfilment of your strivings would be sought elsewhere than in literature. In the face of this severity on your part, my praises beat a retreat, shamed at the thought that they must now strike the recipient as so much flattery. Today you have buckled on your wings again. You have written a beautiful and original book, whose cruel dénouement is most profound since, the substance of jealousy being that two people love each other, it does not cease until only one of them is left, at death. A figurative death, I think, standing for all the deaths that can destroy the being one loves, among which forgetfulness is not the least frequent, nor the least total.[4] With nothing more than the observations scattered through this novel one might compose a very fine and fundamental book of moral reflections. And you have also found your Nucingen, who is admirable and repulsive. Oh, exceedingly repulsive. But admirable all the same:

There is no snake or monster so odious . . .[5]

Please convey my respects to Mme Muhlfeld and rest assured of my sincere admiration.

Marcel Proust

1. Lucien Muhlfeld (1870 – 1902), novelist and critic, was on the staff of the Sorbonne Library.

2. Muhlfeld's novel *Le Mauvais Désir* (Corrupt Desire) was published in October 1898.

3. A review of Anatole France's novel, published in *La Revue blanche*, no. 36 (October 1894).

4. Proust would develop this idea in connection with the death of Albertine.

5. Cf. Boileau, *Art poétique*, Chant III: 'Il n'est point de serpent ni de monstre odieux / Qui, par l'art imité, ne puisse plaire aux yeux.' The crude and ruthless banker Baron Nucingen figures in several of Balzac's novels.

147
TO ERNEST VAUGHAN ?[1]

[26 or 27 November ? 1898]

Dear Sir,

I sent my signature for the Picquart Protest[2] and see that it has not been published. I very much want it to appear. I know my name will add nothing to the list. But the fact of figuring on the list will add to my name: one doesn't miss an occasion to inscribe one's name on a pedestal.[3]

1. This letter, headed only 'Monsieur le Directeur', must have been addressed to the managing editor of a daily paper, either *Le Siècle* (Yves Guyot) or *L'Aurore* (Ernest Vaughan). The latter seems more likely, because Proust's name appears on none of the lists published by *Le Siècle*, whereas it does appear on *L'Aurore*'s third list, published in the supplement for 28 Nov. 1898.

2. The Protest read: 'In the name of flouted justice, the undersigned protest the measures taken against Colonel Picquart, the heroic artisan of revision, just as revision is going into effect.'

3. The end of the letter has apparently not been preserved.

148
TO MARIE NORDLINGER[1]

[Soon after 25 December 1898]
Mademoiselle,

Your Christmas card has given me great pleasure. If we were creatures only of reason, we would not believe in anniversaries, holidays, relics or tombs. But since we are also made up in some part of matter, we like to believe that that too has a certain reality and we want what holds a place in our hearts to have some small place in the world around us and to have its material symbol, as our soul has in our body. And while little by little Christmas has lost its truth for us as an anniversary, it has at the same time, through the gentle emanation of accumulated memories, taken on a more and more living reality, in which candlelight, the melancholy obstacle its snow offers to some desired arrival, the smell of its tangerines imbibing the warmth of heated rooms, the gaiety of its cold and its fires, the scent of tea and mimosa, return to us overlaid with the delectable honey of our personality, which we have unconsciously been depositing over the years during which – engrossed in selfish pursuits – we paid no attention to it, and now suddenly it sets our hearts to beating.[2]

These are some of my excuses for taking so much pleasure in your Christmas card, not to mention the opportunity of apologizing for a silence you may have misinterpreted, and the cause of which is this: I myself was ill at the time when you wrote to me so charmingly, and then Mama underwent a terrible operation. She spent three months in the clinic. She is quite well now and fully recovered.

I hope, though I envy you your life in England, that you will return soon to Paris. I shall be very happy to renew acquaintance with your rare and precious wit and your grace as fresh as a branch of hawthorn. Do be so kind as to remember me to Mademoiselle your sister, to whom I have not dared write directly, since we have never corresponded, and to share with her my humble respects.

Marcel Proust

1. Marie Nordlinger (1876 – 1961), a first cousin of Reynaldo Hahn, spent most of her life in England. She was later to help Proust with his translations of Ruskin.

2. This passage is echoed in *Jean Santeuil*, 464, where, referring to the poetry of the Vicomtesse Gaspard de Réveillon (i.e. Mme de Noailles), Proust speaks

Comte Robert de Montesquiou, in a portrait by Lucièn Doucet. Related to half the aristocracy of Europe, he was a prolific poet and society wit; Proust accepted his patronage but later dined out on his wicked imitations of Montesquiou's mannerisms.

The writer Emile Zola, shown here with his defence counsel, Maître Labori (standing), in February 1898, when Zola was prosecuted for having published his famous open letter, *'J'accuse'*, in support of Captain Dreyfus. Proust and his friends were passionate Dreyfusards

The novelist Alphonse Daudet, photographed by Nadar in 1891. Proust had close relations with the Daudet family, though he did not always agree with them politically. Daudet's elder son Léon *(below)*, remained loyal to Proust even though his own politics were far to the right.

Proust (back row, centre, with moustache) with members of the Brancovan family and others at Amphion, near Evian-les-Bains, in 1899. Prince Constantin de Brancovan is on Proust's left; his sister Hélène (Princesse Alexandre de Caraman-Chimay) is seated at the front (with lorgnon) and his sister Anna (Comtesse Mathieu de Noailles) in the second row at the right. Others are Prince Edmond de Polignac (standing, extreme left) and his wife, the former Winnaretta Singer (seated, second row centre); the writer Abel Hermant (front row, right); and Montesquiou's protégé, the young pianist Léon Delafosse (standing, extreme right).

of 'the essences of things, the memory of herself which she savoured in certain recurring scents – the odour of tangerines in a warm room, the sumptuous festivities of Christmas when we have often brought to the table a heart chockfull of thoughts about somebody who is not there, who will never be there, whose absence gives to the sundering snow without . . . a feeling that is not one so much of absence as of charm. . . .'

149
TO ANATOLE FRANCE

[2 January 1899]

Maître,

I wish you a happy New Year and good health. And, come to think of it, no year has been so fine for you as the one that has just ended. 'It was then that Alexander was given the name the Great . . .' The courage you have so nobly sung – no one has had it in higher degree than you, and the time is past when you could envy the tragic Greek for winning victories other than literary. Indeed, you have participated in public life in a manner unknown in this century, in the manner neither of Chateaubriand nor of Barrès, not to make a name for yourself but at a time when you already had one, and made it weigh in the Balance of Justice.[1] I had no need of this to admire you as a just, brave and good man. Because I loved you, I knew what you had in you. But this has shown to others things they did not know, things they admire as much as the prose of *Thaïs*, because it is just as noble, as perfectly harmonious and beautiful.

Yours,
Marcel Proust

1. A reference to Anatole France's activity in connection with the Dreyfus case.

150
TO ANATOLE FRANCE

[Soon after 1 February 1899]

Mon cher maître,

Rereading *L'Anneau d'améthyste,*[1] I am remembering a time that has remained dear to me, when *Le Lys rouge,* which had not yet been given its name, was known as 'the Novel'. 'The Novel is getting ahead,' Mme Arman would say. And then came the thing, concerning which no one knew at first whether it would have permanence and an identity and which amidst this uncertainty was spoken of as 'the piece in *L'Écho*'. Soon we were able to call it the Bergerets, the last Bergeret, the next Bergeret. It kept that name for a year until one day at a luncheon Mme Arman, who had been scolded for arriving very late, kept sufficient presence of mind to think up 'Under the Elms on the Mall'. And once again Bergeret became *L'Histoire*. I don't know if that was the case in the avenue Hoche. But I incline to think so and that it is only the past periods which come to an end with the titles *Le Mannequin d'osier* and *L'Anneau d'améthyste*. *L'Anneau* is the finest of all. And it is certain that your genius has grown unfalteringly. And what began in a jealously guarded room where no one dared speak, I am referring to M. Arman's study, as the caprice of your idle hours, is on its way to becoming the entertainment and enlightenment of the centuries. The 'piece in *L'Écho*', the 'Bergerets' have turned out to be *L'Anneau d'améthyste*, the most vast *Comédie humaine*, the most complete *Encyclopédie des mœurs du temps*, the *Mémoires* of an equitable and harmonious Saint-Simon. Could anyone have foreseen that the rarest poetic gift might some day become popular? This glory is yours. Everywhere people are citing the predictions of General Cartier de Chalmot (whom M. Forain in the original version wished to call Carré de Chalmot) concerning the Spanish-American War, and the dialogues of Guitrel and de Bonmont.[2] Vulgar memoirs have quoted the sayings of M. Bergeret, who loves the ceremonies of the cult. Your humour, like that of Molière and Cervantes, is relished by simple folk. And by the sophisticated as well.

Accept, *mon cher maître*, my respectful admiration.

Marcel Proust

1. France had sent Proust an inscribed copy of *L'Anneau d'améthyste* (The Amethyst Ring), the third part of his Bergeret chronicle, *L'Histoire contemporaine* (see letter 131), when it was published in book form on 1 February 1899. Proust had read the novel as it appeared serially in 1898 in *L'Écho de Paris*.

2. When France's character General Cartier de Chalmot is asked his view of the outcome of the Spanish-American War, he replies that the Americans, having neither army nor navy, 'have committed an act of folly which may cost them dearly'. At that moment another character reads in the newspaper of Dewey's destruction of the Spanish fleet in Manila Harbor. (*L'Anneau d'améthyste*, chapter IX.) In the same novel, the Abbé Guitrel is made a bishop thanks in part to the support of a converted Jewess, the Baronne de Bonmont.

151
TO LÉON DAUDET[1]

[Soon after 25 February 1899]
Dear friend,

I've just finished *Sébastien Gouvès*, which moved me deeply, it's an admirable book.[2] I am sure that like Tolstoy in *The Powers of Darkness* or Goethe in the [*Elective*] *Affinities*, you built your book round some little news item. But it crystallized the entire content of your intellect, which is so vast that there is no way of foreseeing what your future books will be, as one can with other writers, however great. How could *Le Voyage de Shakespeare* have enabled one to prophesy the novel that followed, or the latter this one? You speak of the scientist as having the same power of reconstruction as the poet. It seems to me that with each book you become more objective, which for you is the most sincere way of being subjective; for your thinking confronts all nature at once and to carry through all your ideas is to describe nature. I am certain that when you seem to be portraying Gouvès and Marianne, you are working with ideas which you have been carrying about with you for a long time, which have intellectual implications for you, which are part of your system, as indeed you show. But since your intellect is so vast and so natural, its creations are living creatures, and in unburdening your brain you seem to be painting from life. It is quite true, to reverse the maxim in your Epilogue, that the strongest are the most sensitive,[3] that those who hold all cities so firmly in their powerful right hand that they can show them to you in a single movement, down to 'the immense cauldron where the horrible simmers with the sublime' (how happy that would have made Balzac; even on the heights of Père Lachaise his Rastignac would not have thought of that), are also those sensitive enough to find such quiet words as 'silent before the smiling life of the waters and the ballet of the dragon-flies'. All of pages 375, 376, 377, 378, 379 are divinely beautiful. But what touches me more than the novel itself, which I prefer to *La Recherche de l'absolu*, is the mortal sadness of Marianne's poisoned happiness; that is the philosophy of all life, which I have felt so often and never seen expressed. As for Mercier, until this past year, I wouldn't have found him credible, because I absolutely did not believe in evil. Now I've had experience of it.[4] There are books which I couldn't understand and which I like now, and a good many of Balzac's, Shakespeare's and Goethe's characters. And now I am ready to understand Mercier. The basic truths carry the secondary truths with them. Accordingly, since this book is true as a psychological portrait, it is also true as a study of history. And it is not least profound when satirizing the Medical School and society. I cannot thank you enough for sending it.

Your friend
Marcel Proust

1. Léon Daudet (1868–1942), elder son of Alphonse Daudet, in 1894 abandoned medicine for journalism; he later involved himself in rightist politics, editing, with Charles Maurras, *L'Action française*. He published a number of novels.

2. Daudet's novel *Sébastien Gouvès* was published on 25 February 1899.

3. The Epilogue of *Sébastien Gouvès* is subtitled 'In which it is seen that the most sensitive are the strongest'.

4. A reference to recent revelations concerning figures in the Dreyfus case. Mercier, the villain of Daudet's book, is in no way connected with the General Mercier of the Affair.

152
TO GASTON DE CAILLAVET[1]

[Thursday 2 March 1899]
My dear, my good Gaston,

I was hoping I'd at least find you yesterday evening and since it was Wednesday I went to the avenue Hoche.[2] You had just left. Accept at least, until such time as I can give them to you by word of mouth, my very, very sincere compliments on your conduct – so fine, so perfect, so 'superb' (in the Latin sense).[3] I was retrospectively alarmed but very glad to see you comport yourself so bravely. Along with my parents' sincere compliments for what you have done, please convey to your wife the humble respects of her old admirer.

Marcel Proust

1. Mathurin-Cyprien-Auguste-Gaston Arman de Caillavet (1869–1915), son of Mme Arman de Caillavet; Proust met him at about the time of his military service. As Gaston de Caillavet he later became a successful playwright.

2. Wednesday was the 'day' of Mme Gaston de Caillavet, née Jeanne Pouquet. Out of discretion, Proust had gone to find his friend at his mother's house, in the avenue Hoche, rather than at home.

3. Deeming himself insulted by an anonymous article in *La Vie parisienne*, Caillavet had challenged the known author, Pierre Veber, to a duel. They fought with sabres on the Île de la Grande Jatte on 28 February 1899, and both were slightly wounded before their seconds stopped the fight.

153
TO GASTON DE CAILLAVET

[2 or 3 March 1899]

2nd telegram

Because I was just going to write to tell you that I went to see *Le Lys rouge* on Monday,[1] that I thought it delightful, and that I know your contribution to the great pleasure being dispensed at the Vaudeville – rather than the disappointment of a butchered novel, the agreeable surprise of a perfect play.

Marcel Proust

1. This telegram is apparently an afterthought to letter 152. *Le Lys rouge*, a play in five acts adapted by Gaston de Caillavet from Anatole France's novel, had opened at the Théâtre du Vaudeville on 25 February 1899.

154
TO ROBERT DE MONTESQUIOU

Tuesday evening [25 April 1899]

Dear Sir,

I was meaning to go and thank you for the trouble you took on my account and the honour you've done me, but a note in *Le Figaro* deprived me of the pleasure and pride I would have drawn from this honour and possibly may have fomented an incident between my family and the 'élite of the scientific world', who were alleged to have been invited,[1] and I was obliged to spend my day with Charles

Ephrussi on the one hand and Bailby on the other, looking for ways of remedying this state of affairs.[2] (In this connection, incidentally, M. Ephrussi made an amazing discovery which I'll tell you about and beside which Picquart's *petit bleu* is a trifle, in addition to being a forgery.)[3] I was expecting you when I came home this evening, but I was given a note from M. de Yturri informing me that he was ill and couldn't come. I shall try to see you tomorrow.

Your grateful admirer
Marcel Proust

1. On Monday 24 April 1899, Proust had given a literary soirée at which the actress Cora Laparcerie (1875 – 1951) read poems by the Comtesse de Noailles (see letter 171) and Anatole France, and some unpublished sonnets by Montesquiou from his forthcoming book, *Les Perles rouges* (The Red Beads; 1899). The poets in question were all present, but *Le Figaro*, in its account of the next day, while noting the presence of 'leading lights of the scientific world', failed to mention Montesquiou or his book.

2. Charles Ephrussi (1848 – 1905), one of the models for Swann, was born in Odessa and settled in Paris in 1871. A scholar and art collector, he became general editor of *La Gazette des beaux arts* in 1894. Léon Bailby (1867 – 1954) was general editor of *La Presse* until 1905, and later of *L'Intransigeant*. Thanks no doubt to theirs and Proust's efforts, *Le Figaro* printed the desired rectification, on 26 Apr. 1899.

3. The *petit bleu* (a letter sent through the Paris pneumatic post) was a torn message which led to the implication of Esterhazy in the Dreyfus case.

155
TO CLÉMENT DE MAUGNY[1]

13 July 1899

My dear Clément,

Our lives have been so affectionately mingled in these last two years that you have a kind of retrospective title to the thoughts and imaginings of my previous life, which, at least so long as we remain friends, I should not dream of questioning. It seems to me that everything that comes from me belongs to the hospitable friend whose house has been my house and whose heart has been my confidant. One often shows a photograph of oneself as a child to a friend who has made one's acquaintance later. So it is with this book,[2] which introduces you to a Marcel you did not know. Can I even say that? You have seen me in sorrow and never made me suffer by any tactless word or unkindness, and, another rare distinction, you have seen the coming and going of spells of sadness, from which those I attempted to describe in these pages will strike you as not very different. What makes us weep changes, but the tears are the same. It seems to me that close as you have been to the wellsprings of my joys and sorrows during the years when you were my confidant and friend, you must, in reading these pages, feel more keenly than would anyone else, what remains in them of storms that will never return.

God knows whether our paths will now diverge. Whatever happens, I shall preserve a pleasant memory of the travelling companion who for no reason was so generously kind, so unalterably sympathetic to sufferings which he had no good reason to understand, to states of fatigue which must have seemed hardly natural to one of his good health, and who charitably adjusted his pace to the dreary step of the companion whom he welcomed and cared for so well. At the moment of parting, affectionately hoping to be able some day to reciprocate your acts so full of delicacy, understanding and kindness, I say to you with all my heart these words in summary: thank you.

Marcel Proust

1. Vicomte, later Comte, Clément de Maugny; his father, Comte Albert de Maugny (1839 – 1918), a diplomat, owned the château of Lausenette, at Thonon, in the Haute-Savoie. The Vicomte and Proust were of an age, and met when they were in their late twenties.

2. *Les Plaisirs et les jours*, a copy of which accompanied this letter.

156
TO JOSEPH REINACH[1]

[Friday 11 ? August 1899]

Dear Sir,

I hear things are going very badly at Rennes.[2] Is it true? Have you any information? I don't dare ask leave to call for fear of disturbing you, because I'm so ill that I can seldom go out except in the evening (this evening, for instance). But I'd better not disturb you, and if you could write me a short note, I'd be very pleased to have some news.

Your admirer

Marcel Proust

Do you think Mercier's bombshell is what *Les Droits de l'Homme* says?[3]

1. Joseph Reinach (1856–1921), a member of the Chamber of Deputies, who as a publicist took an active part in the campaign to rehabilitate Dreyfus. He wrote a seven-volume history of the Affair.

2. The new trial of Dreyfus by court martial took place at Rennes from 7 August to 9 September 1899.

3. On 11 Aug. 1899 the daily *Les Droits de l'Homme* published a story under the headline 'Mercier's Bombshell' charging that the new revelations in the Dreyfus Affair promised by General Mercier – concerning B——, a woman agent of the Ministry of War through whom Generals Mercier and Boisdeffre had supposedly learnt in 1894 of the alleged visits of Dreyfus to the German Embassy – were false.

157
TO FERNAND LABORI[1]

9, boulevard Malesherbes
[15 August 1899]

Homage to the good invincible giant, with whose name, after this bloody consecration, battle and victory can now be linked in a more than figurative sense, and who no longer need envy the soldier's glorious privilege of giving his blood.

Marcel Proust

1. Fernand-Gustave-Gaston Labori (1860–1917), the lawyer who had defended Zola in the action brought against him in February 1898 for his letter 'J'accuse', and later Colonel Picquart, was now defending Dreyfus himself before the court martial at Rennes. At 6.20 A.M. on 14 August 1899, a shot was fired at Labori, injuring him slightly and prompting Proust's telegram.

158
TO HIS MOTHER

[Évian] Sunday half-past one
[10 September 1899][1]
My dear little Mama,

Half an hour after leaving you (I was already consoled) we saw the shameful verdict[2] posted at the Casino to the great joy of the entire Casino staff. Then we went to the Villa Bassaraba[3] for dinner. As I was going into Constantin's pavilion to smoke before dinner, I heard sighs. It was the little Noailles girl (the poetess) passing by, sobbing as though her heart would break, and crying out between sobs: 'How could they do such a thing? How did they dare go and tell him? What will the foreigners think and the whole world? How could they?' I was so moved by her weeping that I began to feel better towards her. The Prince de Polignac, who knows Galliffet well, says he is incapable of indelicacy in money matters.[4] – The weather has changed completely, there's quite a wind, All Saints[5] weather. It may have affected my digestion a little. But I had a good night. I shall write to Papa as soon as I finish this. I'll be going to see Maugny this afternoon but will return here for the night. Don't be too sad about the verdict. It's sad for the army, for France, and for the judges who have had the cruelty to ask an exhausted Dreyfus to make another effort to be brave. But the physical strain of having to display moral fortitude when he is already broken is the last he will have to suffer, and it is now behind him. From now on things can only go well for him, morally in respect of the world's esteem, physically in respect of his freedom, which I assume has been restored to him by now. As to the verdict itself, it will be quashed juridically. Morally it already has been. The Princesse Brancovan and everyone else for that matter, have been charming to me. – Yesterday afternoon at Coppet Mme de Polignac was so injudicious as to tell Mme d'Haussonville I was at Évian. She asked where, she wanted details, said we were very good friends (?). I fear an invitation to lunch . . . especially since, speaking of the Affair, she said to Mme de Polignac: 'Of course I understand that foreigners like you should feel that way about it.'[6] M. de Noailles wired the verdict to his sisters Mmes de Virieu and Henri de Montesquiou, and added: 'As incomprehensible as it is sad.' It's true that 'extenuating circumstances' for a traitor is unusual. But it's not incomprehensible.

On the part of the judges, it's a clear and perfidious admission of their doubts. At the hotel and in town the most absolute calm prevails. I had lunch at half-past twelve (having dined from a quarter past nine to ten o'clock, because the Brancovans stayed on, talking about the Affair, and I went to bed at that same hour). Tell Robert to keep calm. He should bear in mind that any encouragement of disorder would greatly embarrass the government, which would be obliged to punish his friends. It is preferable that Millerand should not be forced to have Jaurès arrested,[7] and that these ministers, whom despite their shortsightedness one is glad, at least on the morrow of the verdict, to see in power, should be given time to take compensatory measures.

A thousand loving kisses to my father and brother and a thousand loving kisses to you.

Marcel

1. Proust's parents, with whom he had been staying at a hotel in Évian-les-Bains, had returned to Paris the day before.

2. At 4.30 P.M. on Saturday 9 September 1899, the court martial at Rennes again found Dreyfus guilty of treason, 'with extenuating circumstances', and sentenced him to ten years at hard labour. A presidential pardon was announced ten days later.

3. The villa at Amphion, near Évian, of the Princesse Rachel Bassaraba de Brancovan, née Rachel Rallouka Mussurus (1847 – 1923); she was the mother of Prince Constantin de Brancovan, and the Princesses Anna (Comtesse Mathieu de Noailles) and Hélène (Princesse Alexandre de Caraman-Chimay).

4. General Marquis Gaston de Galliffet (1830 – 1909), appointed Minister of War on 22 June 1899, came under violent attack from both the left and the right during this revisionist phase of the Dreyfus Affair. One rumour was that Joseph Reinach had loaned the General money – which Reinach denied – in return for his putting pressure to get Picquart appointed to the Intelligence Service.

5. I.e. 1 November.

6. Mme de Polignac, née Winnaretta Singer, was the American wife of Prince Edmond de Polignac (1834 – 1901).

7. Étienne Alexandre Millerand (1859 – 1943), Socialist deputy since 1885, was now Minister of Commerce; Jean Jaurès (1859 – 1914), the Socialist leader, headed the revisionist attack in the Chamber.

159
TO HIS MOTHER

Splendide Hôtel & Grand Hôtel des Bains
Évian-les-Bains
Tuesday two o'clock [12 September 1899]
My dear little Mama,

I have just paid 10 francs 50 for *L'Union morale*,[1] a demand for payment which was sent without an envelope (not *sous enveloppe – sans enveloppe*) as if I were a criminal. Would you please drop them a line cancelling my subscription. Otherwise there's no knowing where it will end. (Unless you think it's because of the Affair, about which they've been very good, and the verdict. Well, see what you think.) –

Yesterday my successive meetings with Dr Cottet,[2] M. de Polignac and then Mme de Polignac made me (because Mme de Polignac had got lost on the road) walk a long way with no feeling of oppression. I slept so little last night that not having slept much the night before I was seized to my dismay with an uncontrollable fit of laughter in front of the Princesse Brancovan, so this morning to avoid another fumigation, etc. I took a little Trional, which was followed by a restorative sleep and really did me good, which is not always the case. Need I tell you that this was an exception and that 'we are not backsliding into medicines'. Anyway, you know I hadn't taken any for twelve days. And this morning the noise of the omnibus at half-past six was exceptional. I didn't go to the Brancovans' yesterday. (My laughing fit occurred on the road, there's no denying that the Princesse Brancovan would give anybody a laughing fit with her outlandish ways. She is a person of great kindness and moral distinction, but compared to her Mme Tirman is calm, she is a combination of nervous twitches and oriental extravagance which makes M. de Noailles smile disdainfully and say: what do you expect, she's nervous.) And in the evening I preferred to walk all alone to the Casino (where I don't set foot) and back. Now I know that the Prince de Chimay is not at the villa, mostly because of the Affair, though quite moderate he doesn't see eye to eye with the rest of the family and they would make life impossible for him. It's also because of the shooting, but I don't believe he'll bag any game that comes up to his wife.[3] – M. de Polignac told me that he (Polignac) had mounted a Boulangist campaign with Barrès and Paul Adam to try and get elected to the Chamber. He made speeches at meetings and he himself jokes very wittily about the insincerity of the attitudes he took. 'When a workman asked me if I was a socialist, I replied: my word, can you doubt it for one moment?' – I don't think I'll stir this afternoon. The weather is still rainy. Perhaps a little walk, but not too far. As for this evening, a wire from Maugny informs me that he's coming to dinner with me. I have no way of calling him off, nor can I afford to have him for dinner. I'll tell him that if ever he comes again I prefer lunch (4 and 4 = 8; 7 and 7 = 14).

I'm enclosing a letter from Poupetière. Speak to Robert about the League for the Rights of Man and *tell me his answer, that is, Abel [Desjardins]'s*. It's very urgent. Otherwise I may take advantage of the presence of M. de Kertanguy, Maugny's friend at Thonon, to see about the Insurance Company. On the other hand (I haven't given him anything for months) the situation strikes me as so serious that I think you should send him 25 francs *in your name* and tell him to expect a letter from me at Renaison (it's Renaison, Loire, M. Pierre Poupetière). You don't say anything about Mlle Bailby. I don't know when she's getting married,[4] so I don't dare write. So find out, and don't let our letters cross in the void, let them *answer* one another. Yours give me infinite pleasure. Make them shorter so as not to tire yourself. Every moment I thank you mentally for thinking of me as you do and making my life so easy, it would be so lovely if I were entirely well. I'm pretty well today. Give Papa and Robert my love. Remember me to Eugénie and the Gustaves[5] and tell them I haven't misled them about the Affair, that if Dreyfus were a traitor those hostile judges wouldn't have modified the sentence of '94, taking so many years off his prison term and making the conditions of confinement less severe – and that two of them are said to have been opposed to his rehabilitation. M. de Polignac tells me that *Le Petit Bleu* appeared in Brussels with a black border. Chevilly[6] writes that at a château near Lyons where he was staying they wanted to drink champagne or light up the place to celebrate the sentence but someone observed that it was too light to rejoice at. Have you seen Forain's caricature? In the same *Écho* there's a very upsetting piece by Lemaître, and so for that matter is Barrès's piece about the verdict,[7] which is as mediocre as the one I gave you was fine, but its apparent sincerity, its conviction, is most disheartening. If you hear any news, let me know. It seems that Chauvelot[8] is more violent than the most violent of Dreyfusards. M. Pina asked for you. I shuddered to think how you must have laid yourself open to Antoine[9] when he brought you the news. I was glad to read about Jaurès saying to a friend who wanted to discuss the sentence with him: Not a word outside, wait till we're among ourselves. I saw *La Petite République* at M. Cottet's; excellent headline, roughly: *Cowardly verdict, why extenuating circumstances.*

Mme Deslandes[10] has just been very ill and takes it as a pretext for asking me to write her a long letter.

Go back to page two of my letter. At intervals of one line you will see Polignac written three times with two different Ps (a subject, as a newspaper would say, for the graphologists and Bertillon[11]). And yet my letter is not a forged document. Apropos of Bertillon, in a game of consequences at the Brancovans' they asked for details about Bertillon (I wasn't there, it's Constantin who told me about it). Mme de Noailles answered: 'I don't know. I never shlept with him.' The husband hears it, the brother reports it. Obviously such things wouldn't happen at the Gomels' or at the elder Waru's.[12] It's true that the verdict wouldn't be greeted with sobs in those quarters.

A thousand loving kisses

Marcel

1. The *Bulletin* of Paul Desjardins's Union for Moral Action; see letter 26.

2. Dr Jules Cottet, a physician practising at Évian, was a brother of the painter Charles Cottet (1863 – 1925).

3. Prince Alexandre de Caraman-Chimay (1873 – 1951) had married in August 1898 Princesse Hélène Bassaraba de Brancovan.

4. Jeanne Bailby, sister of Léon Bailby, married Victor Dupont on 21 September 1899.

5. Eugénie had been the Prousts' chambermaid since 1890. Gustave Clin and his wife were the concierges at 9, boulevard Malesherbes.

6. Pierre de Chevilly; see letter 162.

7. *L'Écho de Paris* for 12 Sept. 1899 carried a cartoon by Forain titled 'The Affair, a tragicomedy in two years' and showing a likeness of Joseph Reinach labelled 'Portrait of the Author'. An article by Jules Lemaître in the same number expressed approval of the verdict, as did that by Maurice Barrès in *Le Journal* for 11 Sept. 1899.

8. Apparently Robert Chauvelot (1879 – 1937), later an advocate in the Appeals Court; he married into the Daudet family.

9. Antoine Bertholhomme, concierge at 102, boulevard Haussmann.

10. Madeleine Vivier-Deslandes, Baronne Deslandes (1866 – 1929), a society hostess.

11. Alphonse Bertillon (1853 – 1914), head of the 'Judiciary Identification Section' at the Prefecture of Police and chief expert at the first trial of Dreyfus in

1894. At the trial of Zola he made himself ridiculous by claiming to have 'not graphic but scientific' proof of Dreyfus's guilt.

12. Charles Gomel and Pierre Laurens de Waru were both railway officials; the wife of the latter was a sister of the Comtesse de Chevigné.

160
TO HIS MOTHER

[Évian] Friday three o'clock
[15 September 1899]

My dear little Mama,

This will be only a short note, because I've had to pay the Cottins[1] a long visit. M. Cottin who hadn't seen me for several days (because I had been gadding about quite a lot) dropped in and told me General Mercier was coming to Évian soon, laughingly, because he knows I'm not exactly in love with him. But of course I won't show my antipathy in any way, because I don't know him. Anyway, I don't know if it's true that he's expected. I'm so horrified at the way the money slips away that I don't dare go out any more. Every time I pay a visit it costs 10 to 20 francs. From that point of view the dilapidation of the *Romania*[2] is disastrous, if it's true, that is. Yesterday I went to Coudrée,[3] and so as to have less of a ride I took a carriage only from Thonon. The Bartholonis are surprised that staying so close to them on the lake this year I don't go to see them more often. The truth is that it's so dreadfully expensive. The people nearest me, seeing I don't know anybody at Évian, are the Brancovans, but even that's a long way and necessitates a carriage. What with cotton wool, *L'Union morale*, etc., the money goes fast. I'm putting on the brakes to recoup, because during the first few days I didn't keep track of what I spent. I got enough sleep last night and no noise this morning, hence no need to fumigate and no oppression at all. I can't tell you how much your letters delight and amuse me. About the hat I'll do whatever you say, but the rain has straightened the straw and it's as good as new. It would break my heart and give me no pleasure at all to spend more money on a mediocre hat. Mlle Kiki is like you. She would like me to be better dressed and says she's amazed that I can't manage it with Eppler in the house.[4] – I went to see Chevilly and his father said to me: There must be a lot of Jews at the Splendide. Seeing he's an old fool befuddled by *La Libre Parole*,[5] I thought I'd be doing his family, who detest him, a favour by not starting an argument, and I replied: I have no idea who is at the hotel, everyone keeps to himself. Even so, he adjured me to stay at Thonon next year, where the society 'is more French, not so cosmopolitan'. You understand that [young] Chevilly is sick over the verdict, he has become another Gohier or Gérault-Richard,[6] the name of Reinach is always on his lips, and the old man doesn't like it very much. I must admit that when I see what a brutal lunatic he has for a father I'm amazed that he has the courage to profess his faith. Robert de Flers has sent me a telegram, something worth keeping because of his way of adapting the telegraph to literary formulas, and worse, obliged me to send Bailby a similar telegram. Mme Cottin is a friend of Marcel Habert's mother (never mind), who said to her when he was put in jail: 'How fortunate! Now at least he won't be able to misbehave for a while.'[7] Being seen at close quarters doesn't help the Cottins' abbé. He doesn't open his mouth and he has a stupid laugh. It's true I only saw him for ten minutes, during which I did all the talking. Forgive me for my useless wire, but I was worried and afraid of seeming callous if he[8] had lost a member of his family. I must tell you, incidentally, that I wired yesterday Thursday at two o'clock and that your telegram arrived today Friday at twelve o'clock. – Could it have been mislaid or forgotten here at the hotel. . . .

I had dinner at the Brancovans' yesterday. I happened to be at the Amphion station, and from there I walked. Which meant one carriage instead of two. And a dinner at least cancels out the expense of dinner. I'm back on good terms with the Noailles. The Cottins send you their best regards.

A thousand loving kisses

Marcel

I'll send your letter to Poupetière.[9]

Forgot to tell you that I haven't once had any hay fever or that kind of thing since you left.

---

1. Henri Cottin and his wife, née Roussel, were old friends of the Prousts; Cottin, a former notary, had drawn the marriage contract of Dr Proust and his wife, in 1870.

2. The Brancovans' yacht, used to ferry guests across the lake to the Villa Bassaraba. In *Cities of the Plain* Proust speaks of 'the hosts' little yacht' which 'would sail across, before the party began, to fetch the most important guests', would serve 'as an open-air refreshment room after the party had assembled,

and would set sail again in the evening to take back those whom it had brought. A charming luxury, but so costly. . . .' (II. 795)

3. The Bartholonis' château near Sciez, ten kilometres from Thonon.

4. Eppler, gentlemen's tailor at 9, boulevard Malesherbes, where the Prousts lived. In *The Guermantes Way*, Jupien has his tailor shop in the court of the Hôtel de Guermantes, to which the Narrator's family move.

5. Comte Marius de Chevilly, probably the same one arrested with Paul Déroulède and members of the Patriots' League and the Anti-Semitic League at the time of the trial at Rennes.

6. Urbain Degoulet-Gohier, lawyer and journalist, and Alfred-Léon Gérault-Richard, deputy and editor of *La Petite République*, both ardent Dreyfusards.

7. Marcel Habert (1862 – 1936), lawyer, nationalist deputy, and member of the League of Patriots, had been sentenced to five years' banishment for his part in Déroulède's attempted *coup d'état* in February 1899.

8. Reynaldo Hahn. In a letter of 14 September Proust had written anxiously to his mother: 'Why do you say *that poor* Reynaldo? The more I think of it the less I understand these words, which refer perhaps to something I couldn't read in your yesterday's letter. I only hope it's not some disaster.'

9. See letter 159. But on 16 September Proust told his mother, 'I've made an eloquent and exacerbated résumé of your letter to Poupetière, but I haven't sent him the original because of the ironic phrase: "the always practical Poupetière". I preferred to say "the absurd Poupetière", which is stronger but less insulting.'

161
TO HIS MOTHER

Splendide Hôtel
Évian-les-Bains
Friday one o'clock [22 September 1899]

My dear little Mama,

I shall try to be brief so as not to tire myself, because I have lots of writing to do.

If my letter reaches you in time, tell me in your reply how much I should give the waiter who serves me at lunch and dinner (the pale Raphael who knows so little French and waited on you the last few days of your stay, did you give him something?). Without wishing to make a martyr of him, I must tell you that what with departures he serves lunch to no one but me. If your letter reaches me

on Sunday morning, I shall be able to take account of what you say
(even if it doesn't come until dinner time). The weather has turned
beautiful again (yesterday and today, that is, the day before we had a
deluge). Unfortunately, I still haven't had a long enough night. I've
been trying for one since I arrived. I'll give you the details of my ills
(or rather my well-being) another time. As for bedtime, I got back
from Geneva very late and went directly to say goodbye to Cottet,
who was leaving this morning, with the result that I didn't get
home until midnight. I haven't got a bandage on my wrist any more or
any pain.[1] Here's why I went to Geneva. The day before, Constantin
sent word that if the weather was fine he would be going to Coppet
with Hermant[2] by motor car (belonging to the Prince de Chimay,
who is still absent, either for the shooting or because of the Affair). It
was raining at the time. Restless night: would they, wouldn't they go?
Up at half-past seven, waiting for a message and scrutinizing the sky.
They went. To spare me exposure to the cold wind, it was arranged
that I should take the train to Geneva, where I met them. (And where
telegrams – I had received your letter too late to send one from
here – cost 2 sous [10 centimes] a word, which came to quite a sum
because the two to you were not the only ones, and they refused to let
me cross out any words. The fact is that if you try to take *one* word
out of a telegram you'll see what a muddle you get into. Try it.)
From Geneva I went to Coppet by motor car. 'Mme la Comtesse' had
gone to Geneva for lunch. But preferring Mme de Staël to Mme
d'Haussonville,[3] I was determined to visit every room in great detail. It just happened to be visitors' day. And that is probably why
they went out, because it must be a frightful bore. There were lots of
people. Besides she went to the station to pick up the Duc de Broglie.
Since she has no day, there was nothing we could do. Still by motor
car we went from Coppet to Prégny and from Prégny to Geneva. (At
Prégny Mme de Rothschild was also out.[4] I left my name on Constantin's card for Mme d'Haussonville and Mme de Rothschild.) When
we got to Geneva the weather had cooled and a wind had come up, I
thought the motor car from Geneva to Évian might bring on an attack, so I left them at Geneva, where I had dinner and took the train.
By the way, when they were trying to persuade me to ride in the
motor car with them, Constantin said I just imagined that cold air was
bad for me, because Papa told everyone there was nothing wrong
with me and my asthma was purely imaginary. I know only too well
when I'm awake in the morning here that it's quite real and I wish in
your next letter you'd say something like: 'Your father was furious
about your riding in a motor car. You know very few things are bad

for you, but that nothing is worse for your asthma than cold air.' I'm writing very badly because I'm delighted and comforted by this delicious sun. I'm on a bench writing on my knees, all warm and radiant with this good balmy air, which I'd call almost maternal if my Mama's absence didn't make me only too well aware of the difference and of the inappropriateness of the term. In the motor car everything naturally struck me as amazing,[5] and I'd like to describe every one of the chauffeur's movements to Dick, who would no doubt say: 'Why, of course.' Luckily for me I'm not Linguet or Deschamps, etc., because for them the arrival of our motor car in old Coppet and 'the terrified shades of Mme de Récamier, etc. . . .' would be a God-given theme, their variations on which I can surmise only too well. Your letter was my first news of Dreyfus's pardon (He must have said to his inflexible partisans who wanted nothing to do with a pardon: 'Dross if you will (or rather wreck, since one speaks of a physical wreck), but my dross is dear to me.' But it's in all sincerity that I say 'the poor man') (God knows that Hermann-Paul has portrayed him in a way one feels to be true, charmingly sensitive and even endowed with a sickly sort of grace) and of Guérin's arrest ('You are an arrant rogue').[6] I don't know who sent *Le Figaro* my name at the Vittas'.[7] It's either them or M. Pateck. – I regret it because it will notify my presence to the lakeshore socialites, all of whom I've avoided up to now (I've kept putting off even Mme d'Haus[sonville] and only gone because of Coppet, which I boned up on first in an idiotic but informative book by Paul Deschanel about Mmes Necker, Récamier, de Beaumont etc. . . .[8] lent me by Mme Cottin). I will make no secret to you of the fact that Dr Cottet seems to have gone quite overboard about me. *Does he spend the winter in Paris?* You realize (and I only add this stupid remark because of my mother's imagination) I say overboard in a good sense, so don't go imagining that it's an evil connection, great gods!!!!!! Which reminds me, send me some cards for me to leave on Mme Pinard (Chefdebien left long ago) and Mme Vitta. What you say about the Oulif couple stupefies me. I thought they were plaster saints and boring for that very reason. The husband is so polite as to be ridiculous and despite the best of intentions the wife is incapable of unbending. Who is this M. Gallard who came up to me the other day though he doesn't know me (it's true that I know his son a little): That gentleman is the Vicomte de Maugny, I trust? Yes, Monsieur. – The Count's son? Yes, Monsieur. – 'I know his father.' Just like that. Like Cordier.[9] And then the day before yesterday: 'You're M. Weil's nephew,' with an air of unmasking me that I didn't at all like. – Call him Jugurtha, that way you can give me a complete account of him without fear. Mme Oulif, Mme Cottin etc. exasperate me by asking me to leave my rooms, which they consider damp. Cottet doesn't think so. And incidentally he thinks I haven't got rheumatism but synovitis. – To think that I was only going to write you a line. But with you I have my 'heart on my sleeve' in a different sense, and I can't stop. If you want to tell me what to give the chambermaid, writing won't do, you must wire *immediately*. I'll know it's in reference to her. I no longer have the *slightest* pain in my wrist. But don't tell anyone, because I can use it to shirk troublesome letters. About Poupetière, I haven't time to tell you my joy. 'The great joys are mute.'

With many kisses,

Marcel

1. I.e. from his supposed rheumatism; see below.

2. The novelist and critic Abel Hermant (1862 – 1950); he wrote for *Le Temps* under the pseudonym 'Lancelot'.

3. The Baronne de Staël-Holstein, née Anne Louise Germaine Necker (1766 – 1817), lived in her family's château at Coppet during the Revolution and later when she was exiled from France by Napoleon. Comte d'Haussonville and his wife, née Pauline d'Harcourt, now owned the château; see Proust's account of this visit in his 'Salon de la Comtesse d'Haussonville' (*Le Figaro*, 4 Jan. 1904; Pléiade v. 485).

4. The Pavillon de Prégny, four kilometres from Geneva, was the property of Baron Adolphe de Rothschild (1823 – 1900) and his wife, Julie, née de Rothschild (1830 – 1907).

5. Proust described his early impressions of motor travel in an article in *Le Figaro*, 19 Nov. 1907. Cf. *Cities of the Plain*, II. 1029 ff.

6. At the behest of General Galliffet and over the opposition of President Loubet, the cabinet voted on 19 September 1899 to pardon Dreyfus. Jules Guérin, anti-Semitic agitator and editor-in-chief of *L'Anti-Juif*, was arrested on 20 September and sentenced to ten years' imprisonment. Proust is echoing Molière: 'Guenille si l'on veut . . . ma guenille m'est chère' (*Les Femmes savantes*, II. vi) and 'le pauvre homme' (*Tartuffe*, I. iv); and Victor Hugo: 'Vous êtes un fier gueux' (*Ruy Blas*, IV. viii). The painter Hermann-Paul was famous for his caricatures.

7. In spite of *Le Figaro*, Proust was not present at the wedding on 18 September 1899 of Fanny-Victorine, daughter of Baron Joseph Vitta, to the explorer Édouard Foa, at a villa near Évian; he complained to his mother in a letter of 16 September that he had not been invited: 'These affairs on the lake are charming when one is "in", but deadly when everybody else is going and only oneself isn't.'

8. *Figures de femmes. Mme Du Deffand, Mme d'Épinay, Mme Necker, Mme de Beaumont, Mme Récamier* . . . (1889). The author (1855–1922) was a future President of the French Republic.

9. Colonel Cordier, deputy chief of the Intelligence Service, an exuberant, emotional witness, was so incoherent when he appeared before the Appeals Court and the Rennes court martial that it proved impossible to obtain any 'clear and sensible' statement from him.

162

TO PIERRE DE CHEVILLY[1]

Paris, Friday [13 October 1899]

My dear Pierre,

The people at Évian have sent on a packet of letters, in which a letter from you and a postcard are distinguished by the charm of the style and at very first glance by the familiarity of the handwriting. You mustn't suppose that I'm hiding somewhere, that I've absconded or am in gaol. As I told you in my note, I left for Paris with a precipitancy to which the Brancovans can bear witness, the sort of precipitancy that, as you know, follows long hesitations which prepare the way for it. I caught cold on the way and I'm not very well. I have renewed acquaintance with the faithful and understanding Oncieu,[2] who with the prestige of an illustrious lineage (an advantage which frankly my imagination has always refused to envisage and which leaves it cold in the presence of Bossuet's tomb or the manuscript of the [Pascal's] *Pensées*), combines the delectable treat of a free and entrancing spirit. He has been kind enough to follow me about, though to be sure I lead him only to such exalted places as the Louvre and the Bibliothèque Nationale (where I have at last found, read, and loved Ruskin's *Seven Lamps of Architecture* in *La Revue générale*, between – O destiny – an article by M. Trogan and a remarkable piece by M. Bordeaux).[3] I often think of our projected lakes, the glaciers we promised ourselves, our chimerical Lombardy, and I dream of the journeys I haven't made, which is an excellent way of making them, pending the day when the law of fulfilment, which always puts our youthful projects on to the stage of life sooner or later, and which carried me to Thonon this summer, the least unlikely pilgrimage to the shores where Fabrice[4] played, is amicably put into practice by the two of us in accomplishment of an old desire, of a dream which is still a dream.

I charge you with my respects or regards, according to rank and age, for all those whose benevolent hospitality I enjoyed at Thonon, from your parents to M. de Pateck and M. Bordeaux. But I cannot resolve to include in a collective homage that unique person Mademoiselle your sister, to whom apply so adorably the lines from 'La Maison du berger' which the other day, to the lulling rhythm of the carriage (Good Lord, I owe you more than 10 francs!), I took the liberty of reciting to her on the darkening road at nightfall.[5] And I don't know whether there was more poetry in those delicious verses or in her. Also pay my respects to Mlle de Foras, and believe me, my dear Pierre, your affectionate

Marcel Proust

1. Pierre d'Humilly de Chevilly (1872 – 1948), who was in the diplomatic service. His family owned the estate of Montjoux, on the shores of Lake Geneva at Thonon.

2. Comte François d'Oncieu de la Bâtie, who was to die in November 1906 at the age of thirty-five.

3. La Revue générale (Brussels) for October 1895 had published a chapter of Ruskin's book in a French translation. Édouard Trogan (b. 1861), who was to marry a cousin of Chevilly, contributed a monthly letter from Paris to the Revue. The novelist and critic Henri Bordeaux (1870 – 1963), whom Proust seems to have met at Thonon, published two articles in the Revue in 1895: one on Pierre Loti and Paul Bourget (July – August) and one on René Bazin (December).

4. Fabrice del Dongo, hero of Stendhal's La Chartreuse de Parme.

5. Marie de Chevilly gives a charming account of Proust reciting Vigny's lines to her on this carriage ride, in 'Marcel Proust en Savoie', Bulletin de la Société des Amis de Marcel Proust et des Amis de Combray, no. 23.

163
TO MARIE NORDLINGER

Tuesday [5 December 1899]

Mademoiselle,

What a pity that you are not in Paris and what a pity that when you were we knew each other so little and that I failed to take greater advantage of the opportunity. Because letters such as the one you did me the honour of writing not so long ago inspire something more than gratitude, namely, true sympathy. And sympathy does not content itself with ideas but calls for personal contact. It is not as philosophical as you are when you say: 'I don't know if I have any living friends.' It needs friends other than books. Forgive me for seeming to contradict you. It is you who make me feel this more demanding and less easily satisfied sympathy which, aroused by your fine words and exquisite attentions, does not stop there but goes out to your person.

I have not been very happy since I had the honour of seeing you. My health, which was none too good before, has got still worse. And unfortunately my imagination, which gave me some pleasure even if it gave none to others (for you are an exception in your taste for my writing, as you are in all things), seems to have been affected by my weariness. I have been working for years on a very long-term project,[1] but without getting anywhere. And there are times when I wonder if I do not resemble Dorothea Brooke's husband in *Middlemarch* and if I am not a collector of ruins.[2] For the past fortnight I have been working on a little piece quite different from what I usually write, about Ruskin and certain cathedrals.[3] If, as I hope, I succeed in having it published in a periodical, I'll send it to you as soon as it comes out. If I had published anything else, I'd have sent it, but thus far I've only encumbered my bureau drawers.

I don't know if I've told you how much pleasure your letter has given me. That is not easy for me, because it would strike me as so ridiculous to appear to attribute what you say about my book[4] to anything other than kindness on your part and to suppose that it corresponds to reality, to a real talent in me, that I don't dare take your compliment at face value. But seeing what pleasure you have given me, perhaps when you have nothing else to do, you will take up your pen from time to time to give me news of yourself. If ever you wish for some information about a French book or a French artist, you would be doing me a great kindness to ask me, and though I am a very poor correspondent because of my poor health, which as it happens is somewhat better at the moment, but even this somewhat better is abominable, I should be very glad to write to you and being consulted would flatter my vanity!

Do remember me to your sister and believe me, Mademoiselle, your most respectfully admiring and grateful

Marcel Proust

1. I.e. *Jean Santeuil,* begun in 1895.

2. 'And now' Dorothea, having promised to devote herself to Casaubon's work, 'pictured to herself the days, and months, and years which she must spend in sorting what might be called shattered mummies, and fragments of a tradition which was itself a mosaic wrought from crushed ruins – sorting them as food for a theory which was already withered in birth like an elfin child' (George Eliot, *Middlemarch,* ch. 48). A French translation of *Middlemarch* had been published in 1890.

3. This 'little piece' of work became the essays that make up the preface to Proust's translation of Ruskin's *The Bible of Amiens;* these were published in *La Gazette des Beaux-Arts* for 1 Apr. and 1 Aug. 1900 and in *Le Mercure de France* for April 1900.

4. *Les Plaisirs et les jours.*

164
FROM ANATOLE FRANCE

[January 1900 ?]

Marcel,

Really, I can't countenance such folly. Only yesterday you brought your ailing old friend excellent syrups, much too many of them. And today you send me an admirable and extremely costly Rubens drawing. I cannot, I cannot allow this. You will make me ill with stupefaction. How can I stop you? Your letter was so good! all by itself it would have cured me. I am racking my brains for a way of putting an end to your follies. And if I still embrace you, it can only mean that I'm very fond of you.
I'm much better.[1]

Anatole France

1. France was recovering from an operation performed on him in September 1899 by Dr Pozzi.

165
TO MARIE NORDLINGER

[Shortly after 21 January 1900]
Mademoiselle,

Learning of Ruskin's death,[1] I cannot help thinking of you so intensely that I *must* write to you. Not that that was needed to make me think of you. I have been ill for some time, unable to write without difficulty and unwilling to dictate a letter addressed to you, so that all my thoughts of friendly gratitude, for your letter, for the book you sent and its precious annotations,[2] have made themselves at home within me, not in some remote recess where one visits them only rarely, but in that chamber of the heart to which one repairs several times a day. Still, when I learned of Ruskin's death, I wished to acquaint you before anyone else with my sadness, a wholesome sadness, let me say, replete with consolation, for I am shown how paltry a thing death is when I see how vigorously this dead man still lives, how I admire him, listen to him, and make a greater effort to understand him than I do a good many of the living. A month ago I should have liked to ask your advice in connection with the essays I am writing about him. But the fear of boring you, which was stupid for I know how you love these things and that one is bored only by what one does not love, stopped me and I consulted an English friend instead.[3] Since then I have often wanted to ask you about a word, a title, a meaning. But then it was not just the aforesaid fear, but my illness as well (a stupid attack of influenza, nothing serious, but it came on top of everything else), which prevented me from writing to you and obliged me to address my questions to persons close at hand, whom I could consult by word of mouth. But you have none of these excuses for not asking me (how fatuous of me to suppose I could have given you any) for pointers on French authors or for my views on life. Just imagine, when you sent me Ruskin's little book covered with your charming notes, which were like dried flowers on every page, one of them culled as it were by the two of us together, since you had delicately taken it from my book, I had just written some sentences which I've forgotten (and shall send you when they appear) about something of Ruskin's, the gist of which is more or less as follows: 'Thus he has given us pleasure after the manner of those who send us something they have long made use of for themselves with no thought of giving it away later on, and to sensitive souls these are the most precious of presents.'[4] And a moment later I receive this book bearing the marks of your personal use, so delicate a gift – and what is it but a book by Ruskin! O pre-established harmonies! –

Has Reynaldo told you about that wicked Ruskin's stipulation that his works were not to be translated into French, so that my poor translations will remain unpublished. But I shall quote long fragments in my essays.

Respectfully your grateful
Marcel Proust

1. *Le Figaro* for 21 Jan. 1900 reported: 'M. John Ruskin, the illustrious art critic, died in London yesterday of influenza at the age of eighty-one.'

2. Mlle Nordlinger had sent Proust her own copy of *The Queen of the Air* (1869), with her notes.

3. Possibly Douglas Ainslie.

4. A roughly similar sentence occurs in Proust's essay 'Ruskin à Notre-Dame d'Amiens' (*Mercure de France*, April 1900).

166

TO MARIE NORDLINGER

[7 or 8 February 1900]

Forgive me for not having thanked you before, I have had so much trouble and illness. Thank you for everything, for so many exquisite thoughts and the precious articles you sent. (If ever you send me fragments of letters or passages from Ruskin, what interests me most at the moment is what he wrote about the French cathedrals other than Amiens – apart from *The Seven Lamps of Architecture*, *The Bible of Amiens*, *Val d'Arno*, the *Lectures on Architecture and Painting*, and *Praeterita*, because I know these books by heart. But if you ever come across something in his other works, or in university dissertations on poetry or architecture or whatever – about Chartres Abbeville Rheims Rouen etc. etc., it would interest me very much. But you mustn't think I want you to search. All my essays are finished, and if in ten years you come across a line of his on these things it will interest me as much as it does now.) As for the Christian name, which comes so naturally from the heart and which it is possible to use without familiarity since 'Ave

Maria', I don't believe I ought to, but as you see I've dropped the Mademoiselle.

Believe me, yours ever,
Marcel Proust

167
TO POL-LOUIS NEVEU[1]

[14 February 1900]
Dear Sir,

It appears that my last year of leave (the fifth) has expired and that I ought to return to the Mazarine, which my health alas! does not permit. Must I tender my resignation, or is there some possible way out, renewal of my leave, postponement of my return, indefinite leave, or something else? I am only asking you for information. Because if there is such a possibility, I don't want you to take any further trouble on my account, you have taken so much already. Just tell me what can be done and I shall attend to it,[2] since I am acquainted with close friends of the Minister.

Your devoted
Marcel Proust

Could you possibly let me know whether the nurse Mme Chivot[3] has been awarded the academic palms?

1. Pol-Louis Neveu (1865 – 1939), former librarian, had since 1898 been chief assistant in the Ministry of Education and Fine Arts, the government department responsible for the Mazarine Library.

2. On 1 March 1900 Proust was considered to have resigned the post as librarian which he had been awarded in 1895.

3. Possibly the widow of the playwright Henri Chivot (1830 – 97), on whose behalf Proust made other enquiries.

168
TO MARIE NORDLINGER

[Early March 1900]

I am more touched than I can say by your kindness to me. But from now on I do not permit you to send me so much as *one* newspaper article. Much as I value the references you give me, which enable me to obtain them, it distresses me to receive all these things which would give me far more pleasure if I rather than you had gone to the trouble of obtaining them. Accordingly, if from now on you send me anything other than such references, it will be disobedience, a word which, believe me, implies no pretension on my part, but only a belief in the rights of a reciprocal authority which two persons who are in sympathy confer upon each other. Your verses are charming and evoke in my memory the delicious bouquet of spring flowers you once brought me from an excursion you went on, such as my hay fever would have prevented me from taking. But you are a poet and have no need of going to the country to bring back flowers. Don't complain of not having *learned*. Strictly speaking, no knowledge is involved, for there is none outside the mysterious associations effected by our memory and the tact which our invention acquires in its approach to words. Knowledge, in the sense of something which exists ready-made outside us and which we can learn as in the Sciences – is meaningless in art.[1] On the contrary, it is only when the scientific relationships between words have vanished from our minds and they have taken on a life in which the chemical elements are forgotten in a new individuality, that technique, the tact which knows their repugnances, flatters their desires, knows their beauty, plays on their forms, matches their affinities, can begin. And that can happen only when a human being is a human being and ceases to be so much carbon, so much phosphorus, etc. Victor Hugo, whose *Shakespeare* I fear I do not like, says

'For know that the word is a living being.'[2]

You know. And consequently you love words, you don't harm them, you play with them, you entrust your secrets to them, you teach them to paint, you teach them to sing. And your horror of Yellow is an exquisite 'Symphony in Yellow'; God seems to have given you a sample of everything yellow he possesses, from the flowers of the field to the light of the firmament. It would not be possible to write that in painting and you have painted it in writing. –

You speak of Ruskin's *Poetry of Architecture*[3] – tell me, is there anything in it about cathedrals? Which ones? And these works you mention – do they speak even incidentally of cathedrals? Do you know anything about an essay of Ruskin's on flamboyant architecture on the banks of the Somme?[4] –

In another letter I'll tell you about Julien Édouard, whom I saw a month ago. But he shows only Saint-Ouen and not the cathedral. What did he say to you about Ruskin? He claims Ruskin told him Saint-Ouen was the most beautiful Gothic monument in the world, but in the *Seven Lamps* Ruskin calls it frightful![5]

Your respectful friend,

Marcel Proust

1. Cf. *Within a Budding Grove* (1. 896): 'Although it is rightly said that there can be no progress, no discovery in art, but only in the sciences, and that each artist starting afresh on an individual effort cannot be either helped or hindered therein by the efforts of any other, it must none the less be acknowledged that, in so far as art brings out certain laws, once an industry has taken those laws and popularized them, the art that was first in the field loses retrospectively a little of its originality. . . .' Towards the end of the novel the Narrator comes back to this question and frames his mature judgement (*Time Regained*, III. 945).

2. 'Car le mot qu'on le sache est un être vivant' (*Les Contemplations*, Bk. I, ch. viii).

3. *The Poetry of Architecture: Giotto and His Work in Padua;* Proust saw Giotto's frescoes for himself when he visited Padua in May 1900, while he and his mother, as well as Mlle Nordlinger, were staying in Venice.

4. 'The Flamboyant Architecture of the Valley of the Somme', a lecture delivered on 29 January 1868 at the Royal Institution.

5. On a visit to Rouen in February 1900, Proust was shown round the church of Saint-Ouen by the verger, Julien Édouard. That Ruskin had changed his mind about Saint-Ouen since 1849 is evidenced by his very severe criticism of the church in Appendix II of *The Seven Lamps of Architecture* (1880 edn.); apparently Proust had even read the appendices.

169
TO CONSTANTIN DE BRANCOVAN

[31 January? 1901]
Dear friend,

I don't dare suppose the brain waves they speak of at the New Institute of Psychology, which can traverse space to attain the object that motivated their dispatch,[1] are real enough for me to credit them with letting you know that I have been down with the grippe since New Year's Day and waiting for a day of good health to tell you how sad your absence makes me and how grateful I am for the affectionate reminder with which you have been kind enough to comfort and console me. Anyone who knows the meaning of friendship would appreciate your kindness. But if you bear in mind that constantly ill, bereft of pleasures, aim, activity, and ambition, fully aware that my life is behind me, knowing the sorrow I bring on my parents, I have very little joy, you will understand what great importance feelings of friendship can take on for me, what sympathy a heart detached from so much else must feel for my friends and how grateful I am to those who like you respond to it with marks of delicate kindness and affection. Thank you with all my heart. Your fine letter was of the greatest interest to me. I take the keenest interest in life plans, being so very much in need of a plan for mine, and even though a few passages are somewhat obscure, not as to thought or style but as to handwriting, and will need clarification which I shall ask of you on your return, everything you say about your 'Vita Nuova' made a deep impression on me and I have often thought of it since. Your New Year's telegram gave me enormous pleasure. I shall never forget the moment when I received it. I felt the physical presence of friendship.

Now, dear friend, I shall express no wishes with regard to you, either for your return or for anything else. My friends' aims are theirs and not mine, and I wish them what they wish, not what I would wish if my desire for their happiness and respect for their destiny were less profound. If Romania is favourable soil, where you can bear richer fruit, stay there, dear friend, as long as necessary.[2] I would make the sacrifice of saying: Stay there for good if you think it best. We owe nothing except to that element of the eternal which is in us, and it is our duty to manipulate ephemeral circumstances only in so far as they can contribute to it most effectively. If nevertheless a bit of Paris seems to you (yours alone to judge, and I believe you have so judged) compatible with the accomplishment of your supernatural duty, no one will be happier than I to see you again and avail myself of your leisure hours for good talks.

With all my heart, your friend

Marcel Proust

1. The Institut Psychologique International was inaugurated on 30 January 1901 at a meeting at which Émile Duclaux, eminent chemist and head of the Pasteur Institute, said: 'If we admit that an instrument – a metallic ear – installed at Versailles, can perceive and register waves coming from Paris, why not admit that an individual with human ears can similarly perceive and register other waves directed towards him by another person?' (*Le Figaro*, 31 Jan. 1901)

2. *Le Figaro* for 25 Dec. 1900 reported that Prince Bassaraba de Brancovan was in Bucharest; *Le Gaulois* for 13 Mar. 1901 noted his return to Paris.

170

TO LÉON YEATMAN

[April 1901]

Dear Léon,

Forgive me for not replying. Went out at a quarter to six (your telegram had not yet arrived), did not come home for dinner, returned only at midnight, found it then and am writing instantly. You take a dreadfully ironic view of the exquisite engaged couple[1] whom you yourself brought together (when will you marry me off?), though I can hear the bride-to-be (who is actually charming) daily lecturing her husband in the words of *L'École des femmes:*

'I've married you, Octave, and you must bless
The star that lit your way to happiness.
Think of your former mediocrity
And marvel at my magnanimity
Which from a lawyer's helper's low estate
Has raised you to the feudal marquisate
With title to the couch and fond affections
Of an angel, who, scorning fortune and connections,
To scores of brilliant catches long denied
The honour she did you in becoming your bride.
Never, dear fellow, cease to bear in mind
How small you were before our knot was joined.

etc., etc.'[2]

Submit to your wife[3] the aptness of this quotation and then deliver this sacrilegious letter to the flames and oblivion.

Affectionately yours
Marcel Proust

1. *Le Figaro* for 23 Apr. 1901 announced the engagement of Mlle Eugénie (Kiki) Bartholoni, god-daughter of the Empress Eugénie, to Octave Deschamps.

2. After Molière, *L'École des femmes*, III. ii, with 'Octave' replacing 'Agnès' and various other changes to suit the circumstances.

3. Mme Yeatman, née Madeleine Adam (1873 – 1955).

171
TO MADAME DE NOAILLES[1]

Wednesday half-past midnight
[1 ? May 1901]
Madame,

I was awaiting your poems with the anxious certainty of one who knows he will have new beauty to admire. I was as sure of that as the prince in the fairy tale, for whom the bees who worked and made the rose bushes bloom, was sure of having honey and roses. For a gifted nature, like nature itself, has its infallibility. And what springs from your brain will always be precious, just as the scent of hawthorn blossoms will always be delicate. Only this was not a tranquil certainty, for these certain miracles which poetic souls perform in accordance with the laws of instinct have about them all the unforeseen character of thought and feeling, since they initiate us into a secret that is at every moment new, a unique reality that will never recur, so that, though only a rose resembles a rose, one poem does not resemble another. I was sure of having one as good as the last, but I was looking forward to something new. And in neither expectation was I disappointed. I read them only a moment ago, for I have just come back from seeing M. de Montesquiou. I was going out when they were delivered and I barely had time to look at them (need I say that I did not mention them to him, since you asked me not to show them to anyone). And I have just put them in an envelope for Mlle Laparcerie.[2] But even so I have seen any number of things I felt sure of loving most particularly, a certain mode of expression, an air of kinship, or rather the air of a person one is delighted to meet again in a poet one prefers to other poets. The Pigeons whose whiteness walks in procession, The Sunlit Road without shadow or bend, the swans dancing in the wind, the intimate land of my tenderness, and the admirable familiarity with which you speak to nature and the infinite, 'the moon with the lovely cheeks', and to Conscience, 'My dear old friend'.[3]

Madame, I don't know how to thank you and I suffer to think how ridiculously diminished these infinite things will be in inhospitable minds.

I thank you for letting these verses alight for an evening like those pigeons which walk in procession this evening but which once stopped to rest at the edge of your sandals.[4] Then they will resume their flight, that will not be interrupted again.

I got home so late from M. de Montesquiou's that here it is one o'clock in the morning. I still have a thousand things to say to you, as Coppée said in a famous line. In particular, that Mlle Laparcerie is going to give you an appointment.

Forgive me for writing at such length and so badly, befuddled as I am by these tedious preparations and by prolonged conversation with so brilliant a conversationalist as Montesquiou. No matter, it's wrong to be sad over the things one hasn't got. True, they usually come when one has ceased to desire them. This at least will not have been the case with your poems, I shall have known them while I still loved them. Two years ago I knew only two lines of yours:

> *But what matters it to the summer, drunk with flowering,*
> *If the dust of the roses irks the winter,*[5]

I asked everyone who might have remembered others, do you know of any, for in hearing those two lines I felt the awakening of a new literary passion which I did not know how to satisfy, comparable to the first time I saw a Gustave Moreau or heard a melody by Fauré (I mention these because they were passions and not for their value, that can be questioned). At that time I did not suspect that an evening would come when instead of two lines I would receive two poems, reworked as it were for me, written in the poet's hand. These are poetic compensations for destiny, the accomplishment of a cherished intellectual wish.

Most respectfully your admirer, Madame,

Marcel Proust

1. Comtesse Mathieu de Noailles, née Princesse Anna-Elisabeth Bassaraba de Brancovan (1876 – 1933), poet and novelist.

2. Mme de Noailles had given Proust two poems from her forthcoming book, asking him not to show them to anyone before forwarding them to Mlle Laparcerie, who was to read them at a soirée Proust was giving later that month.

3. The phrases quoted are all from Mme de Noailles's two poems 'La Conscience' and 'Paroles à la lune', to be included in *Le Cœur innombrable* (Unbounded Heart; 1901).

4. '. . . comme deux pigeons / Posés légèrement au bord de mes sandales', from 'Offrande' (Offering), a poem by Mme de Noailles which had appeared in *La Revue de Paris* for 1 Feb. 1899.

5. 'Mais qu'importe aux étés ivres d'éclosion / Ce que pèse à l'hiver la poussière des roses', from 'Notre Amour' (*La Revue de Paris*, 1 Feb. 1899).

172
TO MADAME DE NOAILLES

Tuesday evening [7 May ? 1901]

Madame,

Many thanks for your letter. To my great pleasure, my eye lit at once on that splendid word 'anger', which took on a new lustre for me when I saw it standing so proudly in 'Conscience'.[1] To tell the truth I had feared that it was in some degree the sin of anger, anger at a less than perfect reciter, which had deprived me of the mysterious pleasure I had been anticipating with delight for several days, the pleasure of seeing you listen to your poetry. But then I learned that this was not so and M. de Noailles told me you were really ill in a tone 'that brooked no reply' and admitted of no doubt. It made me very sad to think of your being ill just then. But one must not rail too much at illness. Often it is under the burden of too great a soul that the body gives way. Nervous states and enchanting poems may very well be inseparable manifestations of one and the same tempestuous power.[2] The spring manifests itself to us no less in mosquito bites than in the smell of roses.

It was very kind of M. de Noailles (with whom, it seems to me, I have hardly made 'a hit') to come without you in spite of everything, to leave you. True, he was reunited with you in my salon, or perhaps he can never be reunited with you since, seeming as he does to be always thinking of you, he never leaves you. Here I would add some beautiful lines of Vigny, which would apply perfectly to you and to him, were it not rather late to be writing such a long letter. In a day or two I shall pay you the visit you did not pay me yesterday evening,[3] beg your pardon once more for the trouble you took for my sake in coming to rehearse with Mlle Laparcerie, and pay you my humble respects.

Marcel Proust

I'm sorry you didn't hear M. France speak of your poems and the enthusiastic remarks of all my friends. There were accents which would have touched you and 'that voice of the heart which alone can reach the heart'.[4] Hervieu[5] didn't come, but he wrote me a note with words of great admiration for you. – Gregh didn't come. I hope you didn't forget to invite him.

1. 'Et j'ai guéri pour vous mon âme violente / Du péché de colère et du péché d'orgueil', from Mme de Noailles's poem 'La Conscience' (see letter 171).

2. Proust would develop this idea in *The Guermantes Way* at the time of the Narrator's grandmother's illness and the consultation with Dr du Boulbon.

3. The soirée which Mme de Noailles failed to attend was to mark the publication, on 7 May 1901, of *Le Cœur innombrable*, her first book of poems.

4. Cf. Musset, 'À la Malibran'.

5. Paul Hervieu (1857 – 1915), dramatist and novelist.

173
TO MADAME ALPHONSE DAUDET

[Saturday 18 May 1901]

Madame,

As in those oriental tales of an awakened sleeper, in which the humblest inhabitant of the city sees the queen most graciously bestowing gifts upon him, you, with a kindness that never stops halfway, amuse yourself reversing roles, twice inviting me to one of those festive gatherings to which by rights I should be admitted only after prolonged supplication which in the end you would perhaps deign to hear. And now, to offer me a pleasure as great as it is undeserved, you carry charity, paradox and graciousness to the point of seeming to be asking a favour of me. A pity that I am not one of those whom the kindness of others render fatuous enough to suppose that it is their due and who find it only natural to be showered with gifts. Alas, I belong to another species. The kindness of a person like you does not magnify me in my own eyes but magnifies that person more than ever. The distance is further increased rather than diminished. And, at that degree of excess and intensity, the feeling of never being able to prove one's gratitude gives it a sad, almost oppressive quality. As for the dinner itself, you will understand why I have not attended – or rather partaken, for it's no consideration of diet that deprives me of the pleasure and Lucien has told me frankly that he has often been 'repelled' by my voracity – when I tell you the next day, since this painful confession is imposed upon me by your infinite kindness, why on the previous evening – the 23rd – I didn't come until after dinner. There is nothing very interesting about my secret and having to reveal it is for me most humiliating. But I should be too unhappy if you were to think it a mere caprice. You will know on the 24th why I couldn't tell you on the 23rd. What complications I seem to be creating and how important I seem to be making myself! Don't you believe it, Madame.

Believe only in the profound and infinite gratitude of your respectful servant and admirer

Marcel Proust

174
TO MADAME DE NOAILLES

Monday evening [27 May 1901]

Madame,

You hadn't come home yet when I phoned you at eleven o'clock and again at 11.10. If I took the liberty of asking for you, it was because I received from Brussels (where he is with Sarah Bernhardt) (*confidential*) a letter from Reynaldo Hahn, who tells me this. He took *Le Cœur innombrable* away with him, he is wild about it and read it to Sarah. She was enthusiastic, thinks you are the greatest of poets, a great genius etc., immediately memorized the 'Offering to Pan' and is going to recite it on Thursday at M. de Montesquiou's.[1] Reynaldo's letter is so full of mysteries I think this must be a secret at the very least and I should be much obliged if you would not repeat it to anyone except

to the Princesse de Chimay
fairer than the month of May

if that would give you an opportunity to tell her I love her madly and would move her to indulgence. Sarah Bernhardt may have notified Montesquiou, who may in turn have informed you, in which case I may be meddling to no purpose. Still, I thought it better to tell you, in case you had anything to say, etc. etc.

I beg you not to suppose that I tell you of this event in the belief that it should fill you with pride! You understand of course that I shall always regard such things merely as flowers in your path to set your feet upon. But I am resolved, resigned and reduced to the role of herald and messenger. In short, I hope I haven't put my foot in it.

Can you imagine, I've finally, either in the Bois or in your book, contracted my hay fever, for twenty-four hours I haven't been able to breathe and I'm suffering terribly. I shall take every medicine that has ever been invented in the hope of being present on Thursday, but I'm useless before nine in the evening and not much better after that. I wouldn't want the Princesse de Chimay or you to witness one of my cacochymic wheezing fits.

I send you a thousand respectful thoughts, and my best regards to Mathieu.

Yours,
Marcel Proust

You're not going to Madeleine Lemaire's tomorrow evening? Wouldn't you like me to announce you?

1. 'Sarah delighted with Mme de Noailles's book, which I brought her,' Hahn had noted in his diary for 23 May 1901 (Reynaldo Hahn, *La Grande Sarah* [1929], 169–70). *Le Gaulois* for 31 May 1901 reported that the programme at Comte de Montesquiou's 'Pavillon des Muses' at Neuilly the previous day had included ' "Offrande à la Nature" (Comtesse de Noailles) recited by Mme Sarah Bernhardt'. (*Le Gaulois* and *Le Figaro* both noted the presence of Mme Proust at the occasion.)

175
TO ANTOINE BIBESCO[1]

[August – early September 1901]

Alas, it's impossible, and I very much regret it. – If you change your mind, I shall be at home until midnight. – Yes, I'm quite sure I shall be able to see you on Wednesday at that time.

As for the cathedrals which I used, in days of better health, to visit each in its distant, sacred place, might they not one evening, in touching concert, now that the friend who loved them can no longer go to see them, appear in the guise of your precious photographs to return the visit I paid them so often. That, I believe, might almost serve as the theme of a story, which one would represent as 'an old French legend', then it may catch the fancy of our 'aesthetes'. But even for so formidable and charming a titan as you, it would be an enormous labour to carry all those tympanums, to move those architraves, to haul so many towers. Don't do it, my dear friend. But soon, if I'm better, before returning to Amiens,[2] Rheims, Chartres, I shall go and see the cathedrals at your place, where your thoughts will surround them with poetry enough. And it will give me pleasure to associate poetry with friendship. – *Aegri somnia*.[3]

M.P.

I adore the Princesse de Chimay.

1. Prince Antoine Bibesco (1878 – 1951), Romanian diplomat and playwright; in 1901 he was attached to the Romanian legation in Paris. He and his brother, Prince Emmanuel (see letter 202), were first cousins of the younger Brancovans.

2. Proust did indeed go to Amiens, with Léon Yeatman, on 7 September 1901.

3. It is said that M. Darlu, having read the first papers written for his philosophy class and identified the best one, Proust's, commented: 'The conceptions of a diseased brain, *aegri somnia*' – a sick man's nightmares (Horace, *Ars Poetica*, II. 7) (F. Gregh, *Mon Amitié avec Marcel Proust* [1958], 25).

176
TO ANTOINE BIBESCO

[August – September ? 1901]

My dear friend (?)

If the Brancovans have not ruined me for ever in your esteem, would you consent to a *closing session* at which I might finally see your cathedrals – those exactly appropriate symbols of your mind which, grave in respect of ideas and sarcastic in respect of men, discovers no doubt in their quatrefoils some part of its devotion to the former and its irony towards the latter, contains like their choirs treasures and images, and raises its ardent scrutiny heavenwards with an impulse whose elevation I have not yet measured exactly but whose numerous concerted streams I admire for their power, their faith and their multiple orientations.

But this time it's your cathedrals, your photographs that I want to see. My *Carne des Heures,* as one of my enemies titles his articles,[1] has changed. Now I get up at about two or three o'clock, dine at about four, and if I haven't gone to Versailles or somewhere else when your answer comes, if you write, I shall be able to call at whatever time you prefer, and just as willingly in the daytime. Maybe we won't recognize each other, having seen each other only by night.

Yours ever,
Marcel Proust

1. Albert Flament wrote a column for *La Presse* entitled *Carnet des Heures* (Book of Hours).

177
TO HIS MOTHER

Saturday [evening 31 August 1901]

My dear little Mama,

'Misery of miseries or mystery of mysteries?' That's the title of a chapter in Dumas, which could apply to me at the present time. After writing to you yesterday, I was taken with uninterrupted asthma and flux, obliging me to walk doubled over, to stop in at every tobacconist's and light [anti-asthma] cigarettes, etc. And the worst of it is, I went to bed at midnight after long fumigations, and three or four hours later came the real summer attack, something quite unprecedented. That had never happened before, outside of my regular attacks. – My asthma has been much better today, I've had just a little this evening (it's half-past seven now), but nothing to speak of, I haven't even had to smoke. If it recurs in the next few nights, I shall have to give up my schedule for a while, because my attacks come in the middle of the night, when there's no one to light my candle or to make me something hot when it's over. It's not Peking any more, it's Fashoda, Marchand obliged to evacuate against his will.[1] But I don't believe this will happen, and I think I shall have good nights again. Obviously I don't attribute these incomprehensible attacks to my new life. They must have a definite cause, but I don't know what it is. It's not the Bois, because I'd given it up and just gone driving with Roche. I thought there might be some odour in his cab, but I won't have him after tomorrow, so we'll see. Marie thought it might be the saffron she uses for your jabots, etc., but I doubt it. And I wondered while reading a page of Brissaud if I didn't have helminths like M. Homais.[2] I wanted to ask [Dr] Bize for advice. But he didn't answer the telephone. Actually I'm fine this evening. At about half-past two in spite of all that, I had a meal consisting of two steaks, which I didn't leave a scrap of, a dish of fried potatoes (about twenty times as much as Félicie used to make), a portion of *fromage à la crème*, a piece of Swiss cheese, two croissants, a bottle of Pousset beer (I don't believe beer can give one albumen?).[3]

I wanted to stay home afterwards to rest. But the Princesse de Polignac had sent word, asking me to go and see her at half-past six, and seeing I wasn't shaved I went out at about five, so as not to be rushed. She made me think of you, my poor little Mama, at Auteuil, wearing yourself out sitting up at night with me, when she told me about the nights she had spent with her husband and how they talked about Mark Twain at three in the morning.[4] She wanted to engage an English nurse to take care of him, but the woman got on his nerves and he kept sending her away, so there was nothing she could do but take her place. All Englishwomen looked alike to him, so when he saw the nurse with her little white collar, etc., he'd say to his wife: 'I have nothing to say to the Princess of Wales at three o'clock in the morning.' She told me that when she married him all those of his relations whom he called 'the red-faced louts', the ones who didn't understand him, had told her she was marrying an unbearable crank – but that on the contrary she had never known anyone so easy to get on with, because he was so afraid of inconveniencing anybody. Her free-and-easy American ways upset him. He had reserved rooms in Amsterdam (because when he stayed in a hotel he made a note of the room numbers and their exposure, to be sure of having the same ones next time), so when he fell sick, she said: I must wire Amsterdam to tell them you won't want the rooms. To which he replied: 'Oh yes, of course, you want to make me look like a flibbertigibbet. They'll think I had no intention of taking those rooms.' And he had worn himself out writing eight pages to the manager of the hotel. – My slight oppression has passed completely in the course of this talk with you, my dear little Mama, because of the affectionate need I felt for you. I shall have a good night and shall probably spend the first days of the week in the country somewhere. Let me know how full or empty the hotel is.[5]

Will you go back to Évian for a few days (Mme de Chimay will be there, so I hear from Mme de Polignac). I thought Maugny's letter idiotic, exactly the kind of letter one shouldn't write. I think it's more likely from Mme Paraf than from my Fame that M. Richelot[6] learned my Christian name. Tell me if André Michel has written a second piece about Amiens.[7] I've seen M. Barrère[8] passing by and he does not look like St Francis of Assisi. Thank Dick for his affection, which was returned to him in advance.

With many kisses,

Marcel

You had better send some money (though I still have some) in case I go away. I shall have spent about 200 francs in three weeks. I know you left me 300, but you know that 40 francs were committed in advance, then I gave Félicie 40 francs and spent a *louis* [20 francs] at various theatres, which I will explain.

Don't blame my hay fever on constipation, because on the contrary, as a result of my oppression or perhaps of something else, my bowels have been loose. As for milk, I seldom take any now, and anyway I was taking less than before because of cutting out *café au lait* and soup. I drink just a little cold.

1. In 1900 the European colony in Peking had successfully resisted Chinese attack, but in 1898 the French troops under Marchand, who had occupied Fashoda (now Kodok), on the Upper Nile, were obliged to retire under orders from the French government.

2. Roche was a coachman with a closed carriage. Saffron was used in laundering lace, to which it gave a delicate yellow tinge. Dr Brissaud, in his *L'Hygiène des asthmatiques* (see letter 107), speaks of 'verminous asthma'; helminths are intestinal worms. M. Homais is the pharmacist in Flaubert's *Madame Bovary*.

3. Proust was to worry for years about albumen. In *The Guermantes Way*, when the Narrator's grandmother tells Dr du Boulbon that she has a little albumen, he replies: 'You ought not to know anything about that' (II. 313).

4. Prince Edmond de Polignac had died on 8 August 1901.

5. Mme Proust was in Switzerland, staying at Zermatt.

6. Dr Gustave Richelot (1844 – 1924), professor of medicine and a colleague of Dr Adrien Proust.

7. The art critic André Michel (1853 – 1925) published two articles on Amiens cathedral in the *Journal des débats* for 13 Aug. and 10 Sept. 1901. In the second of these he alluded to Proust's essay 'Ruskin à Notre-Dame d'Amiens' (*Mercure de France*, April 1900), but only to remark that some people went to

Amiens not so much to admire or study the cathedral as to perform a pious 'Ruskinian pilgrimage'. When Proust published his translation of *The Bible of Amiens* he appended a note to his preface replying to Michel.

8. Camille Barrère (1851 – 1940), French ambassador to Italy 1897 – 1925; it is thought that some of his traits went into Proust's portrait of the Marquis de Norpois.

178
TO ANTOINE BIBESCO

Friday [8 November 1901]
Dear friend,

Thank you for your kind note, I hope it answered a desire on your part, but if its intention was only to satisfy a desire you supposed I had, that in itself would show it was written by a friend. In Pascal and La Bruyère, with whom I have been assuaging my regrets this evening, I keep coming across this very word 'friend', and, what's more, taken more or less in the sense of 'one of the two' or of 'intercessor'. La Bruyère says:

'A man of standing should incline towards . . . persons of intelligence. . . . He should adopt them . . . he cannot requite the help and services he derives from them, even without knowing it, with I shall not say too many benefits but with too many caresses (Salaïst).[1] How much malicious gossip they dissipate (but are you reading me at least, Bibesco, because, if you're not, why should I wear myself out copying this wonderful passage), what calumnies they reduce to fable and fiction (it's too long, I'll skip the best part) . . . in order to avail themselves of every possible occasion to disseminate advantageous fictions and details and to turn the laughter and mockery against those who have advanced opinions to the contrary, etc. etc.'[2]

And Pascal, more succinct and stronger (I am amazed to find him so well informed about what goes on at Mme de Saint-Victor's):[3]

'A friend is so advantageous a thing even for the greatest nobles, to speak well of them and uphold them even in their absence (*even* is brilliant) that they should do everything in their power to have some. But let them choose with care, for if they expend their efforts on fools, it will do them no good, etc., even if they (the fools) speak well of them. And in truth they will not speak well of them if they are the weaker. For lacking authority (sublime), they will slander in droves (1901).'[4]

I would like (it is no longer Pascal speaking, and alas there was no need of telling you so) to have the kind of intelligence that would serve you with others, but you are not utilitarian and I am not useful. You were odious yesterday evening, dear Telephas,[5] you sank. But before that you had found the way to my heart. And so, like a person one has gone to see for the first time, I say to you: 'Now that you know the way, I hope you'll come again.' This conclusion to a sentimental 'tour of the premises' is crude enough to give the Paris public an illusion of great psychological subtlety. Perhaps you could put it into *La Lutte* if you're short of a speech, just as they grafted on to the divine countenance of Demarsy the skin of an inferior being's posterior.[6] And the over-all effect was one of seemliness – or as the Venetians built their basilica, grafting on to their own work pieces brought back from countries they had loved.

Dear friend, enough of letters (I am referring to my letters, which are letters, you never send me anything but messages, which might just as well be telephoned). All this is too much bother about friendship, which is a thing without reality. Renan tells us to shun individual friendships. Emerson says we should change our friends as we go along. It's true that equally great men have said the contrary. But in a way I'm sick of insincerity and of friendship, which is almost the same thing. And speaking as an old coquette of intellectual friendship (a Salaïst), I remember what M. Darlu, my philosophy professor, once said to me: 'Another new friend. What number did you give him when he entered the door of your heart.' Goodbye, dear friend, very much *yours*,[7] since this absurd Anglo-French formula appeals to you.

Marcel Proust

1. A private word derived from the surname Sala (see letter 187) and meaning someone suspected of sexual deviation.

2. Quoted freely from La Bruyère, *Les Caractères ou les mœurs de ce siècle*.

3. Mme de Saint-Victor, daughter of the critic Paul de Saint-Victor, took a passionate interest in political events, and seems to have had a Dreyfusard salon.

4. Pascal, *Pensées*, no. 155; the quotation is not quite accurate.

5. From the Greek, meaning 'he who talks from far away'; Bibesco had a fondness for the telephone.

6. Bibesco's play *La Lutte* (The Struggle) was never produced. The ravishingly beautiful actress Jane Demarsy (real name Anne Darlaud) had made her

début as Venus in Offenbach's *Orphée aux Enfers;* she was the model for
Manet's *Le Printemps,* now in the Metropolitan Museum.

7. In English in the original.

179

TO ANTOINE BIBESCO

[Monday evening 11 November 1901]

Dear friend,

On leaving you I learned that Reynaldo's concierge had come
to tell me he was returning tomorrow (that is, today 'when you will
have this note') (theatre style). Since Haras is performing in a play of
hers the day after tomorrow[1] I ought to have guessed as much. It occurred to me at once that Reynaldo's first call would be paid to Haras
and his second to me. If so, I might by tomorrow evening be in possession of some of Haras's impressions of *La Lutte* (perhaps not). I'm
telling you this to enable you to make an appointment with me for tomorrow evening if you wish to. But bear in mind that Reynaldo may
not have been able to see Haras or may not have seen her alone or that
she may not have spoken to him about *La Lutte.* Be that as it may, I'm
writing to you just in case.

We must have a short frank talk. It will simplify, I won't say
the future of our existence, but the future of that portion of our existence over which will be distributed (whatever the extent, I won't
say of its duration, but of its scope, what gibberish) what it may not
be presumptuous of me to call our friendship. (I'm getting into your
habit of calling women by their Christian names. 'Joanne de Billy' was
perfect. There's something documentary and familiar about it that
reminds me somewhat of Lisotte.) And then we shall have to go into a
few particulars about relations with Reynaldo, who will be informed
as soon as he gets here of the importance assumed in the life of the
moschant by a certain person residing at No. 69 of the same street,[2]
who before his departure played only a subordinate, though picturesque, role (theatre style). I must warn you that tomorrow I shall not
be up before five in the afternoon (and perhaps a good deal later) and
consequently shall not be visible in the daytime or not until very late.
I hope this serious talk won't annoy you. It will be very useful. Your
kindness is my excuse for the importunities which my sincerity im-
poses on me as a duty. As for Salaïsm, aren't you enough of a psychol-

ogist, seeing me as much as you do, to realize that it interests me in the same way as Gothic, though much less, and that in the reality of my life, in myself, in my friendships, etc. (you have one before your eyes) it is as absent as. I can think of nothing as absent. Anyway I don't really care what you think on the subject, since you yourself say that you attach no importance to it.

> *[No signature]*

P.S.   If you like, I'll give you a lesson in 'moschant' language so you can surprise and charm Reynaldo.

1. Haras = Sarah, i.e. Sarah Bernhardt (1844 – 1923), whose one-act play *L'Aveu* (The Confession) was to be performed at the Théâtre Sarah Bernhardt at a matinée, not on the following Thursday but on 12 December 1901.

2. The Princesse Alexandre Bibesco, mother of Prince Antoine, lived at 69, rue de Courcelles; the Proust family had moved in October 1900 to no. 45 in the same street. For 'mosch', and Proust's and Hahn's private language, see letter 98, n. 2. The substantive form 'moschant' is coloured by its resemblance to *méchant*, bad, in the sense of wicked.

180
TO FERNAND GREGH

Thursday [28 November 1901]

Dear friend,

I'm sure I had no need to tell you in the note I left for you on Tuesday that I had just been rather seriously ill. On reading my note you must have realized that I had been obliged for some time to keep my window closed 'to all the murmurs of life and the dispersed voices of my times', which is why I failed to hear those that already were applauding *La Fenêtre ouverte* and was able to think it was a book of poems.[1] Antoine Bibesco had told me the good news: 'Gregh has dedicated something in his new volume to you,' but it never occurred to me that the book might not be poetry. Never mind, it's an admirable book of poetry all the same. I'll write to you about it later, but what I wanted to tell you now was that my joy at having a piece to myself in the book was very much increased when I saw it was our old bells of Honfleur.[2] I had known it to be an admirable prose poem. But I don't believe I had remembered it to be so beauti-

ful. I ask myself if there is another prose poem as beautiful in the
French language, and honestly I don't think so (perhaps I ought to except certain of Baudelaire's prose poems, which certainly vie with
yours but do not excel it, I think). I don't know of any that contains
so much 'Truth and Poetry'. If one wished to praise it, I believe one
would have to proceed more or less like Trissotin,[3] taking it word by
word and going into ecstasies over each one. The consequence of such
richness of thought and feeling is that every epithet, every phrase or
clause, is a small world of profound and concatenated beauty. The
narrow and intimate port, the houses crowding together so that all
may see a little, are already very fine. But the port at the foot of the
house, to which the house communicates some of its gentle warmth,
those are words that penetrate as deeply into the heart as does the
voice of the belfries you speak of further on. And to stop at each
word would not be enough. Over them all hovers an atmosphere similar to the atmosphere between the windows of the houses and the
water of the port. Perhaps this atmosphere is the gentle warmth you
speak of. In any case it is poetry. But though already so beautiful, it is
still the threshold and the ship is still in port, slowly being hauled into
the open. It has not yet set sail. But then all this beauty is set in motion, something new enters into your contemplation, something that
breaks away and moves. When that happens, you find expressions of a
beauty which are to the immobile beauty of the beginning as song to
the spoken word. 'This water which cradles it still' is a truly admirable phrase, containing the hidden richness of ideas, the cloudy depth
of the dissolved images in the water of the port. 'Cradles' is the slow
movement of the water, and also suggests the caress of the motherly
houses and of the port which is their dependent. I don't think there is
anything so gently warm in any of Loti's books as this church which
is as warm as a large bed-closet, and the comparison with cathedrals is
superb. But what I like best of all (until you set things in motion, once
the bells start ringing, they dominate the whole, they drown out everything else and in point of fact sum it up, since what they carry to
the sailors' hearts is the gentle warmth of the maternal soil and, as you
say above, a smile from home on the treacherous sea), what I like best
of all at the hour of the bells is the masts turned to immobile
landlubbers, an admirable image further reinforced by 'like the sailors
etc.' Forgive me, I see, as I said before, that I've been a perfect Trissotin. I shall have great pleasure with this book, every part of which will
arouse so many memories, and the 'Verlaine', for instance, will call to
mind all the fine things M. Darlu said to me about you just after it appeared in *La Revue de Paris*.[4] I was right when I told you the other

day that I thought I was falling ill again. I am ill today, as you must have judged by my difficulty in expressing myself. So I don't dare suggest a meeting with you. Today I went to bed at noon and got up at nine in the evening. This is hardly a convenient situation for seeing one's friends, and to make matters worse it changes every day.

Your very grateful
Marcel Proust

1. Gregh's *La Fenêtre ouverte* (1901) consisted of essays on Victor Hugo, Paul Verlaine, etc. followed by selected essays and prose poems. Proust adapts a sentence from the preface, in which Gregh speaks of 'these prose essays by a poet who through the open window of his house listens as the dispersed voices of his times are wafted in with the murmurs of life'.

2. The prose poem 'Les Cloches sur la mer' is dedicated to Proust in memory of an evening in September 1892, when during a stay at Les Frémonts, he and the author entered the old church at Honfleur at the hour of the Angelus.

3. A character in Molière's *Les Femmes savantes*.

4. The essay 'Paul Verlaine' had first appeared in *La Revue de Paris* for 1 Feb. 1896.

181

TO ANTOINE BIBESCO

Thursday [December 1901 ?]

My dear friend,

I prefer to forget our quarrel at a time when you've had a setback, a stupid setback which makes me quite ill, especially as I have certain things to say to you.

1) You can count on me to give *La Lutte* to Réjane, Franck, Deval, or any director you like, and ask them to expect a visit from Antoine Bibesco, if this first failure hasn't disgusted you for good with my efforts (you just have to drop me a line).[1]

2) As for the merits of *La Lutte* (concerning which I am quite in the dark, it may be a masterpiece and it may be rubbish, I have no idea, although what knowledge I have, not about the work but about the author, leads me to take a favourable view) I implore you not to be discouraged for a single moment by the judgement of a woman capable of solving the difficult problem of being taken for

twenty at the age of sixty by people who once they've seen her close up can't bear to part with her, and who has a kind of genius when she acts – but whose literary judgement (I wouldn't repeat this to Reynaldo) is utterly nil and contemptible, based on nothing at all or on an absence of all feeling, thought or sense of style. It's pleasant to be received by her and still more to be played by her, but to be appreciated by her might give one food for self-doubt. This is the kind of thing you are too elegant to say, but which a friend must tell you in no uncertain terms to prevent you from thinking *La Lutte*, I won't say bad or good, I haven't read it, but less good than IT IS.

3rd point) Don't you think it would be a good idea for a man of letters, and more particularly of dramatic letters, one intelligent enough to understand you but stupid enough to push you (I mean commonplace enough to have authority, energy, etc.) to read *La Lutte*, like it, speak of it, and make wide-awake directors want it. It seems to me that you have an ideal man of this type within reach. Another, who is not ideal, might be the Right One, and why not? Only there you've got to consider intimacy with the Brancovans, gossip, etc.[2] All this is a far cry from my discreet services, but also more effective with those theatre people, whom I don't know and on whom I can't have the slightest *personal* influence. To the names of directors I can intercede with (all of them) I add Bartet,[3] who is not a director but is influential.

You're so discreet that I can't tell whether or not you sleep with Granier.[4] If you do or are inclined to, you should let her read it, make her want to perform it, etc. True, you don't need me for this sort of advice.

Oh yes, did Reynaldo tell you that Sarah wants another play from you? Wouldn't *Le Bon Amant* [The Good Lover] be a good choice? And in that case mightn't *La Lutte* fall back on Deval, we wouldn't want to disappoint him. I'll bet you he's unaware of his good fortune (*fortunatos agricolas sua si bona norint*).[5]

Well, my dear friend, you need only drop me a line. Forgive me for breaking the silence but this thing began at a time when we were very much in harmony and I would think myself cold-hearted were I to let you learn of your pseudo-setback from Reynaldo alone.

And besides I wanted very much for you to know that Sarah's judgement is mathematically equivalent to nil – and that I am entirely at your disposal in this as in everything else and always will be

Your most devoted

Marcel Proust

1. Sarah Bernhardt, approached via Reynaldo Hahn, had declined Bibesco's play. The great actress Réjane (real name Gabrielle-Charlotte Réju, 1857–1920) was the wife of Paul Parfouru (known as Porel), director of the Théâtre du Vaudeville. Alphonse Franck (1863–1932) was then director of the Théâtre du Gymnase; his wife was an intimate friend of Mme Lemaire. Deval (real name Abel Boularan, 1863–1938) was director of the Théâtre de l'Athénée.

2. The first candidate was probably the playwright Henry Bernstein (1876–1953), the second Abel Hermant.

3. Julia Bartet (stage name of Mme Regnault, 1854–1941), Bernhardt's rival, occasionally recited at Mme Lemaire's.

4. Jeanne Granier (1852–1939), an actress old enough to be Bibesco's mother, at that time played chiefly at the Théâtre des Variétés.

5. Cf. Virgil, *Eclogues*, 453: 'O fortunatos nimium, sua si bona norint, agricolas!' (O farmers, thrice happy, though unaware of their blessings!).

PART THREE

[1902 ~ 1903]

INTRODUCTION TO PART THREE

At the beginning of 1902 Proust was still translating Ruskin's *Bible of Amiens*, though his enthusiasm was waning and he was trying to decide how he could manage to write something on his own account; this is the burden of his letter to Bibesco of 20 December (letter 207). By then he was feeling rather better in health, and in March 1903 he wrote testily to his mother (letter 228) about her reluctance to arrange dinner parties for him, since he needed to catch up with his social obligations.

Although the *Jean Santeuil* project was virtually dead by now, Proust occasionally added a character sketch based on someone he met. His sketch of Vicomte Bertrand de Fénelon, whose name comes up often in the letters to Bibesco, was eventually to enter into Proust's portrait of Robert de Saint-Loup. The relationship with 'Blue Eyes' Fénelon became intense and eventually stormy; in many respects it corresponded with the ideas about romantic love that Proust had already set out in *Jean Santeuil* and was to develop in detail and at length in *À la recherche du temps perdu.*

In 1902 he went with Bibesco and Fénelon to hear Wagner's *Tristan.* October 1902 saw him setting off with Fénelon for Bruges to see an exhibition of Flemish primitive paintings. He went on alone to Antwerp, then to Dordrecht, Rotterdam, Delft, and Amsterdam, where he rejoined Fénelon, but went off on his own again to Vollendam, Haarlem, The Hague, and eventually back to Paris.

Bibesco's mother died at the end of October; Proust's letters of sympathy are full of genuine concern and even anguish for his friend.

Towards the end of 1902 Proust was persuading Alfred Vallette to publish his translation of *The Bible of Amiens* at Éditions du Mercure de France. Vallette wanted a Ruskin anthology but turned down the *Bible;* Proust refused the one without the other, and Vallette gave in. Proust then arranged with his friend Constantin de Brancovan, editor of the periodical *La Renaissance latine*, to accept part of *The Bible of Amiens* for his review, played off publisher and editor one against the other to hurry them both into print, and was so successful in his tactics that he could not get his material ready by the times arranged.

He was becoming quite skilled at manipulating people, using a mixture of pathetic need, emotional blackmail, and a technique which consisted of making his exacting requirements quite clear while withdrawing from any responsibility for what might be awkward requests. He contrived compliments so hyperbolic that they would be ludicrous without the redeeming self-consciousness of their own hyperbole. And he reveals sides of himself that he will later mock or satirize in the characters of his novel – a literary careerism as calculated as Bloch's; a cultivatedly excessive sensibility like Mme Verdurin's.

Yet his fundamental seriousness and the true power of his mind show clearly when the occasion calls them out, as in his letter about political action against the religious orders. The dominant Radicalism of the Third Republic was violently anti-clerical. A law of July 1901 asserted the control of the government over the religious orders, and when Émile Combes became Président du Conseil, with responsibility for religious affairs, he applied the law with the utmost rigour. Many religious institutions were closed, including a number of schools; diplomatic relations with the Holy See were broken off. All this was to lead to the annulling of Napoleon's Concordat in 1905, and the separation of Church and State. Proust foresaw a resultant change in the spiritual atmosphere of France, and set out his views in the remarkable letter 251, to Georges de Lauris on 29 July 1903.

Some of the letters show Proust's increasing involvement in the affairs of Louis d'Albufera and his mistress, Louisa de Mornand. (Later Proust was to act as go-between and pacifier when Albufera left Louisa and married.) And the lighter sides of his life are reflected in a number of letters in which he recounts the high spirits and practical jokes of his companions.

The year 1903 ended with the first of Proust's great family griefs. In his 1902 letter of sympathy to Bibesco he had spoken of his mother's inconsolable grief at the death of his grandmother, rather than of his own feelings on that occasion. In November 1903 his father died suddenly of a stroke. As the eldest son, Proust was chief mourner at the national funeral. He thought of giving up his work on Ruskin, but his mother urged him on. So he wrote to Anna de Noailles (letter 262) that his only real happiness had been in the happiness of his parents together, and that he had no aim in life to help him to bear his grief. He was, of course, more ambitious than he himself knew, and was eventually to realize his ambition. But that story is not yet.

J.M.C.

182
TO MADAME ÉMILE STRAUS

[17 or 18 February 1902 ?]

Madame,

Many thanks for your note, which gave me great pleasure. I am still in bed but shall be able to go out any day now and my first or second visit will be to you. Reynaldo's address is 9, rue Alfred de Vigny. But he left the day before yesterday for Monte Carlo, where I don't know his address. But if it would be of any use to you, I can easily have it for you in an hour or two, because his sister is now in Paris. He is spending a month at Monte Carlo and then coming back to Paris. He has enormous admiration for you and adores M. Straus to whom he attributes, among many other accomplishments, the finest pronunciation he has ever heard. I must admit that I don't quite see what he means. But I realize that such a judgement, coming from a singer, must mean a good deal to a lawyer. The other day the same Reynaldo chanced to sing me Holmès's 'Éros'. I can't tell you how moved I was by the 'cruel huntsman with the gentle eyes',[1] I hadn't heard that since the days when you used to sing it after lunch for Jacques [Bizet]'s friends in the boulevard Haussmann. You looked as if you were thinking of something else, of your own friends most likely. That was the time when every day for two months I swore to myself that I'd kiss your hand the next day, but didn't dare. I can't tell you how that melody, not by reminding me of all that, for I often think of it, but by suddenly bringing it back to me with no need of an introductory reverie, conveyed an impression of charm and poetry which in itself it does not possess. Thank you, Madame, for all that as well as for today's kind note, and deign to accept my affectionate respects.

Marcel Proust

---

1. 'Chasseur cruel aux yeux si doux', from the song 'Eros', by the Paris-born Irish woman composer Augusta (Mary Anne) Holmès (really Holmes,

1847 – 1903), a pupil of César Franck. It was perhaps of her that Proust was thinking when he wrote his 'Éloge de la mauvaise musique' in *Les Plaisirs et les jours* (cf. 'In Praise of Bad Music', *Pleasures and Regrets*, 138 – 39).

183
TO ANTOINE BIBESCO

[April? 1902]

Dear friend,

I have just received the edifying and valuable pamphlet, un-doubtedly the cause of the war in China; what troubles me no end is that it will be very hard for me to return it to you: the charming in-scription has the drawback of being indelible, and if anyone were to see it in your library he would suppose it to be a book of mine which you were wrongfully sequestering, and that would really be intoler-able. Many many thanks for this rare and charming present, worthy of him who has sent it. Bibesco the Magnificent has overwhelmed me with the subtle or haughty marks of his benevolence. How shall I ever be able to show my appreciation and thank him fittingly? Until such time, while you are *'dona ferens'*,[1] I remain more grateful than I can say. And since the Magnificent calls the Medici to mind, let me add that these famous and idiotic lines

Medici received it with indifference
As though accustomed to such gifts[2]

express a state of mind diametrically opposed to the one with which I welcome your *Imitation*. I have had some rather profound thoughts about Salaïsm, which will be communicated to you in the course of one of our next metaphysical conversations. No need to tell you that they are of extreme severity. But there remains a philosophical curios-ity about persons. Dreyfusard, anti-Dreyfusard, Salaïst, anti-Salaïst, are just about the only things worth knowing about an imbecile. I forget that you are in the country and consequently less indulgent towards gossip. 'It would set the most inveterate talkers to dreaming,' writes M. de Balzac (the seventeenth-century one) (speaking of a canal).[3] I therefore fall silent and silently press your hand.

Your most grateful
Marcel Proust

1. An allusion to *Aeneid* II. 49 (referring to the Trojan horse), 'Quicquid id est timeo Danaos et dona ferentes' (Whatever this may be, I fear the Greeks even when they come bearing gifts).

2. Cf. Voltaire, *La Henriade*, Chant II, 240, 243: 'Médicis la reçut avec indifférence, / . . . comme accoutumée à de pareils présents'. The head of Admiral Coligny, leader of the Protestant party, has just been brought to Catherine de' Medici. Proust alters the gender in order to compare Bibesco to Lorenzo de' Medici. The gift was a rare edition of the *Imitation de Jésus-Christ*, attributed to Thomas à Kempis (*c.* 1379 – 1471).

3. '. . . un canal qui fait resver les plus grands parleurs, aussitost qu'ils s'en approchent', letter of 4 September 1622 to M. de Lamotte-Aigron, *Oeuvres de J.-L. de Guez de Balzac* (1854 edn.), 428. Proust used the same quotation at the head of 'Versailles', in *Les Plaisirs et les jours* (cf. *Pleasures and Regrets*, 115).

184
TO MADAME DE NOAILLES

Sunday [1 June 1902]

Madame,

I am writing this little note to tell you how very glad I am that you have won the prize and how angry that two poets whose names I cannot remember have stolen half of it from you and that you have been crowned only between these two thieves.[1] Christ suffered the same fate. Posterity has forgotten the names of the two thieves (with regard to your two I am counting on the ignorance of posterity), but the name of Christ is immortal. As yours already is. Be that as it may, I'm very glad you've had the prize, for I like to see the world of appearances and its most futile citizens imitate the real world and the hierarchy of the intellect. That is why I take an interest in academic elections when a great writer, etc., is concerned, although that sort of thing is quite unworthy of true talent. You know I regard yours as unique. So what I have in mind is not one prize from the Academy, but all the prizes for many years, and not one seat in the Academy, nor one bed nor one throne, but an Academy superior to the one with forty members, which would have only one member and that one would be you. That is the Academy of our dreams. But how pleasant it would be if it really existed and if France were governed by this one poet, like the Persian Poet to whom Gustave Moreau gave the body of a woman and who inflames the people with her dress, purple like yours, and with her songs. A comparison that I shall remember in case some Calmette ever commissions me to write an article about you.[2] At least it will have the merit of being laudatory. I would be much obliged if you were to remind the Princesse de Chimay that I love her. Deign, Madame, to accept my respectful homage, and give my warm regards to M. de Noailles, whose charming voice heard over the telephone reminded me recently of how very exquisite, profound, and pure a man he is. I am really fond of him – a fact which, I am sure, leaves him too indifferent to object. Tell Hermant that in the relationship between Donatien and the Writer I seemed to recognize that between Léon de M. (with a dash of Ferdinand de M.) and Barrès,[3] and tell M. Anne-Jules[4] that I well understand his precocious pride at the sight of his mother's laurels.

I kneel to you, Madame.

Marcel Proust

1. *Le Journal des débats* for 1 June 1902 reported that, at a session of the Académie Française on 29 May, 'The Archon-Desperouses prize was awarded as follows: 2,000 francs to M. Ch. Guérin (*Le Semeur de cendres*); 1,000 francs to M. Depont (*Pélerinage*); 1,000 francs to the Comtesse de Noailles (*Cœur innombrable*).'

2. For Gaston Calmette, editor of *Le Figaro*, see letter 248. Proust used the comparison with Gustave Moreau's Persian (or Indian) poet in an article on Mme de Noailles which appeared in the literary supplement of *Le Figaro* on 15 June 1907.

3. No trace of this Donatien is to be found in the works of Abel Hermant; MM. Léon and Ferdinand de Montesquiou were indeed associated with Barrès and his nationalist movement.

4. Mme de Noailles's son, Anne-Jules-Emmanuel-Grégoire, then twenty months old.

185
TO ANTOINE BIBESCO

[Shortly after 6 June 1902]

Ocsebib

I've had a *sublime* idea for Nomara.[1] Unfortunately, as you've written, you can't come to see me any evening soon, and it's too complicated to write. So no sooner is my idea conceived than I give it up. My purpose in writing is not to tell you this, but to warn you not to invite Mme Lemaire and Mme de Pierrebourg together whatever you do, on pain of disastrous conflagrations. I hadn't thought of that. On the other hand, you ought to invite Flament for the pleasure of seeing the look on the faces of Robert de Billy, Léon Yeatman and Gaston de Caillavet. And then perhaps you won't have to invite him to 'the Princesse Alexandre Bibesco's superlatively elegant matinées' and have *Le Gaulois*, always ready to oblige *La Presse*, insert a, to say the least, useless Albert Flament into its otherwise homogeneous write-up.

In any case I advise you to invite him or his friend, but not both of them. When it comes to *faux ménages*, you will do well to invite only those involving unlike sexes to your tea party, especially as you already have a considerable number of this kind, if I have counted right. Since of you I can only expect every sort of kindness and would like to forestall *'the evil consequences of indiscriminate charity'*,[2] I must advise you not to invite Nomara to your tea party. No doubt the ferry crossing would leave room for a Banvillesque

Dans un bac à rame on
Peut voir Bertrand d'Aramon[3]

but not even that, since you say he's so electric. Besides, I don't think he's intellectual enough to enjoy such a gathering, and perhaps

Les Decori
Non sunt illo decori[4]

But most of all because the only person who would take an interest in him, namely, myself, will not be there, for in spite of the vague threat I tried to frighten you with, I shall not attend your rustic tea party. Anyway I'm sure it will be delightful, and truly *La Leçon d'amour dans un parc.*[5]

Do forgive me for all this advice, which I really have no right to give you, but this evening's will be the last. Forgive me and ponder this: don't you think it reflects the jealous, subjective disposition of a male Andromeda chained to his cliff and suffering at the sight of Antoine Bibesco going here, there and everywhere and his own inability to follow him. So that my antisocial advice is perhaps only an unconscious, didactic and pejorative version of the sublime

The poor flower said to the sky-born butterfly:
Don't leave me . . . Off you go, and here I stay![6]

I envy you both, Nonelef[7] and you. I envy you both to be seeing each other, while I shall be changing sides in my bed. But how many leagues I travel in my mind and heart in the course of this apparent repose. And I believe that because my repose is so exclusively physical it cannot be wholly effective. That, at least, was the opinion of Chateaubriand, who said of Joubert: 'In order to recover his strength, he often felt obliged to close his eyes and remain silent for hours. God only knows what tumult and movement went on inside him during this self-imposed silence and repose, etc.'[8] Now here you have a really and truly imbecilic letter. I don't dare write to Nonelef, with whom I am still at the stage of hope. Tell Fénelon that I have a great deal of affection for him and that I should be only too happy if, in exchange for mine which is enormous, he would grant me a little piece of his, which he breaks up and disperses among so many people. I, too, disperse myself, but successively. Each one's share is shorter but larger. Which reminds me, dear friend, that we should have quarrelled long ago. You have infinitely exceeded the maximum of time I allot to my friendships. Quick, let us quarrel.

Yours,
Marcel Proust

1. Comte Bertrand d'Aramon – here spelt backwards – (1876 – 1949), member of the Jockey Club, son of Comte Jacques d'Aramon and the Comtesse, née Fisher.

2. Quoted in English from Ruskin's *The Bible of Amiens*. At the time when the cathedral was built, says Ruskin, the pernicious nineteenth-century nonsense about 'the evil consequences of indiscriminate charity' was still unheard of.

3. Théodore de Banville (1823 – 91), playwright and writer of heroic verse, was known for Byronic rhymes of this kind. The interest of this couplet, meaning literally, 'In an oar-propelled ferry one can see Bertrand d'Aramon', lies entirely in the rhyme 'rame on / Aramon'.

4. 'The Decoris are not to his liking', referring evidently to Félix Decori (1860 – 1915), an advocate in the Appeals Court and his wife, née Perrody.

5. (A Love Lesson in a Park), title of a novel by René Boylesve which had appeared on 22 March 1902.

6. 'La pauvre fleur disait au papillon céleste: / Ne fuis pas. . . . Je reste, tu t'en vas!', from Victor Hugo, *Les Chants du crépuscule*, XXVII.

7. I.e. Vicomte Bertrand de Salignac-Fénelon (see letter 229).

8. Chateaubriand, speaking in *Mémoires d'outre tombe* (Pléiade edn., 1946, I. 450) of his associate, the moralist Joseph Joubert (1754–1824).

186
TO MADAME DE NOAILLES

Saturday evening [28 June 1902]

Madame,

I thank you with all my heart for sending me your book, many of whose masterpieces were already known to me, but which contains even more poems that I did not know and that are at least as beautiful. I shall write to you when I've read it all, but I can tell you now that I think 'Nostalgie', 'L'Année', 'L'Abondance', 'Les Vagues', 'Mélancolie le soir', 'La Nature ennemie', 'La Mémoire', and 'Midi' are at least equal to the poems that appeared in *La Revue des Deux Mondes*.[1] And though I love *Le Cœur innombrable* with all my soul, though I am still resolved to love nothing more dearly, not to forsake it for the volumes to come, not to be unfaithful to it with *L'Ombre des jours*, I nevertheless have the feeling that this volume is something greater, that you have reached a higher point within yourself, that for you, as for a tree, putting forth a new branch has been your way of growing. And beyond a doubt you have grown. I did not believe that anything could be more beautiful than *Le Cœur innombrable*. And yet I have the impression that *L'Ombre des jours* transcends and towers over it. It is the second branch. It is definitely higher. In it the idea of death is different, and so is the idea of immortality. In it you see yourself more clearly than you did, a poet among poets and above them. I loved the epigraph, with the misconstruction and the new avenues by which you secretly transform Racine's line.[2] I will tell you a good epigraph for 'Les Vagues' with its sublime ending,

> *that all tenderness is feigned*
> *which lacks the will of consent.*

It is true that we imagine it differently and transpose it according to what it relates to: drinking foaming beer, bathing in the sea, or breathing the sea wind. A commentary worthy of Mme Caro. I am extremely fond of 'La Petite Ville', in which, quite apart from its profound Beauty, the 'wit' you show in your conversation makes its entrance into your writing.

Would you please convey to M. de Noailles, along with the assurance that I joyfully and with all my heart appreciate the pride, the tender and profound pleasure he must take in your genius and your glory – the following vulgar and contingent request.

For some months I have been looking up passages in the Bible. In copying out certain quotations I find them so pallid, because of the poor translation I have been working with, that I would like to compare it with a more accurate one. He told me once that he has a very good Bible. Whose translation? And might he possibly lend it to me if it is not too enormous? Since my research is all done,[3] I would keep it for only a few days.

It has been said that poets are sublime go-betweens: Would you remind the ingrate at 31 (avenue Henri-Martin)[4] of my sadly disdained and sadly forgotten love. I admire you and love you beyond measure, Madame.

Respectfully yours,
Marcel Proust

1. All the poems named figure in Mme de Noailles's second book, *L'Ombre des jours* (The Shadow of the Days), which had just appeared. Five other poems had appeared in *La Revue des Deux Mondes* for 1 July 1900.

2. The epigraph on the title-page of *L'Ombre des jours* is 'Mes yeux sont éblouis du jour que je revoi' (My eyes are dazzled by the daylight which I see again), from *Phèdre*, I. iii.

3. I.e. for the commentary on *The Bible of Amiens*.

4. Mme de Noailles's sister, the Princesse Alexandre de Caraman-Chimay.

187
TO ANTOINE BIBESCO

[June or July 1902]

P.S. for Bibesco down to the bar (don't tell Mme de Noailles that you know I'm going to write to her). Here is the Sala draft.[1] Considering the information you have given me about Jaucourt,[2] etc., I don't see how I can help you the least bit more. Well, see what you can do. In any case, I think the vaguer you can make it the better. But I'm *aghast* at the attitude of Mme de Noailles. And without mentioning, silence tomb,[3] what she said about Aramon, since I heard about it from you – solely on the basis of what she said about Sala in front of Vacaresco, I shall write her a long letter. We must absolutely stop this horrible business of being the public denouncers of Salaïsm.

My dear little Sala,

It was terribly stupid of me to write to you, because my trifling and unintentional gaffe has now been repaired. It's too complicated to explain in a letter. No one could have guessed that those remarks of mine applied to you, but then by a distinguishing mark which those people knew about but which I could not have suspected they knew, they recognized you. However, I said it was a joke, and that went down perfectly. You would never have known, and it was sheer honesty that made me write to you. But if that has caused you the slightest uneasiness, I am sincerely sorry; it would be too absurd. In any case it has taught me a lesson, to be more careful and never again to breathe a word about anything remotely connected with these things. From this point of view, I'm glad you spoke to me so frankly, because from now on you will have in me a defender all the more ardent and adroit for being less convinced. But there's no need to defend you. Anyway I think people are talking about you less and less. You told me that one of the people who had said that about you was P[roust]. Well, if that is true – I don't know whether it is or not – there has certainly been a change, because he was in the place where that remark was made at the same time as I was, and he said it was absolutely untrue, pure invention, calumny, etc. And as for the lady who, you say, spoke disobligingly of you, I believe the poor thing is now much too busy with her own affairs to think of other people's. In any case, I could easily get her to say something if you like. As for myself, I did commit that gaffe, but it has had no consequences (?). (The question mark is for you.)⁴ But I promise you to keep the most absolute silence from now on and what is more, if necessary, to defend you as adroitly and warmly as I can. Forgive me for upsetting you stupidly and for reasons of remorse and conscientious scruple.

Yours ever,
Antoine Bibesco

I've just received the list of Mme Bessand's lady friends: Mme Girod, the little Dreyfus girls, Mme Maurice Bernard (the lawyer's wife), Mme Maurice Bernhardt (Sarah's son's wife), Mme Decori, Mme

Tripier née Gouzien, Mme Painlevé, Clairin's niece née Villeneuve, Mme Georges Hugo the elder née Ménard-Dorian, Mme de Saint Marceaux, a close friend and neighbour.[5]

1. Comte Antoine Sala, son of Comte Maurice Sala and the Comtesse, née Sanford, was an overt homosexual. Proust is reproving Bibesco for having talked openly about Sala's tendencies, and providing him with a way to smooth matters over. (The P.S. is written at the head of the draft letter to Sala.)

2. The Marquise de Jaucourt, née de Atucha, a lady of fashion admired even by Robert de Montesquiou. She is said to have had a liaison with the Marquis du Lau, one of the few persons given their real names in *Remembrance of Things Past*.

3. A private expression meaning 'not a word of this to anyone'.

4. The bracketed sentence is a note at the foot of the page, addressed to Bibesco.

5. This postscript is of course addressed to Bibesco. Mme Léon Bessand, née Massenet, lived at 25, avenue de Villiers, and Mme René de Paul de Saint-Marceaux, née Fred-Jourdain, wife of the sculptor, at no. 23.

188

TO ÉDOUARD ROD

[Summer 1902]

Dear Sir,

If you did not know that I have been confined to my bed for the last six months (in all this time I have got up and gone out perhaps eight or ten times) you must have thought *L'Eau courante* had not reached me. I did receive it though, not 'smiling like the blue waters of Lake Leman',[1] but with tears, bitter tears that are sooner wiped away than forgotten. Very few books have given me so sad and profound a feeling of life, increasing as it were my power to suffer from it. But at the time I was too ill to write. And my gratitude, and this I am sure is true of many unknown readers, was reflected only in constant meditation on this so simple drama and on the infinitude of life it encloses and discovers, on all that a man can suffer before the trunk of a lime tree has grown perceptibly thicker. It seems that the more you write the more you simplify the technique and subject matter of your work, until there is scarcely any intermediary between the soul and life. And so, much as I have always admired the sequence of masterpieces, your books, in which not the least dead wood is perceptible, in which you seem to offer posterity a selection from your writings embodying only the purest essence of your thought and the precious, intact fruit of your meditation, nevertheless, if I were called upon to state a preference, it would be for one of your most recent books and perhaps for this *Eau courante*, to which I have given a place in my book shelf side by side with another beloved work, *The Mill on the Floss*, whose homespun majesty and concentrated tragedy, likewise in a river setting, it equals. Ah how marvellously it is what it is and what you wanted it to be. I don't believe there can be another such example of artistic proficiency, if at such heights it is permissible to talk shop. The seasons follow one another in the book as they do in the real world it seems to be a part of. One pities Marguerite because she will not live to see the spring, and one is infinitely charmed at the coming of the misty autumn flowers. What an exquisite phrase.[2] Writing to you from my bed, I haven't got the book at hand, but I remember the scent of the pale cowslips, the little African marigolds that are redder than a drop of blood, and the thistles whose hairy stems bend under the weight of their heavy violet flower-heads. But all these charms do not console one for the human wickedness one feels so deeply and the sadness of life which makes one regret not to have 'departed' with those who have died and which permeates Bertigny's retrospective vision of his life, a vision even sadder than his death.

Permit me to assure you, dear sir, of my respectful admiration.

Marcel Proust

1. Rod's novel *L'Eau courante* (Flowing Waters) was published on 28 January 1902. The allusion is to the final words of the novel.

2. Rod's phrase is 'les vagues fleurs de l'automne', from ch. VII.

189

TO ANTOINE BIBESCO

[Sunday evening 10 August ? 1902]
Dear friend,

Here is what I could not tell you before about Nonelef:

1) What you said about 'arranging to see him and not one of your friends when for once you go out of an evening, etc.' gave me

food for thought. It's true. Especially since before the evening at Larue's [restaurant] he wasn't exactly on the upswing. How would I have felt after those two big booms, the Lemaire soirée and the Saturday at Larue's.[1] I'll tell you why. I have to acknowledge what you seem to have diagnosed, to wit, the possibility and perhaps even the beginnings of an intense affection for Nonelef, ephemeral, like all my predilections, and yet, alas, susceptible of continuing for quite some time. And this affection, beyond I believe the shadow of a doubt, could only be a very unhappy one for me. Consequently I have, I won't say a desire, for one never desires to fight off an affection, but the will to suppress this affection before it takes on excessive importance – which it has not yet done. So here's what I've been thinking. You know that in me no affection, however great, can withstand absence – some that were incomparably greater than what I feel thus far for Nonelef have succumbed to it for ever. So if Nonelef were called away to some post, or if I were to go off on a trip, that would be the end of it. But it so happens that he is staying in Paris and that I shall be here too until I leave for Biskra, Cairo or wherever. That will be in a few months and no great harm would be done. But is it certain that I'll go? And if I don't go and he stays in Paris, there is no reason why this affection should not grow, and then I shall be afflicted with it for a year or a year and a half (the term beyond which such affections, or should I say infections, abate and die away. Take, for example, Lucien, Flers, etc., etc., etc., etc.). Well, I wouldn't want things to go so far, because I already have sufficient grounds for sadness without looking for new ones, and because I'm sure Nonelef can never be a 'happy' friend for me. 'Too intelligent or not intelligent enough' is not really true, because I think he will be much more so than he is, with the Virgilian conditional *'eris'*.[2] But what you say of his character is enough to convince me that all I would get from him is grief. Of course there's another remedy besides absence. That is, if he were disagreeable, or at least cold, indifferent, etc. But he has such quick intuitions of character that he has undoubtedly seen – though I've tried to hide it – how free I am from coquetry, how very much kindness and marks of sympathy enhance my own, how inapplicable the adage 'if you don't love me I will love you'[3] is to me with regard to love and *a fortiori* to friendship. The consequence being that although it's entirely a matter of indifference to him whether I like him or not (or not, Bibesco) he will instinctively behave amiably – and I the more so. So after all the only solution is absence, in other words, since we are both in Paris, to stop seeing each other. The fact is that every time he has registered a sharp upswing (his charm at Mme Lemaire's or at Larue's), it has been followed after a few days by a slump, and the flame would die away completely if it were not revived by yet another evening. In spite of that, I am writing to him about Versailles and about Noailles (despite your 'here I fail to understand you', you will understand, my dear friend) because Versailles was arranged with Reynaldo, and as for Noailles I'll tell you later. With all the more reason because there's a very good chance at these soirées of his bringing on a slump with his coldness, as he has done so often. Do you remember what a slump he had before you left for Spain,[4] I thought he would never recover. It was that wretched Lemaire evening and his return. In such cases a vulgarian returns with 'someone else'. One feels rather put out, one has an unpleasant feeling from the start, whereas as it was (coming back with him) one gets the impression that one has been not the only one but the last one, no bad humour mars one's pleasant memories and feelings of affection, no sensation from outside obtrudes, and one goes home enveloped, virtually imprisoned, in a warmth of memories which, far from dwindling, incubates one's nascent affection in the days that follow. Someone who was very good to me (but this was in the realm of love) and who knew that I was trying to liberate myself from my attachment to her, used to say to me imperiously: 'You will take me home.'

Dear friend, I'm so tired I shall put off the rest of this conversation till another day. It would be stupid of me to tell you I had no affection for Nonelef. One doesn't take so many precautions against a nonexistent feeling, and the pleasure one takes in saying one means to give it up proves that one has not yet done so. On the other hand, this letter is a gross exaggeration. All this is the last echo of Larue's. Unless something new happens soon, I shall look on Nonelef exactly as I do twenty other persons and I shall no longer have to struggle with that Siren of the sea-blue eyes, a direct descendant of Telemachus, of whom M. Bérard must have found traces not far from Calypso's island.[5] The poor boy, who obviously doesn't give a damn about me, would be very much surprised at being the subject of so much discussion. I never caught the meaning of these lines from Mme de Noailles's *L'Ombre des jours:*

> *When Fénelon in rustic times*
> *Strolled in the scented evening,*
> *Languishing even then at the thought*
> *Of some day being loved despite himself*[6]

but now I'm beginning to think they apply to Nonelef and myself. In any case, dear friend, whatever happens, (1) don't speak of this to *anyone*. I'll finish this another time, I'm asleep on my feet.

Yours,

Marcel

P.S. Well, now at the last moment I am applying the treatment without further delay. I am going to the Noailles's this evening and not asking leave to bring Nonelef. And I'm going to Larue's alone at half-past eleven without letting Nonelef know. What do you think of that?

Thank you for all your kindness in all this and in everything else, my most sublime friend. Incidentally it's awfully kind of you (and very intelligent) never to run Nonelef down to me. You're very very nice and I'm very fond of you.

1. Mme Lemaire's soirée, to which Proust had invited Fénelon on behalf of the hostess, was on 17 June 1902; the Saturday evening at Larue's was 9 August.

2. For Virgil's 'Tu Marcellus eris', see letter 104, n. 1.

3. A reference to the Habanera in Bizet's *Carmen*: 'L'amour est un enfant de Bohème / Il ne connut jamais de loi / Si tu ne m'aimes pas je t'aime! / Si tu m'aimes tant pis pour toi!'

4. On 12 May 1902 Bibesco had gone to Madrid, in his capacity as secretary of the Romanian legation in Paris, to attend the coronation of King Alfonso XIII.

5. In the first volume of his *Les Phéniciens et l'Odyssée*, then just published, Victor Bérard (1864–1931) situates Calypso's island at the foot of the Atlas Mountains. Cf. *Within a Budding Grove* (1. 1012): 'Geographers or archaeologists may conduct us over Calypso's island. . . .'

6. 'Quand Fénelon au temps champêtre . . .', from the poem 'Parfumés de trèfle et d'armoise', which refers of course to Bertrand de Fénelon's famous ancestor, François de Salignac de la Mothe-Fénelon (1651–1715), Archbishop of Cambrai and author of *Les Aventures de Télémaque*, a treatise on education.

190

TO ANTOINE BIBESCO

[17 ? August 1902]

My dear little Antoine,

I'm dreadfully put out (it really doesn't matter, come to think of it, it's just a bore) by what you said to Constantin [de Brancovan].

Didn't I say silence tomb in my telegram? It seems awfully frivolous for someone who is between life and death, between love and despair, between thought and nothingness, to be upset by such a little thing. But I have three very *serious* reasons, which I'll tell you by word of mouth, for feeling put out.

But since I shall probably see Constantin before I see you, do be kind enough to tell me exactly what you said to him and just why you sent me that 'tell me the name, etc.' wire. Did Constantin arouse your curiosity by talking about him in vague terms. . . . The best, I think, would be to tell Constantin that I was the one who told you. But don't tell him before I give you new instructions, which will depend a little on your reply to this.

((Yesterday evening I saw your friend R. Blum,[1] slender, flushed, untamed, curly and smiling, like a Hippolytus from the best period of Greek sculpture. Flushed chiefly from constipation, which he complains of and which is symbolic of his difficulty in producing. He has the weird habit, in speaking of people he hasn't been to see or hasn't written to, of saying that he has treated them very badly! He is charming and I think he has a truly profound affection for you. This is said sincerely, don't mistake it for soft soap or for Robespierrian Berquinism[2] à la Bertrand [de Fénelon])) to whom – Bertrand – you may communicate these two judgements (on Blum and on him). But I would have to explain the whole thing word for word if you were to conclude that I identify Bertrand – so good (here good diction is necessary) – with Robespierre. But I do think they have one thing in common – they are both Berquinists. So am I at times. That's when I'm nicest. At such times I give people the illusion that I feel a great friendship for them, and the future transforms the illusion into reality. This isn't meant for you, I've always been enormously fond of you, nor, I hardly need say, for Bertrand. I would actually be rather at a loss to say whom it would apply to, I have no need to tell you that this letter is for you alone. The only part you can communicate (if you wish, I don't especially want you to) to Bertrand is the part I've put between double brackets)), but don't say I authorized you to, just make it look as though, carried away by your admiration for my lapidary judgements, you couldn't restrain yourself from sharing your delight with a friend!

Yours ever,

Marcel

((On the other hand Blum (this, too, is communicable) has, as I observed to you on the very first day, a poor sense of the meaning of words. Wanting to say that Lauris[3] is very simple, he declared in tones of enthusiasm: 'He has nothing of the *grand seigneur* about him!' I'm curious to know what Lauris would think of this characterization.))

p.s.   Sincerely, Bertrand *is very very good*. But don't tell him so.

1. René Blum (1878 – 1942), brother of Léon Blum, a man of letters whom Proust seems to have taken as one of his models for Bloch.

2. The sad, languorous plays of Arnaud Berquin (1747 – 91) were ironically dubbed 'berquinades'.

3. Comte Georges de Lauris; see letter 239.

191
TO ANTOINE BIBESCO

[18 ? August 1902]

Dear Antoine,

I've forgotten how much you loaned me, for which many thanks. I do know it was at least 53 francs. Here they are. Tell me how much more there is.

I woke up a little while ago. You can come if you like. This proposal may surprise you. Let me explain. Since despite my warning, my insistence and more, you have allowed our friendship to be shattered,[1] I think it preferable not to leave an interval, because afterwards it is very difficult to resume relations that are not false. – And if we do not leave a gap, we are sufficiently enamoured of the same things and the same ideas to build, on the ruins of our friendship, delightful groves of Academe, where our conversations, no longer carried on in the depths of a deconsecrated bed – one more thing that has gone, as the sentimental Serge Basset[2] would say – will often be peripatetic – hence a charming conversational friendship. We must not leave ourselves time to contemplate the tomb, but quickly cover it with flowers which will not reopen it but will hide it. *Date lilia* (Virgil). *Inde nascentur violae* (Propertius?) but in any case something

> *Dulci dulcius rosa*
> *Tristi tristius elleboro* (Ausonius).[3]

But that is my only reason for asking you to drop in if by chance you have nothing else to do this afternoon. For I am neither sadder nor unhappier today than any other day; not at all, and furthermore you can no longer console me. Besides, the day isn't my bad time. So do whatever is easy for you and seems fitting. Forgive me retrospectively if I made fun of your feeling of friendship for [Henry] Bernstein. I liked him very much, he rather reminded me of Aramon! And now I regard that friendship in a very different light, as excellent and to be encouraged. But it needs no encouragement. Please tell Constantin (as though coming from you) that Nonelef is not some interchangeable friend of mine and that you were only teasing with your inept and odious jokes that would have been more applicable to one of my interchangeable friends. Name any you please. As for Hermant (you can tell this to Constantin, if you don't think he will repeat it to Hermant), he must not be allowed to suspect so much as the existence of these jokes. As for Bernstein, need I tell you! – You have wronged me and hurt me with all this, though it was so clearly understood and I had explained it all so carefully.

I have a message for Hermant but I'm not asking you to deliver it, because I think it would bore you. You keep forgetting *Unto This Last*.[4] My letter is for you and you only, not for Nonelef any more than for anyone else.

Au revoir

Marcel

1. An undated letter of about the same time (*CMP* III. 105) reproaches Bibesco, because, says Proust, 'while I, shunning to leave you in the dark concerning any corner of my life, your life, anyone's life, or Life as such, tell you everything I ought to conceal from you, you systematically hide everything from me, even what concerns me. . . . I find this detestable.'

2. Pseudonym of Pierre Chapoton (1865 – 1917), journalist and playwright.

3. 'Give lilies' (Virgil); 'Thence are born violets' (Propertius?); 'Sweeter than the sweet rose / Sadder than the sad hellebore' (Ausonius).

4. A French translation had recently appeared of Ruskin's *Unto This Last: Four Essays on the Principles of Political Economy;* Proust had asked Bibesco for it in an earlier letter.

192
TO HIS MOTHER

Monday evening after dinner, nine o'clock
dining room, 45, rue de Courcelles
[18 August 1902]
My dear little Mama,

As I didn't write to you yesterday, I shall take up where I left off. Well, the day before yesterday evening there was a temporary let-up in my trouble. I took advantage of it and went to bed at about three o'clock, or even earlier (at night), so as not to take any Trional. I slept in snatches, but well enough on the whole (except for a vestige of asthma) and was amazed to wake up without staring desolation in the face. I took the opportunity to spend twelve hours in bed, my pulse dropped from 120 to 76, and yesterday I was able to dine at Durand's with Brancovan without having an attack either during dinner or after or during the night, which is something new since my daily nights out. What's more, I who had lately been consuming vast quantities of powders (because my asthma had started up again) refrained from smoking until five in the morning, and then only smoked a tiny bit while going to bed, and after that not at all until eight in the evening, in other words, infinitely less than when I didn't leave my bed. I had another twelve hours in bed and got up for dinner at about eight, but then, alas, I had another bit of trouble. – I still haven't taken any more enemas, which proves they are not really necessary. – Your absence, even in so disastrous a phase of my life, is beginning to bear fruit (don't be offended at this, as Mme Roussel would!).[1] For instance, in dressing yesterday evening and this evening, I left off the second pair of drawers, and in my bed last night and during the day, which is a great deal harder, I went without the second thick jersey. Since I caught a chill this afternoon, I don't know if I shall be able to do that again tonight, but all the same it was an accomplishment I'd given up hoping for. My many dinners at restaurants have given me a brand-new stomach. Though I eat much more. But much more slowly. And besides, eating out is my Évian, my travel, my summer resort – all the things I have to go without. Anyway, everyone says I'm looking very well. Since the asthma seems arrested, I believe that if my troubles would go away . . . but alas. – You tell me there are people who have as many troubles as I do but have to work and support their families. I know that. Though having the same trou-

258

bles, much bigger troubles, infinitely bigger troubles, doesn't necessarily imply the same amount of suffering. Because in all this there are
two factors: The substance of whatever it is that provokes the suffering. And the person's capacity – owing to his nature – for suffering.
Nevertheless, I'm sure a great many people suffer as much or more
and manage to work all the same. Then we hear that they've been
stricken with some ailment or other and have had to stop working.
Too late, so I preferred to do it ahead of time. And I was right. Because there are different kinds of work. Literary work makes constant
demands on those emotions which are connected with suffering.

When you have so many other ties with suffering.[2]

It's like making a movement that affects an injured organ
which ought to remain immobilized. When what's actually needed is
frivolity, entertainment. But this is the month of August. Oh well, in
spite of everything I'm better, at the moment at least. Even today I
feel happy! But your criticism amazes me. You complain that it's irregular to take my meal one day at nine in the evening and the next at
one in the afternoon. And so it is. But seeing that I was committing
the irregularity of getting up early and spending the whole day out,[3]
could I (especially when I hadn't so much as *touched* my bed) go
without eating until nine at night? – And when, driven by starvation, I
had eaten at one o'clock, should I have eaten again at nine o'clock and
run the risk of not getting to bed that night? The truth is I should
never tell you anything, because you look at things too much '*ab uno*'.
You're surprised at my consulting Vaquez and say that all doctors say
the same thing. There I disagree, they've all told me something
different. But considering that I had something I had never had before, which forced me to stop the treatment that was doing me good,
I really had to see someone about my heart and stomach-intestines
(which I – mistakenly – thought partly responsible for my spells).
Faisans was away, Papa was out of town, Bize busy, so I thought of
Vaquez, who is a good man, both intelligent and conscientious. I don't
say that I consulted him with the certainty that if there was something
wrong with my heart he would tell me so. But at least it's a good
thing to know there are no special indications and that I don't have to
worry about my stomach. While we're on the subject of medicine, ask
Papa about a burning sensation while urinating, which makes me break
off and start again five or six times in fifteen minutes. Maybe it's from
the oceans of beer I've been drinking lately.

I've asked a favour connected with *Le Figaro* (not for me, for
Fénelon) of Baya,[4] who was most affable. Maybe I was a little too

eager (you see that I'm not afraid of exposing myself to criticism) to anticipate Fénelon's wishes in this matter, because he didn't really want this *Figaro* thing. I don't know yet how it turned out. – I haven't finished telling you about my nights. I'm still doing without Trional and I'm still calm, I've had another fairly good night, half an hour at a time, and I've really been extremely well. Which reminds me, Arthur[5] has spoken to me of

[*End of letter missing*]

1. Proust's parents had been staying at Évian since 12 August 1902. Mme Roussel was the mother of the Prousts' friend Mme Cottin.

2. 'Quand par tant d'autres nœuds tu tiens à la douleur', from Musset's 'Don Paez', in *Premières Poésies*.

3. On 14 August Proust had gone out at noon to take lunch with Brancovan, Bibesco, and another friend.

4. No doubt E. Rabaya, on the staff of *Le Figaro*.

5. A servant of the Proust family.

193
TO JACQUES-ÉMILE BLANCHE

Saturday [September 1902]

Dear friend,

Many thanks for troubling to answer me. Yet your answer has rather grieved me, though clearly by no fault of yours. It saddens me to know that the only time you have seen me this year (without my seeing you) should have been at that party[1] and that on the strength of that one meeting you should have, perhaps not judged me but at least confirmed an old unfavourable opinion, which I believe to be unjust. – I find it all the sadder that the name of a friend such as Fénelon, who far from being a social butterfly is positively anti-social, should lead you none the less to put a worldly interpretation on my behaviour, thus reinforcing your impression. It may be wrong of me to deplore such misunderstandings, since you say they are beneficial, leading us, through injustice and the righting of it, to greater self-awareness. Nevertheless I should be glad if my health were better and I could see you often enough to give you, not a good impression, for that would be false, but a less disagreeable one. Since you are as good as you are severe, you end by granting me what I ask. Or so at least it seems to me. For I presume that a 'thought' signifies a sketch, in the deliberately ambiguous and slightly disingenuous language M. de Montesquiou employs to leave a petitioner with a troubling doubt about the effect his request has had on Montesquiou and how he is likely to respond. I remember once when I sent him a pot of hydrangeas he wrote me that he had presented them to a grave which thanked me and sent greetings, and claimed later on that it was sheer disingenuousness on my part to pretend I hadn't guessed that he had thrown them out of the window. Another time he invited me to lunch, but warned me that it would be served by bats and asked me to bear with him. Which frightened me so that before going I wrote to Pozzi, asking if it were true. A 'thought', of course, could mean a drawing of a thought. That would be perfect. – All this should not be taken to mean that I consider one of your thoughts less desirable than one of your drawings. But I assume that the album appeals to your more celebrated speciality, that is, as a painter. The format of the album is that of small-size letter paper, this paper for instance. Since Mlle de Fénelon is away, it would be best, I think, if you were to be kind enough to do it on a sheet of paper and send it to me.[2] As for what you tell me about Mme de Fénelon, I really can't say, because I don't know her.[3] I met her once some years ago, but I don't believe I spoke with her. – Yes, it would have given me great pleasure to see you in the country, surrounded by all the things that are spiritualized by the interpretations you have given and will give of them and that are beautiful because they are imbued with your gaze and dear to your mind. But I shall not be able to go to Bas Fort Blanc unless there is a change in my health, because although much better – for the last fortnight I have been getting up every day – I am not yet fit to stay 'among others'. Yet I would so much have liked to see you there. But perhaps these dreams will come true one day.

In the meantime, may I ask you to convey my respectful homage to Mme Blanche and to believe in my admiration and affection.

Marcel Proust

The young lady's Christian name is Françoise, but since she has no unmarried sister I believe one addresses her simply as Mlle de Fénelon.

---

1. This may have been the tea party given by Bertrand de Fénelon on 5 September 1902 at the Hôtel des Réservoirs, in Versailles.

2. It appears that Proust had written to Blanche, asking the painter to do a page for the album of Françoise de Salignac-Fénelon (d. 1967), the young sister of Bertrand. She married Comte Pierre de Ritter-Zahony in 1904.

3. The Comtesse de Salignac-Fénelon, mother of Bertrand and the sister of the sportsmen Émile and Pierre Deschamps, may have been one of Proust's models for Mme de Marsantes, Saint-Loup's mother.

194
TO ANTOINE BIBESCO

[9 or 10? September 1902]

My dear little Antoine,

Don't let what I am writing, which is very affectionate, make you angry (I'm not referring to 'doubts'; whether or not I have any has nothing to do with the case). But it horrifies me to have you ask me out loud whether I've asked Lauris if he thought 'His Blue Eyes'[1] (not Lauris's blue eyes!) was nicer or not so nice to me on a certain evening, etc.

Hadn't I made it absolutely clear that you were the *only* person to whom I had spoken of this business, that even Reynaldo doesn't know about it. Without stopping to think, you passed it on to others. I've done all I could to straighten things out. But if you're going to start dropping innuendoes to Lauris, etc.! Think of the impression it would make and what people would think of me. It's true that, especially at times like this when my 'Fin de la jalousie' is causing me mortal anguish,[2] such childishness as what people will think of me seems unimportant. But it's not only on my account, I also owe it to my family not to let myself be taken for a Salaïst, gratuitously since I'm not one. Of course this wouldn't necessarily make me look like a Salaïst. But cut off from the interpretation which your knowledge of my character and of the daily course of events have given you, it would certainly look odd. Besides, my affectation of humility, etc. etc. already makes me look servile enough, without adding to that impression by representing me to Lauris or others as living in expectation of a smile from the King. But the nub of the matter is that what the intensity of my sympathy for you, my absolute confidence in you, and my habit of telling you everything have made me confide in you, should remain privy to you and not be passed on to anyone whomsoever. Neither Lucien Daudet, nor Reynaldo, nor Yeatman, etc. know of it. So there is no reason to speak of it to Lauris, Billy or Constantin. I assure you that you are rather frightening, because you can't deny that I explained this to you at great length. This time, I hope, I have made myself clearer.

I am very unhappy again, my dear little Antoine, and life is not kind to me at this moment. Forgive me for making it too evident to my friends.

Yours,
Marcel Proust.

Are you doing anything this evening? (– this afternoon would be very inconvenient for me) – And when are you off on your long journey? I've forgotten the date. – And when will you be coming back? *What made you laugh so hard as you were driving away* (leaving Larue's with Constantin)?

P.S. Very important and *ultra silence tomb*. Since an entire hidden aspect of 'His Blue Eyes's' life may be discoverable this evening, tell me at exactly what times you will be at home today, so that I can communicate with you if necessary – and more important, where you are going for dinner, where you will be after dinner, during the evening, etc., in case I want to talk with you, because without you I would not be able to learn anything. Keep this letter carefully hidden and bring it back to me when we see each other. – Don't come this afternoon unless I phone you, because I am not at all well.

1. I.e. Bertrand de Fénelon.

2. There seems to have been gossip to the effect that the sexes were transposed in this, the final story in *Les Plaisirs et les jours*.

195
TO MADAME ALPHONSE DAUDET

Saturday [13 September 1902]

Madame,

I am very late in thanking you for the delightful hours spent at your admirable Pray,[1] one of the most beautiful places I have ever seen. But I would have been so happy to see it with you, to speak of it with you, to hear you speak of it, and I was not even able to see you. Accordingly, my stay at Pray was a mingling of happiness and sadness. Still, I'm glad to have gone. If my improvement goes on this winter and if you will let me call again at the rue de l'Université, I shall perhaps have acquired in your eyes the small merit of having seen and admired something you love, of being less a stranger to your memories of Pray than I was, and, when you say the name in my presence, of no longer having merely the letters P-R-A-Y before my eyes, but instead the charming old house which I saw radiant in the morning beside the Loire and amidst flowers and which I found myself even then loving so much that the excitement of our precipitate departure did me a service by rushing me through the pangs of leavetaking from this house which had been unknown to me the day before and which I shall never forget. You were not dressed, and I was not able to see you. Lucien made me shout through the window a ridiculous 'Goodbye, Madame', which remained unanswered. What I should have said is Thank you, Madame, when I think of all the kind attentions which I passed one by one in review that night, finding in my delightful room so many things for warmth, for comfort, and very personally for me. I shall write to Lucien to thank him. But do tell Léon of my joy at finding the same cordiality he had shown me at Fontainebleau – my admiration for him makes it doubly precious to me. I also want you to know that great as my indiscretion may have been, the telegraph should be held responsible for the most ridiculous part of it. I never asked for that *'bouillon à l'esprit de vin'* (or any other), the recipe for which must have given your cook pause. However the problem was solved (and I own that I am curious to know how), the preparations must have kept your people up very late and you must have been quite amazed at my rudeness in refusing the strange concoction I had asked for in my telegram. What I actually asked for was a *'bouillote à l'esprit de vin'*.[2] But I have so much confidence in your kindness that I hope you only laughed a little at my expense when you read the telegram and were not put out with me. With the expression of my profound gratitude, deeply moved at the persistence of your benevolence towards me and at the warmth of your hospitality, I beg you, Madame, to accept my most respectful homage.

Marcel Proust

1. Proust had spent the night of 6 September 1902 at Pray, the Daudets' house at Chargé, near Amboise, before going on the next day by car with Lucien Daudet to visit Mme de Brantes at the château du Fresne, at Authon. He returned to Paris the same night.

2. What Proust had meant to ask for was not bouillon with spirit of wine – i.e. alcohol distilled from wine – but a *bouillote* (a hot-water bottle). Possibly the spirit of wine was thought to make it more comforting.

196

TO MADAME ALPHONSE DAUDET

Thursday [25 September 1902]

Madame,

I wrote to you the other day after considerable delay.[1] But my letter was forgotten, and since it was not posted until several days after it was written, it crossed the parcel with the tie pin and the sweet note you were kind enough to enclose with it. You must have realized as much when you saw in my letter that among all the things I had to thank you for I did not mention the pin. I am really abashed to learn that it was not only my presence that caused so much bother and disturbance at Pray. But that after my departure the bother continued. And that the disastrous consequences of my visit continued to mount up after I left. With the result that during the following weeks I continued to disturb you without being there, like those dead stars that are still sending us their malignant rays. While conversely, now that I am far from you, I continue to receive repeated and charming proofs of your importuned benevolence. One day a valise, another my brushes, another a tie pin. I am infinitely grateful to you but also very much ashamed. I long to see you and yet sometimes have the feeling that I shall never again dare show my face in your presence. I am counting on your kindness to arrange all that and without too much exasperation or rancour to accept the respectful homage of my admiration and gratitude.

Marcel Proust

With two contradictory telegrams Lucien has overwhelmed me with hope and regret. But he hasn't come.

1. See letter 195.

197
TO ALFRED VALLETTE[1]

45, rue de Courcelles
Monday [29 September 1902]
Dear Sir,

I stopped by *Le Mercure* about a month ago, but was not fortunate enough to find you there. Though I am fairly well now, it is not easy for me to go out in the daytime, and that is why I have not been able to try again. I left what information I was able to obtain with the editorial secretary.

Unto This Last sells for 3 francs 50 (I believe I said 3 francs, so I was 50 centimes off; anyway, I left the volume at *Le Mercure* and you can see for yourself). I compared the English text of *Unto This Last* with the English text of *The Bible of Amiens*. Since the latter is much longer, I believe (but is that an adequate reason?) that M. Beauchesne will price *The Bible of Amiens* much higher![2] Though perhaps you will say that my calculations are based on mere guesswork.

As for going to see Beauchesne and asking him how much *The Bible of Amiens* will cost, without even the pretext that it's the first volume announced (*Sesame and Lilies* is the first), I'm afraid that would be rather risky and put them on their guard.

Of course I shall do and say whatever you wish. But don't you think he would have to be half asleep not to smell a rat?

I shall probably take advantage of the improvement in my health to visit the exhibition of Primitives at Bruges. Since it closes on 5 October, I shall probably leave on Thursday if I decide to go,[3] and I don't think there is time for you to write to me before then. But if on my return, which will be in a week no doubt, you could give me an answer about the *Bible*, I should be much obliged. Naturally if a delay would increase my chances of a favourable reply, I would rather you postponed your decision for a while. But otherwise I shall have to look for a publisher, and I had better not wait too long.

Yours faithfully,
Marcel Proust

1. Alfred Vallette (1858 – 1935), chief editor of the literary periodical *Le Mercure de France* and of the publishing house of the same name.

2. Éditions Beauchesne et Cie, having published *Unto This Last* (see letter 191), had announced a series of translations of Ruskin's work. Proust was hoping that Éditions du Mercure de France would publish his own translation of *The Bible of Amiens*.

3. The exhibition of early Flemish art which had opened at Bruges on 19 June 1902 was to have closed on 15 September but had been prolonged into October. Proust left for Bruges, with Bertrand de Fénelon, on 2 October.

198
MADAME ADRIEN PROUST TO ANTOINE BIBESCO

45, rue de Courcelles
[Thursday evening 9 October 1902]
Dear Prince

Ponsard has written

Once the limit is exceeded, there's no stopping,[1]

and having failed to return that same evening, Marcel doesn't seem to be coming back at all. The truth is that Bruges didn't disagree with him, nor did Antwerp, where he wrote to me: 'If you see Bibesco, give him my best regards. I miss him very much. Tell him that being rather tired (but quite well) I have prolonged my trip.'

Planning to send you news of him this evening, I was waiting – in vain – for a second post. This little absence is a great step forward – and he owes a good part of his improvement to your warm, comforting friendship, for which I thank you once again.

Believe me yours affectionately,
J. Proust

As soon as I know the date of his return, I shall write to you. When he says his fatigue is making him prolong his trip, I think it's because he knows he will not be able to take another.

J.P.

1. Cf. François Ponsard (1814 – 67), *L'Honneur et l'argent*, III. v: 'Quand la règle est franchie, il n'est plus de limite, / Et la première faute aux fautes nous invite.'

199
TO HIS MOTHER

Hôtel de l'Europe, Amsterdam
Friday [17 October 1902]

My dear little Mama,

I've just received your two little letters. Forgive me for not writing more. But I am doing this trip so conscientiously – and, I might add, so intelligently – so thoroughly that I haven't had a minute. I often go out at half-past nine or ten in the morning and I don't get back until very late. The day before yesterday I took the boat to Vollendam, a very curious and, I believe, little visited place. Today to Haarlem to see the Frans Halses.[1] I've been alone here since yesterday. I am in so disastrous an emotional state that I was afraid of poisoning poor Fénelon with my dreariness, and I've given him a breathing spell, far from my sighs. I'll see him again at The Hague, but I shall come back to Amsterdam for the night and return to Paris either Sunday or Monday, overjoyed to embrace my little Mama and little Papa after so long an absence. I might not have had the courage to bear so long a separation if I had not decided on it all at once. But I've prolonged it almost from day to day. Fifteen times I've thought I would embrace you the next day. I never imagined that I could go a fortnight without embracing you. This also applies to my little brother, unless his success in life makes him impervious to my importunate effusions. I'm awfully unhappy about that theft, which is making my trip a heavy burden to you. Apart from this catastrophic adventure, I have been balancing my budget with the ingenuity of a Rouvier.[2] This hotel is so wildly expensive that to avoid paying 10 francs for a modest dinner, Fénelon hasn't taken his meals here for the last two days. But who is to blame? And why did he choose it and to all intents and purposes force it on me, seeing that I was in Antwerp when he reserved my room. And worst of all, how could this have been done on *Yeatman's* advice?[3] The fact is that if I take another trip I shall have to choose second-class hotels, where one is just as comfortable and doesn't pay exorbitant prices for a little extra luxury, especially as one hasn't even the pleasure of being 'classified', because there isn't a single Frenchman in this town. The trip in itself is not expensive. The most interesting excursions have cost us next to nothing. I value your advice about going to the country, all the more so as the hot-air heating frightens me and I believe that if I haven't had so much as a *trace of asthma* here (and I haven't) it's because the hotel is heated by hot-water pipes. But my state of mind does not permit of such an experiment, which could only do me *great harm*. Fénelon was *the only person* I could go away with. If I were not afraid of boring him with my present moroseness and not afraid of running out of funds (that is the real reason and I don't really mind telling you because since you will see me almost at the same time as this letter and will not be able to answer, it can't look as if I were preparing you for a 'touch' later on) I would spend another week in Holland or Belgium. But going to Illiers or anywhere else, especially at the present time, would be true madness.

Coming back to Paris, even with Bibesco (if he hasn't gone), Reynaldo, etc., will be hard on me, like any change of scene. But at least it's a place I know. Illiers would be terrible, and so would any other place – *just now*.

Fénelon is as kind as he can be. You wrote him a charming letter, addressed to M. de Fénélon.[4] That acute accent on top of the K in BibesKo . . . doesn't matter in the least. Have you any information about Fromentin's life? It's a bore to be so ignorant about someone I've just spent a fortnight with at the hotel.[5]

A thousand affectionate kisses,

Marcel

I suspect you of not reading my letters, which would be horrid. Since this one has been written during a pseudo-remission, do at least read it.

1. In *The Guermantes Way* (II. 544), the Duchesse de Guermantes speaks of the Frans Halses in the Haarlem museum, and the Narrator comments ironically on her way of looking at paintings.

2. Maurice Rouvier (1842 – 1911) had recently been appointed Finance Minister. Proust had apparently reported the loss of some money in an earlier letter to his mother.

3. Léon Yeatman had made the same tour with his wife not long before, and had given Proust an itinerary of places to stay and things to see.

4. In *Cities of the Plain* (II. 799), Proust assigns his mother's mistake (though in pronunciation rather than spelling) to Mme Poussin, a Combray lady, who in speaking of the author of *Télémaque* felt that the extra accent made the name sound softer.

5. Before travelling to Holland, Proust had borrowed a copy of *Les Maîtres d'autrefois*, by Eugène Fromentin (1820 – 76), and had then bought the book to take with him.

200
TO ANTOINE BIBESCO

[Probably Tuesday 28 October 1902]
My dear Antoine,

I am ill (caught cold) in bed. Though I haven't insisted on seeing you these past few days, I'm so exasperated with lying in bed that it would be ever so kind of you to pay me a little visit either before going to dinner (now, for instance) or about eleven o'clock on your way back from Mme de Peterborough's.[1]

As for the letter I've been wanting to write you for several days, this is what it is. I've noticed that it distresses you when I ask for news of the Princesse Bibesco.[2] On the other hand, it distresses me to have none and to have no answer to these questions that are constantly on my mind.

Is there anything in your mother's condition that worries you, that is, leads you to suppose that, when she recovers, some part of her present trouble will still be with her.

Don't you think you might postpone your holiday and go away with her when she is better, if she needs to be in the south somewhere. Wouldn't that make you happier?

If that would be difficult – or if it wouldn't be good for your mother, who is very highly strung, to have you with her at a time when you are rather worried and upset, wouldn't it be more soothing to your nerves if you were to leave before she comes back, so as to spare you both the excitement of a reunion followed by a parting, the opposite of the Beethoven sonata.[3]

I know how wildly indiscreet these anxieties are, but I can't help having them and would be ever so grateful if you'd set my mind at rest with a line (at least about the first question, the real state of your mother's health), since, and this I fully understand, you dislike speaking of it.

If you dine with the Strauses[4] – and even if they don't come to the dinner – I beg you not to joke, in an access of innocent but not inoffensive exuberance, about my affection for Nonelef (who in retrospect, incidentally, is getting most amazingly on my nerves); just say that we're very good friends, that he's one of my best friends, but not 'how he adores Nonelef, etc.' and other things that even my worst

270

enemy would not have the wit to dream up. You can tell Mme Straus
that I'm ill.
Until very soon, moschant, I hope.

Marcel

If you come towards midnight, I shall have a key brought down for
you, ring three times even so, but come in without waiting for anyone
to open. – If you don't find a key, come up and ring. It will mean that
there's someone to open the door.

1. Proust is anglicizing Pierrebourg.

2. Antoine's mother, the Princesse Alexandre Bibesco, née Hélène Costaki
Epureano. The sister-in-law of the Princesse de Brancovan, and like her a pianist, she had known Liszt, Wagner, Renan, Puvis de Chavannes, and many
other musicians, artists, and literary men of the day.

3. The three movements of Beethoven's Sonata in E-flat major, opus no. 81a,
dedicated to the Archduke Rudolph on his enforced departure from Vienna in
1809, are titled 'Les Adieux', 'L'Absence', and 'Le Retour' (Farewell, Absence,
Return).

4. That is, if M. and Mme Émile Straus were present at Mme de Pierrebourg's
dinner party.

201
TO ANTOINE BIBESCO

Monday [3 November 1902]
My dear little Antoine,

When I think that you wouldn't even let me talk to you about
what I did not yet realize was worrying you so, I am afraid that at
this particular moment you will throw away a letter from me in
anger. I am fully aware that I, like all those who did not know your
mother very well, who cannot recall to you any memory of her, have
become a stranger to you. But even so allow me, without for one moment intruding upon your grief, to tell you how deeply I am afflicted
by it. My poor friend, if you knew how many times since this morning I have lived through your journey, the moment when you learned
the worst, your arrival too late, and everything that must have followed.[1] I fear the violence of your grief, I would like to be with you

without your knowing it. It would make me very unhappy to see you in that state, but less so perhaps than to know nothing, to tremble every moment and tell myself that at this very moment you are racked with sobs. My affection for Mama, my admiration for your mother, and my affection for you – all these combine to make me feel your suffering more than I had thought it possible to suffer from someone else's misfortune, even when that someone had become a part of myself, so deeply had I got into the habit of owing him the greater part of my happiness, which is destroyed along with his. When I think that your poor eyes, your poor cheeks, all those features that I love so much because your thought and feeling dwell in them, are expressed by them, never cease to come and go in them, are at this moment, will be for so long, will always be, full of sorrow and are now bathed in tears. It hurts me physically to think of you in this state. I'll write to you or not, I'll speak to you of your sorrow or not, I'll do whatever you wish. I don't ask you to feel affection for me. All other feelings are certain to be shattered. But I never knew that I felt so much affection for you. I am very unhappy.

Marcel Proust

1. The Princesse Alexandre Bibesco had died in Bucharest on 31 October 1902, before Prince Antoine was able to reach her bedside. Proust must have read the obituary which appeared in *Le Figaro* on 3 Nov. 1902.

202
TO ANTOINE BIBESCO

Monday [10 November 1902]

My dear little Antoine,

I don't know anything about you – and yet I know too much, because when I think of you, which is all the time, I have the same feeling as in jealousy, though there's no connection. I mean that, without knowing anything precisely, I keep imagining everything best calculated to torture me, at every moment I see you either so shaken by sobs that it drives me to despair or so terrifyingly calm that it depresses me not to see you weeping, for that might comfort you a little; and I not only imagine your sad face, your sleeplessness, or if you do sleep your horrible dreams, and if they are pleasant, your even more horrible awakenings! – I also imagine your thoughts, and they are what pain me the most. Nevertheless, I say this to myself: Princesse Bibesco admired her son enormously. After all, Antoine should regard it as a duty to think she is still with him, that she is miserable, suffering to see him destroy himself with so much sorrow, and try not to grieve less, not to forget – that you will never do – but to make his grief compatible with the intellectual energy, which alone – forgive me, my dear little Antoine, for trying even now to encourage you – will enable you to become what your mother wished and to achieve the triumphs to which she aspired for you. At present, no doubt, they will give you no joy, since the thought of pleasing her was your strongest incentive and you will no longer be able to see her smile and bring her your laurels and lay them at her feet. But you will lay them on her grave. My dear little Antoine, in days of unhappiness I conceived a great affection, which has remained with me, for some words of Ruskin. My only reason for holding them to be true and certain is that a mind like his, so much greater than ours, a mind which must have perceived far more quickly than ours the arguments to the contrary but had gone beyond them, held these words to be true and certain:

'If, parting with the companions that have given you all the best joy you had on Earth, you desire ever to [meet their eyes again and clasp their hands, –] where eyes shall no more be dim, nor hands fail – if preparing yourselves to lie down [beneath the grass in silence and loneliness,] seeing no more beauty, and feeling no more gladness – you would care for the promise to you of a time when you should see God's light again, and know the things you have longed to know, and walk in the peace of everlasting Love etc.'[1]

If you think your brother[2] might at this time listen to such accents and find them sweet, quote this passage to him. I wrote to him two days ago, but I did not dare cite these words. But I remember all the good they did me. And I do not believe their power to soothe can ever be exhausted.

The people I care for just now are those who can speak to me of your mother or of you.

Believe, my dear little Antoine, in my profound affection.

Marcel Proust

Will you be back soon? I think they will make me leave Paris this winter, but I would rather not go until I have seen you.

1. Quoted in English from *The Bible of Amiens*, ch. IV; the words in square brackets were omitted by Proust in copying out the quotation. Proust also omits the first part of the sentence and, more significantly, this conclusion: '*then*, the Hope of these things to you is religion, the Substance of them in your life is Faith.'

2. Prince Emmanuel Bibesco (1877–1917), later a member of the Romanian parliament.

203
TO CONSTANTIN DE BRANCOVAN

[Shortly before 24 November 1902]

Dear friend,

I have various things to ask you, and since I don't know when I shall be able to see you, I am writing you this short letter.

You have been kind enough to ask me for things of mine for *La Renaissance latine*.[1] I have thought of something which, while a response to your gracious request, might perhaps be more to the taste of your subscribers than my modest prose. I have just completed a translation of an admirable and essentially 'Latin' book by Ruskin, *The Bible of Amiens* (Latin, because it is the history of Christianity in Gaul and the Orient, explained by the Amiens cathedral). The book will be published I think by *Le Mercure*, in February or March, I suppose.[2] Because of the great interest I think it holds (I can say this because, apart from the translation, it is none of my doing) I was hoping to publish if not the whole of it, because there are dull passages, at least the greater part in a magazine. Would you like this magazine to be *La Renaissance latine?* This would be the first periodical publication of Ruskin. And I believe it would be of considerable interest to your readers. Tell me what you think and how long you think the instalments should be. –

Something else. I know you are close to M. Bernstein. Would you happen to have seats you are not using for his *Joujou?* If so, I would be very glad to see it.[3] But of course this indiscreet question calls for an equally frank answer. It doesn't really matter much one way or the other.

I keep writing to Antoine and never receive the ghost of an answer. I am tormented and sad at having no news of him. If you know anything, you would give me great pleasure by passing it on to me.

Affectionately yours,
Marcel Proust

1. The issue of *La Renaissance latine* for 15 Nov. 1902 carries the name of Prince de Brancovan as editor-in-chief.

2. See letter 197. In fact Vallette was still hesitating over an offer of publication. Moreover, as usual Proust was too optimistic about the time it would take him to complete the work in hand; his translation did not appear in book form until 1904.

3. Proust did attend the dress rehearsal of Bernstein's *Joujou*, which took place at the Théâtre du Gymnase on 24 November 1902.

204
TO ALFRED VALLETTE

Thursday [27 November 1902]

Dear Sir,

I wrote to you on receiving the telegram you were kind enough to send me so promptly. But I am sure I forgot to post the letter, though I am quite unable to find it. So I don't know whether I may not have posted it without thinking. Anyway, I'm not sure, so just in case, I am going to repeat everything I said in it. I shall probably use the same terms. If you've received my letter, please forgive the resemblances. If I could remember it accurately, I would manage to avoid repetition by saying the same things in a different way. But precisely because my memory of it is vague, I shall not know if a sentence expressing a particular thought is identical with the one in which I expressed the same thought the other evening. Consequently, if whole sentences are the same, it will not as usual be because of too much, but because of too little, memory. So you don't want my poor *Bible of Amiens*, and I must confess that I fail to see why. Even if, as you say, it would be meaningless published by itself, such a publication would present no financial risk, since I would bear the costs,[1] and it would certainly not dishonour *Le Mercure*. For it is undoubtedly a beautiful work, apart from being curious and unknown. Can you really think *Le Mercure* would suffer by publishing a work by Ruskin, believed by many to be his finest? In saying this I am quite sincere, for out of all his works it is this one that I chose to translate. And if only one of Ruskin's works were to be translated, it is the *Bible* that should be published, even if it were not the finest. Because it is the only one that deals with France – at once the history of France, a French city, and French Gothic. If for no other reason than to enable the reader to verify and compare, since it is easier after all to go to Amiens than to Verona or Padua. And it is more relevant to our preoccupations. That is why the Société d'Édition Artistique wanted to begin its translations with this one.[2] I believe also that I once quoted to you the passage (which alarmed me at the time but which I invoke today) in a book by M. Brunhes, where he says that if any of Ruskin's books should arouse the interest of us French, it is *The Bible of Amiens*, the only one dealing with our history and our monuments.[3] And finally, as you know, Ruskin thought it eminently representative of his system. –

I shall send someone to *Le Mercure* Monday morning. If all these arguments have not moved and convinced you, if your decision remains unchanged, don't trouble to reply, just give the messenger my manuscript: that will be the black sail of Theseus. – But then, like Moreau's woman bearing the *Head of Orpheus*, I shall have to embark on dreary wanderings in search of a shelter for the genius. And this duty seems so urgent that until it is accomplished I shall not be able to give you a reply about the Ruskin *Pages choisies*. I have perused the only two books that have been written about Ruskin, and the quotations amount to so little that to tell the truth there would be hardly any overlap, which disposes of one of my objections. But the other holds good. Just the sort of book to dampen the enthusiasm his genius should arouse! In place of a living cathedral a cold museum full of odds and ends. It will make known the works in which he resembles other great writers, not those in which he differs.[4] In any case, I must first, even if I drop 'Of Kings' Treasuries',[5] find a home for the wandering and banished *Bible*. And if, citing itself, it can say to *Le Mercure*: 'I knocked at your door and you did not let me in,' imagine how it will be when I call on other publishers who are probably illiterate.

Forgive my insistence.

Yours faithfully,
Marcel Proust

---

1. In the contract eventually signed by Proust and Vallette on 26 February 1904 Proust was granted the usual royalties. He was later to make the same ges-

ture, of offering to bear the costs of publication, in connection with
Du côté de chez Swann – with deplorable consequences.

2. The Artistic Publishing Company seems to have brought out only one volume (containing *The Crown of Wild Olive* and *The Seven Lamps of Architecture*), in 1901, of a projected complete edition of Ruskin's works in translation, before going bankrupt sometime before 1904.

3. H. J. Brunhes, *Ruskin et la Bible: pour servir à l'histoire d'une pensée*
(1901); the H. J. stood for Henriette and Jean, a wife-and-husband team.

4. Proust was later to express a very different opinion on the *Pages choisies*
(Selected Pages), which in the end he agreed to edit for Éditions du Mercure de
France.

5. The title of the first essay in Ruskin's *Sesame and Lilies* – suggesting that
Proust had already begun to translate that work.

205
TO ANTOINE BIBESCO

Thursday [4 December 1902]
My dear little Antoine,

Never for one moment have I stopped thinking of your cruel
grief, and yet when I saw your poor letter, when I saw your dear
handwriting utterly changed, barely recognizable, with its shrunken,
diminished letters, like eyes contracted from weeping, it came as a
fresh blow to me, as if I had for the first time become clearly aware of
your distress. I remember when Mama lost her parents, her suffering
was so great that I still wonder how she could go on living. I had seen
her every day and every hour of the day. But then I went to Fontainebleau and spoke to her on the phone. And suddenly, over the
phone, I heard her poor broken, tortured voice, changed for ever
from the voice I had always known, now full of cracks and fissures;
and it was on hearing those bleeding, broken fragments in the receiver
that I had my first terrible inkling of what had broken for ever within
her.[1] The same with your letter, in which I felt how infinitely it fatigued you to write, regardless of whether or not you spoke of your
grief. In a manner of speaking, your letter gave me pleasure, but it
also made me very unhappy.

As for my coming to see you, you haven't understood my
suggestion.[2] On the one hand I shall *have to* leave Paris, but on the
other hand it is almost physically impossible for me to leave immediately. And though the reason is still an absolute secret, I shall reveal it

to you if you like, so that you may judge. I won't ask you to write, now that I can sense what an effort it is for you. But couldn't you arrange for someone to tell me your plans and let me know whether my idea of spending March, April, May, and June if you like (and if there are no flowers) would appeal to you. I have a feeling that you will be coming back to Paris just as I am getting ready to leave, and that makes me miserable. Or rather, it doesn't make me miserable, because if you arrive, I simply won't leave, but will somehow arrange to spend a good month near my poor little Antoine, weeping beside you, or rather not weeping, but trying to revive your interest in life, being as good and kind as I possibly can. Alas, I was beginning to feel I had done wrong in speaking of nothing but your grief in my letters, and I was resolved to start speaking of other things, starting with those which would give least offence to your grief and those which, by offering some interest for the intelligence or some appeal to habit, might with the least violence open the 'way to your heart'. But your poor letter hurls me back to the bottom of the slope I had climbed with my odds and ends of news which might perhaps not hold your interest, but would at least divert your attention. And I feel that you are so exhausted, so detached – or absorbed, that I don't dare say anything more or tell you any of the things I meant to. I am going to tell you (swear not to repeat it) what it is that prevents me from leaving straight away (unless you think my presence indispensable, in which case I would leave regardless). It's because my brother is probably getting married, and I shall have to call on the girl,[3] whom I don't know, etc. etc. But no one knows this, nor should anyone know. –

If in December you want to do something without me after all, don't go to Egypt, you'd do better to go to Constantinople, where you would see Bertrand.[4] Your visit would sweeten the beginnings of his exile and his unaccustomed solitude. And all things considered, your long-standing friendship for him would make his company rather enjoyable, since he is not one of those unbearable people in whose presence one is obliged to stifle one's sorrow. Everyone speaks of you with deep and afflicted sympathy. Several friends of yours whom I have met recently, such as Mme Le Bargy and Mme Tristan Bernard,[5] spoke of you in a way that moved me deeply. But let me tell you what touched me the most. The other day I went to Gallé's to have something engraved on a vase. The assistant tells me that no work is being done because the elder M. Gallé had died that very day.[6] I remark that this must be a cruel blow to young M. Gallé. 'Monsieur Gallé doesn't know,' he tells me. 'How is that?' I ask. 'He is in such a state of despair, it has so shaken his health that we don't

dare tell him the news, for fear it might kill him.' – 'Over his father's
illness?' I ask. – 'Oh no, he didn't even know his father was ill. A month
ago, M. Gallé lost the person he admired most in all the world, Princesse Bibesco, and he has been so dejected ever since that the doctor
has ordered total rest and seclusion. And Monsieur, we all understand,
she was such a fine woman, etc.' – And this assistant had no idea that
I knew you. It's the hundredth time I've heard someone say those very
words. –

Forgive me, my dear little Antoine, I only tell you things that
are likely to make you sad. But that's all over now. I won't write to
you any more and when I see you, I shall speak to you only of innocent trifles. If you don't feel up to reading me, you won't read me,
and if you don't want to listen to me, you'll leave me, but this
complicity with your grief would be wrong and I will countenance it
no longer. Your mother would be furious with the criminal friend
who, hardly for pleasure but driven by weakness and desolation, keeps
her son's tears flowing. I am sure that if we were together serious occupations would enable us to find a compromise between consolations
that you would reject and amusements that would not amuse
you – and a sorrow which you really must prevent from engulfing
you, if only to preserve the force, fullness and purity of your memory,
your vision of a past which tears would finally blur and darken.

This marriage comes just at the wrong time. But even before I
knew of it for sure, I told you that my suggestion applied only to the
end of February, March, April, and as long after that as you wish.
About that I would really like an answer, though of course I could
come at once if the thing were to be broken off. As for spending the
whole winter in Paris, that would be both physically and psychologi-
cally impossible for me. Still, if you come back in January – or whenever you do come back – I shall postpone my departure to be near you
for a while, if you think you would like to have me around for a
while and that my grief over your misfortune will make my attempts
to revive your interest in life, in the various forms of intellectual life,
and in human activity more bearable to you.

Mme Le Bargy was not at all as I expected and exactly as you
told me, very very intelligent. I met her on the night of the dress rehearsal of *Joujou*. Sée took me to see her at two in the morning to tell
her it had been a flop.[7] – And once you meet people, you keep running
into them. That same week I sat next to her twice at dinner, once at
Mme de Pierrebourg's and once at Mme Straus's, and I was really very
much taken with her. This evening I had dinner at the Noailles's with
your cousin Marghiloman,[8] whom I know you like, but I had no op-

portunity to speak to her. And several times I dined at the homes of your cousins, who are charming women. But you are the only person I would really like to see at the present moment. And I embrace you as I love you, with all my heart.

Marcel Proust

1. See letters 107, 108. Proust would recollect this 'broken' voice on the telephone in connection with the Narrator's grandmother in *The Guermantes Way* (II. 136).

2. In a letter of 23 November 1902 (*CMP* III. 177), Proust had offered to come to Romania early in 1903, to stay near the Bibescos' country estate of Corcova: 'If I don't get asthma there,' he said, 'I could stay through February, March, April if you're still there, and May if there are no flowers. I wouldn't bother you, for I would be some distance away, but able to come and talk with you on days when you wanted to see me, but not on days when you would rather I didn't.'

3. Mlle Marthe Dubois-Amiot, whom Robert Proust married in February 1903.

4. Bertrand de Fénelon left Paris on 8 December 1902 for a posting as attaché in the French Embassy at Constantinople.

5. Mme Le Bargy, née Pauline Benda (b. 1880), a well-known actress at the Comédie Française and the wife of one of the shareholders; Mme Bernard, née Bomsel, wife of the playwright and novelist Tristan Bernard (1866–1947).

6. Charles Gallé, noted glassmaker and ceramist, died at Nancy on 3 December 1902 at the age of eighty-four. His son, Émile Gallé (1846–1904), was a glassmaker and botanist.

7. Having fallen ill at the end of October, while playing in Henry Bernstein's *Détour,* Mme Le Bargy had been obliged to drop the part she was rehearsing in *Joujou;* hence her interest in the fate of the dress rehearsal (see letter 203). Edmond Sée (1875–1959) was a playwright and drama critic.

8. Mme Alexandre Marghiloman, née Princesse A. Stirbey.

206

TO HIS MOTHER

[Saturday evening 6 December 1902]

My dear little Mama,

Since I can't speak to you, I'm writing to tell you that I fail to understand you. You could guess, if you don't know, that from

the time I come in I cry all night, and not without reason; and all day
long you say things to me like: 'I couldn't sleep last night because the
servants were up and about until eleven o'clock.' I would be only too
glad if that were what prevented me from sleeping! Today, because I
was suffering, I committed the crime of ringing for Marie (to bring
me my asthma powders) who had come and told me she had finished
her lunch, and you punished me, as soon as I had taken my Trional,
by making people shout and hammer nails all day. Thanks to you, I
was in such a state of nerves that when poor Fénelon came with Lauris
I flew at him, because of something he had said – something very disagreeable, I admit – (Fénelon, not Lauris) with my fists. I didn't know
what I was doing. I picked up the new hat he had just bought,
stamped on it, tore it into shreds, and finally ripped out the lining.[1]
In case you think I'm exaggerating, I enclose a piece of the lining, so
you can see I'm telling the truth. But don't throw it away, I want
you to return it to me in case he can still make use of it. Of course,
if you see him, not a word of all this. I must say, I'm glad the victim
was a friend. Because if Papa or you had said something disagreeable
to me at that particular moment, of course I wouldn't have done anything, but I don't know what I might have said. After that I was so
hot that I couldn't get dressed and I sent to ask you if I should have
dinner here or not. While I'm on the subject, you seem to think
you're pleasing the servants and punishing me at the same time when
you put me under interdict and tell them not to come when I ring or
wait on me at the table, etc. You're very much mistaken. You don't
realize how uncomfortable your footman was this evening at not
being able to serve me. He put all the dishes down right beside me
and apologized: 'Madame's orders,' he said, 'I can't help it.' – As for
that night table you took away from me, as though depriving me of
dessert, I can't do without it. If you need it, give me another or I'll
buy one. I would rather do without chairs. – As for the servants, you
know what a keen psychologist I am and what flair I have, and I assure you that you're quite wrong. But that's no concern of mine, and
I shall always be glad to fall in with your views in such matters,
provided you let me know what they are, because how am I to guess
that when Marie has finished her lunch I am running the risk of having her sacked when I ask her to make a fire in a room where Fénelon
and Lauris, even with their coats on, couldn't stick it out, and to bring
me my asthma powders. What afflicts me – though in my present distress these petty quarrels leave me indifferent – is not finding the moral
comfort I thought I could expect from you in these truly desperate
hours. The truth is that as soon as I feel better, the life that makes me

feel better exasperates you and you demolish everything until I feel ill again. This isn't the first time. I caught cold last night; if it turns to asthma, which it's sure to in the present state of affairs, I have no doubt that you'll be good to me again, when I'm in the same state as this time last year. But it's sad, not being able to have affection and health at the same time. If I had both at this moment, it would be no more than I need to help me fight against an unhappiness which, especially since yesterday evening (but I haven't seen you since), has become so intense that I can no longer contend with it. So I'd have wished, but too late, to get back my letter to M. Vallette.[2] I may write to him again, changing my mind. We'll speak of it another time.

A thousand loving kisses,

Marcel

1. The scene is echoed in *The Guermantes Way*, where the Baron de Charlus is the butt of the Narrator's 'wild rage' (II. 580): '. . . I seized the Baron's new silk hat, flung it to the ground, trampled it, picked it up again, began blindly pulling it to pieces, wrenched off the brim, tore the crown in two, heedless of the continuing vociferations of M. de Charlus.'

2. In a letter of the same date, 6 December 1902 (*CMP* III. 187), Proust had undertaken to complete his translation of *The Bible of Amiens* by about 1 February 1903, and thereafter to compile a volume of Ruskin's *Pages choisies* for Éditions du Mercure de France.

207

TO ANTOINE BIBESCO

Saturday [20 December 1902]

My dear little Antoine,

Every night before going to sleep I read your dear letters and fall asleep with sad but pleasant thoughts of you. There were two until a while ago (Mama had given me hers). Now there are three and the last is the nicest of all. But it has upset me terribly. I shall try without getting too confused, though my thoughts are very much so, to tell you why.

1st For various reasons too complicated to explain, it is next to impossible for me to go to Egypt. Apart from the fact that the journey would be so fatiguing that I'd be afraid to make it alone, that with you I could have made it, but not otherwise, – I don't believe it's desirable from your point of view. Because you say 'we', which means no doubt that your brother is coming with you. Well, no one could be nicer. But he doesn't know me, and all the good he can do you and you him would be ruined by the presence of an outsider, which would irritate him at any time and would be odious to him in his present state of mind. But most of all, as I've told you – and you know it's a secret, even the girl's brothers don't so much as suspect it! – my brother is getting married. And I can't go off on such a trip at the risk of not being able to come back for the wedding if I'm ill or even tired.

2nd   Since I nevertheless find the thought of not seeing you utterly distressing, especially as I shall have to leave Paris this spring or rather late this winter. And if the marriage had not been put off until almost the first of March, there would have been a possibility of my not being here on your return! But in any case I'd have arranged to be here, because the need to see you has lately become so cruel as to keep me awake at night. On the other hand, I must deliver my Ruskin to *Le Mercure* on 1 February, not a single day later, and between now and then begin a second for that same *Mercure*, write an article or two a week, etc., etc., and I don't see how I could take my Ruskin, that is, 30 volumes, and my manuscripts (because I put references all over [*illegible*] *The Bible of Amiens*) away with me.

So how would this appeal to you: that I should go and spend 24 or 48 hours at some place not too far from Paris, because you know I'm always ill after a journey, and with only a day to spend I shouldn't want to be too ill, Munich, for instance, if, as I believe, it is only twelve hours from Paris and consequently half-way between Corcova and Paris (I shall check the distances on a timetable, but I haven't got one here and I wanted to answer you straight away). Even if it's fifteen hours, I'll do it, and if I'm too tired I'll stay three days. But I can't stay any longer. That could be about 10 January or even the 7th or 8th (on the 2nd and 5th there are anniversaries[1] for which I ought to be at home. But if you very much preferred, I could manage). But perhaps your grief has brought on a physical reaction and the thought of 12 hours in the train frightens you, especially in the direction of the cold weather, and besides you will have so much fatigue to contend with on your trip to Egypt. In that case I shall bear my hardship, my yearning for Antoine, with patience, and will wait until the 1st of March for the sorrowful joy of seeing you again. If before then I see a possibility of making myself free for ten days, I shall go and spend eight days (plus the trip there and back) near Corcova, at Strehaia,[2] I suppose. But I don't think it likely that I'll be able to do so before 20 January, when you tell me you are leaving. No, I really don't.

And this so-called work I've taken up again – it plagues me for several reasons. Most of all, because what I'm doing at present is not real work, only documentation, translation, etc. It's enough to arouse my thirst for creation, without of course slaking it in the least. Now that for the first time since my long torpor I have looked inward and examined my thoughts, I feel all the insignificance of my life; a thousand characters for novels, a thousand ideas urge me to give them body, like the shades in the *Odyssey* who plead with Ulysses to give them a little blood to drink to bring them back to life and whom the hero brushes aside with his sword. I have awakened the sleeping bee and I feel its cruel sting far more than its helpless wings. I had enslaved my intelligence to my peace of mind. In striking off its fetters I thought I was merely delivering a slave, but I was giving myself a master whom I have not the physical strength to satisfy and who would kill me if I did not resist him. So many things are weighing on me! when my mind is wholly taken up with you. I never cease to think of you, and when I write to you I keep talking about myself. If my friendship can be of any comfort to you, then bear in mind that my constant sadness over your desolation has infinitely reinforced and magnified it.

Yours,
Marcel

I can't give you any news of Bertrand. He left for Constantinople a fortnight ago next Monday. But we haven't yet written to each other. He was rather tired when he left.

1. I.e. of the death and burial of Mme Proust's mother.
2. A town in south-western Romania, near the Yugoslavian border.

208
TO ANTOINE BIBESCO

[22 – 24 December 1902]

My dear little Antoine,

You say my telegram is unintelligible. What do you think of this one: 'Received letters today sorry Asti i at 10 o'clock Munich will write una deco toi. – Antoine.' (I enclose the original so you can give the telegraph office at Corcova a piece of your mind.) As for the one that came to you so absurdly garbled, it was: 'You haven't answered me about Munich.' It was written out in my best hand. But if you were in one particular place, how is it that you haven't received my two letters suggesting Munich (I said Munich as I might have said any place half-way between Paris and Corcova). And if your post was not forwarded, how is it that you didn't find my letters there before you wrote, and how is it that you don't tell me in your letter that you have just been away? If I still had the same suspiciously affectionate feelings towards you as in the old days – my grief over your misfortune has effaced them completely by making me incapable of any sorrow other than the sorrow it gives me to think of your sadness – what a splendid occasion for persecution mania all these coincidences would have offered me!

I would gladly give you an idea of what's going on, but I've been living entirely in my books. I had dinner yesterday at the Noailles's, where I dine fairly often. Apart from the usual company, young Guiche was there, a matter deserving of no special mention if Lucien [Daudet] had not been placed beside him, which had such an effect on Lucien that he talked in a steady stream, I'd never seen him so voluble, as joyful as Mme Bovary when she looked at herself in the mirror and cried out: 'I have a lover, I have a lover!'[1] As for me, it made me sad to see him sitting so close to the bacillus (of snobbery), only too eager to succumb to the infection. But this is what happened (all this is strictly in confidence, a mere attempt to speak to you of something that isn't sad, *for I will never speak sadly to you again*, my poor boy): Lucien was convinced that if the Gramonts had stopped inviting him it was because of his brother (*Libre Parole* and the Duchesse née Rothschild).[2] This certainty overwhelmed him but at least it accounted for his not being invited. Towards the end of the dinner the innocent Guiche asked him: 'Do you have a brother?' Lucien in his stupefaction would have liked to take advantage of this blessed ignorance, this *sancta simplicitas*, and say: 'No, I haven't, and if you ever hear that a Daudet has said anything about the R[oth-schild]s and the J[ew]s, it has nothing to do with me.' But your implacable cousin had heard the question and looked straight at him. So that after a painful hesitation he replied: 'Yes.'

Another trifling anecdote. Gregh is getting married. The 'Forsaken Woman', who had not yet been informed, was visiting Mme Baignères with a Mme Sichel (for your internal *Tout-Paris*, I add: Sichel-Dulong, widow of the dealer in Japanese artefacts, friend of the Goncourts, children died of tuberculosis).[3] Since illness had for some time prevented this Sichel woman from going out, she didn't know about the Forsaken Woman's liaison with the young Poet. She says: 'I hear Gregh is getting married.' Old Mme Baignères breaks out in a cold sweat, denies it, protests, tries to change the subject. Mme Sichel says: 'Actually I was surprised to hear it, he's so ugly, bald, vulgar, etc.' Renewed protestations from Mme Baignères. The Sichel woman begins floundering and finally says: 'Well, anyway, I don't find him attractive'; (a silence); then, at last realizing her gaffe, she says in a loud, clear voice: 'Not at least for a young girl!'

My brother's marriage has been brought forward to 2 February! It's intolerable!

Yours ever,
Marcel

P.S.   Your brother has written me a letter so exquisite that I don't believe I have ever received one so involuntarily beautiful. I told the Noailles about it and they spoke of him with the most fervid praise.

I apologize for putting 'tenderly' at the end of my telegram. That was idiotic. And your 'affectionately' made me aware of it. Forgive me. When one feels that those one loves are sad, one hopes that affection will make them forget it.

1. Cf. Flaubert, *Madame Bovary*, Part ii, ch. 9. Armand Agénor Auguste Antoine, Duc de Guiche (1879–1962), was then twenty-three years old; Lucien Daudet was twenty-four.

2. Léon Daudet wrote for *La Libre Parole*, the self-styled 'anti-Semitic and independent' daily; Guiche's mother, the Duchesse de Gramont, was a Rothschild by birth.

3. The *Journal des Débats* for 9 Jan. 1903 announced the engagement of Fernand Gregh to Mlle Harlette Hayem, daughter of Mme Jules Comte and stepdaughter of the editor of the *Revue de l'art ancien et moderne. Tout-Paris* is a directory, 'Who's Who in Paris'. The 'Forsaken Woman' is unidentified.

209
TO ANTOINE BIBESCO

Monday [19 January 1903]
My dear little Antoine,

Having so offended you the other day in spite of myself, I don't want to do it again and I shall try to answer you very precisely in such a way as not to vex you again. Actually, only the first part of my letter will be ticklish in this respect. I don't believe I shall be running any risk in the second and third.

PART I

If in the fragment of your letter that I enclose with mine the word underlined (by me) is 'or' [*ou*] (I myself think it is 'by' [*dès*]), which would make your sentence: 'So I believe I can conclude that you would come to Constantinople only if you received my telegram in three or four days – *or* after 2 February' – I must alas reply that you are under a misapprehension, which seems incomprehensible in view of my many long letters.

You see, since the wedding is on the 2nd, the civil marriage will take place on the 31st; and so, even if I am able to miss all the dinners, etc., I shall have to be back on the 30th, and for that I should have to leave Constantinople on the 27th or 28th (on the supposition that I can do the trip non-stop, which is unlikely, considering that I was planning to make two stops even on the way to Strehaia). A telegram from you in three or four days means on the 21st or 22nd. In other words, even if I left the *same day*, which is impossible, I'd arrive in Constantinople on the 24th or 25th, which would mean staying *two days*. You see it's impossible.

PART II

But if it is 'you must have a telegram by two or three days after 2 February', then my reply is this (in so far as I can foresee the state of my health and how much the wedding will have fatigued me, etc.): Since I'd have gone to Strehaia to see you, I shall be just as glad to go to Constantinople. Only I don't want to go to Strehaia unless I can stay at least a month. *A fortiori* to Constantinople, which is a much more fatiguing trip. But at Strehaia I don't know what I'd have done if you had gone away and left me, whereas in Constantinople you wouldn't have to worry about that, because I have Bertrand who would prevent me from being bored if my need for rest requires me to stay longer than you (if you are not planning to spend that much time in Constantinople). You will say that under these conditions, and if we are not returning to Paris together, it would be more practical for me to stay in Paris, where we shall have a longer time in which to see each other. But since they want me to go away, I don't know if we shall see each other for very long. So it wouldn't be so impractical.

PART III

But in all this it would be *absurd* of you to subordinate your plans to mine for one *minute*. If Constantinople suits you at the present time, go there – and if you mean to return at just about the time I

287

could go, I shall be delighted, because then I won't go, I shall wait for you in Paris and see you just as quickly and as soon as if I were in Constantinople. Moreover, even if you didn't go to Constantinople until about the 7th or 8th (my time), my arrival there to join you would not be absolutely certain, though highly probable, and besides, to give me the pleasure of your company for any length of time, you would have to stay at least ten days or a fortnight.

But since every prospect of a long journey is for me a source of great agitation, do please, *as soon as* you envisage a probability, that is, as soon as you are able to say, 'It has become probable that I shall not go to Constantinople and shall return to Paris on the . . . , so don't go [to Constantinople]' 'It has become probable that I shall go to Constantinople about 8 February, so do join me there', tell me so without delay, so as not to prolong my useless agitation and uncertainty, on top of the idiotic agitation of these last few days, consisting of: 'Will I burst into giggles while passing the collection box at Saint-Augustin – or while listening to the Mayor's speech?'[1] 'Will I be able to deliver Ruskin to M. Vallette on 1 February?'

But once again, don't change your plans in any way on my account. Constantinople tempts me a great deal but frightens me a little, especially because I'm afraid that you will leave the day after I get there and that I will be reluctant to stay on. So do it, don't do it, do it with me, do it without me, do it exactly as you please, and don't let the thought of my arrangements, or the very notion of my existence, play any part whatsoever.

Yours ever,
Marcel

I shall probably write to Bertrand but shall not mention the probability of my or your coming to Constantinople, since it looks so vague to me and since I don't know whether you want me to speak of it. It will always be time enough to speak of it if our plans take shape. But you may speak of it if you like. If you do go to Constantinople in the next few days, don't tell Bertrand the stories I told you (paltry gossip) in my last letter,[2] I'll tell you why.

Marcel

In case you do speak to Bertrand of your Constantinople plans, it would be preferable for you to tell him you haven't yet mentioned them to me, that you are going to ask me to come but haven't yet done so; then he won't be surprised at my not having mentioned it to him. And tell me what you have done about this. – But here's what I've been thinking. Even if you aren't going until about the 6th, wouldn't it be better for me to stay in Paris and for you to have a good visit with Bertrand alone. Then you'd see me in Paris and you'd be spared a fatiguing conjunction? – I mean this in an extremely friendly way, and I beg you to read it in that light.

As I reread your letter, the *context* seems to prove that 'or' is impossible. But in the land of '*filioque*'[3] my subtlety won't surprise you too much.

1. Proust was to be best man at his brother's wedding, at the church of Saint-Augustin on 2 February 1903; the religious ceremony was preceded by a civil ceremony at which the Mayor of Paris spoke.

2. See letter 208.

3. A reference to Romania as a Greek Orthodox country; though in fact the doctrine of *filioque* was repudiated by the Eastern Church and accepted by the Roman Catholic Church.

210
TO CONSTANTIN DE BRANCOVAN

[Second half of January 1903]

Dear friend,

You know how fond I am of you. And especially at a time when you've been so good to me and my Ruskins, I don't like to seem to be finding fault with you – but I find it incredible that, knowing as you do that I've been working for four years on a translation of *The Bible of Amiens*,[1] that my translation is soon to be published, that it has given me a great deal of trouble and that I attach a great deal of importance to it – I find it incredible that knowing all this you should say to me in front of Lauris (or anyone else) as you did just now: 'It must be full of mistakes, because you don't really know English.' My dear Constantin, I'm sure you meant no harm. *But could someone who detested me and wanted with a few words to destroy the fruit of my four years' labour*, carried on in the midst of illness – I ask you – could someone who wanted my translation to be read by no one and utterly ignored, *have said anything worse?* Repeat only that to three people, and I might just as well not have spent a single one of the thousand (and how many more!) hours of work this book has cost me. –

As for the work itself, you know I'm not in the habit of over-rating my achievements or boring people with my productions. But I do believe – not because of my talent, which is negligible, but because of my conscientiousness, which is infinite – that this translation will be virtually unequalled, a veritable reconstruction. If you knew that for every ambiguous expression, every obscure phrase, I have consulted at least ten English writers and amassed a whole file of correspondence, you would not speak of 'mistakes'. And by delving into the meaning of every word, the implications of every turn of phrase, and the con-nections between ideas, I acquired so precise a knowledge of this text that when I consulted an Englishman – or a Frenchman well versed in English – about some difficulty, he usually took an hour to detect the difficulty and congratulated me on knowing English better than an Englishman. In that he was mistaken. I don't know a word of spoken English and I don't read English easily. But having worked on *The Bible of Amiens* for four years, I know it entirely by heart, and it has become so nearly assimilated, so transparent to me, that I am able to see not only the nebulosities resulting from the inadequacy of my scrutiny but also those resulting from the irreducible obscurity of the thought itself. On more than a score of sentences d'Humières[2] said to me: 'That is impossible to translate, the English is meaningless. If it were up to me, I'd skip it.' In the end, by dint of patience, I found meaning even in those sentences. And if there are still any mistakes in my translation, it is in the clear and simple passages, for the obscure ones have been meditated, scrutinized and reworked over a period of years. – [3]

Telling you all this, dear friend, is hardly in my character. I don't believe I have ever in all my life talked so much about myself to anyone. But your injustice made me rather angry, and I was rather frightened at the possible consequences of your words for me. When you see Antoine Bibesco, ask him if he thinks I have a good under-standing of Ruskin's text. He has often seen me hesitating over a meaning when he thought there was no room for doubt. And then, lis-tening to my explanations, he saw that there was a basis for my doubt. And when he saw how I finally resolved the problem, he would say: '*I wouldn't have thought it possible to translate anyone so well.*' It's a bit ridiculous giving you all these references, but isn't it necessary? And yet, if you were to ask me in English for something to drink, I would not understand you, because I learned English when I had asthma and couldn't talk, I learned with my eyes and am unable to pronounce the words or to recognize them when pronounced by others. I don't claim to know English. I claim to know Ruskin. And you know that I haven't many pretensions. Perhaps you are still convinced of the contrary and believe my translation to be a series of absurdities. But in that case, do refrain out of friendship for me from telling anyone, let the reader find out for himself. Forgive my frankness and believe in my grateful affection.

Marcel Proust

P.S. The corrected proofs are with my concierge. I have nothing more to change. But if your magazine usually sends two sets of proofs, I can read the second proof to make sure my corrections have been fully understood. (When I say 'nothing more to change', I believe that to be the case.) But of course I shall change anything you want me to. – Still, I am afraid we shall lower Ruskin in the reader's esteem and detract from his strange charm if we turn him into some sort of Mérimée.

1. In fact he had begun work on the translation in October 1899, a little more than three years before.

2. Vicomte Robert-Aymeric-Eugène d'Humières (1868 – 1915), translator of Kipling. Proust had known him since 1895 and consulted him on his Ruskin translations.

3. There is no lack of mistakes in Proust's version of *The Bible of Amiens*, of which his mother supplied him with a rough translation that he then proceeded to polish. Yet much of what he says here is true, and his translation of *Sesame and Lilies* was to be impeccable.

211
TO ANTOINE BIBESCO

[Monday evening 26 January 1903]

My dear little Antoine,

1st I'm fonder of you than you think, and the thought of spending five days with you and staying on in Constantinople while you run off to Paris is odious to me. So I shall remain in Paris (I shall not go to Constantinople), I shall see you five days later and shall not see Bertrand – which grieves me – I shall not see Santa Sophia – which, though people mean more to me than things, upsets me in a different way – I shall not see the Golden Horn, a thought which gives me palpitations – *But,* five days later I shall see Antoine, and if my parents and my health don't drive me out of Paris too soon, I shall spend a good month with him in Paris (whereas, supposing I'd found myself in Constantinople, exhausted by the trip, God knows when I'd have been able to join you in Paris).

If it seems to you that this resolution (which I simplify because I am very tired and this written résumé will soon be backed up by an oral commentary) shows a lack of affection, you are very hard to please. – As for going to Constantinople, to stay there for five days and come back to Paris with you might not mean certain death, but would at least tire me beyond all reason.

2nd Seeing that I'm worn out with work, etc., etc., there may be no urgent need for me to tell you here why I wired you this morning: 'Since when has Bertrand known?' I'll explain when I see you. Anyway it's of no interest. But could anyone possibly imagine a reply more horrid (if you hadn't written it, I'd have said idiotic, but since you're not an idiot, I can only put it down to perversity) than this:

'Since I wrote to him.'

I send you a telegram with reply prepaid. Showing that I attach some importance to the answer to my question. The question was: 'Since when has Bertrand known?', in other words, 'When did Bertrand receive the letter in which you told him?', in other words: 'When did you write to him and how long do letters take from Bucharest to Constantinople?'

All this would have cost me 50 francs to telegraph to Bucharest, so I summed it up intelligently as

'Since when has Bertrand known?'

'Since I wrote to him' is an answer to which Flaubert would have given a place of honour in his *Dictionnaire de la bêtise humaine*[1] and which I simply inscribe on the title-page of *The Golden Book of Antonine Cruelty*. Because, seeing how eager I was to know, it was pure Satanism to reply: 'Since I wrote to him, but as you don't know when I wrote and as that is just what you are asking, I am leaving your thirst unslaked, my good friend.'

All the same, keep me informed of your plans as soon as they take shape in one direction or another, for though I have no share in them they agitate me nevertheless (because of my absurd nervous state brought on by the fatigue of correcting proofs, this marriage, etc.).

The only situation, one that as far as I can see will not arise, which would take me to Constantinople would be if your affairs kept you in Bucharest for another month or three weeks. Then I would go and spend those three weeks near you at the Hôtel Boulevard (a charming name) and I would be less unhappy about abandoning you in Constantinople, since I'd have seen you quietly first.

But five days after so long an absence – and what an absence – are beyond the strength of your affectionate

Marcel

I am nevertheless *exceedingly touched* by your Constantinopolitan project and *I will never forget it.*

1. (Dictionary of Human Stupidity); cf. Flaubert's *Dictionnaire des idées reçues*, intended as part of the unfinished *Bouvard et Pécuchet*.

212
TO ANTOINE BIBESCO

Wednesday evening [28 January 1903]

My dear little Antoine,

I almost changed my mind about Constantinople! By a strange coincidence Constantin, who was not supposed to go to Romania this month, is leaving for Bucharest on the 6th. The thought of having a travelling companion made it all seem so simple that I hesitated for a few minutes. But then the reasons I gave you seemed better after all, so I am standing by my original decision. I told you those things would appear any day in *Le Figaro* and now that they haven't, you probably think I was joking. It's because the Breton fishermen take up a lot of space, and so would my article.[1] We'll have to wait till they stop starving and I'm not yet man of letters enough to think their hunger is less interesting than my gossip. When you see Bertrand, tell him to swear never to say a word to anyone about a letter I shall write him soon, and which I shall distinguish from others by signing myself *Le Cobaye* [The Guinea Pig]. You will convey his oath to me by word of mouth. I'd rather he didn't mention it if he writes to me in the meantime.

Ever yours, my dear little Antoine,

Marcel Proust

1. Throughout January 1903 *Le Figaro* devoted much space to the misery in Brittany resulting from a disastrous fishing season. Proust's article was the first of his 'Salons' (see letter 227), one of which was to contain a portrait sketch of Bibesco.

213

TO CONSTANTIN DE BRANCOVAN

Thursday evening [29 January 1903]

Dear friend,

Here are the revised proofs for 15 February. I shall send you those for 15 March tomorrow.[1] Your very kind note saying you would be glad to have me with you on your trip to Bucharest gave me great pleasure, because there are times when I suffer from a slight persecution mania and think everyone is bored with me. Unfortunately, I'm very much afraid, almost sure in fact, that I won't be able to go. In the first place, the 6th is a little too soon for me. And actually I believe I won't go at all. I'd have been so glad. But it would have disappointed me to leave you as soon as I got to Bucharest (I wouldn't have stayed there, I'd only have picked up Antoine), and to miss the chance of seeing you in your life there, which is unknown to me and which I am so curious about. All that politics, farming, friend-of-the-people side of you escapes me, I admire it, and would love to see you in that incarnation. I do hope I shall get to Romania some day and that then no part of you will remain alien to me.

Until Monday, I hope, dear friend, at Saint-Augustin and the avenue de Messine.[2]

Your devoted
Marcel Proust

You would have had the 15 March packet at the same time as this one if Mama, suffering from an attack of rheumatism, hadn't forgotten to send it to the copying bureau.[3] You will have it tomorrow.

There's only one thing that worries me. When I substitute a word or sentence for another, is it clear that the original sentence is to be deleted? I say this because in my proofs the new phrase and the old one were often printed side by side. – I believe the type face of the signature *John Ruskin* is much too small. As small as that of the notes. I trust that will be changed in the page proof.

1. *La Renaissance latine* published two extracts from Proust's translation of *The Bible of Amiens*, in its issues of 15 February and 15 March 1903.

2. Following the wedding of Robert Proust and Marthe Dubois-Amiot, on 2 February 1903, the bride's parents gave a reception and lunch at their home in the avenue de Messine.

3. The advertisement of one of these bureaus read: 'Manuscripts copied on patented typewriters.'

214
TO ROBERT DREYFUS

[Late January 1903]

My dear friend,

Our relations were fated to be complicated. Now it turns out that a hundred or more! of the invitations to my brother's wedding have not arrived. I hope yours is not among this number and that you received both announcement and card a week ago. But on the chance that you didn't I thought I'd remind you that we are counting on you Monday at twelve o'clock at Saint-Augustin, and afterwards at the home of Mme Dubois-Amiot, 6, avenue de Messine. Unfortunately I cannot notify all the people who *may* not have received the invitation. And how many of them will be enemies for life!

Warm regards,

Marcel Proust

If you see Daniel Halévy, you could tell him the same thing, though he has probably received his announcement.

215
TO CONSTANTIN DE BRANCOVAN

[Sunday 1 February 1903]

Dear friend,

Here at last is the end of the *Bible* copied. I've reread it very summarily, being hard pressed by the misfortunes that have hit me in connection with the marriage (Mama so ill she was unable to attend the civil ceremony and will have to be taken to the church in an ambulance) (and half of our announcements lost in the post and not received). I've corrected the most glaring errors. If you like, we can look through it together *this evening* (but not at my place, in some café at about half-past ten or ten o'clock). Then I'd be able to call on your mother for a moment Tuesday after dinner. She was kind enough to invite me to dinner but, fearing I would be tired, I declined and said I might come after dinner.

La Renaissance latine, I believe, carries no illustrations, otherwise I would suggest we put in a photograph of the porch of Amiens; it would be very helpful for the description. But perhaps you could insert the enclosed plan, which please return, in the text. Because, if any of your readers – and it's quite possible – want to take *La Renaissance latine* to Amiens with them, this would be a big help. The part I am sending is sold separately in England (in English, of course, since it has not been translated) to serve as a guide to the cathedral. And innumerable art pilgrims go to Amiens provided with this viaticum. Though I don't dare hope as much of the French, it might be a good idea, if only for the sake of one or two intelligent persons – who are after all the public that counts –, to append this little plan.[1] Tell me what you think of the idea and also of the text, which is a bit long, I'm afraid. And yet I've already cut a good deal, more than fifty pages. But we could easily save space wherever it says

Faith
Under St Paul

by putting 'Faith under St Paul', 'Courage under St Peter', etc. on one line. – And the same for the Prophets.

Affectionately yours, 'my dear editor-in-chief'

Marcel Proust

P.S.   Come to think of it, I shall be dead this evening (I haven't been to bed for three nights now). If I see you at the marriage or at the lunch, we can decide when to meet.

Read this letter to the end, because it's a 'business letter'.

1. The plan of the west porch of the cathedral did not appear in *La Renaissance latine*, but was reproduced at the end of chapter IV of *La Bible d'Amiens* in its Éditions du Mercure de France edition.

216

TO LOUISA DE MORNAND[1]

Wednesday [4 February 1903]

Dear Mlle de Mornand,

The sore throat which made me write to you yesterday that I would probably be confined to my room for two or three days seems to be a little more serious than I thought, and I'm afraid I won't be able to get out for a week. I may be mistaken and I hope it won't be so long. In any case I shall let you know. But on the chance that you would be free before then, I wanted to spare M. d'Albufera and yourself the inconvenience of giving you an appointment that I would not be able to keep.

Rest assured, Mademoiselle, of my sincere respects.

Marcel Proust

1. Louisa de Mornand (real name Louise Montaud; 1884 – 1963), an actress of no great talent whom Proust was to take as the principal model for Saint-Loup's mistress, the actress Rachel. In real life she was the mistress of the Marquis d'Albufera (see letter 258).

217

TO ANTOINE BIBESCO

Thursday [5 February 1903]
(This morning I received your letter dated Sunday.
What a long time everything takes.)

My dear little Antoine,

'Thank you for your good letters' – a sweet and generous, not to say prodigal thing to say in a telegram at so much the word – is much truer of yours which give me the greatest pleasure. It's strange what contrary gifts you and Bertrand have (I'm not speaking of letters, because Bertrand hasn't written to me for a long time, but just in general, apropos of nothing): he the gift of arousing suspicion, you of dissipating it. Consequently, you're both sure to have enemies. But yours will always be people who don't know you yet and are likely to become friends if you want them to. Whereas his enemies will always be former friends. In this case the vulgar, hypocritical and base dictum, 'I have a right to say such things about him because I say them to his face', becomes legitimate and acceptable by reason of being true. Which doesn't prevent me from loving Bertrand tenderly. And at bottom, nothing is more unjust than the affection of those whose partiality blinds them, who shut their eyes to the possible faults of a friend they cherish, for fear of loving him less, and by that same token blind themselves to his good qualities. I had proof of this recently with Maugny, for whom, as I grew to like him more, I felt less esteem, convinced that my affection was mere indulgence. I realize now that he was infinitely superior to what my consciously partial and for that very reason deprecatory friendship supposed. And that he could only have gained by being seen through the eyes of a severe, clear-sighted and just friendship. All this I've put down, I don't know why.

Let me explain this morning's telegram. *In any case* it is impossible for me to go to Constantinople, because I've caught cold. I've stayed in bed today, I shall probably get up tomorrow, and it will be some days (Constantin is leaving tomorrow) before I am in any condition to travel.

Something else. I'm very tired and long to go somewhere, anywhere, I long for 'light and for flaming skies'[1] after so many electrically lit nights at my desk. But on the other hand my work is very much in arrears. It won't be finished before the 1st of March. I could go away before that, but I'd have to take 25 volumes of Ruskin, and that would be a nuisance. All the same, I'd like to go. When you're back in Paris, wouldn't you like to go to Nice or a villa somewhere? I hope it's humorous kindness and friendly solicitude that make you say: 'I won't go to Constantinople if you don't go.' Because I'd die of grief (an exaggeration, but basically true). Go to Constantinople. I'd gladly go, but I repeat that if it's a matter of seeing you for five days and then not seeing you any more, I'd rather wait for you in Paris and see you a little longer, and then, after getting a good look at you, go away (to Constantinople or somewhere else, preferably somewhere else).

Unless (as I've said) you first stay longer in Romania, where I could see you as in Paris, say for three weeks – and from there we'd go to Constantinople. Most of all I want you to do what you would do if I did not exist (a hypothetical situation in which you would have been a lot calmer and happier. Why did you have to know me?) and I shall see you on your return if that is all right with you. Not for long hours because I work so much and sleep so much, etc. (I'm not feeling at all well at the moment), but for a little while every day if you have the time. But with none of the old tyrannical avidity.

Most affectionately,

Marcel

I hear your brother has been elected deputy.[2] It was only fitting that his great heart and great intelligence should find a means of acting on men. Is it that or is it nothing? In any case I'm glad of his success. But I don't want to bore him with a letter. But tell him that I congratulate him with all my heart. But remember to tell him, moschant. Don't forget, I mean.

1. Cf. Baudelaire, 'Le Voyage', in *Les Fleurs du mal:* 'Pour n'être pas changés en bêtes, ils s'enivrent / D'espace et de lumière et de cieux embrasés.'

2. *Le Figaro* for 10 Feb. 1903 reported that Prince Emmanuel Bibesco had been elected deputy in his home country of Romania, but was expecting to rejoin his brother, Prince Antoine, in Paris at the close of the Romanian parliamentary session.

218
TO MADAME ALPHONSE DAUDET

Sunday [8 February 1903]

Madame,

I didn't answer you straight away because I've been ill these last two days just as I was a year ago, and it would have been physically impossible for me to write a single line. Papa assures me that it's a mere chill that has brought on this incredible attack of asthma. If he's not mistaken, it may clear up in the next few days. If so, I shall be able to get up, begin to take nourishment again, go out, and possibly go and see you on Sunday. That's still a week away and I'm much better, infinitely better today (though still unable to speak, eat, drink, get up, or stretch out for any length of time, etc.). But I beg you, don't disarrange your table by counting on me for dinner, it's become too unlikely with this illness. I had accepted invitations to *Siegfried* and *Andromaque* for the last two evenings and though these are the only things I've wanted to see for a long time,[1] I don't have to tell you that I was unable to go! It seems quite unlikely that I shall be able to come to dinner Sunday, even if my attack lets up by Tuesday or Wednesday, in the hope of which I am going to take every existing medicine. And if on Saturday or Sunday one of your guests is ill, and if I have sufficiently recovered to come to dinner, I'll come.

Now that I'm really ill, I feel the absurdity of the times I declined 'for fear of being' so and how irritating that must have been. But this time it's not at all the same! I am really in despair, Madame, at never being anything more for you than an odious, indiscreet thing, who appears to put on airs and who strains your inexplicable benevolence by always creating complications. But it's really not my fault. In any case, till Sunday evening, as I am now seriously beginning to hope, and in the meantime, Madame, I beg you to accept my respectful and grateful homage.

Marcel Proust

1. Wagner's *Siegfried* was performed at the Opéra on 6 February 1903, and Racine's *Andromaque*, in a new production with a score by Saint-Saëns and with Bernhardt as Hermione, at the Théâtre Sarah-Bernhardt on the 7th.

219
TO LUCIEN DAUDET

[Saturday 14 February 1903]

My dear little Lucien,

Complication of complications, read me with patience and answer me with kindness. I was convinced that you were no longer expecting me for dinner[1] (I even wrote to Mme de Noailles that I'd been invited only for the evening). But in the hope of being well enough to come in the evening I've been taking admirable care of myself (I've been in bed for *eleven days*, oh yes, my boy). To tell the truth, I've been so ill that after I told your mother all about it I hoped you'd come and see me. Some people whom I never see came to enquire how I was getting on. (Take this as a friendly regret, not as a horrid reproach.) Then today I woke up with a cold, a slight fever and a bad cough. I was horrified because of tomorrow (after dinner, as I supposed). And now comes a note from d'Humières, who tells me he's going to London tomorrow and is coming here for dinner at seven this Saturday evening in case I need help with my English. I was feeling so ill that I hesitated to get up. And then your kind telegram arrived. I hastily read 'Till tomorrow, I hope' etc., which seemed to confirm my belief that I was no longer expected for dinner, so I decided to tell d'Humières to come to dinner this evening (not the evening of your dinner, you understand, but after such an effort I'm sure to be ill). I start to dose myself so as to be able to get up for d'Humières. On rereading your message I see: 'It's so long since you've come here *for dinner*.' I'd only read 'come here', because 'for dinner' is hardly visible, 'din' at the end of one line and 'ner' at the beginning of the next. I can't call off d'Humières, who told me he was going to visit a factory before coming here. And seeing that I'm already ill today you can imagine the state I'll be in tomorrow. Nevertheless, it goes without saying that if you're counting on me for dinner, I'll be there dead or alive at eight o'clock, even if it means taking to my bed for six months afterwards. But hasn't there been some *roumestanerie*[2] on your part? Wasn't your message sent unbeknownst to Mme Daudet? And won't she on catching sight of me cry out: 'Who is this ridiculous individual? We shall be thirteen at table.' Your table, it seems to me, must have been 'conceived' either without me or with me. If without me, as I believe, my coming will be as disastrous as in the contrary case my absence (you understand that my absence in this context = one less person, and not the absence of me Marcel, who can be counted on to charm all present). If it's without me, I shall come immediately after dinner, and perhaps have a better chance of 'living to tell the tale' than if I come for dinner. A charming formula, which I recommend to you, for accepting an invitation!

I have no doubt that you bring me bad luck (I'm getting more and more gracious without trying). Because whenever I've been taken seriously ill it has been on days when I was supposed to be doing something with you. And now that I know it, my dread of being ill on the day when you invite me has become a phobia which makes me fall ill (you see what I mean, for fear of not being able to come).

Affectionately yours,
Marcel

In short, I'll do anything you say and thank you in advance.

1. See letter 218.

2. I.e. a promise one has no intention of keeping, or a generous offer made in the hope that it will be refused. Cf. Alphonse Daudet's novel *Numa Roumestan* (1880), the portrait of a politician in the South of France.

220

TO LUCIEN DAUDET

[Sunday 15 February 1903]

My dear little Lucien,

You're too sweet, I can't tell you how sweet I think you are ('I'm expansive' as you said unkindly on the way to Fresne, because the motorcar made me happy).[1] Of course I'll come if you're counting on me. See you at eight then. (I didn't answer sooner because I've just woken up and found your telegram on waking.) But it's silly to tell me who's going to be there. Mme Daudet told me a week ago. And I assure you it's not because of the guests that I'm glad to dine with you, whoever they may be. I'm so glad to *dine at your house* that I don't just say with you, but in your dining room. I am quite exalted in advance.

Yours,
Marcel

1. See letter 195, n. 1.

221

TO MADAME ANATOLE CATUSSE

Sunday [15 February 1903]

Madame,

Before answering you, I was waiting to see how I was. But truthfully, despite the great pleasure it would give me to see you, I don't dare. I would have been so glad to spend an evening in your home, full of an old charm that I haven't forgotten, to climb the stairs to Charles's[1] room, to believe myself a character in Balzac and feel that I was visiting you. It seems to me that I would have enjoyed Reynaldo's music more, and I was no less incited by gourmandise . . . I feel that you, Reynaldo, Charles and I would have been an artistic and gourmand 'Society of the Four Friends', worthy of this exquisite setting and glad to be gathered together. But truthfully, since Robert's marriage, which literally killed me (I can't claim to have been dead for a hundred years like M. Champion,[2] but for a fortnight I have been), I am not up to it, I am too ill. I'll ask Reynaldo to come and see me the next day to tell me all about it. . . .

Au revoir, Madame, I hope you will soon come and see us at home, in a setting which you embellish even if you cannot give it the charm of yours, and where you will not dine so well. Then at least I shall see you. Until then, Madame, please accept my most respectful regards.

Marcel Proust

1. Charles Catusse (1881 – 1953), only son of Mme Catusse and the late Anatole Catusse.

2. Unidentified; the name has perhaps been inaccurately transcribed.

222
TO ANTOINE BIBESCO

Monday [evening 16 February 1903]

My dear little Antoine,

I'm caught between two fires. If I keep this up, you will think me tedious, ridiculous, and not very nice. On the other hand, it may be stupid to have begun this admirable psychological discussion and to let good manners deter us from getting to the bottom of it.

So here's an answer to your letter. Your letter explains everything (or rather, as you'll see, nothing). As you've received no letter from Bertrand about *my* journey but have had one about *yours*, there's not a shadow of unlikelihood. I'll explain by word of mouth (silence tomb) why it was impossible for you to receive one about mine. – However, this is the first time you've put the question in this form. Before this your question related to an answer by Bertrand to your letter speaking of your journey (and mine). And now, pay close attention, I am going to raise a shattering objection.

If you were referring to a letter from Bertrand about *my* journey (assuming that he had answered you about *yours*) how is it that my previous objection struck you as so convincing (as you say in your letter) that 'you came very close to thinking *you* had been mistaken' (your letter of this morning). Yes: how could it have struck you as so convincing? Because, if you recall, my objection was as follows: 'It seems unlikely that when you announce your arrival to Ber-

303

trand, who has been separated from you for so long, he would not reply, would not give you a definite appointment, etc.' But how could this objection have struck you as convincing, since you knew he had replied to you, and since my objection had to do with your journey and not with mine. You are too intelligent, my dear little Antoine, not to realize that what impels me to go on with this debate is the pleasure of discussion, the love of logic, a passion for investigation – and not any doubt, distrust, suspicion, or anything of the kind.[1] – And if at the start there was distrust, suspicion or doubt, it related not to Bertrand (as I shall easily prove to you when I see you) but to you (a sentence which looks moschant but is quite the contrary, because it means that in this affair what matters to me is you, your friendship and truth-fulness). – And I vehemently reject the idea of drafting a letter for you to send or of your writing such a letter. But in addition I adjure you not to tell Bertrand about our correspondence, because he might think that what interests me in this matter is he and not you, which would cast us back into the false relationship from which we had so much difficulty in extricating ourselves, which had no other justifica-tion but sincerity and which, if I brought falsehood to it, would be-come unpardonable. Lastly, I don't remember if I wrote to you about the epistolary sequel to my telegram about Clairval,[2] the story of that affair, and the imprudence of your wire. If not, and if the little I know is of interest to you, it is at your disposal, my dear little An-toine, in the same measure as my heart, my strength, my life, and the little utility I may occasionally have in life, in other words, totally. In writing to you, it goes without saying, I am conscious of the slight ag-itation that inevitably accompanies such vehement assertions, and I press your hand most affectionately.

Marcel Proust

Your cousin Noailles is far above anything I can say. Did you know (silence tomb) that the heroine of the second issue of *La Renaissance* (the mother-in-law) is your cousin Marghiloman?[3]

---

1. In *Remembrance of Things Past*, the Narrator's relations with Albertine are marked by plenty of doubt, distrust, and suspicion as well as a passion for in-vestigation. Proust is intent on finding out from Bibesco how Bertrand de Fénelon has received the news of his, Proust's, proposed visit to Constantino-ple.

2. The young actress Aline Clairval was about to make her début in a one-act play, *Black and White*, which she herself had written. Proust was present at a

performance of the play, presumably its première, on 4 April 1903, at the Théâtre des Mathurins.

3. Mme de Noailles's novel *La Nouvelle Espérance* (The New Hope) was appearing serially in *La Renaissance latine*. In the second instalment, which appeared on 15 Feb. 1903, the character of the mother-in-law, Mme de Fontenay, seems to have been based on Mme Marghiloman.

223
TO PIERRE LAVALLÉE

[About 17 ? February 1903]
45, rue de Courcelles

My dear friend,
Would you be so kind as to let me know, if you are still at the Bibliothèque des Beaux-Arts, what days and what hours, *daytime* and *evening,* you are there, and under what conditions I might borrow a book by   [1] to take home.

Because it is my intention to go and work there once or twice in the next few days, and it would make things much easier for me if I could do it under your protection. I say nothing of the pleasure it would give me to see you, because where self-interest is involved I don't like to tinge it with sentiment.

I know how broken up you must be by the death of your uncle.[2] I was deeply grieved for your sake, for he was a charming man. I was unable to go to his funeral. I have spent more than a year in bed, without getting up for so much as half an hour a day, and though much better now, I am still often obliged to stay in bed for several days at a time. It took place on one of those days.

With affectionate regards,

Marcel Proust

1. Proust leaves a space here and neglects to identify the author.

2. Mme Alphonse Lavallée's brother, Émile Chaperon, a retired engineer, formerly active in the administration of the French and Algerian railways, had died at Cannes on 3 February 1903 at the age of fifty-seven.

224
TO ANTOINE BIBESCO

Tuesday evening 17 February [1903]

P.S.

I forgot to tell you in my letter that I was fully recovered (*unberufen*),[1] hence prepared, it's up to you, *to go to Turkey, Romania, Italy, or to wait for you in Paris,* which seems best if you are coming back soon.

Marcel P.

Tuesday evening 17 February

(I put in the date because that makes it easier for us to keep track.) I forgot to tell you that (if it is not an indiscretion) it would amuse me no end to see Bertrand's letters. (Not especially those relating to the journey, *distrust has nothing to do with it!!*) Come to think of it, we could make an exchange.

P.S. 2 Don't answer my long letter (not this one) of this evening.[2] I brought up that objection to display my talent for logic, I assure you I don't give a damn about the substance of the matter. I don't care in the least whether Bertrand wrote or not, whether he approved, disapproved, etc. I wanted (in offering to meet you wherever you liked) to show you my desire to please you. If I succeeded, good, if I didn't, it's not my fault, and I can't keep saying the same thing every day. Let's say no more about it.

1. A German colloquialism meaning roughly 'Touch wood!' The P.S. is evidently to letter 222.

2. I.e. of Monday evening, 16 February (letter 222).

225
TO PIERRE LAVALLÉE

Saturday evening [28 February 1903]

My dear little Pierre,

Suffer one who can call himself an old friend – whose friendship with you was once close and intimate – who at the news of the terrible misfortune that has struck you feels all his old affection for you reviving, to come to you through this brief note – not to intrude on your great sorrow but to communicate from the bottom of his heart the depth of his sympathy. We shall never see your brother – so wise, so charming, so good, who so loved and admired you – we shall never see him again.[1] At this awful truth I despair and rebel. I hadn't seen your brother for a long time. But in the isolation to which illness has reduced me I have got into the habit of turning my thoughts often and for no reason, to those for whom I have felt sympathy and friendship, and thinking of them so intensely that their spiritual companionship is equivalent to a real presence. I did not know your brother well, but his charming features, his exquisite distinction and warmth had remained alive in my memory and I often called him to mind, wishing fervently that he should be happy, that his life should be happy and long. Alas! And how terribly, as you must imagine, my grief and undying regret are intensified when I think of you and his delightful young wife, so gentle, one of the most accomplished persons I have ever known, and the despair that has descended upon you all. Your grief, in particular, my dear little Pierre, is so painful to me, it is almost physically impossible for me to imagine. I am writing to you in bed, and these few lines, a mere fragment of my constant thoughts, which have been with you, with him and with you all ever since I learned of this dreadful misfortune, and will be for a long time to come, are all the sympathy and friendship I can bring you, since to go out is almost impossible for me. But if, once these first days have passed, you should welcome a talk with someone who asks only to weep with you, I would come any evening you please, every evening for a while if you like. I am all yours and entirely at your disposal for anything you wish. But let me know. For I don't wish to intrude, and I know there are times when even those who are most afflicted by our sorrows mean nothing to us, as they remind us so little of the one we love that we cannot bear the sight of them. You will see how you feel about this and whether you think my sincere sympathy and grief would do you more harm than good.

With all my heart in these terrible days,

Marcel Proust

1. Robert Martin-Lavallée, mayor of Saint-Sulpice-de-Favières (Seine-et-Oise), died in Paris on 27 February 1903. Proust had not been aware of his illness when he wrote to Pierre Lavallée about 17 February (letter 223).

226

TO ANTOINE BIBESCO

[First days of March 1903]

Joy, tears of joy, joy.[1]

It is *physically impossible* for me to receive you just now. But tell me if I can see you this evening (have dinner with you if you are alone, etc.). If not, I shall stay in bed, for I am not very well. But I want to tell you the following in case you see Lauris, etc. As they might have supposed that I wanted to go to Constantinople on Bertrand's account, and that I had suggested such a journey to you, I've told them that I had suggested joining you anywhere at all, but that when you suggested Constantinople I didn't want to go, because I would have been going entirely on your account and I thought you would not be staying there long enough. . . . But that you told Bertrand about it before knowing my answer and I was afraid he'd be disappointed at my not coming.

[*No signature*]

1. 'Joie, pleurs de joie, joie': Proust expresses his emotion at learning of his friend's return to Paris in these words from Pascal's 'Mémorial', a document found sewn into the lining of his doublet at the time of his death. This unsigned note was apparently sent out to Bibesco when he called in unannounced at the rue de Courcelles upon his arrival.

227

TO ANTOINE BIBESCO

[First days of March? 1903]

My dear little Antoine,

On leaving you I *chanced* to run into the Yeatmans (charming, *really delightful*) and Peter, and gave them the glad tidings,[1] as I had told Lauris a while ago. That's four people I've made happy in one day, so I haven't wasted it. I thought your *brandy*[2] idea was abominable. Deep down you're not as good and kind as I manage to suppose when hypnotizing myself in solitude. And even with me, whom you've been so good to (said with an air of compunction),

Lucien Daudet, younger son of the novelist, in a portrait by Albert Bernard. Proust's particular friend from about 1895, Lucien was an art student when they met, and later a writer.

Bertrand de Fénelon, Vicomte de Salignac, the young diplomat who became the focus of Proust's emotional life in 1902. He and Proust toured the Low Countries together that October.

Prince Antoine Bibesco, with whom Proust corresponded intensively from 1902. He and his brother, Prince Emmanuel, were Romanian aristocrats; their mother, Princesse Alexandre Bibesco (below, photographed by Nadar), was a talented pianist.

An 1898 portrait of Marie Nordlinger, the English bluestocking who encouraged Proust's interest in architecture and helped him with his translations of Ruskin.

Mme de Noailles, the former Princesse Anna de Brancovan: a French bluestocking whose poetry Proust admired and who became his close friend and confidante.

Veiled enchantresses: the famous courtesan Laure Hayman, whom Proust had known from boyhood and who contributed to his sentimental education when he was barely twenty-one; and the great actress Sarah Bernhardt (below, photographed by Nadar), who was still fascinating young men, including Proust's friend Reynaldo Hahn, when she was in her sixties.

Above, Louisa de Mornand, the young actress whose admirer and friend Proust became about 1903; she and her lover, Louis d'Albufera, were often in his company that summer and autumn.

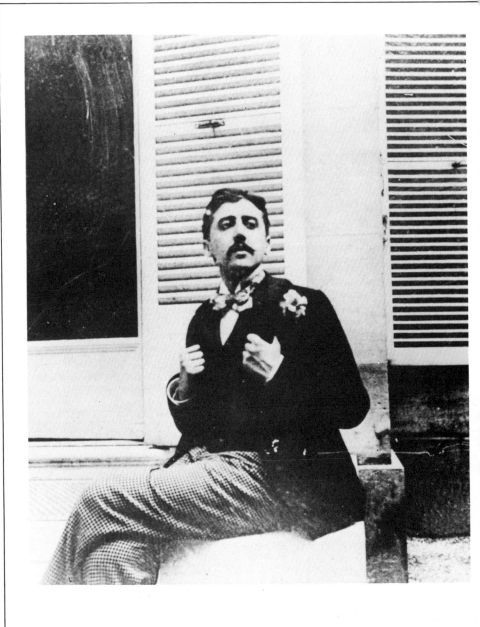

Proust after the death of his father: in the garden of Reynaldo Hahn's house, sometime after 1903.

your 'oh me oh my' is ever present, even when unexpressed. *À bientôt,* my little Antoine.

> Yours ever,
> Marcel Proust

Remember, don't let anyone suspect about the articles,[3] which no one alas dreams of suspecting.

P.S. Be very careful with Lauris. Remember that he is first and foremost 'Bertrand's friend', and that though we can sometimes trust him, we can't be too sure. So don't tell him I told you to tell Mme de Fénelon that I was an anti-literary influence on Bertrand (I mention this just as an example). Lauris and Henraux[4] (so singularly and recently allied) are all for Bertrand and for him alone. – Apart from this, they are capable of friendship with others, and Lauris is very fond of you.

1. I.e. of Bibesco's return to Paris. René Peter (1872 – 1947) was the future playwright; his father, the late Michel Peter, had been a colleague of Professor Proust at the Academy of Medicine.

2. English in the original.

3. Proust's articles on the 'Salons' were appearing anonymously in *Le Figaro*. The first, on the salon of Princesse Mathilde, had been published on 25 Feb. 1903 under the pseudonym 'Dominique'.

4. Lucien Sancholle Henraux (1877 – 1926), a collector of oriental art.

228
TO HIS MOTHER

[Monday 9 March 1903]

My dear little Mama,

Even with a mother's inverse prescience, you couldn't have devised a more untimely means than your letter of nipping in the bud the triple reform which was supposed to go into effect the day after my last dinner out (the one last Thursday at the Pierrebourgs'), which was delayed by my most recent cold.[1] It's a pity, because afterwards it will be too late. Even if I had previously been getting up at five o'clock in the morning, I wouldn't from May to the end of July have got up before seven in the evening under any circumstances, for

I know too well what the result would be for my asthma at that season. But you should have realized that if I had any intention of changing it was enough to say: 'Change or you'll be deprived of your dinner', for me immediately to abandon all thought of doing so – thus showing myself to be not frivolous and capricious but serious and reasonable – and that, if I were not disposed to change, no threat or promise would make me do so, for, if it did, what would I look like in my own eyes or yours?[2]

As for the dinner itself, to which you refer with so much delicacy as a dinner for cocottes, it will take place on a date which has not yet been set but which will probably be 30 March or possibly the 25th, because I cannot do otherwise and the importance to me of it taking place before Easter outweighs the damage the bankruptcy into which it will throw me can do. For I shall inevitably give the dinner at a restaurant, since you refuse to give it here. And I am under no illusion: though you say you are not trying to punish me, you will not, for giving it at a restaurant, provide me with a sum equivalent to what it would cost to give it here. What makes all this especially odd is that, quite apart from other, perhaps more serious arguments that I needn't mention here, Calmette, for one, or Hervieu, is as important to me as Lyon-Caen to Papa[3] or Robert's chiefs to him. The disorder you complain of does not stop you from giving the dinners they desire. And the state I happen to be in does not stop me, however ill, from attending those dinners when the day arrives. So you won't easily make me believe that this isn't a punishment, since what's possible for them becomes impossible when it's for me. The fact is that I ought to give four or five dinners, in any case one for Cardane[4] and one for Vallette. But I can't have them with the fashionable people Calmette wants to see, any more than I can have Hervieu with Mme Lemaire, so I'm obliged to begin with one of them and have the other afterwards. So I fail to see why such dinners, which are possible when they are useful to Papa or Robert, and for which I have never withheld my cooperation, though harder for me to give in the state of my health than yours is for you, become impossible when they would be useful to me. Or rather I do understand, but my interpretation is different from yours. – I worked on Ruskin last night with a high fever and I'm very tired, which is my prevailing state in the face of all the obstacles which, one after another, life puts in the way of all my attempts to resume it, so I won't write any more now. I remember telling you, early in December, when you complained of my intellectual inactivity, that you were really too impossible, that confronted with my veritable resurrection, instead of admiring it and loving what had made it possible, you insisted on my starting to work at once.⁵ But I complied, and took up just the work you wished. If I had been able to do it in a healthier place, capable of being heated by any means but hot-air ventilators, it might have been less exhausting, but to tell the truth I doubt it. Be that as it may, I'm still more or less alive, and despite the enormous amount of work I've turned out, you keep telling me day after day how amazed and pleased So-and-so was to see me so well, and I did manage, crushing as it was for me, to attend Robert's wedding. All this isn't enough for you, or rather it's nothing to you, and you'll continue to disapprove of everything I do until I fall ill again as I did two years ago. Even that wretched *Renaissance latine*. You manage to poison the day it comes out for me. And you must know that in the state of mind I'll be in I won't get much more pleasure out of the second issue⁶ than thanks to you I got out of the first. – And as there won't be a third – But I don't aspire to pleasure. I gave up hope of that long ago. And this particular pleasure was really too frivolous. – Still, I fail to understand why, just when you're asking me to keep accounts, etc., you push me back into the red by forcing me to give a dinner at a restaurant. This dinner was supposed to take place *before Robert's engagement* – but then you asked me to postpone it until after 3 February. I waited too long, that's all. Instead of sleeping just now, I wrote to you and I'm racked. I don't know yet if I'll be able to eat in the dining room. Try to have the room good and warm. The day before yesterday it was so freezing that I caught cold, what with my present fatigue. Unable to bear it, remember, I went out in spite of the fog, to warm myself and caught the fever I have now. You can't do me any positive good, and you're not on the way to learning how. But by helping me not to catch cold too often, you'd be doing me a lot of negative good. It would remove one complication from my life, which for many reasons I would like to lead in separate quarters. But considering that I pay for my own powders (which everyone finds incredible but which seems perfectly natural to me), perhaps I should also pay rent. So I resign myself to life as it is. I can't deny that the unhappiness of my life provides me with a good deal of philosophy. The trouble with philosophy is that it makes one take other people's unhappiness almost as much for granted as one's own. But if I make you unhappy, at least it's over things outside my control. In all others I do my best to please you. I can't say the same for you. I see myself in your place, having to refuse you not one but a hundred dinners! But I'm not reproaching you, I ask you only to stop writing me letters requiring an answer, because I'm racked and all I want is to avoid all this fatigue as much as possible.

A thousand loving kisses,

Marcel

1. This triple reform called for a change (a) in his bedtime, so as to sleep at night rather than in the daytime; (b) in his mealtimes; and (c) probably the discontinuance of sedatives.

2. In *Cities of the Plain* (ii. 1051 – 52), Proust was to give a faithful account of his capricious attitude towards his parents and his abortive attempts to correct his faults. The Narrator contemplates breaking with Albertine, but when his mother reproaches him he finds that 'that life which I intended to change at any moment, choosing a moment of calm, became suddenly necessary to me once more when, by these words of Mama's, it seemed to be threatened.' And at the end of the passage he records an altercation of the kind reflected in the present letter: 'She remembered all the years in which my grandmother and she had refrained from speaking to me about my work and the need for a healthier way of life which, I used to say, the agitation into which their exhortations threw me alone prevented me from beginning, and which, notwithstanding their obedient silence, I had failed to pursue.'

3. Charles-Léon Lyon-Caen (1843 – 1935) was an influential member of the Académie des Sciences Morales et Politiques in the Institut de France, to which it was Professor Proust's ambition to be elected.

4. Jules Cardon, known as Cardane (1859? – 1908), was editorial secretary of *Le Figaro*.

5. See letter 206.

6. I.e. the second issue, that of 15 Mar. 1903, to publish a part of *La Bible d'Amiens*; see letter 213, n. 1.

229
TO BERTRAND DE FÉNELON[1]

[10 or 11 March 1903]

My dear Bertrand,

I'm afraid you didn't know that I've been back in Paris for some ten days. So I have no longer any hope of going to Constantinople. Three weeks ago Sunday I was within two hours of going, but at the last moment it fell through. I'm writing you this, though I fail to understand why you've given up all correspondence with me. If it bored you to write directly, you could have sent me a message through Marcel. It would have reached me, for he and I wrote to each other regularly twice a week. In fact I asked him about you on my return. He told me he hadn't heard from you since 25 December! Is that true? But he has heard indirectly that you have been admirably successful in Constantinople. Congratulations, old man. It gave me no pleasure to see him again, I no longer feel any friendship for him. He is even stupider than when I went away. I've seen Ees, who is terribly upset by Faguet's incredible article on *L'Indiscret*. He is on the outs with the Otropehcirs, who, to tell the truth, are on the outs with everyone, even with Noel Mulb.² I met your brother-in-law, who told me he was living in the rue Copernic now. I'll go and see Didi one of these days.³ *Au revoir*, old man, if you need books or anything else, don't hesitate to ask me. Have you seen what André Beaunier said in *Le Figaro* about Marcel's translation, which is appearing in *La Renaissance latine* at the same time as Anna's novel.⁴ You've no doubt heard about Dracip's fight with Tezib.⁵ Emmanuel told me you wrote him a very charming letter on the occasion of his appointment as deputy. Though I haven't been appointed anything at all, I hope you won't leave me without news of you too long.

Yours ever,
Antoine Bibesco

Through whom did you hear [*su*, literally 'know'] I had talent? I shouldn't say know, one knows only what is true, so I seem to be saying I have talent. I'm only taking up your phrase: 'I've heard [*su*, literally 'known'] you had talent.'

1. Vicomte Bertrand de Salignac-Fénelon (1878 – 1914), a young diplomat whom Proust later took as one of the principal models for Saint-Loup. This letter, though signed 'Antoine Bibesco', is in Proust's handwriting; he sent it to Bibesco intending him to copy it in his own hand and post it to Fénelon.

2. Many of the names mentioned are anagrams. 'Ees' = Sée, whose play *L'Indiscret* had received a scathing review from Émile Faguet in the *Journal des Débats* for 9 Mar. 1903. 'Otropehcirs' = the Porto-Riches, Georges de Porto-Riche (1849 – 1930), well-known playwright, and his wife. 'Noel Mulb' = Léon Blum.

3. Fénelon's sister Marie-Louise de Salignac-Fénelon, called Didi, had married Comte Louis de Montebello (1874 – 1912) in June 1900.

4. The critic and novelist André Beaunier (1869 – 1925) had devoted sixty-one lines of a review in *Le Figaro* for 19 Feb. 1903 to Proust's 'fine translation' of *The Bible of Amiens*. For 'Anna's novel' see letter 222, n. 3.

5. In a letter in *Le Figaro* (24 Feb. 1903), Jacques Bizet ('Tezib') had accused the playwright André Picard (1874–1926) ('Dracip') of having based his play *Bonne Fortune* on a subject supplied by Bizet at a time when they had worked together. Picard denied the charge, and the disagreement led to a duel in which Picard was wounded.

230
TO ANTOINE BIBESCO

[March – mid-April 1903]

My dear little Antoine,

I've just sent back the pelisse (for I suppose that's what it is), but I can't do it without first telling you how very touched, how moved I was by your kindness, and then giving some explanation of why I had to return it.[1]

Dismayed as I may be that you wouldn't listen to me, that you paid no attention when I asked you not to give me a pelisse that I could not accept, regardless of the trouble I have had in sending it back to you – I don't wholly regret your giving it to me, because this memory will remain one of those that most strongly symbolize your extraordinary kindness to me, that best distinguish your kindness from anyone else's, that most solidly confirm me in the extreme, excessive, almost poetic idea I have formed of the free genius of your heart and the marvellous inspirations of your friendship. I therefore beg you to believe that you would be gravely misinterpreting my return of the pelisse if you took it for a cold display of misguided dignity or for the narrow, insensitive pride of one who is unwilling to owe anything to anyone. – But what makes such a gift unacceptable in principle – as you understand as well as I do – is reinforced and sharpened in this particular case by incidental but irrefutable considerations which I have already pointed out, but of which I shall now remind you. When my brother married, he wanted to make me a present, specifically in consideration of my having been his best man. He offered me a pelisse. I refused it. Which was stupid of me, because from a brother nothing could have been simpler and more natural. If I accepted yours, you see what an affront it would be to him. Moreover, I changed my mind recently and told him I would accept one. If I took yours, I would have no use for his gift, coming a few weeks later. I would be most unkindly cutting the ground from under his feet. And there is still another incidental reason. As you know, I am now keeping my own accounts, and not being able to make ends meet, I complain to my family, who are annoyed with me.[2] In accepting your pelisse, I would seem to be appealing to public charity for what because of my family's parsimony I cannot afford, to be protesting in an unkind, undignified way against an allowance which my parents are perhaps unable to make more lavish.

I hope for all these reasons that my decision – which distresses me – will strike you as reasonable. In any case, nothing can change it – or my affection for you.

Marcel

1. 'A friend who had just come from Romania', writes Bibesco, 'brought me a pelisse as a gift. I had several, so I decided to make Marcel a present of the last to arrive. It was a cold winter and he had no pelisse.' (*Lettres de Marcel Proust à Bibesco* [1949], 83)

2. See letter 228.

231
TO ANTOINE BIBESCO

[Between 25 and 30 March 1903]

My dear little Antoine,

(You see that I'm not taking an angry tone. – Actually, one should never get angry except over unimportant things, and besides I think these incidents occur too often to warrant wasting much emotion and nervous energy on them each time.) I wanted to give you a few *ultima verba*, after which arguments of this kind will cease for ever. Today I was punished by Nemesis for trying to exceed the bounds imposed by fate –

1) in thinking I could form a friendship untrammelled by the usual restrictions

2) in violating for my friend all the most sacred pledges of secrecy undertaken towards others, etc.

In part, I must say, you are the cause of the latter offence against the laws of *fas* and *nefas*.[1] Have you not said on several occasions that to sacrifice to you what had hitherto been a permanent trait of my character, my inability to repeat calumny, was the only proof of friendship I had not given you.

Alas, I lent credence to an insensate lover.

As it happens, to stay with *Andromaque*, I had no sooner done just this, with shame at violating an oath, at betraying a friend, at immolating a conscience, than you punished me by the most Machiavellian of responses. The consequence is the most tragic situation known: which is why Racine could express it only in the sublime line which I would not repeat, except that by now I just don't give a damn!

Thanks be to the gods, my misfortune exceeds my hope.[2]

Practical conclusion: let us, if you agree, abandon the cruel and impossible pact which has already done me so much harm. I am choosing an odd moment to denounce it, since I have made you a thousand revelations and you haven't told me the most trivial tale. It's not the moment I would have chosen to share the profit and loss, since I have given all and you nothing.[3] I'm selling my shares at a bad time. No matter, provided this be the end of it, once and for all. But not of our friendship. I shall be every bit as nice to you as before. But no more confidences, no more alliances, no more secrets of the tomb.

I send you herewith a great deal of friendship,

Marcel

I could strongly 'motivate' this letter. There's no need to, is there?

P.S. Does Saussine (without his wife) bore you? I didn't dare invite him[4] without asking you, but the letter is written and only awaits your decision.

Be sure to tell Constantin and Hermant if you see them that I attach importance to *lounge suits,* which makes it possible for me to invite one or two more friends without making a *dinner* of it, which I want to avoid at all costs.

Ask your cousin [Princesse de] Chimay to come to dinner on Wednesday in a *high-necked dress* or a house gown. If it bothers you to ask her, I'll write to her. Tell her it will be deadly, just a way of seeing each other, and ask her if there's anything special she would like to eat.

1. I.e. licit-illicit from the standpoint of (Roman) divine law.

2. Cf. Racine, *Andromaque:* 'Hélas devais-je en croire une amante insensée' (v. iii); 'Grâce aux Dieux mon malheur passe mon espérance' (v. v).

3. Bibesco (*Lettres*, 120) says on the contrary that, with one exception, 'Marcel . . . did not play the game I proposed; he never betrayed any confidences to me.'

4. Comte Henri de Saussine (1859 – 1940), novelist and composer. The dinner party in question took place on 1 April 1903.

232
TO ANTOINE BIBESCO

[6 or 7 ? April 1903]

My dear Antoine,

As Cardane had told me that my article was too long and that my addition about you would add another 18 lines of print (I can't see why) I went to *Le Figaro* at half-past one in the morning to tell him he could cut 18 lines wherever he pleased, but that he should keep these.[1] – That will be done. – (As a matter of fact, there was no hurry, because the article won't appear before next Thursday at the earliest, because of the enormous amount of space it takes up and because of the Chamber, and the tiara of Saites or whoever.[2]

I ran after you this evening. When I couldn't find Casa Fuerte,[3] I did the boulevards again and the faubourg Saint-Honoré, but to no avail.

Yours ever,
Marcel

Never come here with your brother.[4] Naturally, I have nothing against him, he's charming, and I'd be delighted to see him. But for the following reason, which I know you will understand. I wouldn't let him into my room, and anyway Mama wouldn't allow it, I wouldn't want to receive him in my soiled jerseys, etc. – The consequence would be that I wouldn't receive you either, and little by little you would move into the category of friends I receive only when fully dressed, in the dining room, in other words, seldom. We would see each other less often and would come to be less fond of each other. – On the other hand, if your brother wants to see me (which I

317

don't believe!) (it was the exclamation mark that made the mess all by itself)[5] we can easily meet all three of us any evening he likes, that is, never, or one day if he cares to visit a church in the provinces, but before my hay fever sets in, that is, before 15 or 20 April.

Tibi

1. The paragraph on Bibesco, when it finally appeared in *Le Figaro,* came to twenty lines. But, for its eventual publication, see letter 238, n. 2.

2. Extensive accounts of the transactions of the Chamber of Deputies appeared almost every day in *Le Figaro* until 9 April 1903, when the Chambers adjourned until 19 May. A tiara thought to be that of the 3rd-century-B.C. King Saitapharnes had been acquired by the Louvre on 1 April (!) 1896; a long-running controversy over its authenticity ended in 1903, when it was revealed to be a modern Russian forgery.

3. The young Marquis de Casa Fuerte; see letter 241.

4. Prince Emmanuel Bibesco arrived in Paris in April 1903 to visit his brother.

5. Large ink blot after 'believe'.

233
TO ANTOINE BIBESCO

[Wednesday evening 8 April 1903]

My dear little Antoine,

You haven't sent me any message, so I am going to bed (with a bit of fever, by the way, I caught a chill this evening), not knowing which of three possibilities is going to materialize:

1) We go in open and closed cars to Provins Saint-Loup Dammarie on Friday;[1]

2) We go by train (Henraux perhaps in an open car, I think he wants to go regardless of the weather) only to Provins – or only to Saint-Loup, or something of the sort;

3) We do nothing on Friday and put it off till later.

If the first possibility comes off, one of you, since I won't be up tomorrow, will have to order a closed car for me, and I believe it would be best to do it through François de Pâris,[2] who gets the best rate, I think. In any case, telephone Henraux, etc. a hundred times rather than once about all this. And seeing that I'm slightly ill this evening, it would be safest to hire the car for me as late as possible. In any case, try to let me have definite word before five this afternoon, so I can know whether to get up, stay in bed, etc. Let Lauris know what you decide, in short, be nice. Forgive me for giving you this chore (actually I give them all chores), but you know I can't do anything in the daytime, especially the day before a possible trip.

Yours ever,
Marcel Proust

Being ill, I'd rather put it off, as I'm saying in my letter to Lauris, but the uncertainty upsets me so much that I'd rather get it over with. The two cancel each other out. What I'd like best of all would be if I could decide tomorrow evening (Thursday evening). But then the rest of you would have to decide everything that depends on you.

I wouldn't want the closed car to cost more than 100 francs. – If it costs more, you could, in my name, ask the Billys to come (at their own expense). I would take them with me in the car. That way I'd only have a third to pay, so you could go as high as 300 francs.

1. Apparently Good Friday, 10 April 1903, when Proust visited Laon, Coucy, Senlis, Soissons, and perhaps some intermediate churches by car in the company of Emmanuel and Antoine Bibesco, Georges de Lauris, and Robert de Billy.

2. The Vicomte de Pâris; see letter 251.

234
TO ROBERT DE MONTESQUIOU

[Friday 10 ? April 1903]

Dear Sir,

I learn to my joy that the waves have at last brought back to us the vessel bearing Virgil. No, not that: whatever pleasure a deferential friendship, that 'gift of the gods', may find in such comparisons with another poet, it is rather of apostolic history, of those military vessels that ploughed the seas on their way to conquer, like you, under the exclusive sign of the Holy Spirit, whose 'not only Pythic but also Christian oracle' you are, that one is reminded by your fabulous journey as an evangelist of the spirit (since there is a baptism by the spirit as well as a baptism by water), in which journey your admirable ardour to conquer and convince has found expression. What pleasure it would give me to hear you say: 'I was there, and this and that befell me,' pending such time as I shall read joyous 'Bostonneries' in the vein of *Parcours du rêve au souvenir*, or of sterner studies.[1]

But I only wanted to strike up the 'Chant du retour',[2] and tell you of my joy at the thought that a journey, perhaps necessary for your spiritual design and for the evangelized populations,[3] has ended to the satisfaction of your deprived and impatient friends.

Respectfully yours,
Marcel Proust

My regards to Timothy, Mark or Barnabas, I mean Yturri, who accompanied you as they did St Paul.

1. *Le Figaro* for 10 Apr. 1903 announced the arrival, 'coming from New York', of Montesquiou and other persons of importance. Cf. La Fontaine, *Fables*, 'Les Deux Pigeons': 'J'étais là, telle chose m'advint.' In his *Parcours du rêve au souvenir*, of 1895, Montesquiou had used the headings 'Bretonnances', 'Néerlandises', 'Engadinages', etc. for groups of poems on particular places.

2. (Song of Return), a play on the title of the famous revolutionary anthem 'Chant du départ' (Departure), of 1794.

3. Before his departure on a lecture tour of the United States, Montesquiou had published an article in *Le Figaro* (5 Dec. 1902) entitled 'Missionnaires de Lettres' (Missionaries of Literature).

235
TO ANTOINE BIBESCO

[Thursday 16 April 1903]

My dear little Antoine,

I've spoken with Ettemlac [Calmette]. The upshot of our conversation, to my great regret and for a reason I do not fathom, is that he wants me to give him another article before the one that was supposed to appear. So I'm giving him without delay the one about Mme Eriamel [Lemaire]. (Since he now wants them to appear regularly every fortnight, if the Ehlufferg [Greffulhe] article is really to follow this one, it will be in a fortnight, but whether that is certain is what I don't know.)[1] Under these circumstances, wouldn't you like me to move the little medallion of my dear friend from the Ehlufferg to the Eriamel salon. That would not stop me from saying some more about you in the Ehlufferg salon. But it seems to me that this 'bird in the hand' might be preferable to the one 'in the bush', though that too is quite certain. So if you see no objection, that's what I'll do. I've told Ettemlac and Enadrac [Cardane] that I wanted to move someone from one salon to the other. Of course I didn't tell them it was your portrait I wanted to move! They implored me, each separately, not to do anything of the kind, said it was perfect as it is (!), and I'll tell you what I believe their reason to be. But I'd like to do it if you have no objection. *I beseech you to want it.*

Do you want [Paul] Deschanel to question you on the Macedonian question? Or [Georges de] Porto-Riche? Or Grosclaude?² Or whoever you wish. Because I can't put Hervieu into a salon where he never sets foot.

Would you like me to put what I say about you in the plural and make it apply both to Leunamme [Emmanuel] and to you? But wouldn't it be better to leave it in the singular and put Leunamme in another salon? Give me an answer about all this before five o'clock. But don't come yourself, because I don't want to be waked up; have your letter left downstairs so they don't wake me. I'll ask for it when I wake up. On the other hand, try to come and see me (if you want to come to dinner with Leunamme, write Mama a note to let her know) (she keeps asking me when you're coming to dinner) (if tomorrow doesn't suit you, name any day you please) because I want to talk to you about this conversation with Ettemlac, which seems pretty mysterious to me. What are you doing this evening? I met Flers and Caillavet who thought etc. etc. and invited me to the first night of *Vergy*,³ the second night, etc. etc. I thought up marvellous excuses, but I wonder now if it will be possible to get out of it for ever and if I wouldn't have done better to go tonight (Thursday), in which case I may phone them, but I really think I won't.

Yours ever,
M.P.

Keep this letter and give it back to me.
*Reply urgent.*⁴

P.S. This evening you brought up the business of the pelisse.⁵ I didn't answer because I thought you were joking. You know it would pain me to return it to you, but I would do so instantly. But I do think you were joking and that I needn't cross this bridge, which would be terrible for me, but I wouldn't hesitate for one instant to send the pelisse back to 69, rue de Courcelles.

1. For reasons unknown, Mme Greffulhe seems to have opposed publication of Proust's article about her salon. The piece never appeared and has apparently been lost.

2. Étienne Grosclaude (1858 – 1932), a journalist famous for his puns.

3. *Le Sire de Vergy*, a comic opera by Gaston de Caillavet and Robert de Flers, music by Claude Terrasse, had its première at the Théâtre des Variétés on 16 April 1903.

4. These two lines and the P.S. are written at the top of the first page.

5. See letter 230.

236
TO MAXIME DETHOMAS[1]

[Latter half of April 1903]

Dear Sir,

I decided, though not at all well, to get up to attend your exhibition and have come home filled with wonder. Sadness as well, because so profound an initiation into the understanding of nature as your work affords is bound to be a source of great unhappiness to one who, confined to his room by illness, cannot upon leaving you go and see actors, priests, common people, Parisiennes, and those distant patches of blue sky which grace the horizon of your *Homme de la campagne* [Country Folk]. Upon leaving you, one has the impression of having received new eyes with which to view life and men and even those little windows on the Grand Canal which I should like to confront with yours.[2] And when the conditions of our existence prevent us from satisfying the longing for reality that an artist has instilled in us by clothing reality with a very special beauty (which he has simply extracted from it, forcing it so to speak to lift its mask and show its colours) we suffer all the more from being outside of life.

When you told me the other day, apropos of my so remarkable enemy M. Flament, that it was a good thing to paint before speaking of painting, you were saying implicitly that it was very dangerous to speak of painting without ever having tried one's hand at it.

And indeed, I have said too much about it. Luckily, since I am writing to you with the reverse side of a pen which refuses to trace proper lines, you will, when what I say is too unsound, put it down chiefly to illegibility, and blame the flaws in my style on my handwriting. Nevertheless, I hope that in this letter you have gained a clear reading of my sincerest admiration.

Marcel Proust

1. Maxime Dethomas (1867 – 1929), an artist to whose studies of Venice Proust gives the highest praise in his *Séjour à Venise* (Pléiade III, 626). An exhibition of Dethomas's drawings was held at the Durand-Ruel gallery 15 – 29 April 1903.

2. No. 29 in the catalogue of the exhibition: 'View of the Grand Canal in Venice.' Here Proust suggests an idea which he would later develop (cf. *The Guermantes Way*, II. 338 – 39; *The Prisoner*, III. 259 – 60; *Time Regained*, III. 944), that the work of an original artist lends us 'new eyes' with which to view the world.

237
TO HIS MOTHER

[Spring? 1903]
[First pages missing]

impatience the time when my extra-familial income will be such that I shall no longer have to live at your expense. I hope this will be soon and, considering my need of being near you, you can be sure that you will not be abandoned and that I shall come twenty times a day – except at mealtimes! What had left me some hope that you would continue to see things in the same way as Robert and myself was that the really superior part of your nature, the part that is really you, stood clear like the high peaks which are later obscured. Thus it is splendid and striking that the one thing you have spent money on without stint has been our private lessons. The more I was tutored in law, philosophy and Latin, the happier you were. And yet the expense was enormous. And that is the argument I have always advanced when trying to convince myself that you were right in your attitude towards other expenses. This I can no longer do. But all those lessons with Darlu, Mossot and others rehabilitate you magnificently, in part, and I don't see why a trip to London or Rome should not be included. Now you can come and talk to me some more about all this, I'm in bed, I can't get away, and like it or not I shall be obliged to listen, so perpetuating my fever, etc. But I'm sure you will prefer not to poison my existence, which is just what these matters are beginning to do, and simply pay me a friendly visit now that we have converted our debtor-creditor relationship into one between a mother and her most affectionate son

Marcel

238
TO ANTOINE BIBESCO

[Shortly before 11 May 1903]

My dear Antoine,

I am writing to you out of excessive scruple and my persistent fear of the hypocrisy involved in substituting one sentiment for another, the expression of which may endure in someone else's mind as the statement of a constant truth (what a style!). This is a very disagreeable thing for me to write and actually it may not be true, if by true you mean something that has become fully operative, whereas this is a truth in process of becoming, etc. I wanted to tell you that your new (and quite natural) attitude towards me, one of mystery – or rather absence of confiding, of questioning, in a word of *oneness* – has encountered in me someone who is not what he was before we met, whom you made what he is and who had got into the habit of no longer living for himself alone, of widening the horizons of his life to take in another being and consequently of channelling into this indistinguishable extension of his self whatever jewels or muck his day-to-day life carries along with it, just as he finds them, with all the sights that life had surprised and reflected, the secrets that had come its way.

And now, losing my second self (that is, you) through your new attitude, I have been unable to change the new form you gave to my first self. And just as a river whose natural flow has been walled in by a dike – a high, impenetrable dike – overflows in a different direction, obedient to the law of its being, perhaps to fertilize new lands and perhaps to lose itself in them – that self has been obliged to pour into a new confidant what you were no longer willing to receive from it, for confiding became a necessity to me once you had accustomed me to it.

Behold, this word once dropped will make me die of shame![1]

Cardane has sent word that I would have the proofs today. So I believe my sufferings at the thought that I was keeping you waiting for 'La Colère de Mario' will soon be over and the article will appear without delay.[2]

Young women really have very different ways of dealing with their pregnancies, *Mme Yeatman* doesn't dare go to *Senlis*, and *Mme Louis de Montebello* goes to *London* to attend a wedding. (Raoul-Duval).[3] *Mme Yeatman* has the right idea. Let's hope Bertrand's future nephew or niece, apart from the industrious activity she will naturally inherit from her parents, will not suffer later on from having been thus prematurely shaken up.

Yours,
Marcel

Return this   *Return this letter*
letter by the bearer   *by the bearer*

1. Cf. Corneille, *Le Cid* (v. ii): 'Adieu, ce mot lâché me fait rougir de honte.' Proust substitutes 'Allons' for the first word.

2. An allusion to Vigny's poem 'La Colère de Samson'; Proust throws self-esteem to the winds in referring to himself as Mario, a stock character in Italian comedy. The passage in question seems to contain a veiled reference to his relations with Fénelon, as 'an affection that was later to bring us nothing but repeated betrayals and final enmity'. The article, which also contained Proust's fulsome portrait of Bibesco, appeared in *Le Figaro* for 11 May 1903. (Cf. 'Le Salon de Mme Madeleine Lemaire', Pléiade v. 462 – 63.)

3. Mme Léon Yeatman gave birth to a son, Laurent-James, on 30 June 1903, and Fénelon's sister, the Comtesse Louis de Montebello, to a second son, Gérard, on 6 September. The marriage of Robert Raoul-Duval to Miss Myra-Rose d'Adler took place in London on 29 April 1903. Raoul-Duval's *Au Transvaal et dans le Sud-Africain avec les attachés militaires* (1902) is the sort of book that interests the Narrator in *Cities of the Plain*.

239
TO GEORGES DE LAURIS[1]

[Tuesday evening 12 May ? 1903]

Dear friend,

I am exhausted after two days not only without sleep but without going to bed. I can't make up my mind to lie down! Before finally closing my eyes, which are full of sand, as children say, I cast them a last time at the singular personage I was with this afternoon,[2] and I here submit to you the (very uncertain) lines of a portrait I might draw if I were not so tired.

Though it is difficult, what with his doubly hereditary stupidity, to disentangle the slender imbecility of the Parisian from the heavy stupidity of the Eskimo, he looks at first sight and at a distance like a distinguished young man patiently cut out of sealskin for some exhibition of the products of the Urals, all in all a rather competent imitation. His eyes have, if I may say so, a kind of superficial depth, an apparent sparkle, a squint suggestive of independence, a myopia that gives an impression of concentration, and are to two thinking eyes what the mottled plaster of a slum stairway is to a Byzantine mosaic. But crude as it is, this *trompe-l'œil* rather fools one at a few yards' distance, and one is tempted to say, as in the presence of certain animals or in a waxworks museum: If only it could speak. If the eyes are those of a thinker, the nose is that of a royalist dandy. This nose bristles, bridles, rebels, declares its independence, it is the nose of a moujik, broad and flat; it wants to be the nose of a patrician. It is a nose that has distinction and poise, that aspires to arrogance; it is an eccentric, waggish nose that parts company with the rest of the face (here a few lines that might be more easily spoken than written). I ought to tell you that some months ago, conscious of its importance and of its independent existence, this nose decided it could afford the luxury of a large pimple all its own, which would gleam complacently on its flank, like a castle on a hillside or the purpure on an escutcheon. And he placed it on the left, slightly to the side of the tip, in the Russian style.[3] This young man is articulated, his head nods, his shoulders shrug; his frock coat is insolent and his jacket offhand. He says 'grandma' and 'papa' with the shade of respect one owes to a cocotte or an Academician. He also says 'Good day, Monsieur So-and-so' and 'Goodbye, Monsieur So-and-so' and can, if one doesn't make him talk at the same time, put on an expression at once clever and good-natured. Still, one has to be some distance away from this sealskin young man; for he is like those dolls which, seen at a distance, smile, but on closer scrutiny seem to be making faces or spitting sawdust. My dear friend, I'm at the end of my strength, I can't go on with this beautiful sketch. [*Illegible*] then burn it *immediately and for ever.*

Yours,
Marcel

1. Comte Georges-Alfred de Lauris (1876 – 1963) had a doctorate in law; he published a novel and critical essays.

2. Apparently Henry de Vogüé, son of the Vicomte Eugène-Melchior de Vogüé (1848 – 1910), author of a once-famous book, *Le Roman russe* (The Russian Novel). Henri de Régnier speaks in his memoirs of the unhappiness which the 'imbecile' son caused the Academician father. The younger de Vogüé seems to have picked a quarrel with Proust at a soirée at Mme Lemaire's on 12 May 1903.

3. Cf. Proust's portrait of the Marquis de Cambremer in *Cities of the Plain* (II. 943): 'By a transposition of the senses, M. de Cambremer looked at you with his nose. This nose of his was not ugly; it was if anything too handsome, too bold, too proud of its own importance. Arched, polished, gleaming, brand-new, it was amply prepared to make up for the spiritual inadequacy of the eyes. Unfortunately, if the eyes are sometimes the organ through which our intelligence is revealed, the nose (whatever the intimate solidarity and the unsuspected repercussion of one feature on another), the nose is generally the organ in which stupidity is most readily displayed.'

240
TO HIS MOTHER

[May 1903 ?]

My dear little Mama,

My going out gave me no congestion, but I was stupid enough to walk home and came in frozen stiff and etc. But I thought of you with so much affection that if I hadn't been afraid of waking you I'd have gone to your room. Is it to the return of my asthma and hay fever, my real physical nature, that I owe this surge of my true spiritual nature? I don't know. But it's been a long time since I thought of you with such a paroxysm of emotion. Tired as I am, writing only with the tips of my fingers, I am afraid of saying badly what I would like to say: That unhappiness makes for selfishness and prevents one from being as affectionate. But most of all that for some years now any number of disappointments you've caused me with words which, rare as they were, left a lasting memory with their contemptuous irony and harshness (though that seems paradoxical), very largely stopped me from cultivating a tenderness that met with no understanding. But all this is absurd, I'm tired, I cannot at this moment express all I was thinking a while ago.

> 'And the least word I could say
> If I tried it on my lyre
> Would break it like a reed.'[1]

A thousand loving kisses,

Marcel

The barber is coming at twenty past six, a quarter past six or half-past seven – You must wake me at half-past five.

1. Cf. Musset, 'La Nuit de mai': 'Et le moins que j'en pourrais dire, / Si je l'essayais sur ma lyre, / La briserait comme un roseau.'

241
TO CONSTANTIN DE BRANCOVAN

[Late May or early June 1903]

My dear Constantin,

You are as kind as can be, and if I had received your letter before dinner, I would, since it held out the possibility of a visit from you, have arranged to be ready to receive you. Unfortunately, I didn't get it until ten o'clock at night. And since I hadn't planned my toilette so as not to miss a visit I was not expecting, I was unfortunately in my bath when you came, that is, dripping wet, on the point of throwing towels round me to rub myself dry, in any case, unable to see you without risking certain bronchitis on top of a bad cold if I had remained naked and wet while I talked with you instead of giving myself a rub-down, which I wouldn't have done while talking with you even if you had allowed it, because it would have made me gasp for breath. –

You have been too kind about Casa Fuerte's translation.[1] But don't put such pressure on yourself. I only wanted to ask you not to take too long and it's terribly kind of you to accede to my request. But obviously a day or two doesn't matter.

I shall arrange with Antoine [Bibesco] for us all to meet one of these days. I know this is not easy for you and that you haven't much time. I shall be all the more grateful if you can set aside an evening for me. As I don't go out at all, it will be easy for me to be free whenever you and Antoine decide. Until that happy time, which will give me the utmost pleasure, accept, dear Constantin, my warmest regards.

Marcel Proust

1. In a letter of towards the end of May 1903 (*CMP* III. 329), Proust had asked Brancovan to look at a translation of some d'Annunzio poems by his young friend Illan, Marquis de Casa Fuerte (1882–1962). 'Since these poems have not been translated,' said Proust, 'whether good or bad they are certain, because of the author's name, to attract readers to the issue in which they are published. And since Casa Fuerte knows Italian almost as well as an Italian (indeed, he is half a one) and writes French very nicely, I imagine the translation is harmonious and faithful.' The poems did not appear in *La Renaissance latine*.

242
TO LOUISA DE MORNAND

Tuesday [evening 2 June 1903]

Mademoiselle,

A thousand thanks for your delicate thought, which moved me deeply. Unfortunately I cannot accept your charming invitations because I *never* go out in the daytime. I should be delighted at any other season to make an exception for you. But every year from 15 May to 15 July I suffer from an absurd – but very disagreeable – ailment which is called hay fever but is actually flower fever,[1] during which time it is quite disastrous for me to go out in the daytime. At the end of June I begin to venture out before sunset, but very seldom. So I shall have to forgo (much to my sorrow, believe me) both your invitation to lunch and the pleasure of going to applaud you at the Bouffes.[2] Actually the only way of seeing me at this season (and the one I prefer at any season) is in the evening, from eight o'clock on, until any hour of the night (however late). If you are not still playing in that curtain-raiser – (as *Le Coin du feu* doesn't begin before eleven o'clock, I believe)[3] – tell me a day when you are

329

free and give me the great pleasure of joining me at dinner wherever you like with M. d'Albufera. If you are still playing in the curtain-raiser and it goes on *every night,* the best would be for us to meet *after* the theatre. Anyway Bertrand [de Fénelon] will be arriving soon and will provide us with the occasion, I hope. In the event, which I would regret, that you can't have dinner with me, the best would be to wait for Bertrand's arrival, which should be fairly soon.[4] In any case we must have a serious talk. M. d'Albufera has told me of your desires which – assuming that they are practicable – really call for advance consultation, by word of mouth I must add. Things that are ever so complicated to write can be said very quickly. –

I call to your friend's attention an article in this evening's *Presse* (the *Presse* dated Wednesday 3 June, appearing Tuesday evening) which will please you, I hope, and what makes it all the more 'helpful' is that this Martin Gale is about the only thing anybody reads in *La Presse* (precisely because he's so very *gale* [nasty]. Not to you, you must admit. On the other hand you've seen no doubt that my efforts with *Le Soleil* have ended in utter fiasco, as Léon Daudet compliments you in the same breath as Mme Milo de Something-or-other and Monsieur (the run-of-the-mill actor whom you dislike – in the play – because he's a cuckold). Which doesn't prevent Léon Daudet from finding him charming![5]

To recapitulate, tell me if you can have dinner with me one evening at eight or a quarter past (not for the next two or three days, because I'm slightly ill), on condition, however, that you be my guest, since I alas am older than you and M. d'Albufera, and I can't allow you to slight the sad privilege of age. Otherwise (if you are not free) and if M. d'Albufera does not want to leave you alone (and does not want to come to dinner with me) let us have a *souper* together one evening when Bertrand is back. Actually your plans (the Croisset play)[6] are so long term that there's no hurry.

Give your friend my regards and accept, Mademoiselle, the expression of my sincerest homage.

Marcel Proust

I'm enclosing the tickets for the Bouffes and registering this letter to make sure they don't get lost.

1. 'La fièvre des fleurs'; in English it is known as rose fever.

2. *Les Nuls* (The Nobodies), a play by the Baron Loïe de Cambourg in which Mlle de Mornand had a small part, was announced for performance at the Bouffes-Parisiens from 5 June 1903.

3. The curtain-raiser at the Théâtre des Mathurins was *On n'a pas le temps!* (We Haven't the Time), a one-act comedy by Quillardet and Murray. It was followed in the bill by *Le Coin du feu* (The Chimney Corner). Mlle de Mornand had roles in both plays.

4. Bertrand de Fénelon returned on leave from Constantinople about 1 July 1903.

5. In *La Presse* for 3 June 1903 'Martin Gale' (the pseudonym of Albert Flament) mentioned Mlle de Mornand as 'a true comedienne, in whom one senses the precious gift of shedding tears as freely as she spouts laughter'. In *Le Soleil* for 1 June, Léon Daudet spoke of *Le Coin du feu* as 'a charming little piece in which M. Bergeret, Mlle Mylo d'Arcylle and Mlle de Mornand act with simplicity and charm'.

6. The Belgian playwright Francis de Croisset (real name Frantz Wiener; 1877 – 1937) was a friend whom Proust saw frequently at this time. He was the author of several successful comedies.

243
TO PIERRE LAVALLÉE

Saturday [6 or 13 June 1903]

My dear little Pierre,

It gave me great pleasure to learn from the little announcement you sent me yesterday that clement nature in its cruelty had granted you the happiness of a child in the midst of the cruel grief for which you will never be consoled, but which such true joys will at least soften.[1] Don't fail to tell your mother, whom I've often thought of in these terrible days, that the comfort of being a grandmother will at least give her some surcease from the despair she must feel as a mother.

But your poor sister-in-law – what has she got left? Tell her, if you think of it, that I sympathize with her from the bottom of my heart and have forgotten neither her nor the one she mourns.

I would rather have told you all these things by word of mouth, my dear little Pierre. But after two fruitless attempts (once I left a note which you must have found) my hay fever started up again – it had never really stopped – and then I was in bed for a fortnight with bronchitis and a high fever – and when I'm well I go out about twice a week, but so late that I'd wake up not only the inhabitants but even the concierge in the rue de Vézelay. And so it is only from here, telling you how much closer your sorrows have brought

you to my heart, more tenderly united with you – that I most affectionately press your hand.

Marcel Proust

1. See letter 225. The Pierre Lavallées' daughter Arlette was born on 20 May
1903.

244
TO ANTOINE BIBESCO

[Monday morning 8 June? 1903]

Dear Antoine,

I've had an idea. Would you like me, instead of going over
the part of my translation which I haven't yet had time to check with
d'Humières, as I was going to do with Mlle Nordlinger (a young English artist who is very fond of me), to go over it with you? But it
would undoubtedly take three long sessions of at least an hour each.
Would you like that, or wouldn't you? Tell me the truth, because
Nordlinger would be just as easy for me. Here is what might decide
the question: If we did it together, I would make the little sentence
about you refer to the engravings lent by your brother, and thank you
in the preface for helping me. But since I address the same thanks to
d'Humières, don't you think it might look rather Salaïstic, and
wouldn't you rather not? In that case I'd better stick to Nordlinger,
because if it doesn't help with the sentence about you, there's no
reason why I should make you rather than her waste three hours, trying to figure out whether or not the antecedent of '*its*' is '*faith*', and
suchlike questions.[1]

You were *very kind* this evening. But even so, you are the
buyer of my soul and I wish I could return all your kindnesses and
take it back again, and find it as it would have been if I hadn't sold it,
with its secrets unbetrayed, its innocence unspoilt, its tombs and altars
inviolate. At times there rises up before me the dead, reproachful face
of 'what might have been and is not',[2] that is, the better being I would
have been if I had not, to keep you informed at all costs, sold what no
one should be able to buy and what in reality only the Devil buys. But
alas, '*it may not be mended and patched and pardoned and worked up
again as good as new*.'[3]

On the question of collaboration you must answer me today if you come or in a note, because it should be done this week, and preferably this very day (evening), since I shall not be free Tuesday or on the Mornand day (I don't know which)[4] or on Sunday. And besides the proofs[5] may come any day, and in that case I shall have to put in the sentence about you once and for all. And I prefer to do my going-over first. It consists in this: wherever I have a doubt I put a ? in the margin. – We leaf through the book and every time I see a ? that I haven't asked d'Humières about I ask you (or Nordlinger).

Yours,

M.P.

Come to think of it, since d'Humières has a great reputation as a translator, it wouldn't look Salaïstic.

1. Marie Nordlinger supplied the help in question. There is no mention of either Antoine or Emmanuel Bibesco in either of Proust's two Ruskin translations, *La Bible d'Amiens* and *Sésame et les lys*.

2. Adapted from Dante Gabriel Rossetti's sonnet 'Stillborn Love', in *The House of Life*.

3. Quoted in English, and drawn, except for the first four words, from *The Bible of Amiens*, ch. IV.

4. The opening of *Les Nuls* (see letter 242, n. 2), at the Bouffes-Parisiens, had been postponed until either 13 or 14 June 1903.

5. Of *La Bible d'Amiens*.

245
TO MADAME DE PIERREBOURG[1]

Wednesday evening
[24 June or 1 July 1903

Madame,

I had just been thinking, at this time of the year's fullness and fulfilment, how empty my life is of the pleasures that would be most welcome to me, in a word, how little I had seen of you, when your book arrived, bringing me by a kind of enchantment your presence, invisible to be sure, yet not to be doubted, your 'real Presence', to speak the language of the religion towards which in the first part of *Le Plus Fort* I found you so unjust, and which the second part made so odious to me that I can't help wondering how you yourself, in the last pages of the book, can seem to insinuate that 'Julia's noble tormentor was perhaps of an essence superior to hers'.[2] In this case I admire you for being so magnificently Cornelian (and indeed I know of no loftier psychological 'situation', of no more tragic 'peripeteia' of the passions than the duel, so naïve, so unprecedented, so hitherto undreamt-of, and yet so human), but I prefer you as tenderly Racinian as you are the rest of the time, and indeed in the entire secret intention, the entire tacit predilection of the book, if not in its explicit philosophy.[3]

I hope to get over this, for I love Catholicism and want to love it. But this evening all I can see in it (for this marvellously chosen case is symbolic – which is why it is so broadly human – of millions of absurd sacrifices and willingly accepted torments) is a source of suffering, one of the great sunderers of souls in this life which is already sad enough without it, where happiness has so much difficulty in finding its place and kindred souls in coming together, and I detest it as Julia detested the God Bernard demanded she call upon. For your book, profoundly philosophical as it is, is also so much alive that one cannot help adoring Julia from the first minute on, from her appearance in the box where she rehabilitates Gounod[4] and turns out such a pretty 'stylistic modulation' on the phrase 'Pure Angels' (capable of carrying away all hearts along with Marguerite's, etc.), from the appearance, too, of the husband (oh! that glacial handshake between the crude sensualist and the man of feeling, how often I have experienced and detested such handshakes) to the 'painful' and 'inimitable' life that opens up on the day when she promises a friendship which she will never betray. If slight details of orchestration, lightly brushed-in background painting did not as it were sustain, as in life itself, the central voice of thought and love, the book would not be so alive.

Which is to say that I have deliciously enjoyed all the figures who, from Mme Travel (whom we both love and whom you have painted superbly in spirit and in truth) (As a matter of fact the painting outdoes the now-defunct model in universal truth. 'The torturing instinct of every hostess', 'giving in to the need to keep inviting people no matter to what', 'she did not acknowledge the possibility of shirking any obligation, etc.' – Yes, the shades of feeling aroused in the old lady by Julia's youth 'still capable of loving' infinitely surpass the memory, however venerable, of your old friend.)[5] – What was I saying? I was saying, I think, that all these secondary characters are charming, even those philosophical spongers, the Kloses I believe,[6] whom you have sketched so swiftly. In all this there is a philosophy I would like to go into more deeply, to ask you, for instance, if it is really true that life grants us the happiness we desire, on condition that we sacrifice the rest. If one thought it might serve some purpose to sacrifice the rest, one would lose no time in doing so. But the rest stultifies, prevents one from looking one's suffering in the face. Anyhow, it's hard to say. But you are right.

And now, Madame, that I've admired your fine book, mightn't it be possible to see you? I'm still very ill, worse than when you saw me, a little better than these last few weeks, which have been awful.

As Bertrand de Fénelon is here, couldn't we see you one evening together? Or some other combination at your convenience. But I would be glad to thank you again and to bring you directly the homage of your admirer

Marcel Proust

On finishing the book I chanced to open it to the first page. With how many meanings Musset's exquisite lines were suddenly enriched! Here they are, grown to immensity. – I adore the grace of 'And followed Virtue'. I look them up in *Rolla* to reread them. But horrors! I find

He saw Pleasure, etc.
He followed Virtue[7]

So even in Musset's lines the grace was yours, or is my edition at fault?

1. Baronne Aimery Harty de Pierrebourg, née Marguerite Thomas-Galline (1856 – 1943), who wrote novels under the name Claude Ferval.

2. In *Le Plus Fort* (The Strongest One), by Claude Ferval, published on 16 June 1903, Mme Julia de Mieris falls in love with Bernard Aurain, who, after getting her with child, leaves her to become a monk.

3. Corneille's plays depict characters whose will (or reason) dominates their passions; the reverse is true of Racine.

4. Julia to Bernard at the opera during the last act of Gounod's *Faust:* 'Since you love music, Monsieur, listen with us to the moving trio. Fashion has been unjust to Gounod.'

5. The 'now-defunct model' for the aged Baronne de Travel was undoubtedly Mme Aubernon (see letter 29), who died in 1899.

6. The characters of Professor Savreux and his wife were supposedly modelled on a certain Gaston Claus, a broker, and Mme Claus, née Bachelet.

7. Cf. Alfred de Musset, *Rolla,* Chant II (of Hercules): 'Il vit la Volupté qui lui tendait la main: / Il suivit la Vertu, qui lui sembla plus belle.'

246
TO MADAME DE PIERREBOURG

Thursday evening
[25 June or 2 July 1903]

Madame,

It is too kind of you to have taken the trouble to read my cold dissertation on the ardent life of your book. And I'm overwhelmed at your taking the trouble to answer it. How could you suppose that my remark about Musset concealed a reproach?[1] Antoine Bibesco can tell you that some days ago, when I hadn't read your book yet and had only seen the epigraph, I praised the inimitable grace of those lines. He disagreed with me, objecting to the bad French of *'entre un double chemin'* [between a double path, i.e. between two paths]. But to me the grace of 'And' mattered more.

He saw Pleasure, etc.
And followed Virtue.

We would all have written: 'He saw Pleasure. He saw Virtue too, But followed Virtue.' Only Musset could have found that delicious short cut: 'And followed Virtue.' I see it wasn't Musset. You say your memory failed you and attribute your inspiration not to your good taste but to your memory. Let me tell you that one has only the memory one deserves, the memory that goes with one's good taste. The memory that improves on Musset so exquisitely is, even unconsciously, a most artistic memory. You almost go so far as to say you've made a mistake. Let me say to you, again like Bernard's teachers: *'Felix culpa!'* [A happy mistake!] I can permit myself this 'Latin nomenclature', as you call it, since you yourself quote the Psalmist in Latin: *Levavi oculos meos in montem.*[2]

As for the philosophy of choice, I believed it was based entirely on the observance of a law which in its essence remained mysterious. From your letter, I see on the contrary that you have found a psychological basis for it. But alas, I have the feeling that the violence of our desire can change nothing in the world around us, or at least can effect no change in the one thing that matters to us, in the longing of another heart that we wish to incline towards us.

> *For God who created happiness and the Harmonies*
> *Created love out of an unanswered sigh.*[3]

Still, I know that shared loves exist. But alas, I do not know their secret. Nevertheless, I have a feeling that compensates for this in some measure, which is, that everything, *even* what we desire, comes to us in the end, but only after we have ceased to desire it. There are some things, though, which I am beginning to believe will never come. But perhaps because I desire them with a little too much persistence. They are waiting, no doubt, for the moment when I cease to desire them, but I keep trying in vain to hasten it!

Au revoir, Madame, I hope your pretty and priceless fish are well and are still making the frail vitrine that protects them equal to those of the most dazzling jewellery shops. I couldn't help thinking of them when you compare the eddies in a river to silvery fish leaping to the surface.

Very respectfully yours, Madame,
Marcel Proust

But I'd forgotten the practical purpose, the *raison d'être* and excuse for this letter. Yes, I shall be delighted to come to dinner. But I don't know when Bertrand de Fénelon will be free. I'll write to him tomorrow and tell him to make arrangements with you. Naturally I myself am extremely free when I'm well enough. But I'm not at all well at the present moment.

1. See letter 245.

2. Cf. Psalms 121:1. In the King James version, 'I will lift up mine eyes unto the hills.'

3. Cf. Sully Prudhomme, 'L'Art sauveur', in *Poésies 1866 – 1872:* 'Car Dieu, qui fit la grâce avec des harmonies, / Fit l'amour d'un soupir qui n'est pas mutuel.'

247
TO LOUISA DE MORNAND

Thursday [9? July 1903]

Dear friend,

Your remembrance is precious to me and I thank you for it. How I would love to stroll with you in those streets of Blois, which must be a charming setting for your beauty. An old setting, a Renaissance setting. But also a new one, since I have never seen you in it. And in new places those we are fond of seem to us in a sense renewed. To see your lovely eyes reflect the soft-hued sky of Touraine, your exquisite form in profile against the old château would move me more than seeing you in a different gown, wearing different jewels. Side by side with the delicate embroideries of certain blue or pink dresses that you wear so well, I would like to test the effect of the fine stone embroideries that the old château also wears with a grace which for being rather old is no less becoming. I am writing you all this with a pen so bad that it can only write upside down. My brain, too, is somewhat upside down. Don't be astonished if the result isn't brilliant. Besides, I can only tell a woman that I admire her and am fond of her when I do neither one nor the other. And you are well aware that I admire you very much and am very fond of you. So I shall always be reduced to telling you so very badly. I beg you not to suppose that this is an indiscreet, pretentious and awkward way of courting you. Though it would be pointless since you would soon send me packing, I would rather die than cast covetous eyes upon the woman adored by a friend whose noble and delicate heart makes him dearer to me with each passing day. Perhaps at least a little friendship and a great deal of admiration are still permitted me. . . . You will decide that as you wish. Pending the verdict, risking all for all with a boldness which is perhaps a consequence of the considerable distance between the rue de Courcelles and La Chaussée Saint-V[ictor],[1] I shall (mentally asking A[lbufera]'s permission) do something that would give me no end of pleasure if it could some day be done otherwise than in a letter; my dear Louisa, I embrace you tenderly.

Marcel Proust

If, as I hope for him and for you (for the hours you spend apart seem very long to me when I think of his sadness and yours), A[lbufera] is with you again, tell him, first to stop calling me Proust and incidentally that I am very fond of him. My very best regards to your sister,[2] whom I don't know but who must be very charming if she is like you. If she also has your gentleness and your *loyalty* (the qualities I value most in you if I am not mistaken, the future alone will tell me), she must be an accomplished person. But I feel that I prefer you all the same.

1. A town in the Loir-et-Cher department, three kilometres from Blois.

2. Mlle de Mornand's sister, Suzanne Montaud; she played at the Bouffes-Parisiens under the name Jane Moriane.

248
TO GASTON CALMETTE[1]

Saturday evening [11 July 1903]

Dear Sir,

I am getting up a small dinner party chosen from among the people who happen to be still in Paris (a matter in which I am anything but well informed, because I've been quite ill lately), to be held next Thursday, 16 July, at my home at 45, rue de Courcelles, at eight o'clock. I should be most sensible of the honour and it would give me great pleasure if you consented to be among my guests that evening. I hope you will be good enough to come to dinner at my home, and while I am writing, I should take the opportunity to point out that my incognito of Dominique is much more serious than you think. I was seriously irked when you unmasked me to Mme Lemaire, and I adjure you not to do it again.

The fact is I have just about decided to stop the contributions, the sole justification for which was a certain regularity which would enable the readers of these imperfect chronicles to find in their continuity an interest which each, taken separately, could not hope to provide. The long intervals that M. Cardane has left between one chronicle and the next make them utterly meaningless and almost unintelligible. But even if I so decided, I certainly want you, even as to past articles, to keep my identity *rigorously* secret.[2]

All this is only by way of precaution in case there should be talk of Dominique at my table, where I should not like you to betray me and where I hope you will do me the favour of occupying the place of honour on Thursday.

Your most devoted
Marcel Proust

1. Gaston Calmette (1858 – 1914), editor of *Le Figaro*, to whom Proust was to dedicate *Du côté de chez Swann* in 1913.

2. Proust published four more of the 'Salons' in *Le Figaro* under the pseudonym 'Horatio', and a last one signed 'Écho'.

249
TO HIS MOTHER

[Thursday evening 16 July 1903]

My dear little Mama,

Many thanks for your note. I was very glad to have it because I had gone out and came home regretting that I had not been able to thank you for the charming dinner, and gratefully reading your letter was like having a little chat with you. Thanks to your kind fore-thought and your talent for organization, it was indeed, as you say, 'a charming party'. All the same I was in tears afterwards, less perhaps because of the unpleasantness caused by Bibesco's ridiculous sally – and Papa's unjust repartee – than at seeing that no one can be trusted and that those who seem to be one's best friends have such incredible flaws that all things considered they may be even worse than other people. I've told Bibesco a thousand times how the interpretation you put on my way of life poisons my existence, and how, recognizing as I do that I shall never be able to prove you wrong, my legitimate concern for you is even greater than your gratuitous concern for me. Wishing to be extra careful, I reminded him before dinner: 'Please, no jokes about tipping, and another thing, don't ask Papa silly questions like: "Monsieur, don't you think that if Marcel didn't bundle up so", etc.' – There's a trace of the savage in him, he was angry because I had told how he had played 'En revenant de la revue' in church,[1] and he got even – he has protested since that he had no idea of the conse-quences – by saying the very things I had told him not to say (the kind of thing, that is, because of course I hadn't told him not to say that I'd given 60 francs [as a tip], since I had actually given 50 cen-times). I believe the sight of my misery made him repent. But I don't care, I refused to forgive him. He's neither a child nor an imbecile, and if he is capable, after being warned, of so exacerbating the misun-derstandings between Papa and me that it's no longer in my power to dispel them, if accordingly he strikes at me in my family affections, which matter more to me than my affection for my friends, then he is as much to be distrusted as a man who may have a good heart and no end of estimable qualities but who at times, through the effect of drink or something else, will stick a knife into you. I know that I'm making him miserable by refusing to forget as he would like me to – and perhaps as the sincerity of his repentance deserves – the horrid thing he has done. But I can't. And whatever pleasure it may give me to have friends at the house, to see them so kindly and brilliantly entertained, I'd rather not have them at all if the most intimate gatherings, which should also be the most cordial, degenerate into quarrels that leave deep marks in Papa's mind and reinforce prejudices which all the evidence in the world would be powerless to banish.

Good night, my dear little Mama. Thank you again for the kind and charming dinner. I've caught a bad chill, and so I leave you. I'll deal with the financial question another time, because now, this evening, I've written more than I meant to. I won't dine at the same time as you tomorrow. Because if I have a cold, I'll get up a little later than today and you dine earlier. On the other hand, I don't think I'll eat dinner without getting dressed, because then I'd be stuck for the evening. Because according to the note Vallette wrote me this evening, I won't have my proofs from *Le Mercure*[2] yet.

A thousand loving kisses,

Marcel

1. According to Georges de Lauris ([Marcel Proust], *À un ami* [1948], 19), this incident occurred at Saint-Leu-d'Esserent during the motor tour of churches Proust made with him and the Bibesco brothers in April 1903 (see letter 233, n. 1). For 'En revenant de la revue', see letter 3.

2. I.e. proofs of *La Bible d'Amiens* from Éditions du Mercure de France.

250
TO ROBERT DE BILLY

[Monday 27 ? July 1903]

My dear little Robert,

'Joy, joy, tears of joy'
(Pascal).[1]

I'm delighted. In matters of friendship I'm a *bourgeois*, not a metaphysician, and my friends' 'distinctions' give me a naïve and family-like satisfaction. I have all the most vulgar sentiments where my friends are concerned, first and foremost an intense pride. And I'm just as hoipolloily happy about your being decorated as if I were your brother if you had one – or your concierge. I lost no time in asking Albu[fera] to announce the good news to Fénelon, but too late (because I didn't open your letter until six o'clock, when I woke up), for when Albu saw Fénelon, as Albu told me this evening, he had already had your visit and knew of your appointment. Anyway, my dear little Robert, it's a great joy for me, a beautiful feeling that an absurd injustice has been righted, and gives me great hope that in future you will try a little harder to see to it that your high merit occupies a prominent place not just in the esteem of intelligent people, but also in the social scale of honours and offices. This is something you should wish for, if only to make the real community more like the ideal community that will be constructed on the model of your intelligence. I embrace you with all my heart and shall embrace you even more warmly when you are an officer of the Legion of Honour. Q.E.D.

With all the joy of a member of your family, which must indeed be overjoyed in the circumstances, I am, my dear little Robert,

Yours ever,
Marcel Proust

1. Billy, 'Embassy Secretary of the second class', had just been appointed a chevalier of the Légion d'Honneur. See letter 226, where Proust uses the same quotation to express his delight at Bibesco's return to Paris.

251
TO GEORGES DE LAURIS

[Wednesday evening 29 July 1903]

Dear friend,

Since Albu left, I have been thinking some more about your blasted laws, and in a state of incredible depression and dullness (perhaps inseparable from the position I am going to defend) I am setting down my humble little reflections, the product at best of common sense, on a level very much inferior to those of Yves Guyot and, I venture to say, to that at which our discussions on this subject have hitherto been carried on.[1] So tear this letter up straight away, I blush at the thought that someone else might read it. Until now I have thought only of the virtues and dangers of Christianity, of its right to existence and freedom. But now I shall try to get down to the substance of your laws and what they may mean to you; I simply fail to see what you want. To make *one* France (as your subsidiary ideas on Saint-Cyr,[2] which are too specialized for me to discuss, seem to suggest)? I do not think you want all Frenchmen to be alike, a dream that is fortunately stupid, because it is unrealizable. But I trust that you do want all Frenchmen to be friends, or at least, setting aside the special and individual reasons they may have for hating one another, capable of being so, and accordingly that you hope that no a priori enmity will ever, in any situation, pervert the course of justice, as happened some years ago. And you believe that free schools teach their pupils to hate Freemasons and Jews (this evening indeed it was education more than anything else that seemed to arouse your anger after Albu left, to the point of making you doubt my good faith in the matter of Cochin, etc.).[3] And it is true that in the past few years those educated at such schools have ceased to admit Jews to their social circle – a fact which in itself doesn't trouble us, but is a sign of the dangerous state of mind to which the [Dreyfus] Affair, etc. gave rise. But I must tell you that at Illiers, a village at whose school prize-giving ceremony my father presided the day before yesterday, the priest has not been invited to the prize-giving since Ferry's laws.[4] The pupils are taught to look upon all who associate with that priest as persons to be avoided, so that this camp just as much as the other does its best to create two Frances. And I, who remember this little Beauce village, where all eyes are turned towards the niggardly earth, mother of avarice, where the sole striving towards the sky, sometimes mottled with clouds but often divinely blue and every evening at sunset transfigured, where the only striving towards the sky remains that of the church's pretty steeple – I, who remember the village priest, who taught me Latin and the names of the flowers in his garden – I, who above all know the mentality of my father's brother-in-law,[5] the anti-clerical deputy mayor, who hasn't spoken to the priest since the 'Decrees', who reads *L'Intransigeant* but who since the Affair has taken also to reading *La Libre Parole* – I don't think it's right to have stopped inviting the old priest to the prize-giving, since in the village he stands for something more difficult to define than the social function symbolized by the pharmacist, the retired tobacco-monopoly engineer and the optician, but which is every bit as worthy of respect, if only because of the intelligence of the pretty, spiritualized steeple, which points towards the setting sun and melts so lovingly into its pink clouds and which I am sure, to the stranger arriving in the village, looks finer, nobler, more disinterested, more intelligent, and, what we want most of all, more loving, than any of the other buildings, including those decreed by the most recent laws. In any case the gulf between your two Frances is deepened by every new development of anti-clerical policy. Which is quite natural. True, you can say this in reply: If you have a tumour and go on living with it, in order to remove it I am obliged to make

you very ill; I'll give you a fever, you'll need a period of convalescence, but afterwards at least you'll be well. That was how I
reasoned during the Affair. So if I believed that once the teaching orders were eliminated the ferment of hatred among Frenchmen would
be eliminated with them, I should consider it a very good thing to do.
But I believe exactly the opposite. For one thing, it is only too obvious
that what we can legitimately detest in clericalism, first of all anti-
Semitism, and clericalism itself for that matter, represent a complete
break with Catholic dogma. It seems to me that we should not gener-
alize on the basis of radical anti-Semites like Humbert and Cavaignac.[6]
And tolerant priests, even if they're not exactly Dreyfusard, strike me
as tolerable precisely in so far as they are tolerant. Today (and it is
the shame of Catholicism to have accepted their support, but don't
forget that we accepted Gohier and how many more *evil* men, anti-
Semites at bottom) the mainstays of the Catholic faction (Barrès,
etc.) are not believers. And the clericals don't mind. Because they
know that a village priest, a monk, a bishop, a Pope, can make his
peace with the government, but that an editor of *La Libre Parole* cannot. And they give full absolution to those who stay away from
church (except on the days when Charbonnel[7] shows up), who insult
practically the whole clergy, from the Pope on down. Once the orders are gone and Catholicism dead in France (if it could die, but its
ideas and beliefs are not killed by laws, they die when their content of
truth and social utility is corrupted or diminished), there will be just
as many clericals – clerical unbelievers – more rabidly anti-Semitic,
anti-Dreyfusard, and anti-liberal than ever, and they will be a hundred
times worse. Moreover, it's not teachers, even bad ones, who shape
young people's opinions (except for those who go on to higher education and become equally fervent followers of a Boutroux or even of a
Lavisse, regardless of whether they are products of Stanislas or of Condorcet);[8] it's the press. If it were possible to restrict the freedom of the
press, rather than of education, the ferments of division and hatred
might be somewhat diminished. But *intellectual protectionism* (and
the present laws are a form of Mélinism a hundred times more odious
than Méline)[9] would also have its drawbacks. And thus far we have
been speaking only of the other camp, of those who hate us. But what
about ourselves? Have we the right to hate? And is one France to
mean not the union of all Frenchmen but the domination, etc. (I
won't go on). Take an example in which there is no hatred, on the
contrary a good-natured little joke of yours and Bertrand's. When
Bertrand laughs at the idea of nuns 'obliged to travel', when you are
annoyed at seeing a cleric reading *La Libre Parole*, really your state of

mind, though not exactly hateful, is not appreciably different from that of an amiable officer who is annoyed at seeing a Jew in a railway carriage reading *L'Aurore* when he is himself reading *La Libre Parole*. Minds that will never open have *L'Écho* or *L'Éclair* as their teacher, these are the newspapers of their social group, which in turn feed and form their conversation and ideas, if such words are applicable to them. Whereas the opening mind has a Sorbonne professor (or an abbé with *modern ideas*) as its teacher, and then regardless of whether the mind is that of a Fénelon, a Radziwill, a Lauris, a Gabriel de la Rochefoucauld, a Guiche (I purposely choose persons of very unequal intelligence), or simply Marcel Proust, the ideas will be similar (and so for that matter will those of the most advanced Catholics). Rest assured, the fact that a *licence* in literature is required for military service has done more for the cause of the advanced liberal Republic than any expulsion of monks. The others, those who haven't been to university, Pâris, Albu, [Muller],[10] stick to the political ideas of their social group, that is, *of their newspapers*. All this, of course, barely skims the surface of the question. And it's not as simple as you think. For instance, we speak – I do, and so does Albu – very lightly of the Jesuits. But if we were better educated, certain facts about the Jesuits would give us food for thought, and most particularly, that Auguste Comte, whom General André[11] admires, but his knowledge of whom is probably not as complete as it might be, had such admiration for the Jesuit order and was so strongly convinced that nothing of any moment could be done in France without its help, that he arranged a meeting with the General of the order to discuss the possibility of merging the school of Positivism and the order of Jesuits into a single organization. The General of the order was suspicious and the negotiations fell through. We are constantly told that the absolute monarchies could not tolerate the Jesuits. But is this so much to the Jesuits' discredit? Even so, I think I'd be against them in the last analysis, though I wish at least that anti-clericals would draw a few distinctions and look closely at the great social edifices they want to demolish before setting to work on them. I don't care for the Jesuit spirit. But just the same there's a Jesuit philosophy, a Jesuit art, a Jesuit pedagogy. Will there ever be an anti-clerical art? All this is far from as simple as it looks. What is the future of Catholicism in France and in the world, I mean, how long and in what forms will its influence endure – this is a question one can't even ask, because Catholicism is engaged in a process of growth and transformation, and since the eighteenth century, when it seemed to be the last refuge of ignoramuses, it has acquired, even among those who combatted and resisted it, an influence that no one could have foreseen in the last century. Even from the standpoint of anti-Christianity, the distance travelled from Voltaire to Renan (travelled in the direction of Catholicism) is immense. True, Renan is still an anti-Christian, but a Christianized one: '*Graecia capta*, or rather *Christianismus captus ferum victorem cepit*.'[12] The century of Carlyle, Ruskin and Tolstoy, even if it was the century of Hugo, even if it was the century of Renan (and I'm not even saying that it should also be regarded as the century of Lamartine and Chateaubriand) is not an anti-religious century. Baudelaire himself is tied to the Church, at least by sacrilege. In any case this has nothing to do with the question of the Christian schools. First of all, because closing the Christian schools will not kill the Christian spirit, if it is doomed to die it will perish even under a theocracy. And secondly, because the Christian spirit and even Catholic dogma have nothing to do with the partisan spirit which we want to destroy (and which we imitate).

Exhausted, I shake your hand and adjure you to burn this idiotic letter immediately.

Yours ever,
Marcel Proust

Yes, I would be beside myself if anyone saw this inept letter.

As for Denys Cochin (I'm not speaking of Aynard, who is an admirable man, a great mind),[13] he must, I presume, be thoroughly infected with conservatism, reaction and clericalism. Since he speaks admirably and expresses ideas that appeal to me, and is especially liberal at the present time because he quite naturally desires nothing but freedom (just as we spoke only of justice and love at a time when we were asking only for an act of justice and love), his speeches delight me. I wouldn't go so far as to offer him a cabinet post. But a ministry supported by him would frighten me no more, though I am very progressive, than in 1898 M. de Witt, though a royalist, was frightened by a ministry supported by the collectivists.[14] For the pressing need then was to correct the injustices of the General Staff, while today it is to correct the injustices of the government, if we do not want a formidable party to rise up against us with the power of growth characteristic of parties swollen by Justice (Dreyfusard socialism, for instance). At the present time the socialists make the same mistake by being anti-clerical as in '97 the clericals did by being anti-Dreyfusard. They are expiating today. We shall expiate tomorrow.

1. '. . . One evening,' recalled Lauris, 'I defended the Combes anti-clerical laws. I believe I did so not in opposition to Marcel but to someone else who was present' (*À un ami*, 23). The someone else was clearly Louis d'Albufera. Justin Louis Émile Combes (1835 – 1921) was Premier of France 1902 – 5. Yves Guyot (1843 – 1928), economist and publicist, former Minister, was the political editor of *Le Siècle*. He was a partisan of freedom and free trade, and opposed to socialism.

2. The leading French military academy, corresponding to Sandhurst or West Point.

3. In France in 1903 the overwhelming majority of 'free schools' – i.e. schools not operated by the State – were operated by the Catholic Church. Denys Cochin (1851 – 1922), conservative deputy from Paris, was opposed to the radically anti-clerical Combes.

4. Ferry's 'Laws' or 'Decrees', sponsored by Jules Ferry (1832 – 93), then Minister of Education, and promulgated on 29 March 1880, called for the dissolution of the teaching order of Jesuits.

5. Jules Amiot, owner of a haberdashery at Illiers, married Élisabeth Proust, Professor Proust's sister, in 1847.

6. Alphonse Humbert (1844 – 1922), journalist contributing to the right-wing papers *L'Éclair*, *Le Petit Parisien*, *L'Intransigeant*, etc., deputy 1893 – 1902. For Cavaignac, see letter 140, n. 2.

7. Victor Charbonnel (1863 – 1926), priest and publicist, who left the Church in 1897 and gave a series of anti-clerical lectures.

8. For Boutroux, see letter 15, n. 5. The historian Ernest Lavisse (1842 – 1922) had resigned his teaching post at Saint-Cyr in order to retain his freedom of expression over the Dreyfus and Picquart affairs. The Collège Stanislas is a Catholic institution, while the Lycée Condorcet is a state school.

9. Jules Méline (1838 – 1925), deputy, then senator, and Premier 1896 – 98. A leader of the Progressive Republican Party, he advocated economic protectionism and opposed revision of the Dreyfus case.

10. Vicomte François de Pâris (1875 – 1958), member of the Jockey Club and the Yacht Club. The third name is illegible; Proust may mean Maurice Muller, member of the Automobile Club.

11. General Louis André (1838 – 1913), Minister of War 1901 – 4.

12. 'Conquered Greece – or rather conquered Christianity – has conquered the victorious barbarians.'

13. Édouard Aynard (1837 – 1913), deputy, defender of liberal ideas, member of the Académie des Sciences Morales et Politiques.

14. Conrad de Witt (1824 – 1900), agronomist, deputy from the Calvados department 1885 – 1902, the only right-wing deputy to vote for revision of the Dreyfus case.

252
TO MARIE NORDLINGER

[Early August 1903]
Dear Mlle Marie (or dear friend, would you like that?)

I certainly won't ask you for more advice about Ruskin. For this reason. I've lost all the sheets on which I noted your precious corrections. I'm no longer following them, and besides I haven't got the proofs any more (those were the same sheets, and I don't even know if my exasperated publisher will be willing to publish a translation by someone so disorganized and tiresome).

But couldn't I say goodbye to you without benefit of Ruskin? – Or rather, shall I be able to? I'm in a terrible state, which Reynaldo didn't know about, because it didn't begin until after his last visit, and though trembling with fever and suffocating with asthma, I've been going out almost every day to see a friend who is ill but who is going back to Constantinople soon for heaven knows how many years and whom selfishly I try to see as often as I can.[1] Nevertheless I shall try to come and say goodbye to you and if I don't manage it, I'll go and see you at that divine Varengeville,[2] near the delightful little cemetery which prefigures the eternal silence (which its dead bask in and our living ears cannot hear) with the relative silence, made more profound by the regular and repeated beat of the waves so far below. On the pretext of going to the races in Dieppe. I'm returning the beautiful and aesthetic impressions, which though somewhat impenetrable to me because I'm so poor at languages, are beautiful all the same, and send you my respectful regards.

Marcel Proust

1. Bertrand de Fénelon left Paris on 8 August 1903 for Constantinople; however, he was transferred to St Petersburg in November of the same year.

2. Varengeville-sur-Mer, a resort on the English Channel eight kilometres from Dieppe.

253
TO LÉON YEATMAN

[Saturday 15 August 1903]
Dear Léon,

It's not nice of you not letting me know about Bourges and Vézelay, I'd have done them with you, and I'll certainly be going there soon by myself.

Today, I'm making an exception and staying in bed, because of leaving at seven tomorrow morning (to spend the day at Trouville, visiting Mme Straus).

If you aren't doing anything this evening, come up and see me (if it's before ten), but without Mme Yeatman, whom I could see any evening but this one, when I'll be in bed, and it would break my heart to know, and not for the first time, that she is here and I'm unable to see her (Mama would disagree). You could give me a few pointers so that if by chance I don't come back until Monday I'll know the best things for me to see on the way back from Trouville – Bayeux, Caen, Dives, Lisieux, etc. etc. etc.

But I think I'll be back tomorrow evening. Try to come and say good night to me, Léon. Thank Mme Yeatman for the other lovely 'Madeleine',[1] whose photograph she has sent me and whom I'd have liked to visit with your exquisite Madeleine.

Affectionately,
Marcel

1. Madeleine Yeatman seems to have sent Proust a reproduction of an Italian primitive painting of Mary Magdalen (in French Marie-Madeleine).

254
TO GEORGES DE LAURIS

Thursday [20 August 1903]
Dear friend,

After asking in vain for the enclosed information about Brittany, I proceeded to mislay it. I add the following observations about the few places I know. Beg-Meil is an apple orchard sloping down to the Bay of Concarneau, which is the noblest, gentlest, most delightful place I know. I think the Gulf of Morbihan must be very beautiful too. You can't omit the Pointe du Raz; historically and geographically, you know, this gigantic granite rock – surrounded by an always furious sea, dominating the Bay of the Shipwrecked opposite the Isle of Sein – is literally Finisterre (the end of the earth). These are sinister places with famous curses on them; they mustn't be missed. But I own that I infinitely prefer Penmarch, which you can skip, a sort of mixture of Holland and the Indies and Florida (according to Harrison).[1] Nothing could be more sublime than a tempest seen from there.

Dear friend, you have got me into a lot of hot water by not (ever!) telling Picard the truth at Bertrand's. Since I was on the lookout for a way of convincing him of my good faith and friendly feelings, I didn't dare miss the opportunity he gave me by asking me to be his second. Which put me on the outs with the Strauses and the Le Bargys, not to mention a thousand other repercussions.[2] I'm not giving you any news of Bertrand, because I think you know more than I do, as does Henraux, the favourite. He (Bertrand) left Paris a week ago Saturday, I think (a fortnight the day after tomorrow). I had dinner that evening with Antoine and the two of us put him on the train, in rather good spirits. Antoine has left Paris, he's angry with me. He seems to be in England. I long to see you, dear friend. Give Henraux my regards. I don't dare ask you to give your parents my respectful greetings, which (since I don't know them) is a pity, considering that I admire and pass on your father's witticisms. How dismal it is to see Labori turning the Humbert case into a parody of the Dreyfus case, with him playing the part of the General Staff with his absurd secrets which he keeps promising to divulge.[3] I have only one regret about being a Dreyfusard, that it upsets the noble and loyal Albu. True, he has asked me to explain the Case to him so he can share my convictions, but I'm not up to it. I hope Brittany will appeal to the noble and charming strains in your intelligence, which by a rare miracle of nature are combined with grave, austere ones. If you were to say to me: I shall be on such-and-such a day at Paimpol, or on the Isle of Bréhat, etc., I'd jump on a train and join you (if I'm still in Paris at that time). Once again my regards to Henraux. I won't give you any messages for Pâris, because all things considered his conduct towards me has not been very satisfactory. Besides, I can't even manage to remember him, and if ever I see him in my imagination, it is handing out cotillion favours, though I've never seen him at a ball!

Yours ever,
Marcel Proust

1. The American painter Thomas Alexander Harrison (1853 – 1930), whom Proust and Reynaldo Hahn met at Beg-Meil in September 1895, was to be one of Proust's models for Elstir. Cf. *Within a Budding Grove* (I. 913), where Elstir says of Carquethuit, in Brittany: 'I know nothing in France like it, it reminds me rather of certain aspects of Florida.' Harrison knew Florida, having spent some years there making topographic drawings.

2. Proust thought the Strauses bore him a grudge because he had agreed to act as second to André Picard in his duel on 19 August 1903 with Auguste Le Bargy (1858 – 1936), of the Comédie Française; Picard had fought a duel earlier in 1903 with Mme Straus's son, Jacques Bizet (see letter 229, n. 5).

3. Fernand Labori, who had defended Zola, Dreyfus, and Picquart, had undertaken the defence of Frédéric Humbert and his wife, Thérèse, on trial for a huge and notorious swindle. At the trial Thérèse Humbert promised sensational revelations which never materialized.

255
TO GEORGES DE LAURIS

Splendide Hôtel, Évian-les-Bains
[8 or 9 ? September 1903]

My dear Georges,

Thank you with all my heart for the nice things you say. I'll be able to answer better when I see you. But why do you hark back to 'the early days of our friendship'? Do you think the other days inferior? And there's another thing I don't understand. But then you probably said all that out of pure kindness, to give me pleasure, and you yourself don't remember what you said. Since you ask me for news of my health, here it is. After I left you, the tonic company of the two Albus[1] wasn't enough to bring my fever down, and I took the train in an indescribable state. The possibility of sleeping in the train didn't even occur to me. I saw the sunrise, something I hadn't done for a long time, it's beautiful, an inversion, more charming to my taste, of the sunset. In the morning a wild desire to rape the sleeping little towns (don't mistake towns [*villes*] for girls [*filles*]!), those to the west in a dying remnant of moonlight, those to the east full in the rising sun, but I restrained myself and stayed on the train. Arrived at Avallon about eleven, saw Avallon, hired a car and reached Vézelay in three hours, but in an incredible state. Vézelay is a fantastic place, in a sort of Switzerland, all alone on a mountain towering over the countryside, visible from all directions for miles around, in the most strikingly harmonious landscape. The church is enormous and resembles a Turkish bath as much as it does Notre-Dame, built of alternately black and white stones, a delicious Christian mosque. If I weren't so tired (I've sent postcards and yours is *the first letter I've written*) I'd tell you what one feels on going into it, something curious and beautiful. That will be for my next, I'm not up to it now. In the evening I returned to Avallon with such a high fever that I couldn't go to bed. I walked about all night. At five in the morning I heard there was a train at six. I took it. I caught sight of an admirable medieval town called Semur, and at ten o'clock arrived at Dijon, where I saw some beautiful things and those enormous tombs of the Dukes of Burgundy, which the plaster casts give no idea of, because they're polychrome. Then at eleven that night I arrived at Évian. But this frantic, sleepless race against illness, this 'race to death', had changed me so much that I hardly recognized myself in the mirror, people in the stations asked me if there was anything I needed, and I understood the kindly wisdom of your advice (which touched Mama in the extreme) not to travel in such a condition. I've spent all the time since trying to recover. And now I'm pretty much as I was before going away (before being ill) but because of the superstitious importance you attach to it, I've been getting up every day at two or three in the afternoon. I'm worried sick about the events in Turkey[2] because of Bertrand. I'll be easier in my mind when he gets a posting nearer home or in some quiet America, safe from the Bulgarians. I believe you must have plenty of company and I'm glad of that. In your letter for the first time you refer again to Madame ——.[3] I'd never mentioned her to you, because I didn't know the state of your heart. In the calm and happy tone of your letter I sense the charm of convalescence, or the anxiety that comes of a renewal. May that sentiment be blessed, dear friend, by all the capacity for life and happiness with which you are already endowed and which your friends so fervently wish for you.

Marcel Proust

I haven't seen Mme de Noailles, who had already left Évian. My best regards to Bertrand. I won't give you any messages for Antoine, because I'll be writing to him soon, in the meantime give him my regards. I shall write to you about my plans, which are still vague. As for the hermitage, I haven't given it any more thought and I don't take the idea very seriously, but don't mention it to anyone, because it won't be a hermitage any more if everybody goes there.

1. Presumably Louis d'Albufera and his mistress, Louisa de Mornand.

2. The papers were full of acts of terrorism committed by Bulgarian nationalists in Macedonia and the district of Adrianople.

3. Possibly Mme de la Salle, née Madeleine de Pierrebourg, whom Lauris married in 1910.

256
TO MARIE NORDLINGER

Sunday [18? October 1903]

My dear friend,

Don't imagine that I've forgotten the fresh Rose of Manchester – or disdained the faded heather of Varengeville. But I have carried across France, from Romanesque vestibules to Gothic chevets, an ardent curiosity and a more and more ailing body. And of the monuments I've visited only the Hospital at Beaune was suited to my acute state of illness. I have no doubt that I would have been admitted as an emergency patient. Viollet-le-Duc said it was so beautiful it made you want to fall ill at Beaune.[1] He obviously didn't know what it was to be ill. Since like me you are in Paris (Reynaldo told me you were here, that's how I know where to write to you) we might, if I get better, see each other one of these days. Until then, along with my gratitude for your fragrant gift of amethyst and gold and the cherished memory that perfumes it, accept my friendly respects.

Marcel Proust

1. Cf. *Dictionnaire raisonné de l'architecture française du XIe au XVIe siècle* (1863 edn.), VI. 114: 'Anyone who takes the slightest interest in our old buildings has visited the charming Hôtel-Dieu of Beaune, built in 1443 by Nicolas Rolin, chancellor of the Duke of Burgundy. . . . The courtyard of this establishment, smiling and well-proportioned in aspect, still containing its fifteenth-century well, its wash trough and its pulpit, would almost make one wish to fall ill at Beaune.'

257
TO MADAME DE NOAILLES

Monday [26 October 1903]

Madame,

You are infinitely kind. I should be delighted to dine with you on Wednesday. But I'm obliged to go out on Thursday, an engagement that has already been put off four times because I've always been ill.[1] And I can't go out two evenings in a row, because every time I go out it takes me several days to recover. There are times when this life, in which every pleasure has to be paid for without even being enjoyed, fills me with a sort of 'sad loathing', the wretched sort of despair the poor, dear, sublime Sabine felt when she saw the furniture in her living room being moved about and her valet sweeping.[2] I would at least like to be living a withdrawn, laborious and fruitful life in some monastery, with you, all in white, as its admirable abbess. (Though my clericalism has – temporarily – fallen off, because I've just been rereading the history of the emancipation of the towns, and I see what those poor enthusiastic burghers and peasants suffered at the hands of all those swine.[3] What made this impression particularly vivid was that the most dismal story, which gives one the worst 'civic shudders', as you would say, concerns the unfortunate town of Vézelay, where I went a month ago – at the cost of what attacks of asthma! – to admire, ingenuously and without rancour, the marvellous abbey, without suspecting the cruelty of the Abbé Pons de Monboissier.) But I'll forget all that because of my love of churches, to which I always return

'As the wasp flies to the flowering lily'[4]

and also because the burghers were if possible even more ferocious.

Besides I don't know the first thing about history. And I've just read Lenôtre's *Vieux papiers, vieilles maisons* and *Batz*. And you'll have to admit Clemenceau is going a little too far when he identifies himself with the Terror and refuses to dissociate himself from the Bloc.[5]

Madame, you are not my confessor, I don't know why I burden you with every last one of my absurd thoughts. I can only try to efface this heedless effusion with the most passionate respect.

Marcel Proust

Tell Régnier how much I admire him and Beaunier how much I like him.[6]

1. Proust seems to have spent the Thursday evening in question dining at Larue's with Albufera and Louisa de Mornand.

2. An allusion to Mme de Noailles's novel *La Nouvelle Espérance*, which had appeared in March 1903.

3. Cf. Augustin Thierry, *Lettres sur l'histoire de France* (1827).

4. Cf. Paul Verlaine, *Sagesse*, II. iv, poem 7: 'Comme la guêpe vole au lis épanoui'.

5. Georges Lenôtre, *Paris révolutionnaire. Vieilles maisons, vieux papiers* (1900), and *Le Baron de Batz. Un Conspirateur royaliste sous la Terreur* (1896). The '*Bloc*' was a coalition of the Radical and Socialist parties from roughly 1899 to 1905. Georges Clemenceau had written in *L'Aurore* (23 Oct. 1903): 'The policy of the *Bloc*, our policy, is to unite all republicans in resuming the work of the French Revolution, stopped in its course on 18 Brumaire and by the monarchy of 1815, when foreign baggage waggons brought it back from the Army of Coblenz.'

6. The Symbolist poet Henri de Régnier (1864 – 1936). For André Beaunier, of the *Figaro* staff, see letter 229, n. 4.

258
TO LOUIS D'ALBUFERA[1] and LOUISA DE MORNAND

30 Oct[ober] 1903

To your reproaches last night at that Larue's which is sadly dear to me because many of my friendships were virtually born there, in the rather garish purple of its furnishings (like those emperors termed Porphyrogenetoi for that reason – many of whom died young),[2] I reply nobly with the allegorical gift, in the form of this flowery book,[3] of a large part of my past. Our books are never anything other than retrospective confessions to those who did not know us. This one is already very old and resembles me only vaguely, like a photograph of a child who has greatly changed. Not to his advantage, alas, and you will not be able to apply to me the time-honoured words employed in such cases: 'You've grown so much I hardly recognize you.' It would be truer to say that I've shrunk. May your friendship restore a little of my confidence in a life that has wounded me. And may you in return, when you turn the pages of this book, take some pleasure in hearing me relate my dreams.

Marcel Proust

1. Louis-Joseph Suchet, Marquis, later Duc, d'Albufera (1877–1953), one of Proust's models for Saint-Loup.

2. Porphyrogenetoi, 'born in the purple', was the name applied in the Byzantine Empire to children born to the emperors after their accession to the throne. It was doubtless at Larue's that Proust witnessed Fénelon's feat, which he would describe in *The Guermantes Way* (II. 427), where Saint-Loup, wishing in a crowded restaurant to bring the Narrator a cloak to protect him from the cold, climbs nimbly on to the railing and along the benches to reach him.

3. *Les Plaisirs et les jours.*

259
TO ANTOINE BIBESCO

Friday evening [30 October 1903]

My dear Antoine,

I was going to ask you – knowing how sensitive you are about such things and anxious to have your feelings respected – if you would like me to attend the service tomorrow morning or not.[1] But I was foolish enough to go out yesterday and I'm in such a state again that though asthma sometimes takes amazingly little time to clear up, it seems unlikely that I shall be well enough to go out tomorrow morning. But I'm thinking of you with the same sorrow as last year, when I suddenly learned that your greatest source of joy, affection, advice and comfort was gone and that an immense grief would weigh for ever on your life. I never speak to you of this, for I respect your particular form of sensibility, with whose strict dictates you have made me acquainted. But my thoughts remain unchanged, and I require no effort of memory and no help from the calendar to find in my heart the same grief as last year, which I have never ceased to feel and which for several weeks drove me almost mad with despair at the thought that your happiness – which was then inseparable from mine – had been destroyed. And every time I've seen you since then it has seemed to me afterwards that you missed your mother more and more, that this was the cause of the great changes which have taken place in your character, or else that if other grounds for sorrow en-

tered in, she alone (your friends proving helpless) could have comforted you and destroyed their power to hurt you. And so my
thoughts turn constantly and very sadly to her, who died before her
maternal task, which was dearer to her than any other, was done, and
who, if there is such a thing as personal immortality, grieves at being
unable to come to you now to comfort and embrace you. I haven't
waited till today to say all this to myself. I haven't spoken to you of
these things because you don't like me to, but today, having as it were
to apologize for not, because of the state of my health, asking you if I
should go to the rue Daru, I have for once the right to speak of them.
I'm told that Emmanuel is not in Paris. Being far from you, he must
be even more unhappy today. My anxious thoughts go out to both of
you in mournful affection, flitting in distress from one of you to the
other.

Marcel Proust

1. *Le Figaro* for 29 Oct. 1903 announced that a service would be held the
following Saturday at the Russian church in the rue Daru to mark the anniversary of the death of the Princesse Alexandre Bibesco.

260
TO MAURICE DE FLEURY[1]

[Friday 27 November 1903]

Dear Sir,

In the midst of our immense grief, we owe you a most pleasant emotion, for which we shall always be profoundly grateful.[2] The
portrait you have drawn of my father, the work of a great writer, has
brought him back to us with observations so striking and yet so subtle – that you seem to know him better than we do. The spectacles
worn somewhat low, the head held rather high – if you had been writing about someone else, I should have admired these as the strokes of a
great novelist, marvellously evoking a physiognomy. But in the presence of this portrait, proclaiming the true being of one who was with
us three days ago exactly as you paint him and as we shall never see
him again, we could only weep, and our tears were gentler because he
was in some measure restored to us.

Thank you again, dear sir, for Mama, my brother and myself.

Marcel Proust

1. Maurice de Fleury (1860–1931), a medical man, member of the Permanent Commission for Defence against Tuberculosis, at the Ministry of the Interior.

2. Professor Adrien Proust died suddenly on Thursday 26 November 1903. On Friday the 27th, *Le Figaro* published a long obituary signed 'Horace Bianchon', the pseudonym of Dr Fleury.

261
TO HIS MOTHER

[December 1903 ?]

My dear little Mama, I can't sleep, so I'm writing you this note to tell you that I'm thinking of you. I would so much like, I so much want, to be able soon to get up at the same time as you do and drink my breakfast coffee with you. To feel our sleep and our waking distributed over the same hours would be, will be, such a delight to me. I went to bed at half-past one with that in mind, but then I had to get up a second time to go to the lavatory, and I couldn't find my safety pin (the one I use to close and tighten my drawers). Naturally the night was over for me, there was nothing to hold my stomach. I looked for another pin in your dressing room, etc. etc., and succeeded only in picking up a bad chill from my wanderings (bad is a joke) but no pin. I went back to bed, but by then sleep was out of the question. Now at least I while the night away with plans for an existence such as you wish, brought closer to you materially by living by the same timetable, in the same rooms, at the same temperature, on the same principles, with mutual approval, even though satisfaction, alas, is now forbidden us. Forgive me for leaving the smoking room in disorder. I was working hard up to the last moment.[1] And as for this beautiful envelope, it's the only one I had. Make Marie and Antoine keep quiet and keep the kitchen door closed, so their voices don't come through.

A thousand loving kisses,

Marcel

I feel that I'll sleep very well now.

1. Proust had resumed work on the proofs of *La Bible d'Amiens*.

262
TO MADAME DE NOAILLES

Thursday [3 December 1903]
Madame,

You are too kind. I can see why people loved the Blessed Virgin in the age of belief, for allowing the halt and the blind, the lepers and paralytics, all the unfortunate, to touch the hem of her garment. But you are better still, and at every new revelation of your great, unbounded heart I understand more clearly the indestructible foundation of your genius. And in case it makes you a little cross to be a still-better Blessed Virgin, I'll say you are like that Carthaginian goddess who inspired thoughts of lust in all and in some a yearning for piety.[1]

Madame, you mustn't feel sorry for me, even though I am very unhappy. It's my poor Mama, I haven't even the courage to *think* honestly of what her life will be when I consider that she will never again see the only person she lived for (I might even say the only person she loved since the death of her parents, since every other affection was so far from this one). To a point that would not be credible to one who hadn't seen it, she gave him every minute of her life. And now, emptied of what was their joy and *raison d'être*, the minutes bring home to her, each in a different form, like so many wicked fairies ingenious in devising methods of torture, the grief that will never leave her. But this is something that no one will ever see. Mama has such energy (an energy which never gives itself energetic airs and never lets anyone suspect the measure of her self-control) that there is no apparent difference between her present self and what she was a week ago. But I, who know the depth and violence of the tragedy and how long-lived it is sure to be, cannot help being afraid. I cannot think of my own grief. And yet I'm very sad. You, who saw Papa only two or three times, cannot know what a very sweet and simple man he was. I tried, not to live up to his expectations – for I'm well aware that I was always the dark spot in his life – but to show him my affection. And still there were days when I rebelled against the excessive certainty of his opinions, and the Sunday before last, I remember, in a political discussion, I said some things I shouldn't have. I can't tell you how sad that makes me now. It makes me feel as if I had been hard on someone who was already unable to defend himself. I don't know what I'd give to have been all gentleness and affection that evening. Still, most of the time I was. Papa's nature was so much nobler than mine. I'm always complaining. When Papa was ill, his one thought was to keep it from us. But these are things I'm still unable to think about. They make me too unhappy. Life has begun again. If I had some aim, some ambition, that might help me to bear it. But that's not the case. My bit of happiness was only a reflection of the happiness I saw around me between Papa and Mama, not untempered by the remorse – so painful now – of feeling that I was the only cloud on it. Now all the little things in life, which to me made up its joy, are painful. But at least they are life, it has begun again, and no longer the quick, sudden despair that strikes once, and then is ended. Soon I shall be able to see you again and I promise to stop speaking selfishly of things that I cannot even explain to you because I have never spoken of them before. I can almost say that I never thought of them. My life was made up of them. But I didn't notice them. Tell the Princesse de Chimay that I'd been meaning to write to her soon, before starting to answer letters [of condolence], which will be dreadfully fatiguing. But now Mama, hearing that I'd abandoned Ruskin, has taken it into her head that this was the one thing Papa desired, that he'd been looking forward to seeing it published any day now. So I've had to countermand instructions and now I'm starting in again on the proofs, etc. So tell the Princesse de Chimay that I may not write to her for a few days, but that I won't let a single minute pass without anointing myself with the only balm I know, her incredible words of kindness, the kindest anyone has written me.

Accept, Madame, my respectful regards.

Your grateful admirer,
Marcel Proust

1. Cf. Flaubert, *Salammbô*, ch. III.

263
TO ROBERT DE MONTESQUIOU

[December 1903]

Dear Sir,

Speaking for Mama and my brother and myself, I thank you with all my heart for your sympathy and compassion in thinking of us in our misfortune and for the priceless words with which you have honoured my father's memory. I don't know if you realize how very much he admired you. For some years, after I stopped going out, I spent so much more time with him that I had more opportunity than before to speak of you to him, though less to acquaint him with some new quip of yours, since I was virtually deprived of the pleasure of seeing you. Now I bless those hours of illness spent at home, which during these last years enabled me to enjoy so much of Papa's affection and company. Now they seem to me the happiest years of my life, those when I was closest to him; but I'm very unhappy now. Still, I know he would have been very proud and very glad of the mark of good will and affection you have given him. Allow me, dear sir, to thank you with all my heart.

Your respectful and grateful admirer,

Marcel Proust

264
TO MADAME LAURE HAYMAN

[10 or 11 December 1903]

Dear friend,

When the thing you could not have borne to see happened – Papa, who had gone out looking so well in the morning, *carried* home on a stretcher – one of the first persons I thought of as soon as I could think of anyone other than Papa and Mama – was you. Papa was so very fond of you. And I've heard since from my brother that you sent such admirable flowers. Thank you with all my heart for always being so kind to Papa and for still being so kind, I'm sure you'll remember him always. He spoke of you whenever he wanted to cite an example not only of youthful elegance and beauty, but also of intelligence, taste, kindness, tact, and refinement of feeling. You know, I'm sure, that you had become a subject of conversation in our family. Long ago, before I fell ill and before people came between us, every time Papa saw you and through you learned some little thing about me, what great and obvious pains he took to keep me from knowing who had told him. 'You were seen . . .' 'It seems that . . .' Etc. And I would guess instantly that you'd been to see him that day. Some years ago that ceased to be possible. But he spoke to me of you no less. And only recently, wanting to put a crowning touch on his praise of a certain woman's heart, mind and beauty, he added: 'She almost – though not quite – reminded me of Laure.' For some years, thanks to my poor health, which I bless, I had been living on much closer terms with him, because I never went out. In this day-to-day life, I must have attenuated, sometimes in retrospect I have the illusion that I suppressed them altogether, certain traits of character or thought which may well have displeased him. So I think he was fairly well pleased with me. This intimacy of ours was not interrupted for a single day, and I am especially sensible of its warmth now that even the little things of life have become bitter and hateful to me. Other people have some sort of ambition to console them. I have none, I had only this family life, and now it's for ever barren.

I thank you with all my heart, my dear friend, my dear Laure, for sensing this, and, you who are so good to all unfortunates, for the thought that led you to write those kind and compassionate lines. I embrace you very sadly.

Respectfully,
Marcel Proust